PORTABLE MODULA-2 PROGRAMMING

THE McGRAW-HILL
INTERNATIONAL SERIES IN SOFTWARE ENGINEERING

Consulting Editor

Professor D Ince
The Open University

Forthcoming Titles

Software Engineering: Analysis and Design
Software Documentation
SSADM – A User's Guide
Practical Formal Methods with VDM
Introduction to Compiling Techniques

CONTENTS

PART II—MODULA-2 REFERENCE

12 Syntactic Notation

13 Modules

PART III—PROGRAMMING FOR PORTABILITY

PREFACE

It is not usual for a programming book to begin with a declaration of faith, but we feel the need to declare ourselves fans of Modula-2! The reason for this urge to proclaim from the rooftops is that the title of this book contains an implicit criticism of the language which is its subject. While this criticism cannot be denied, it must be seen in the context of most languages being used for production programming; most programs are difficult to transport from one implementation of a language to another. The reason for this difficulty is the lack of precision in the definition of programming languages, and we assert that most languages are at least as bad as Modula-2 in this respect. It is because we believe that Modula-2 has much to offer software developers, and that the portability problems can be identified and avoided, that we have written this book. We also believe that it is a disservice to programmers, including inexperienced programmers, to avoid these issues when introducing a new language.

With one exception, the authors of this book have come to Modula-2 via Pascal. We were, therefore, predisposed to the language and welcomed its advent. We found that those parts of the language which looked like Pascal had more or less the same meaning as in Pascal, and that the new features offered us just those facilities which we had learnt, over the years, were missing from Pascal. In short, we hailed Modula-2 as an advance in programming language development.

However, any initial euphoria was diminished by the realization that Modula-2 programs were not as portable as we had hoped they would be. For a start, the fundamental characteristic of the language—its ability to express programs as a collection of modules—allowed implementors to provide simple input/output facilities in a variety of ways. And, of course, in order that Modula-2 compilers generate efficient programs, they have been unable to escape the constraints of the operating systems and hardware configurations for which they have been designed. (In this respect, Modula-2 is like other languages intended to be used for producing efficient code.) None of the portability problems deterred us from using the language: there were too many advantages in using it. Instead we learned how to surmount the problems and what aspects of the language it might be worth avoiding. This book distils what we have learnt.

INTRODUCTION

Modula-2 is a modern procedural language which allows for, and encourages, the development of large programs in a systematic and modular fashion. Because of the structured nature of its constructs, and its emphasis on readability, it is also suitable for teaching software design and implementation. The language has a deserved reputation for its provision of many high-level principles of software engineering. Why, therefore, should the portability of such a high-level language be an issue worthy of a book? The answer to this question is in three parts.

First, the language is not stable yet; it is in the process of being standardized, but the impact of the standard may take two or three years to take effect. Modula-2 was developed in order that its inventor, Professor Niklaus Wirth, could write an operating system for a new computer. The design criteria for Modula-2 were established by the original requirement for the language, and this led to a language which needed further work done to it. In particular, some features which could have been included in the language were not, while others were not well defined. (Chapter 1 contains a résumé of the history of the language and its main features.) Also, like most programming languages prior to standardization, Modula-2 has suffered from a diversity of compilers which implement different dialects—providing extensions and interpreting ambiguities differently.

Second, it is not possible, in practical terms, to make any language truly portable. There are always inherently unportable facilities in a language: such as the range of whole numbers and precision of real numbers. These are as problematic in any other language as they are in Modula-2. Some implementations have attempted to alleviate these problems (with varying degrees of success) by providing a variety of numeric types. (See Chapter 17 for a discussion of these.)

Third, Modula-2 deliberately omits facilities which are difficult to make portable (such as input/output). One of the most significant omissions from Modula-2 is input/output. Nothing is provided in the language which will allow the beginner to write `Hello world!` to his or her screen; nor is anything provided to allow the professional programmer to implement a 'quick sort-merge' program. Modula-2 was designed (to some extent anyway) to implement file systems and so it did not make sense to build input/output into the language. Instead, a library of modules which includes input/output is usually supplied with a compiler, usually called `InOut`. Unfortunately, no two `InOut` modules are the same.

Relationships with the forthcoming standard and published reports

Currently Modula-2 is 'defined' by a number of publications by Professor Wirth and others from his institution (ETH, Zürich). Wirth has produced four reports on Modula-2 as part of the four editions of his book *Programming in Modula-2* (Springer-Verlag, 1982, 1983, 1985 and 1988). He has also published other versions of the report and with colleagues has published manuals which document implementations of Modula-2 produced at ETH. These reports and ETH manuals are not complete (in the sense that they allow implementors undesirable freedoms) nor are they consistent with one another. Consequently there are too many differences among Modula-2 implementations, despite the fact that at least 90 per cent of the language is common to all.

Obviously an international Modula-2 standard is required; work started on the standard in 1985 and the draft standard is expected in 1989. The uncertain state of the language might be thought to leave this book in somewhat of a predicament. This is not the case: in this book we describe Modula-2 as we expect it will be defined in the standard. That is our fixed point. We then point out how Modula-2 implementations differ from the forthcoming standard. For the reader of this book (and the designer of portable Modula-2 programs) this allows one to restrict one's use of the language for now and for the future.

As well as referring to the forthcoming standard, we will cite the third edition of Professor Wirth's *Programming in Modula-2* (and sometimes the second edition). At the time of writing, the third, corrected edition is considered to be the current definition. (The fourth edition has not been published long enough to have had an effect.) Inevitably, you must refer to the documentation for your implementation of Modula-2 to determine the rules and idiosyncrasies of the implementation. At least, this book will provide a context within which to place such interpretations of what is Modula-2.

How to use this book

The premise on which this book is based is that programming is a practical activity which exposes the programmer to imperfect technology and forces compromises and the revision of designs when they are least welcome. We believe that these issues should not be obscured and that the novice may as well develop skills of dealing with them as his or her knowledge increases, rather than during some crisis which exposes his or her lack of 'real experience'. Therefore, the book aims to introduce Modula-2 with a frank discussion of its weaknesses, as well as its strengths, and to provide reference material for the experienced programmer. To this end, all chapters include a discussion of the portability issues relevant to the chapter's subject. In the early chapters, these introduce the notion of portability; in the later chapters, more complex portability problems are explained.

The book is organized into three parts, 26 chapters and a set of four appendices. The book may be read through from cover to cover, but can be dipped into, as explained below.

Part I of the book, *Beginners' Modula-2*, is essentially for the student or novice Modula-2 programmer, including undergraduate and BTEC courses. It presents the elements of Modula-2 in a bottom-up fashion—starting with the simplest features and the building up towards the more complex—and is intended to read through sequentially. In Part I it is assumed that the reader has at least a little experience of programming—using Pascal or BASIC, for example. Chapter 1 provides an overview of the language—its history and main characteristics. Chapter 2 describes the structure of Modula-2 programs, in particular their modular nature. (The language's module construct is introduced in Chapter 2.)

Note that Chapter 2 also describes the way in which Topspeed Modula-2 is used for implementing the programs used in the book. As authors of a book on portable Modula-2 it would ill behove us to insist on a particular compiler. We chose Topspeed Modula-2 because it is a robust and exceptionally fast implementation which can be used to produce portable Modula-2.

The rest of Part I introduces the language, beginning with the basic elements in Chapter 3 and progressing to programming with dynamic variables, in Chapter 11.

The full list of Part I chapters is given below:

Chapter 1   What is Modula-2?
Chapter 2   Structure of Modula-2 Programs
Chapter 3   Basic Elements
Chapter 4   Assigning Values to Variables
Chapter 5   Control Structures
Chapter 6   Programmer-defined Types
Chapter 7   Structuring Data
Chapter 8   Organizing Programs into Modules and Procedures
Chapter 9   Simple Terminal Input and Output
Chapter 10   Strings
Chapter 11   Dynamic Variables

Note that Chapter 9 introduces our portable I/O module and Chapter 10 describes our portable string processing module.

Part II, *Modula-2 Reference*, is both for the beginner who has worked through Part I and for the programmer who has experience of a block-structured language such as Pascal. It is organized in a top-down way; that is, it follows roughly the order with which a compiler processes a compilation unit in the language. Chapter 12 introduces the syntactic metalanguage which is used to define Modula-2 grammar thereafter, and so must be read. Chapters 13 to 23 give detailed descriptions of aspects of Modula-2 in a stylized fashion dictated by the chapter's subject matter, and may be read in a random fashion.

Chapter 12　Syntactic Notation
Chapter 13　Modules
Chapter 14　Procedures
Chapter 15　Data Declarations
Chapter 16　Expressions, Types and Type Compatibility
Chapter 17　Elementary types
Chapter 18　Statements
Chapter 19　Arrays
Chapter 20　Records
Chapter 21　Sets
Chapter 22　Pointers
Chapter 23　Built-in Procedures

Note that because Part II is for reference purposes, there is a degree of overlap among the chapters. Where appropriate, a topic is described in the context of some other discussion, even if the topic is covered in depth elsewhere. This is a deliberate policy which has been adopted to minimize cross-referencing, and to improve context-dependent explanations. Despite the reference nature, we have supplied exercises to aid the student (and the enthusiast). In general, therefore, subjects which are introduced in Part I appear again in Part II, where they are discussed in depth. There are two exceptions to the rule: terminal I/O is only described in Chapter 9; and the use of character arrays as representations of strings is only described in Chaper 10.

Part III, *Programming for Portability*, is devoted entirely to facilities in Modula-2 which help make portable software, which is usually thought to be difficult to reimplement (systems programming is an example of this type of software).

Chapter 24　Developing Portable Software
Chapter 25　Systems Programming with Modula-2
Chapter 26　Coroutines

The book finishes with four appendices. These include a collected syntax of the language, in textual and diagramatic forms, a description of Topspeed Modula-2 extensions, example implementations of modules used in the book, and answers to questions and answers.

This is not a book on software portability *per se*. We do not attempt to introduce principles of portable programming and then follow them with examples of how they may be applied using Modula-2. Instead, portability principles are examined as they occur in Modula-2 in the section on portability issues in each chapter. The *Portability Issues* section of Chapter 1 explains what we mean by 'portability'.

Typographic conventions

There are two main typographic conventions used in the book: the main text font is used for referring to technical material when the latter is considered in the abstract. The typewritten font for Modula-2 code is used in the main text to refer specifically to symbols in Modula-2 programs or for data which is input to or output from a program.

Note that the syntax rules of Modula-2 are expressed informally in Part I of the book. In later parts of the book the rules are given formally, according to the notation described in Chapter 12. These formal rules are displayed in boxes, and so are easily found in the text.

Implementing software for the book

The book assumes the availability of two portable modules—one for input/output, the other for string processing. These are called `PortIO` and `PortStrings`, respectively. The latter is large but easy to implement on any Modula-2 system. The former is smaller but more complex. Chapter 9 describes `PortIO`, and Chapter 10 describes `PortStrings`. An implementation is given in Appendix 3.

To obtain a machine-readable copy of this and other software in the book please send a formatted floppy disk to the authors ^c/o the publisher at the local address.

Acknowledgements

The authors wish to acknowledge the enormous contribution which the British Standards Institution Working Group (IST/5/13) on Modula-2 has made to their ideas. In particular, we acknowledge the sterling work of Derek Andrews, Barry Cornelius, Susan Eisenbach, Roger Henry, Don Ward, and Brian Wichmann.

We also thank Brian Souter for his comments on an early draft. Thanks are also due to Jensen and Partners International, for the loan of computers and Topspeed Modula-2 software, and for answering our pedantic questions, often late at night. We acknowledge Paul Bacsich of The Open University for his help and support, and for producing the MoreMath font that we used. We would also like to thank Apple Computer (UK), who came to our aid with the generous loan of two Macintosh SEs.

Last, and in no measure least, we thank Pauline Graham for her patience in tolerating the late nights and lost weekends working on our behalf. Without her organizational and word-processing skills this book would still be a gleam in our collective eye.

Trademarks

IBM is a trademark of the International Business Machines, Inc.; Topspeed is a trademark of Jensen and Partners International Ltd.; UNIX is a trademark of AT&T; MS-DOS is a trademark of Microsoft, Inc.

PART I—BEGINNERS' MODULA-2

1 WHAT IS MODULA-2?

1.1 INTRODUCTION

Modula-2 is a general-purpose programming language whose most salient characteristic is its ability to express software as a hierarchy of component 'modules'—hence the name. It is difficult to state any specific area of application for the language; if Modula-2 actually has any particular area of application, it is that of large programs such as:

- database systems;

- communications systems;

- operating systems, compilers, editors, etc.;

- transportation control systems;

- computer-aided design systems.

In other words, Modula-2 was intended for complex software systems whose construction might benefit from the structuring facilities the language provides.

Actually, to describe Modula-2 as general-purpose ignores its history and admits to no particular area of application having emerged by the late 1980s. Therefore, this chapter opens with a brief history of the language. It is useful to have a little of the history of any programming language when first learning it, or indeed when tackling large applications for the first time. Inevitably you will find yourself in some situation when you say 'Why didn't I think of using that feature?' or 'Why can't I do it this way?'. If you know the background to a language you might be able to ask the first question less, and accept answers to the second more readily.

After the history lesson, the main facilities offered by Modula-2 are outlined; these include its module facilities, data types and statements. The chapter concludes with an introduction to the aims of portable programming and the portability issues that Modula-2 raises.

1.2   HISTORY OF MODULA-2

Modula-2 is a descendant of the programming language Pascal and was invented by the latter's originator, Professor Niklaus Wirth of the Institut für Informatik, Eidgenössische Technische Hochschule (ETH), Zürich; consequently Modula-2 superficially resembles Pascal. The similarity between the languages is the result of the equivalence between corresponding statements in each language, and from the large number of symbols (especially keywords) which are common to both.

After the success of Pascal, Niklaus Wirth began to experiment with implementing multiprogramming operating systems using high-level programming languages. (Traditionally, operating systems have been implemented using low-level languages such as assemblers.) From this work Wirth published a language called Modula, a number of compilers for which were implemented in the mid 1970s.

Modula differed from Pascal primarily by providing modules which could be used to compile separately collections of data structures and the procedures which manipulate them. Modula's syntax is very like Pascal's but is less redundant; that is, less symbols are required for structuring program text in Modula. For example, sequences of statements do not have to be bracketed using BEGIN and END, as in Pascal. On the other hand, all but one of the structured statements (i.e. those which control other statements) do need a terminating symbol END after the statements they control. The exception is the REPEAT statement which is terminated by UNTIL, as in Pascal. Significantly, Modula did not have a type defined for handling real numbers (such as 291.3456) since they are not generally needed when implementing operating systems. It did have primitive facilities for implementing the concurrent execution of programs; these are essential for operating systems and the like. Modula-2 is a direct descendant of Modula.

Wirth developed Modula-2 after having spent a year's sabbatical at the Xerox Palo Alto Research Center during 1976–77, after completing his work on Modula. There he studied the language Mesa which was developed for implementing the prototype WIMP (windows–icons–mouse–pull-down menus) systems which are so common today. After his time at Xerox PARC, Wirth returned to ETH in Zürich and the strands of Pascal, Modula and Mesa came together in Modula-2. Like Modula, Modula-2 recognizes the need to break up software into chunks which can be compiled separately. These chunks, or modules, maintain type-checking across interfaces and permit the separation of the definition of their interface and their implementation. Modula-2's syntax is very like Modula's (and thus Pascal's). Like Modula it provides primitive operations for concurrency, and like Pascal it provides the type REAL for real numbers. (Indeed most implementations include a variety of numeric types; see Chapter 17 for details.)

An implementation on a PDP-11 computer resulted, followed by an extraordinary project which essentially built a computer around Modula-2. The computer, called Lilith, was programmed in Modula-2 and included much WIMP software and, of course, a Modula-2 development system. Both the aforementioned ETH implementations are significant because they have influenced the language's development. Many other implementations have appeared since, both from ETH and independent software developers. Some of the latter implementors have based their products on ETH compilers. However, since the ETH compilers have differed in their interpretation of some aspects of the language, programmers have formed different views on what constitutes valid Modula-2; this is the reason for many of the portability problems addressed by the book.

By 1985, the qualities of Modula-2 had become recognized by software engineers to the extent that a project to standardize the language and to define a standard library (more on libraries below) was initiated by the British Standards Institution (BSI) which had produced the international Pascal Standard. That project became international in 1987 and a draft standard should emerge during 1989. In this book we describe Modula-2 as we believe it will be defined in the British and international standard and what aspects of Modula-2 can be considered to be portable.

1.3   OVERVIEW OF MODULA-2

In this overview of Modula-2 there is an assumption that you know a little about other programming languages, such as Pascal, C, or BASIC. Do not worry if you do not have this background, because (Chapters 2–11) provides an introduction to Modula-2. The main features of Modula-2 are outlined below.

Modules

As discussed earlier, the most significant feature of Modula-2 is its provision for splitting up software into components called 'modules'. Other languages also claim to provide this facility, but you should find that Modula-2 goes beyond what you might have encountered elsewhere. The problem lies in the term 'module'. It has been used in computing for a number of years and its meaning has changed over the years. The oldest and simplest concept of a module is an identifiable piece of program design or source text (rather than executable code). In other words it is a piece of program that has a name by which it can identified. This definition made module synonymous with subroutine or procedure, but this is now considered to be inadequate. The notion of a module has been extended to include the separation of interface and implementation (see Chapter 2). There are many ways of organizing program text which would now be considered to be modular. For example, it is now known that one of the best kinds of module is one which implements a single function of a program, and does that by collecting together both the variables and any procedures (i.e. subroutines) which act upon them.

If one considers a module to be an abstract structuring device, then certainly, for many programming languages, a procedure is the only construction which is available for implementing a module. In such languages, the procedures have to operate on global variables, and this fact leads to lots of problems in program design and implementation. Basically, because all of the program can access global variables, inadvertent interaction can be caused between the variables. Also, because you, as a programmer, can see the identifiers (both physically and via program access) you may make some assumptions about the way global variables are implemented. This is particularly the case if you are working with others on a project.

Being forced to over-use global variables is one of the weaknesses of Pascal which Modula-2 overcomes. In Modula-2, modules can (and often do) contain both variables and procedures. They may also include the names of constants and types. The identifiers for these constants, types, variables, and procedures can be made available to other modules, or kept private. This alone is a comparatively rare facility which Modula-2 offers and is of huge importance when developing large programs.

Another practical advantage of modules is that they may be separately compiled. This means that different components of a software system may be developed separately—either at different times or by different people—and they can be combined to make up the whole program.

This may appear at first sight not to be out of the ordinary, but the way Modula-2 does it is. First, very few programming languages provide *type secure* separate compilation. That is, most languages allow procedures to be compiled independently of each other, but the programming environments (the compiler/linker) do not provide secure type checking. For example, implementations of languages which allow independent compilation of procedures cannot guarantee that the parameters of a procedure call will match exactly the parameter specification in the procedure's declaration, if the latter had been compiled independently of the text containing the call.

Also, Modula-2 implementations enforce what is known as *version control*. This is where the environment ensures that the private (implementation) part of a module matches the public (definition) part. It is not possible in Modula-2 to make a mistake by plugging in a component which looks like it fits in the program but which does not.

Another huge advantage of the modular nature of Modula-2 is that the language does not have to include every facility which every programmer in the northern hemisphere, or the southern hemisphere, might want. A 'library' of modules can be built or bought to suit the needs of particular programmers. For example, it has already been observed that WIMP systems are very common, but it would be wrong to include support for them in Modula-2 (i.e. in the language). It is sensible, on the other hand, to provide a module to allow those who wish to write such systems to do so with ease. This is exactly what Modula-2 implementations do.

This separation between programming language and the supporting library is important and will crop up frequently when writing Modula-2 programs. Also, the lack of a standard library presents problems when trying to write portable programs.

The basic ideas of how to structure modules are introduced in the next chapter. Chapter 8 describes how to construct modules in Modula-2.

Data types

The richness of data types in a language often determines its usefulness to programmers. The competent programmer makes use of most data types a language offers, and will therefore relish what Modula-2 has to offer, whilst the poor or inexperienced programmer will avoid these, muttering excuses about how some other language is just as good. (Of course it is not.)

Data types define the values which a variable may take, and the operations which may be used on the variables. Data types can be split up into *elementary types*, which define values such as numbers or characters, and *structured types*, which define aggregates of variables of some type or types. In the case of structured types, the way a variable is composed of other variables is also specified.

Among the elementary types are basic numerical types. Modula-2 has four predefined numerical types:

- CARDINAL, which is for variables that only take non-negative whole number values, such as 0, 1, 2, 3...

- INTEGER, which is for variables that take negative and non-negative whole number values, such as ...−5, −4, −3, −2, −1, 0, 1, 2, 3, 4, 5...

- REAL, which is for variables that are used to approximate numerical values which are like the mathematical real numbers, e.g. 71.22348.

- LONGREAL, which is for variables requiring extra precision than that offered by REAL.

The type CARDINAL is not found in Pascal, for example. As you will discover it is an extremely useful type. In fact it is probably the most commonly used data type in Modula-2.

Modula-2 also provides a character type and a Boolean type (the latter being used for holding truth values):

- CHAR, for variables which hold both printable and unprintable characters. On microcomputers these values usually include the 128 values of the ASCII version of the international character set and a further 128 defined by the hardware manufacturer.

- BOOLEAN, which has just two values—FALSE and TRUE.

Like Pascal, subranges of most of the above simple types can be specified, so as to define more tightly the possible values which a variable may take. Also, you can create your own elementary types (called *enumeration types*) by defining a list of identifiers to represent the values. These are described in Chapter 6.

There is another elementary data type, or set of data types, known as the *pointer type*, which is used to construct variables while a program is running. Dynamic variables are introduced in Chapter 11. (Chapter 22 gives a full description of pointers.)

Modula-2 provides two *type constructors*; for building aggregates of variables. These are the array and record constructors:

- ARRAY , which allows a table of variables of identical types to be defined.

- RECORD , which allows a collection of variables of different types to be constructed.

Modula-2 also allows sets of *values* (rather than variables) to be constructed.

However, unlike Pascal, Modula-2 does not have a file (or sequence) data structure. Neither does it have any input or output statements. There are a number of reasons for these omissions. The most important one is that file-handling programs are notoriously difficult to make portable (i.e. easy to re-implement on other computer systems). Because Wirth intended Modula-2 for programming on complex and diverse systems, he decided that there was little advantage in cluttering up the language with them and has left their provision to implementors of Modula-2 development systems. We shall describe a portable terminal I/O module which is suitable for the examples in the book, called PortIO in Chapter 9, and a file I/O module in Appendix 1.

Also note that Modula-2 does not provide a string data type, but does allow character arrays to be easily used to represent strings. We will define a module called PortStrings which contains procedures for handling such strings (see Chapter 10).

Statements and expressions

Modula-2's statements are much like Pascal's. They do differ in a number of fairly small ways which together are a considerable improvement.

To begin with, assignment statements and procedure calls are much the same as Pascal's. Two small improvements do make life easier:

- String literals (i.e. a sequence of characters in quotes) may be assigned to character arrays which are at least as long as the literals.

- Similarly, array data structures of various sizes may be passed to the same procedure, depending on how the procedure's parameters have been declared (more on this in Chapter 8).

The other difference between Pascal and Modula-2 which is related to statements is the evaluation of Boolean expressions. In Modula-2 they are evaluated from left to right and the evaluation is *short-circuited* by skipping some parts of the expression if the answer becomes obvious. (For example, if Boolean terms are combined in an expression with AND they must all be true for the whole expression to be true; if the first term is false, then the other two will not be evaluated since the whole expression must be false.)

All Modula-2's *structured statements* (those which control other statements) are terminated by a keyword such as END or UNTIL (and therefore BEGIN...END bracketing is not required).

The *selection statements* IF and CASE are much the same as in Pascal, but have been improved: IF has an ELSIF part which allows alternatives to be checked for one after the other; CASE has an ELSE part which allows a default to be specified.

Of the *iteration statements* only the FOR is radically different, although both WHILE and REPEAT are affected by the short-circuit evaluation of Boolean expressions described above. The FOR statement does not have a 'down to' form but does allow a constant expression to specify the size of increment (or decrement) which is to be used on each iteration.

WHILE and REPEAT loops are greatly simplified by short-circuit evaluation as this virtually eliminates the need for the Boolean flags used when searching arrays in Pascal, for example.

Modula-2 provides a very general iteration statement called a LOOP. A LOOP statement will cause a sequence of statements to be repeated forever, unless one of them executes an EXIT statement. (The EXIT statement is provided for use with LOOP only.)

One other advantage of Modula-2 is its provision of a RETURN statement which is used to terminate a function procedure and to return the result. RETURN can also be used to terminate prematurely procedures and modules before they reach their end.

Type checking

Modula-2 enforces type-checking like Pascal, but is even more rigorous. Pascal is fairly relaxed about numerical expressions: it allows INTEGER values to be assigned to REAL variables. Modula-2 adopts the attitude that because you have decided what types your variables should be, you should not expect the compiler to compromise the type checking, which, after all, is intended to help the programmer. However, Modula-2 does recognize the need to convert values between types (particularly the numerical types) and provides fairly simple mechanisms for doing this. These *type conversions*, as they are known, are not 'hidden': it is always clear when you use them that you intend to convert values between types.

Circumventing type checking is often required when systems programming; the bit pattern representing a value of one type must sometimes be interpreted as a value of another type. Chapter 25 describes in detail this sort of use, which is known as *type transfer*.

Declarations

Modula-2's declarations are a lot easier to use than Pascal's. In Pascal, declarations are only allowed at the beginning of programs or procedures or functions. In Modula-2 they may appear anywhere except where statements are used. They may be in any order, although, in general, an identifier must have been declared before it can be used in the declaration of another.

Within a module or procedure there may be many declarations of constants, types, and variables. All the constants do not have to be declared together, nor do all the types have to be declared together, nor all the variables. Indeed, one useful practice which Modula-2 encourages is the declaration of constants, types, and variables just before the procedure or module which needs them.

From the last paragraph you might already have picked up the fact that you can declare local modules as part of other modules (or even as part of procedures), rather than define and compile them separately. These *local modules* are discussed fully in Chapter 13.

Modula-2 also overcomes the weakness of the way constants are defined in other languages. Modula-2 allows *constant expressions*; these are expressions involving constant values which the compiler can work out while compiling a module. This allows constants to be expressed by formulae containing constants.

For example, if three arrays are needed in a program—two to hold different numbers of values and a third to hold both sets of values—then the constant which is the maximum index of the third array can be worked out in a constant expression which adds the maximum indexes of the smaller two. This facility allows different versions of a program to be generated by changing just a few constants, but only as long as you have defined other constants in terms of the few, and have defined types using constant identifiers (rather than numbers, say).

Systems programming

Modula-2 is often used for systems programming, such as the implementation of compilers, input/output systems, storage allocation systems, etc. (Indeed the Topspeed Modula-2 compiler and the Topspeed library of modules are implemented in Modula-2.)

Modula-2 has many facilities to aid the systems programmer. Systems programming necessarily involves working at a low level with the computer and operating system and often this forces the systems programmer to use low-level languages, or to use high-level languages which do not object to 'breaking the rules'. Modula-2 allows programmers to continue to write high-level programs but to access low-level entities or to 'break the rules' in a structured way.

Also Modula-2 encourages the programmer to come clean about any systems programming in a module; for example, if facilities from the special module SYSTEM are needed, then those facilities must be imported (see Chapter 25) and this is like holding up a red warning flag. There are none of the covert operations which other languages encourage and which only obscure the meaning of programs.

Procedures

Modula-2 procedures come in two flavours, which roughly correspond to procedures and functions in Pascal. Except for the use of the RETURN statement mentioned above they are very like Pascal. However, there is no keyword 'function' as in Pascal: function procedures are recognized by the fact that they return a value of some type. More on this later.

There are two procedure innovations which Modula-2 includes. The first is that procedure types, and thus procedure variables, are provided. This means that you can specify the type of a procedure and use that to declare a procedure to have an array of procedures which can be indexed in the normal way. (All these possibilities are described in Chapter 14.)

The second innovation in Modula-2 is *open array parameters*. These are array parameters which allow arrays of different sizes (and thus strictly speaking different types) to be used with the procedure. This eases the development of procedures for processing arrays which have the same type of components.

When open array parameters are used whose components are the smallest addressable unit of the implementation (see Chapter 25), then any type of parameter will match it. This is a tremendously powerful feature for implementing software for general use (such as library modules).

Concurrency

Most computers process programs sequentially. They perform one operation followed by another, followed by another (and so on). The world is not like that and software which has to interact with the real world often needs to reflect the concurrent nature of the world, rather than the sequential nature of the computer or the operating system. Many software designs are made overly complex by trying to make them sequential.

Modula-2 allows parallel execution of software to be simulated using a device known as a *coroutine*. Coroutines essentially allow procedures to be executed concurrently; part of each is executed before control is transferred to another. Full details are given in Chapter 26.

1.4   TOPSPEED MODULA-2

The implementation we have chosen for our examples of portable Modula-2 in this book is JPI's Topspeed Modula-2. The Topspeed implementation (release 1.15) is as close as any compiler we have seen to the emerging standard for Modula-2. Differences from the proposed standard have not prevented us from providing programs and program fragments which exhibit the design principles we extol to achieve portability.

Topspeed was chosen for a number of reasons, the three most significant being that, at the time of writing, it is one of the cheapest Modula-2 compilers available for microcomputers, it is a high quality implementation and it produces the fastest executable code on computers running the MS-DOS Operating System. While cost and code speed may not be sufficient reasons for a programmer to choose a particular implementation, we felt that these factors, together with its other virtues, would guarantee a significant market share to JPI. The compiler is pleasant to use, and it has allowed us to demonstrate our approach to portable Modula-2 programming.

Nevertheless, it should be stressed that it is not necessary to have Topspeed Modula-2 to make good use of this book. Although Topspeed is used throughout the book, it is the principle of the techniques being applied which is significant.

1.5   PORTABILITY ISSUES

To close this chapter we will look at the notion of program portability and how Modula-2 programs can be portable.

Before looking at the ideals of portability, we should establish why program portability is desirable. The primary consideration is an economic one: an implementor may want to provide a version of a program for a variety of computer systems without having to rewrite the software completely. Software is expensive to produce and implementors are eager to protect their investment. This economic factor is one reason for the popularity and usefulness of high-level languages.

A second motivation is quality. It has been observed that programs which have been designed to be portable are usually well engineered: they do not fail often and are comparatively easy to maintain. The care which is required when designing for portability has a side-effect of introducing care into programming.

But what do we mean by 'program' or 'portable' or 'computer system'? We tend to be imprecise when discussing software. For example, we often use the term 'program' to describe several different entities, thus:

- A program is a document containing text which has apparently been written according to the rules of a programming language; the text may or may not adhere to the rules and thus may or may not be a valid program.

- A program is a disk file containing binary codes which are ready for execution. (Alternatively the binary file may have to be linked to others to form a 'program'.)

- A program is a sequence of binary codes in execution. (The codes are usually in memory, but sometimes on disk pending transfer to memory.)

While we can usually rely on the context of a technical discussion to resolve any ambiguity, this is not the case when discussing portability issues. When it comes to portability issues, we must be precise.

Having established that we may be concerned with programs at different levels, we must determine what programs execute on. We will use the term *computer system* and define it to be a configuration of a processor and memory with backing store devices and an operating system.

Portability is best defined by a set of goals. Starting with the ideal form of portability we can define four goals:

1. being able to execute the binary code generated on one computer system on another;

2. being able to execute the binary code generated on one computer system on another after re-linking the code on the target system;

3. being able to execute the binary code compiled on the target system from unchanged program source;

4. being able to execute the binary code compiled on the target system after minor changes of program source text.

Although some programming systems have achieved goals 1 and 2 with some success, neither are usually considered when addressing portability problems. Even goal 3 is considered to be almost unattainable for all but the smallest of programs. We will adopt goal 4 as our ideal.

For program texts in a language to be portable, the language itself must have been designed with portability in mind. Modula-2 facilitates portability in a number of ways which we shall discuss. Most importantly, the language which Professor Wirth designed was reasonably portable itself, and the standardization process (the preliminary results of which are used in this book) has been oriented towards a truly portable language.

The module facility is itself a boon to portability. Non-portable, system-dependent software can be isolated within a module and access to it restricted through the interface definition. This technique will be used extensively throughout the book.

The problems with Modula-2 portability arise from the divergent implementations described earlier. These will be avoided in the examples given when introducing the language in Parts I and II, but will be described in the

Portability Issues section of each chapter. Part III is about improving the portability prospects of inherently system-dependent software.

1.6   REVIEW QUESTIONS

Q1.1   Who invented Modula-2?

Q1.2   What does 'short-circuit' evaluation mean, and why does it only apply to Boolean expressions?

Q1.3   What is the iteration statement offered by Modula-2 but not by Pascal?

Q1.4   How does Modula-2 help to avoid the problems of using global variables?

Q1.5   How are strings provided in Modula-2?

Q1.6   Why might the type rules of Modula-2 need to be broken?

2

STRUCTURE OF MODULA-2 PROGRAMS

2.1 INTRODUCTION

The purpose of this chapter is to introduce you to the main components of Modula-2 programs, i.e. modules. A Modula-2 program typically consists of a number of component modules. We look at the general structure of both program modules and component modules.

2.2 PROGRAM MODULES

In Modula-2, programs themselves are called modules. This might seem strange at first, but will seem less so when you encounter other modules. The difference between a *program module* and a component module is that the program module is the centre of control for the whole program; ultimately, the program module directs how other modules are to be used. Also, the program's environment (e.g. an operating system from which you might start the program executing) will identify the program by the program module.

The first program module you should look at is the trivial one which does nothing and, except for the passage of time, whose execution will go unnoticed:

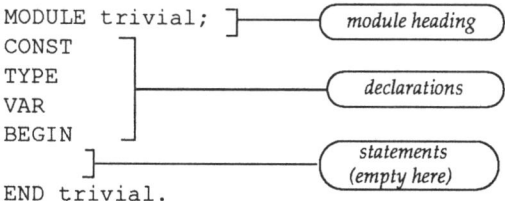

The first thing to notice is that the module begins with a heading which starts with the identifier MODULE followed by the name of the program—in this case trivial.

After the module heading comes declarations of constants, types, and variables (indicated by CONST, TYPE, and VAR respectively). All these are introduced fully in Chapter 4.

The identifier BEGIN indicates the start of the program module's statements; these are the instructions which specify what the program is to do during execution. The matching END terminates the statements and the module and is followed by the module's name and a full stop.

In fact, the program is so trivial that a lot of the above can be omitted; the program does not use any constants so the CONST declaration part can be omitted. Nor does it declare variables, so neither the VAR nor TYPE declaration parts are needed. Finally, it does not contain any statements and so the BEGIN can be omitted. Therefore the trivial program could just as well be written as follows:

```
MODULE trivial;
END trivial.
```

You will, no doubt, never write such a program, but understanding it will help you understand the form which modules take.

The uselessness of the program trivial is not just because it does nothing. You will recall from Chapter 1 that Modula-2 has no input or output statements, and so even if we had calculated something, we could not have observed the result (without looking at the physical memory or registers of the computer!). What we need are some output facilities from somewhere.

Since we are concerned with the construction of portable software we need to have a portable input/output module available to our programs. We call this module PortIO. (PortIO is described fully in Chapter 9.) This module has been designed to provide input/output facilities using the Modula-2 procedure mechanism. Procedures are like mini-programs; they have their own data and statements. Their usefulness comes from being able to encapsulate operations which you might want but which the language does not provide. They often take a data value as a parameter which the procedure's statements make use of. (Procedures are introduced in detail in Chapter 8.)

Therefore, what we need to develop is a program whose execution we can observe in the form of output produced by procedures from PortIO. The following program module prints the message Hello world on the screen. To do so it must indicate its use of the procedures WriteString and WriteLn from the module PortIO. These procedures output a string of characters and cause the printing position to move to a new line, respectively. WriteString operates on a sequence of characters which is given to it as a parameter between parentheses (see below).

The module hello is said to *import* WriteString and WriteLn. The particular form of import instruction used in the example below makes WriteString and WriteLn appear as if they were identifiers which had been declared in the module `hello` itself. (There is another form which you will see later.) By importing `WriteString` and `WriteLn` from `PortIO`, `hello` has made two extra statements available to it (special-purpose statements for outputting characters and new lines). These can then be placed in the statement part of a module in the order in which they are to be executed. The module `hello` is given below:

```
MODULE hello;
FROM PortIO IMPORT WriteString, WriteLn;              ⎤───⟨ import list ⟩
BEGIN
  WriteString('Hello world');         ⎤─────────⟨ statement part ⟩
  WriteLn
END hello.
```

Therefore this module will output the words `Hello world` on the screen, and will move the printing position to the line below, under the `H` as shown below:

```
Hello world
^
```

The reason that it is possible for `hello` to import `WriteString` and `WriteLn` is that the `PortIO` module exports them. The two-faced nature of separately compiled modules has already been mentioned: they are split into a definition module and an implementation module—the public and private parts, respectively. A little bit of the definition module of `PortIO` is given below, just to illustrate how this import–export mechanism works (and because you will see `PortIO` a lot). Do not worry about the syntax or meaning of it for the moment; we will look at these details in due course.

```
DEFINITION MODULE PortIO; ⎤──────────⟨ definition module heading ⟩
PROCEDURE WriteString(v: ARRAY OF CHAR);⎤
PROCEDURE WriteLn;
...                                       ⎦──⟨ declarations of procedures
END PortIO.                                    being exported by PortIO ⟩
```

Note that the definition module of `PortIO` given above is not complete, but the omissions need not worry us now.

A comparison of the program modules `hello` and `trivial` should suggest to you that even the simplest programs have to use other modules; this is certainly the case. In fact, most programming languages have facilities built into them which Modula-2 has abstracted from the language. The omission of input/output facilities from the language is an example of this abstraction. Languages which do include input/output facilities often hide the fact that they are provided by a special-purpose piece of software which remains in the background. It is not Modula-2's style to keep things in the background. If you have designed your software so that it is made up of a number of components, then Modula-2 requires you to make that explicit. In the long term this will help you, but it immediately helps anyone you are working with who needs to understand what you are doing.

2.3   SOME MODULA-2 SYMBOLS: KEYWORDS, IDENTIFIERS, STRINGS

Before proceeding we need to look more closely at some of the symbols of the Modula-2 language which are used in the rest of this chapter. You have already encountered a number of Modula-2 symbols; you have met several *identifiers* and *keywords*, and one *string* value. An *identifier* is a name which is used to denote some entity in a program, such as the name of a module or procedure. For example, the identifiers, `trivial`, `hello`, and `PortIO` are the names of modules; `WriteString` and `WriteLn` are the names of procedures.

A *keyword* is an identifier whose use has been reserved for particular situations. So far you have seen MODULE, IMPORT, FROM, BEGIN, END, and PROCEDURE. (Notice that all the keywords in Modula-2 are spelled using capital letters only.)

A *string* is a data value which is composed of a sequence of characters. A string value is denoted by a *string literal* which is a sequence of characters between quotation marks. The string literal you have seen is `'Hello world'`.

For a Modula-2 program to be valid, the symbols of the language must be combined in a way which the syntax rules of the language permit. The full range of Modula-2 symbols are discussed in the next chapter; the syntax rules are given informally throughout Part I and are precisely defined in Parts II and III of the book.

2.4   SOFTWARE COMPONENTS AND MODULARIZATION

In Chapter 1 we asserted that the modular design of software usually leads to well-designed software, and software which is easier to implement and test, and, most of all, easier to get right. The following two criteria may be used for judging how well a Modula-2 module has been designed:

1. The degree to which the whole of the module is responsible for a single aspect of the program. This can usually be determined by whether the variables in the module are related to each other and if the procedures in a module operate only on those variables.

2. The number of identifiers which have to be imported from a module to use it should be fairly small. That is, the size of its definition module should be fairly small, or at least another module should not have to import too many to carry out a task.

If both of these criteria are successfully applied to modules when they are designed and implemented, then it is possible to consider them as replaceable components. This can be a great help when developing software, especially if you are not sure just what is required. For example, if you decide to have a module to input transactions from the terminal, but you are not sure what kind of interface is required—whether to use a menu or form system, or whatever—then you can choose the simplest to implement as a prototype. Then, if you have specified the definition module properly, you will be able to replace the implementation module when you have decided what is needed. The idea of a software component should encourage you to produce programs whose component modules can be easily replaced by improved versions, just as the engines of well-designed automobiles can be replaced by more powerful ones. Designing programs as if they were to be built from components also helps minimize portability problems.

As a general software development strategy, this evolutionary approach is to be recommended. If you design your program as a collection of modules and fully specify the definition modules (compiling them if your implementation requires this), but have dummy implementation modules, or do not produce any, then you can get a Modula-2 implementation to check your design. All you have to do is compile the program module which imports the others. This will check the interfaces without needing implementation modules. If you implement dummy or prototype versions of these then you can begin to execute the software fairly early during development and build it up bit by bit.

The way in which separately compiled modules have public and private parts has been alluded to before. The overall structure of how this works is now presented. The example includes the use of a module which has been compiled separately from the program module. Not a lot of detail is given about what the statements do. The following chapters will deal with these details.

The example is a simple one which in reality might not actually warrant a separate module; however, it is a useful illustration of separate modules.

The program is to output both informative messages and error messages, and you have decided that one module should have the responsibility of outputting messages, no matter what type. You must decide first what the public part of the module must contain.

A useful way to decide this is to consider the module as being a service company which offers services to clients who are willing to pay. Clients are happy to pay for what they need but they do not want to have to use a lot of services to get at what they want. Let us say that error messages must be preceded by sounding the terminal's bleeper and by the word `Error:`. You have a design choice to make: you could include a procedure (described in Chapter 8) to sound the bleeper and a procedure to output `Error:` and a procedure to output information or error messages. However, a simpler approach, which is in keeping with the idea of the client/server relationship, is simply to have an information message procedure and an error message procedure.

(Notice that a decision in favour of the second option allows the rules for error messages to change without having to change the public part—the definition module.)

The definition module for the message module is now specified as follows. It consists of a number of declarations of identifiers which the module makes available to its clients. In this case, the identifiers are Messages, InfoMessage, and ErrorMessage. The first identifier is the name of the module. The second and third are the names of the procedures, and are followed by notation which allows strings to be passed to the procedures. (The meaning of this syntax is fully described in Chapter 8.)

```
DEFINITION MODULE Messages;
PROCEDURE InfoMessage(Message: ARRAY OF CHAR);
PROCEDURE ErrorMessage(Message: ARRAY OF CHAR);
END Messages.
```

The general strategy for testing a design specified by a definition module is to compile another module which makes use of the definition module. Therefore the test module needs to import from the definition module whose design is being tested. The following program module, TestMessages, tests the definition of the Messages module by importing its procedures and using them:

```
MODULE TestMessages;
FROM Messages IMPORT InfoMessage, ErrorMessage;
BEGIN
   InfoMessage('This is a test information message');
   ErrorMessage('This is a test error message')
END TestMessages.
```

Assuming TestMessages has already been typed in and stored in a suitable file, then TestMessages can be input and compiled. (In some implementations, the Messages definition module will have to be compiled before TestMessages.) Successful compilation of TestMessages will confirm that the interface is correct, and give you some confidence about the design of Messages.

Before proceeding with the design of our program, it is worth pointing out that the way in which the names InfoMessage and ErrorMessage have been imported from the Messages module makes them appear in TestMessages as if they had been declared there. To identify completely these procedures their names should be *qualified* by preceding them by the name of their module and a period, thus:

```
Messages.InfoMessage and
```

```
Messages.ErrorMessage
```

If we preferred to use this form of identifying the procedures we imported, we would have to use a different form of the IMPORT statement:

```
IMPORT Messages;
```

For simplicity, we will use the FROM form of IMPORT throughout Part I. (Chapter 13 describes when qualified importation is required.)

Returning to the design of `TestMessages`: you should note that you do not need to implement `Messages` before compiling `TestMessages`; indeed, you should not, because you may find that there are problems with the definition module.

Of course, to execute `TestMessages`, you will eventually need to implement the `Messages` module. You have not been introduced to enough Modula-2 yet to understand every detail of the implementation module below, but you should be able to pick up the main points from what you have already seen.

```
IMPLEMENTATION MODULE Messages;
FROM PortIO IMPORT WriteString, WriteLn, WriteChar;
PROCEDURE InfoMessage(Message: ARRAY OF CHAR);
   BEGIN
      WriteString(Message); WriteLn
   END InfoMessage;
PROCEDURE ErrorMessage(Message: ARRAY OF CHAR);
   CONST bleep = 07C;
   BEGIN
      WriteChar(bleep);
      WriteString('Error: ');
      WriteString(Message); WriteLn
   END ErrorMessage;
END Messages.
```

implementation of procedures declared in Messages definition module

The essence of the implementation is that it imports the necessary output procedures from the module `PortIO`. You have met `WriteString` and `WriteLn` before; `WriteChar` simply outputs a single character and is needed for sounding the bleeper in the `ErrorMessage` procedure. (The definition `bleep = 07C` defines a character which is commonly used for sounding the bleeper on a terminal; the notation is explained in Chapter 3.)

This implementation module can now be compiled. To execute the complete program usually involves a linking process which connects the program module and separate module for execution. This process may be explicit (as it is in Topspeed Modula-2) or automatic. We will use the term *link* to refer to whatever process your implementation requires.

Therefore, having successfully compiled the implementation module of `Messages`, it should be linked with `TestMessages` and the latter executed. This will test that you have actually implemented the `Messages` module properly.

You should now have a broad understanding of the structure of Modula-2 programs. The next chapter describes the elements of Modula-2, and the rest of Part I introduces most of the facilities of the language.

As a postscript to this description of a model Modula-2 implementation, it is necessary to distinguish between two types of fault in a program. The first is an *error*[1] which is a fault in the form of a program text; if a compiler detects that a program is not *well formed* it must report the error and prevent executable code being generated. On the other hand, an *exception*[2] is a contravention of the rules of the language which occurs during the execution of a program, thereby making it an invalid program. However an exception need not be detected by an implementation; the detection of some exceptions would be too expensive to implement. (Accessing the 'value' of an unassigned variable is typical of this kind of exception.)

2.5   PORTABILITY ISSUES

Fortunately, there are few portability problems with the way in which program modules make use of separate modules. Three portability issues are worth noting here, but we will only look at one at this point:

1. Modula-2 implementations divide into two sets: those which implement definition modules according to the syntax presented above, and those which require the exported identifiers to be explicitly exported (see below).

2. Some identifiers are automatically exported when a type is exported. (See Chapter 13 for details.)

3. Some implementations place restrictions on the identifiers used to name modules, because of limitations on their linkers.

The syntax problem arises from Professor Wirth's earlier editions of *Programming in Modula-2*. In editions 1 and 2, the identifiers being exported by a definition module had to be included in a list preceded by the keywords EXPORT QUALIFIED. Many implementations are based on the second edition and use this syntax. Others, despite being based on the third edition use the syntax because of the apparent ability to control the automatic exporting of identifiers (see Chapter 13). In practice this difference in syntax is not a problem. For example, to re-implement a definition module written using Topspeed Modula-2 for a compiler which required an export list means collecting together all identifiers which a client module might use and preceding them with EXPORT QUALIFIED. The definition module of Messages would be rewritten thus:

```
DEFINITION MODULE Messages;
EXPORT QUALIFIED InfoMessage, ErrorMessage;
PROCEDURE InfoMessage(Message: ARRAY OF CHAR);
PROCEDURE ErrorMessage(Message: ARRAY OF CHAR);
END Messages.
```

There may be a few more problems re-implementing syntax based on edition 2 of *Programming in Modula-2* because the programmer who wrote the original

---

[1]The terms *compile-time error* and *compilation error* are also in common usage.
[2]The terms *run-time error* and *execution error* are often used in this context. However, they usually refer to exceptions which have been detected.

definition module may have used facilities which allowed the export of identifiers to be controlled; more on this in Chapter 13.

2.6   REVIEW QUESTIONS AND EXERCISES

Q2.1   How does a program module begin and end?

Q2.2   What is the instruction which allows you to use procedures (or whatever) from another module?

Q2.3   Non-trivial programs do not always need to use other modules. True or false?

Q2.4   The use of upper- and lower-case letters in identifiers does not matter in Modula-2. True or false?

Q2.5   What is the significance of EXPORT QUALIFIED in definition modules?

Q2.6   Type in the Messages definition module. Then type in the TestMessages program module and use it to check the interface to Messages. Finally implement Messages and execute the test program.

Q2.7   The style of the error messages provided by the Messages module is to be changed: instead of preceding a message with a bleep and the prefix Error:, a prefix *** ERROR *** is to appear on a *separate* line before the message. Reimplement Messages to effect this change and test it using TestMessages.

3 BASIC ELEMENTS

3.1 INTRODUCTION

'Twas brillig, and the slithy toves
Did gire and gimble in the wabe:
All mimsy were the borogoves,
And the mome raths outgrabe.'

The above gibberish (from *Jabberwocky* by Lewis Carroll) looks like English; you can even make it sound like English. The author made his poem conform to the lexical and syntactic conventions of English; he put letters together to form words, and used punctuation properly. However, the meaning, or semantics, of the quotation is open to question. This chapter is about the fine grain of Modula-2 programs—how character sequences make up the symbols of the language. For a program to be valid, it must have the correct form and to describe such forms we must be able to identify the words, numbers and punctuation symbols which are used.

3.2 THE LEXICAL ELEMENTS OF MODULA-2

Modula-2 is a free format language, which means that unlike FORTRAN, for example, no significance is attached to the column in which a particular language symbol is placed, or to the number of spaces and new lines which are placed between any two language symbols.

In Modula-2 your program text is considered to be a sequence of symbols or tokens. These *tokens* are delimited by punctuation characters, spaces or end-of-lines (and so no token may include either a space or an end-of-line). The fact that some tokens are made up of strings of alphabetic or alphanumeric characters, and some are made up of punctuation symbols is of no consequence to Modula-2.

What it must distinguish between are the tokens which fall into the four classes: symbols of the language, identifiers (defined by the programmer or predefined), literal constants and comments. These are discussed next.

Symbols of Modula-2

These are alphabetic words, such as `MODULE`, `BEGIN` and `FROM`, and other symbols such as `;` , `=` and `+`. The alphabetic words are called keywords or *reserved words,* the latter because they cannot be used as identifiers denoting constants, types or variables.

Programmer-defined or predefined identifiers

These are words which begin with a letter and may contain other letters and digits (and the underscore character `_`). However, there are portability problems with underscores (see below) and so we will avoid using them. Identifiers are used to name variables, modules, procedures, etc. For example: `Count`, `Message`.

Literal constants

These tokens denote actual values. They include numeric literals and string literals. Numeric literals are unsigned whole numbers, positive or negative whole numbers, positive or negative real numbers, and numbers in scientific notation for the real types. For example:

```
0, 25, 6456, -13, -678, 1.234, -3.124E2, 'A', 'hello'
```

Comments

A comment is a piece of text which has no effect on the execution of a program. Its purpose is to inform the reader.

3.3   IDENTIFIERS

Identifiers are sequences of letters, underscores, and digits. The first character of an identifier must be a letter or underscore.

Examples of *correctly* formed identifiers are:

```
LineNumber, Date, string1, New_word, a99,
NumberOfPackets, x, Storage.
```

Examples of *incorrectly* formed identifiers are:

```
A$, 1x, Line Number, New-word
```

There is no maximum length of identifiers specified for Modula-2. (In most implementations there is a *very* high maximum length, which is usually adequate; for example, in Topspeed Modula-2 the maximum length of an identifier is 255 characters.) All characters are significant. Modula-2 is case sensitive, which means that upper- and lower-case letters are not considered to be the same, and so all the following are *different* identifiers:

- `ThisMonth`

- `thismonth`

- `thisMonth`

- `THISMONTH`

- `THISmonth`

All the keywords of Modula-2 are in upper-case, which makes them easy to recognize. You are encouraged to use mixed case for identifiers, like in `ThisMonth`: start the identifier with a capital letter and use lower-case letters until what would be the beginning of the next word in English. Begin subsequent words with a capital. This style is used throughout the book, except for single-character identifiers which are used in simple examples.

Identifiers must be separated from numbers and reserved words by either a space, a comment, or a new line. They may be juxtaposed with non-alphanumeric symbols (such as punctuation symbols, arithmetic operators, etc.).

3.4   NUMERIC LITERALS

Numeric literals are used to denote either whole numbers or real numbers. Whole numbers are usually denoted by a sequence of digits which may or not be preceded by a plus or minus sign, for example:

```
0,  472,  -456,  +23400
```

However, it may be convenient to denote a whole number value using either hexadecimal or octal notation. This is done by adding a suffix to the sequence of digits: if the digits are followed by an H they represent a hexadecimal value; if the digits are followed by B they represent an octal value. When the octal notation is being used, only the digits `0..7` may precede the B. When the hexadecimal notation is being used, the digits `0..7` and the letters `A..F` may precede the H. For example:

- `10B` is the octal representation of the decimal number `8`.

- `327B` is the octal representation of the decimal number `233`.

- `4D4H` is the hexadecimal representation of the decimal number `1236`.

- `0FF77H` is the hexadecimal representation of the decimal number `65399`.

Note that hexadecimal numbers must begin with a digit in order to distinguish them from identifiers. (`0FF77` is a number expressed in hexadecimal, whereas `FF77` is a valid identifier.)

Octal numbers may also be used to specify a character value: by using a C suffix instead of a B suffix, a number can be used to denote a character according to how characters are implemented by a particular compiler. The C is needed to distinguish character values from numeric values. (See Chapter 17 for further details.)

Real number literals have both an integer and a fractional part, and possibly a scale factor. The integer part consists of a sequence of digits. This is followed by the fractional part which begins with a decimal point. The decimal point may be followed by a sequence of digits. After the fractional part a scale factor may be used to indicate whether the preceding decimal number must be multiplied or divided by a power of ten. The scale factor consists of the letter E optionally followed by either a plus or minus sign followed by an integer. For example, 2.651E-4 has an integer part of 2, a fractional part of .651, and a scale factor of -4. The number this denotes is 0.0002651.

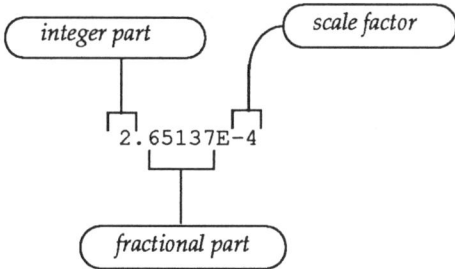

Other valid real literals are:

```
0.23   1.E12   5.   234.573E-3
```

To conclude this section, the following table lists some examples of tokens which will be recognized by Modula-2 as numbers and what they denote.

Numeric literal	Meaning
29	whole number 29
OAF22H	the hex denotation for 44834
3.	real number 3.0
333.023	real number 333.023
33.5E-7	the real number 0.000000335
32B	the whole number 26

3.5   LITERAL STRINGS

In the same way that numerical values may be denoted by literals, string values may be denoted by literal strings. A *literal string* is a sequence of characters enclosed by quotation marks, or apostrophes. The enclosing character may not be one of the characters used in the literal string. Therefore, in order to include quotation marks in a literal string you must enclose it using apostrophes, and to include apostrophes in the string you must enclose it in quotation marks. The following are examples of strings:

```
'A'
"Hello World"
"abcdf'45+=--\"
'"I am angry", exclaimed Bert'
```

A literal string may not be spread over more than one line.

3.6   RESERVED WORDS

Modula-2 has 41 special identifiers[1] which are the keywords of the language. They cannot be used for variable names, and they must be separated from other identifiers and numbers by a space or a new line.

The reserved words are:

AND	ARRAY	BEGIN	BY
CASE	CONST	DEFINITION	DIV
DO	ELSE	ELSIF	END
EXIT	EXPORT	FOR	FROM
IF	IMPLEMENTATION	IMPORT	IN
LOOP	MOD	MODULE	NOT
OF	OR	POINTER	PROCEDURE
QUALIFIED	RECORD	REM	REPEAT
RETURN	SET	THEN	TO
TYPE	UNTIL	VAR	WHILE
WITH			

The meaning of the reserved words will be explained in subsequent chapters.

3.7   SPECIAL CHARACTERS

The special characters presented here are operators, brackets, and delimiters; they are listed below with a brief description of their purpose. (Note that some have more than one role, and that some have alternative representations, as described in Section 3.9.) The details of each symbol are discussed as they are needed in the rest of Part I.

Special character	Purpose
+	addition or set union operator
−	subtraction or set difference operator
*	multiplication or set intersection operator
/	division or symmetric set difference operator
:=	assignment operator
&	logical AND
=	equal
# or <>	not equal
<	less than
>	greater than

---

[1]Note that additionally the identifiers NIL and FORWARD are frequently implemented as reserved words and so should not be used as program identifiers.

Special character	Purpose
<=	less than or equal, or set inclusion
>=	greater than or equal
()	parentheses
[]	index brackets
{}	set braces
(* *)	comment brackets
^	dereferencing operator
, .;:..|	punctuation symbols

3.8   COMMENTS

Comments are any sequence of characters enclosed within the comment delimiters (* and *). They are treated by a Modula-2 compiler like a space, and should be used to provide information about what the program is supposed to do for subsequent readers of the source program.

Some examples of comments follow:

```
(* Program to sort a linked list *)

(* A comment spread
   over two lines *)
```

Note that the second example begins on one line and ends on the next; comments may cover any number of lines. This means that if you forget to finish a comment, the compiler will discard *all* the text following the start of the comment until an end of comment is found, this would lead to the module failing to compile. Modula-2 also allows nested comments (unlike some other languages such as C). That is, a compiler counts the number of (* symbols in a comment and only ends the comment when it finds an equal number of *) symbols. This is useful for 'commenting out' code fragments with comments in them. For example, consider the following source code. It includes an IF statement which detects an exceptional situation in a module, and includes a comment to that effect. When the programmer has decided that he or she has removed this possibility, he or she may effectively remove it by commenting out as shown. (WriteCard outputs the value of a cardinal, as we shall see.)

```
(* debug code commented out
IF Count > 100 THEN    (* this should never happen *)
   WriteString('Value of variable Count=');
   WriteCard(Count);
   WriteLn
END;
*)
```

In many, if not most, implementations comments which have a special form may be used to give instructions to a compiler. These instructions are called *compiler directives*. They often begin with a $ symbol, such as:

```
(*$B-,I-,S- ...*)
```

There are no standards for the form or meaning of compiler directives, and they are rarely discussed in texts on programming languages. However, in the context of portable programming, their use is significant. We shall only refer to Topspeed Modula-2 compiler directives when appropriate.

3.9   PORTABILITY ISSUES

There should not be portability problems with the basic elements of a language. However, there are problems with all languages at this level. The problems may be categorized thus:

- use of alternative symbols and character sets;

- implementation restrictions;

- extensions.

For most programmers in the USA and Europe, there is only one set of character codes and graphics—the one defined by the ASCII table. (This is compounded by nearly all programming text books including it.) However, the ASCII set is a variant of the international 7-bit character set, known as ISO 646 (the number of the standard which defines it) and which contains 128 character values. The differences are small and arise because ISO 646 specifies that certain codes may be used for national symbols. For example, the currency symbol may be $ or £ or ¥.

Modula-2 programs must be represented using the symbols described above, all of which are found in the ISO 646 set. For convenience, this book uses the ASCII variant for expressing program source code. However, some of the special symbols in the last table occupy positions in the character set which are defined by ISO 646 to be available for national variants. (The square brackets are affected by this.) The following table shows the 'standard' symbol and an alternative proposed for adoption in the Modula-2 standard:

Standard symbol		Alternative
#	(not equal)	<>
[]	(index brackets)	(. .)
{}	(set braces)	(: :)
^	(dereferencing operator)	@
|	(case alternative symbol)	!

Note that although # is considered to be the standard not-equal symbol, it is subject to much variation, and so we use the more portable <> pair for not-equal.

The question of what character set should be used to represent source code is different from the question of what character set may be used for characters. Although the CHAR type should include the symbols needed to represent Modula-2 programs, the other character values may come from any implementation-defined set. For example, the Japanese character set would be permissible for characters. Indeed, at the time of writing most implementations use an 8-bit, 256-value character set.

The use of the underscore character in identifiers may also cause problems. Its use was sanctioned late in the development of the language and not many implementations permit it. (Some allow it but ignore it, so that `This_Month` is considered to be `ThisMonth`. This seems contrary to the spirit of a language which distinguishes between upper- and lower-case characters.)

We have already mentioned that the significant length of an identifier may be restricted to a large number (255 characters in Topspeed Modula-2). This will normally not be a problem. However, if you build software to generate Modula-2 programs which have *very* long identifier names, you may have to reconsider your identifier generation algorithm!

Similarly, there may be a maximum length of line of text which a compiler can accept, and string literals are often restricted to this length. Topspeed Modula-2 does not have static limits on the size of string literals.

Another restriction on what a compiler can process often occurs because of the evolution of Modula-2. For example, the remainder operator, REM, which was introduced late in the development of the language, is simply not provided by many implementations. (See the exercise in Chapter 17 on how to simulate MOD.)

Finally in this section, we consider *extensions*. All Modula-2 implementations offer facilities to the programmer which are not specified as part of the language. Often, these are what is known as *pure extensions*, which are extensions which do not effect the meaning of source code written using standard Modula-2. (Topspeed Modula-2 provides bit-shift operators >> and <<; these are not defined for 'Standard' Modula-2 and so are pure extensions.) However, some extensions are the result of decisions which an implementor has taken which fundamentally effect the way in which a compiler processes all source code. We are concerned here with three extensions which are not pure.

Many implementations define more than the 41 reserved words listed above. Many define FORWARD, CODE, and NIL as reserved keywords. This has the immediate effect of making them unavailable as programmer identifiers.

FORWARD is used to postpone the full definition of a procedure and is used in implementations which cannot process a class of Modula-2 source programs. The effect of this is significant and is discussed in detail in the section on portability issues in Chapter 14.

CODE is used to permit assembler code to be included in procedures. This facility is generally not portable.

NIL is used with pointer variables (see Chapter 11). Most implementations have it as a predefined identifier, and this means it can be redefined by the programmer who is not using pointers. Other implementations have it as a keyword. For the sake of portability, it is better to treat it as if it was a keyword.

In general, you cannot avoid the use of all possible reserved words. However some which are known to the authors and should be avoided are LONG, SHORT, FAR, LVAR. Using lower-case letters in identifiers should avoid clashes with most extra reserved words.

3.10 REVIEW QUESTIONS AND EXERCISES

Q3.1 What are tokens?

Q3.2 What kind of tokens are the following: `1,432,-5454,1.0E-10, 'help'`?

Q3.3 Give an example of a string literal which includes an apostrophe string delimiter

Q3.4 Write 0.000012 in scientific 'E' notation.

Q3.5 What is the effect of an implementation defining FORWARD as a keyword?

4 ASSIGNING VALUES TO VARIABLES

4.1 INTRODUCTION

To some degree or other a computer program deals with data. If it deals with large amounts of data the program is usually called a *data-processing* application; if it does not process too much data but has to process it quickly, in response to events which occur in its environment, then it is called a *real-time* application. In both cases (and all the cases in between), data must be stored and manipulated, or changed.

The way in which data manipulations are performed varies from language to language. Modula-2 has a fairly simple model of how this happens: a data value is stored at a location in a computer's memory, and may be replaced by storing a new value at the location using an assignment statement. New values are calculated by evaluating expressions. This chapter introduces the basic data values which Modula-2 provides and shows how they can be manipulated.

4.2 VARIABLES AND DATA

Data values in languages like Modula-2 are placed in storage locations called *variables*. Variables are so called because they usually contain different values during the execution of a program. At the beginning of a program's execution, the variables in the program are not defined to contain a value, and any attempt to use a variable which does not contain a defined value invalidates a program (although it may continue to execute). Storing an initial value in a variable is called *initialization*.

Once a variable has been initialized, the value it contains may be extracted and stored in another variable. Alternatively it can be combined with other values in an expression. The result of such an expression can then be stored back in the original variable, or stored in another variable.

The Modula-2 operation for storing a value in a variable is called *assignment*. The *assignment operator* is a special symbol of a colon followed by an equals sign:

```
:=
```

Variables must be created before they can be used. When they are no longer needed they should be disposed of. For the most part you do not need to be concerned with how this is done. The most common kind of variables are those which are introduced in the text of modules and procedures by a mechanism called a *declaration*. (You will see examples of variable declarations later.) When your program source text is successfully compiled, the compiler ensures that code is placed at appropriate points in your program to create and dispose of the variables which you have declared. We term the period of program execution between the creation and disposal of a variable its *lifetime*. Because their lifetimes are determined by the unchanging text of your Modula-2 program, rather than by its execution, variables which are created in declarations are called *static variables*.

(There is another kind of variable which can be created and disposed of explicitly during program execution. These are called *dynamic variables* and are not discussed in this chapter. You should consult Chapter 11 for an introduction to dynamic variables.)

In the case of static variables the compiler arranges for them to be created in response to variable declarations in your program. These declarations can appear anywhere in a module before the statement part of a program or implementation module (see Chapter 8). Variable declarations can appear anywhere in a definition module.

Typically, more than one variable is declared at a time in a sequence of declarations which is preceded by the keyword VAR. To declare a variable requires an identifier which names the variable and information concerning the values which the variable may store.

This information is called the variable's *type*. A type is a set of values and the set of operations which are permitted on those values. (Examples of these attributes are given below.) Modula-2 provides a number of built-in types, the simplest of which are identified by predefined identifiers.

A *variable declaration* consists of one or more variable names (separated by commas), then a colon, and the type of the variables preceding the colon. The declaration is terminated by a semicolon. Thus the general form of variable declarations is:

```
VAR
    variable1, variable2 : type1;
    variable3 : type2;
```

The following is an example of a list of variable declarations (with line numbers in comments for later reference):

```
VAR                                        (* 1 *)
    Count: CARDINAL;                       (* 2 *)
    Character: CHAR;                       (* 3 *)
    CurrentTemperature, MaxTemperature: REAL;  (* 4 *)
    Danger: BOOLEAN;                       (* 5 *)
    Balance, Transaction: INTEGER;         (* 6 *)
```

Line 1. The keyword VAR begins the declarations; you do not have to have any declarations after VAR, but it is usual to have some, as in the example above. There is no particular keyword to finish declarations. The occurrence of any other declarations terminates them (typically, this will be a procedure declaration, as you will notice).

Line 2. A variable called Count is declared to be of type CARDINAL, which is a predefined type name which denotes non-negative whole number values, beginning with zero. (In theory, CARDINAL should include all the natural numbers; in practice the range is restricted according to the way in which the values are represented by a compiler. Topspeed Modula-2, like many implementations, have CARDINAL as the range 0..65535. This portability issue is discussed later.)

Line 3. The variable Character is declared to be of type CHAR which means it can take values which represent both printable (e.g. A, B, x, and %) and non-printable characters. An example of a non-printable character would be a character to cause a particular printer to feed through a sheet of paper. The specific values of CHAR depend on the computer or the implementation.

Line 4. This declaration specifies two variables CurrentTemperature and MaxTemperature which may take real number values (such as 64.894589 and −0.89478).

Line 5. The penultimate declaration tells the compiler to create a variable called Danger which can take either of the values TRUE or FALSE. This type of variable is used to store logical information. The built-in type BOOLEAN contains only the values TRUE and FALSE. (It is named after the 19th-century English logician George Boole.)

Line 6. Finally, two integer variables, Balance and Transaction, are declared. In mathematics integers contain all negative and non-negative whole numbers, but in Modula-2 the built-in type will have some finite range, such as −32768..32767. (See *Portability Issues* below.)

The type of data values a variable can hold should be dictated by the problem for which the program is a solution. Hence, a need to store whole number values should lead you to consider either CARDINAL or INTEGER, and to choose the former if no negative values should occur, and the latter if negative values are a possibility. The name of a variable should be suggestive of the kind of data which it is to store and its purpose in the program.

4.3   ASSIGNMENT AND EXPRESSIONS

To store a value in a variable, the value must be *assigned* to the variable. A value may be a constant value or may be calculated from a combination of values. Constant values are usually denoted by literals (such as 1, 6.78, 'abc') which were described in Chapter 3.

The combining of values in order to calculate a value to be assigned is called an *expression*. An expression is a combination of other expressions or constant values. It may contain literal constants such as 45 or 'X', or it may include the name of a variable which denotes the value currently held by the variable. These various components of an expression are called *operands* and they may be combined using *operators* such as + and −, which are allowed for values of the numerical types, and AND, =, and OR which are allowed for values of the BOOLEAN type. The following are examples of the simplest kind of expressions:

```
2234
(1 + 2) * 3
54.0/8.2E-3
'p'
```

All the above are *constant expressions*; i.e. their operands are constant values (which is the case here) or their operands are constant expressions. The first expression has the value 2234; the second has the value 9; the third has an approximation to the mathematical value of 54.0 ÷ 0.0082. The last value of the expression is the character value p.

Note that, because constant expressions contain no reference to any variables, they can be evaluated *before* the execution of any program which uses them. This fact results in a useful facility in Modula-2, as we shall see.

The real benefit of expressions comes from their ability to manipulate values which are stored in variables. The occurrence of a variable name as an operand in an expression causes the value of the variable at that point in the expression to be extracted and used in place of the variable operand. In other words, a variable identifier in an expression denotes the *value* stored in the variable. Examples of this are:

```
Count + 1
MaxTemperature - CurrentTemperature
Character = 'p'
```

The first expression would evaluate to a value which is one more than the value currently in Count. The second would result in a value which is the difference between the current values stored in the variables MaxTemperature and CurrentTemperature respectively. The third would result in a Boolean value: TRUE if Character does have the value 'p', and FALSE otherwise.

Expressions occur most frequently when they are being used to calculate a value which is to be assigned to a variable. In Modula-2 the *assignment statement* is used to evaluate expressions *and* to assign the resultant value to a variable. The assignment statement consists of a ***designator*** which identifies the variable (the one in which the value of the expression is to be stored), followed by the assignment operator `:=`, followed by an expression. Thus the general form of an assignment statement is:

```
designator := expression;
```

The following are examples of assignments:

```
Character := 'A';
Count := Count + 1;
Danger := CurrentTemperature > MaxTemperature;
```

The first of these examples, `Character := 'A'`, is the most straightforward. The CHAR value denoted by `'A'` is stored in the variable `Character`.

In `Count := Count + 1`, the expression `Count + 1` must be evaluated before `Count` can be updated. What happens is that the current value in `Count` (i.e. the one which is to replaced) is extracted and 1 is added to it. The result of evaluating the expression is then stored in `Count`. (When the value of a variable is replaced by a value which has been calculated using itself, we often say that the variable has been *updated*.)

The third example requires a little more evaluation on the right hand side of the assignment. The expression is more complex than the others: it contains two simple expressions—`CurrentTemperature` and `MaxTemperature`—the results of which are compared using the greater-than operator (>). Thus, these simple expressions are evaluated as the REAL values stored in each of the variables, and it is the results of these evaluations which are then compared. The result of the comparison is a BOOLEAN value—which is TRUE if the value in `CurrentTemperature` is greater than the value in `MaxTemperature` and FALSE otherwise.

During this discussion, pains have been taken to explain that variables themselves are not affected during the evaluation of an expression. Rather, variables can only be changed when the values calculated by evaluating expressions have been assigned to them. Instead of using a lot of words by continuing to be meticulous in our use of English in these explanations, we will adopt a shorthand which is widespread but which tends to suggest that the variables are operated on. Take the last two examples of the assignment statement. They are more usually described by phrases like 'increment `Count` by 1' and 'check whether `CurrentTemperature` is greater than `MaxTemperature` and store the result in `Danger`'. For convenience, this book uses this type of description as freely as other textbooks.

However, you should try to remember that a shorthand is being used and that values (the results of evaluating expressions) are being manipulated in expressions, not variables.

We can now develop a simple module to calculate the square and cube of a non-negative whole number, to store the results in variables, and to print the results. The number can be input using the ReadCard procedure from PortIO. The following module is a possible solution to this problem:

```
MODULE pwr2and3;
FROM PortIO IMPORT ReadCard, WriteCard, WriteString, WriteLn;
VAR
  N, SquareOfN, CubeOfN : CARDINAL;
BEGIN
  WriteString('Input number: ');
  N := ReadCard();
  SquareOfN := N * N;
  CubeOfN := N * N * N;
  WriteString('The square of the number is ');
  WriteCard(SquareOfN);
  WriteLn;
  WriteString('The cube of the number is ');
  WriteCard(CubeOfN);
  WriteLn
END pwr2and3.
```

There are two points to be made about this module. First, the calculation of the cube of the number N is a little inefficient. A simpler way of calculating the cube would have been to use the square, thus:

```
CubeOfN := N * SquareOfN;
```

In general, the more operands and operators there are in an expression, the more execution time is required to evaluate it. This is not important in such a simple calculation as a cube, but complex expressions can be very slow to evaluate, and can slow the execution of a program when used repeatedly. (See Chapter 16 for more details of expression evaluation.)

The second point is that the problem was over-specified, and the solution over-engineered. There is no need to use variables to store the square and cube of N. As we shall see, certain procedure parameters may be expressions, and this is the case with the output procedures of PortIO. Therefore, the expressions which calculate the required powers may be used with WriteCard, but this solution removes the option of simplifying the cube expression—because the value of the square has not been retained:

```
MODULE pwr2and3;
FROM PortIO IMPORT ReadCard, WriteCard, WriteString, WriteLn;
VAR N: CARDINAL;
BEGIN
  WriteString('Input number: '); N := ReadCard ();
  WriteString('The square of the number is ');
  WriteCard(N * N,); WriteLn;
  WriteString('The cube of the number is ');
  WriteCard(N * N * N,); WriteLn;
END pwr2and3.
```

Layout of programs

At this point we mention our policy on program layout. There are no absolute rules on how to lay out Modula-2 programs. We have adopted a number of practices which we hold to be beneficial to understanding source code. First, we use indentation to emphasize structure, and generally we have only one statement per line. However, in a book space is limited and we do not indent as much as we would normally advocate, and frequently have more than one statement per line. Second, we use mixed upper- and lower-case in identifiers to improve readability.

Our punctuation style is more variable. We do not feel that it is necessary to be rigid on matters such as the use of spaces before colons, or whether an extra semicolon is used at the end of a statement. (Compare the declarations and final WriteLn statements in the last two programs.)

4.4   TYPES

Recall that the type of a variable determines what values that variable can hold. Declaring the type of a variable thus places the requirement on the expression on the right hand side of an assignment that it must evaluate to a result which in some sense matches the type of the variable. In other words, the value on the right hand side of an assignment operator must be one of the values of the type of the variable on the left. The expression is therefore assumed to have a type which determines the values which the expression may have when evaluated.

Programming languages like Pascal, Ada, and Modula-2 are all said to be *strongly typed* languages. This means that they enforce strict type checking rules which ensure that when the value resulting from evaluating an expression is assigned to a variable, it must be the same type as the variable, or at least a compatible type (compatibility is discussed later). There are lots of good reasons for strong type checking.

The essential reason is that by declaring what values a variable may take by specifying its type, you are making an assertion about the solution to your problem which the compiler can check. If you violate your own assertion by breaking the type rules, then you have made a mistake. The mistake may just have been a simple typing one (i.e. a keyboard input mistake—no pun is intended), or the mistake may be more fundamental: your solution might be in error and thus your assertion (the declaration of the variable's type) might be wrong.

For the most part, a Modula-2 compiler checks type information while compiling your program. Therefore most type errors can be detected before you (or your customer) start to use the program. This is clearly an advantage.

However, some type errors can only be detected during program execution, but even then it is surely better to know that you have got something wrong than carry on in ignorance until 'the world falls apart'!

The facilities for specifying data types in Modula-2 are extensive. So much so that there is an extensive vocabulary for describing different classes of data type (see Chapter 16). The simplest types are those classed as *elementary types*. These include the predefined, *basic types* most of which we have briefly described:

- CARDINAL—for non-negative whole numbers;

- INTEGER—for negative and non-negative whole numbers;

- REAL—for approximating real numbers;

- LONGREAL—for approximating real numbers more precisely than REAL;

- CHAR—for characters;

- BOOLEAN—for holding logical values.

All the above, *except* the two real types, are known as *ordinal types*. This means that they correspond to whole (ordinal) numbers. Ordinal types share a lot of properties and can be used with a large number of predefined procedures, as you will see.

Unsigned whole numbers

Unsigned whole numbers in Modula-2 are representations of the mathematical set of the non-negative integers. They are termed *unsigned* because they may not be preceded by a unary sign operator (e.g. if c is a unsigned whole number then +c is not allowed). There are theoretically an infinite number of unsigned whole numbers, but they cannot be represented on a finite computer. A subset is therefore provided by the built-in type CARDINAL.

The actual range of numbers provided by a Modula-2 compiler depends on how CARDINAL values are implemented. A common representation uses 16 bits for each value (see Chapter 17). Such a representation would provide for values in the range 0..65535.

We will assume this range for our examples, but this clearly has portability implications which will be discussed later.

The type CARDINAL is arguably the most commonly used type in Modula-2. It is the natural choice for counting—for example:

```
VAR
  NumberOfTransactions: CARDINAL;
BEGIN
  NumberOfTransactions := 0;
  ...
  NumberOfTransactions := NumberOfTransactions + 1;
```

The usual mathematical operators are provided for use with values of the CARDINAL type. They are:

Operator	Purpose
+	addition
−	subtraction
*	multiplication
/	whole number division[1]
REM	remainder
DIV	division by positive numbers
MOD	modulo (i.e. remainder after DIV)

Some examples of expressions which use these operators and the resultant values are given below. Note that the division operators can result in an exception. (An exception is an event which occurs during program execution and which invalidates the program.) Dividing by zero is an example of an exception.

```
256 + 89 = 345
7345 - 6 = 7339
OEH * 57 * 1B = 6384
65/8 = 8
64 DIV 8 = 8
65 DIV 8 = 8
24 REM 5 = 4
24 MOD 5 = 4
```

(Note that because CARDINAL values cannot be negative, / and DIV are effectively the same; similarly REM and MOD are the same for CARDINAL values. Their differences are explained below in the discussion of signed whole numbers.)

Because CARDINAL has a minimum and a maximum value which can be represented by a given implementation, care must be taken when an expression may calculate a value outside the range, as this would invalidate the program. Exceeding these values is a portability issue and is discussed later.

Values of the type CARDINAL may be compared using the relational operators which result in a BOOLEAN value (either TRUE or FALSE):

Relational operator	Purpose	Relational operator	Purpose
=	equality	<>	inequality
>	greater than	>=	greater than or equal to
<	less than	<=	less than or equal to

For example:

```
NumberOfTransactions > 200
Count <= MaximumAllowed
```

---

[1]The whole number operators / and REM are not yet widely available in Modula-2 implementations. Most implementations only allow / with real numbers.

```
PriceInPennies = 0
```

See Chapter 17 for more details of the CARDINAL type.

Whole number subranges

Frequently, the full range of values is more than is needed. For example, if you are sure that the number of transactions in some system could not exceed 1000, you should make this clear in the declaration of any variable used to store the number. To enable you to do this Modula-2 allows you to define a new type which is a *subrange* of another type. If you wanted to state that the variable NumberOfTransactions could not exceed 1000, the subrange would be a subrange of the type CARDINAL. The type on which a subrange is based is called its *host type*.

A subrange type is declared by giving the lower and upper bounds of the range of the host type. For example, to restrict NumberOfTransactions to values between 0 and 1000, the following could be used:

```
VAR
   NumberOfTransactions: [0..1000];
```

Introducing a new type in this way is generally not considered good programming style. The subrange can be named in a type declaration (similar to that for variables).

As before, NumberOfTransactions may be assigned the value 0. However, it should not be assigned the value 2000.

In the introduction to types we described how a compiler helps you check your logic by ensuring that you generally do not mix types. Unfortunately, because it is usually desirable to allow values of a host type to be assigned to a subrange variable, the majority of subrange type checking has to be postponed until a program is executing. This results in compilers having to generate some extra code which is subsequently executed by your program (with an attendant decrease in performance). Consequently, not all compilers generate the necessary checking code under normal operation: the programmer must explicitly instruct the compiler to insert the checks in the program's code. (This has some portability consequences which we will return to later.) Throughout this book we will assume that subrange checking is being enforced.

Note that subrange types are not restricted to the CARDINAL type; a subrange can be a range of consecutive values of any ordinal type (see Chapter 6).

Signed whole numbers

Signed whole numbers in Modula-2 are representations of the mathematical set of the integers. They are termed *signed* because they may be preceded by a unary sign operator (e.g. if i is a signed whole number both +i and −i are allowed). There are theoretically an infinite number of signed whole numbers, but they cannot be represented on a finite computer. A subset is therefore provided by the built-in type INTEGER.

The actual range of numbers provided by an implementation depends on how INTEGER values are implemented. A common representation uses 16 bits for each value (see Chapter 17). Such a representation would provide for values in the range -32768..32767.

We assume this range for our examples and discuss the portability consequences later.

The following example involves two INTEGER variables—Balance and Deposit. The assignment statement adds whatever has been deposited to the Balance.

```
VAR
   Balance, Deposit: INTEGER;
BEGIN
   Deposit := 23;
   Balance := 0;
   Balance := Balance + Deposit;
```

The same mathematical operators are provided for using with values of the INTEGER types as for CARDINAL. They are:

Operator	Purpose
+	addition
−	subtraction
*	multiplication
/	whole number division
REM	remainder [1]
DIV	division by positive numbers
MOD	modulo (i.e. remainder after DIV)

Some examples of expressions which use these operators and the resultant values are given below. The most complex operators are the division operators, DIV, /, MOD and REM, and even with them the only real difficulty arises from the use of negative numbers. Negative operators on the right hand side of DIV and MOD are not permitted. (However, many implementations allow this and generate unpredictable results.)

The unary operators + and − are available for INTEGER values. + leaves a value unchanged; − negates a value.

```
-256
+89
345 - 3245 = -2900
65/8 = 8
65/-8 = -8
64 DIV 8 = 8
```

---

[1]The operators / and REM are not widely available for whole numbers.

```
65 DIV 8 = 8
-65 DIV 8 = -9
65 DIV -8 should cause an exception
24 REM 5 = 4
24 REM -5 = -4
24 MOD 5 = 4
24 MOD -5 should cause an exception
-24 MOD 5 = 1
```

As for CARDINAL, care must be taken when an expression may calculate a value outside the range of numbers which an implementation provides for INTEGER (see *Portability Issues*).

Values of the type INTEGER may be compared using the relational operators which result in a BOOLEAN value:

Relational operator	Purpose	Relational operator	Purpose
=	equality	<>	inequality
>	greater than	>=	greater than or equal to
<	less than	<=	less than or equal to

For example:

```
Balance > -20000
x <= y DIV -4
```

As with CARDINAL, it is often the case that the full range of values is more than is needed. Therefore you may define and use subranges of INTEGER. For example:

```
VAR
   Balance : [-500..20000];
```

The above declaration introduces the variable Balance and restricts the values it may hold to the range -500..20000. The host type of the subrange [-500..20000] is the type INTEGER; this is obvious since it contains whole numbers which include negative values. However, this would not have been obvious if no negative had been included. The host type may be explicitly given in such circumstances by preceding the subrange with the required host type. For example:

```
VAR
   Balance : INTEGER[500..20000];
```

See Chapter 17 for more details of the INTEGER type.

Real numbers

Mathematical real numbers can only be approximated on a digital computer. Modula-2 provides two types for approximating real values: REAL and LONGREAL. The two types differ in the precision which they offer and consequently in the storage which is required to hold values of the types. The values which can be represented by the types depend on their implementations. Two common sizes for representing REAL and LONGREAL, respectively, are 32 bits and 64 bits.

As an example of the use of REAL variables, consider the following:

```
VAR
   Height, Length, Depth, Volume: REAL;
...
   Volume := Height * Length * Depth;
```

The mathematical operators +, −, *, and / are provided, as shown in the table below.

Operator	Purpose
+	addition
−	subtraction
*	multiplication
/	real number division

All the relational operators are provided for the real types:

Relational operator	Purpose	Relational operator	Purpose
=	equality	<>	inequality
>	greater than	>=	greater than or equal to
<	less than	<=	less than or equal to

However, testing for equality is not usually used between real values because of the way they only approximate the mathematical quantities. A test which checks if numbers are approximately equal (i.e. within some tolerance) is more appropriate. For example, if ApproxEqual is a BOOLEAN variable:

```
ApproxEqual := (Height - Length) <= 0.0000005;
```

Unary + and − are also provided for the real types.

As well as the arithmetic and relational operators, a number of the predefined function procedures may be used with real types. The procedure ABS takes a REAL or LONGREAL value and returns the absolute value; thus a negative value is returned as a positive value. FLOAT and TRUNC are also available to allow the assignment of whole number values to real variables, and the truncation of real values to CARDINAL variables. A new function called LFLOAT has been defined in the forthcoming standard but it is not yet widely implemented. LFLOAT converts a whole number or REAL to a LONGREAL. The following examples show typical results of these functions:

```
ABS(-93792.34) = 93792.34
FLOAT(457) = 457.0
FLOAT(-1) = -1.0
TRUNC(2.34068E3) = 2340
```

Other mathematical functions, such as the trigonometric functions, are provided by library modules provided by an implementation.[1]

Subranges of the real types are not permitted since neither REAL nor LONGREAL are ordinal types.

See Chapter 17 for more details of the REAL and LONGREAL types.

Characters

The type CHAR is an ordinal type which contains character values that are determined by the computer or the compiler which you are using. The first 128 are the same for most American computers: they are the values of the ASCII character set. Because most microcomputer implementations of Modula-2 (including Topspeed Modula-2) implement an extended version of ASCII, we will assume ASCII for most of our examples. This portability issue is discussed later.

Variables of type CHAR and of a type which is a subrange of CHAR may be declared as shown in the following:

```
VAR
   Symbol: CHAR;
   KeyPressed: CHAR;
   Digit: ['0'..'9'];
   CapitalLetter: ['A'..'Z'];
```

In the above, Symbol and KeyPressed are defined as CHAR variables. The variable Digit may only take values which correspond to digits; hence the subrange ['0'..'9']. Similarly, CapitalLetter is restricted to values corresponding to upper-case letters.

There are two kinds of literal constants for values of type CHAR. The most common is used to denote printable characters; the character is placed between apostrophes or double quotes. For example:

```
Symbol := "*";
Symbol := '*';
Digit := '7';
```

It does not matter whether you use apostrophes or double quotes; the first two assignments to Symbol are identical. However, to denote the value for an apostrophe, it must be included between double quotes. To denote the value for a double quote, it must be included between apostrophes, thus:

```
Symbol := '"';
Symbol := "'";
```

Non-printing characters can be denoted as a literal using an octal number followed by the suffix C. However, a simpler way to represent the value of a non-

---

[1] All implementations supply a module of mathematical functions for REAL or LONGREAL. You should consult the documentation for your Modula-2 implementation.

printing character is to use the built-in function procedure CHR. CHR takes a CARDINAL value and returns the character at that position in the *character set* (the character 'set' is actually ordered). In the ASCII set, the character at position 3 is a control code called ETX (which stands for 'end-of-text'). To assign the value for ETX to KeyPressed you can use either the octal notation 3C or CHR(3):

```
KeyPressed := 3C;
KeyPressed := CHR(3);
```

Character positions begin at zero; therefore the evaluation of each expression will result in the fourth value (counting from 0) in the type CHAR. CHR is simpler when larger numbers are used, because you do not have to perform a conversion to octal. For example, the character A has the value 65 in the ASCII set. This is 101 octal. Therefore:

```
'A' = CHR(65) = 101C
```

Note that the built-in procedure ORD complements CHR; ORD takes a value of any ordinal type and returns the position of that value in the type. For CHAR, this means that ORD('A') = 65, and so:

```
ORD('A') = 65 = 101B
```

The relational operators are defined for values of type CHAR. The ordering is defined by the implemented character set. If the ASCII character set is used, the ordering is defined by the position of the characters in the table. Therefore the following is true:

```
'A' < 'B' <...< 'Z' <...< 'a' < 'b' <...< 'z'
```

because:

```
ORD('A') < ORD('B') <...< ORD('Z') <...< ORD('a') etc.
```

No other operators are provided for CHAR. However, two predefined procedures are defined in Modula-2 which are of particular help when handling non-numeric ordinal types. These are INC and DEC. INC increases the value in a variable to the next value in that type; DEC decreases the value in a variable to the previous value in the type. The following module will print B and then y. This is because B is the next value in the type CHAR after A, and y is the value before z in the type. The B is generated by applying INC to Character when it contains A, and the y is generated by applying DEC to Character when it contains z. The module uses the output procedure for characters, WriteChar, which is imported from the module PortIO (see Chapter 9).

```
MODULE IncAndDec;
FROM PortIO IMPORT WriteChar, WriteLn;
VAR Character: CHAR;
BEGIN
  Character := "A";
  INC(Character);
```

```
      WriteChar(Character); WriteLn;
      Character := "z";
      DEC(Character);
      WriteChar(Character); WriteLn
   END IncAndDec.
```

Boolean values

The ordinal type BOOLEAN is used for recording logical values. Consequently it has only two values, which are denoted by the predefined identifiers FALSE and TRUE.

Boolean values are encountered most usually as the result of Boolean expressions which are used to compare values. They occur in all the structured statements of Modula-2.

The use of Boolean variables is fairly restricted. Their simplest use is as flags: a Boolean variable is set to FALSE and this *flag* is subsequently tested by the program and while it remains false the program executes one sequence of statements. At some stage the flag may be set to TRUE and subsequent tests will result in different code being executed. A variant on a flag is a *switch* which alternates between FALSE and TRUE. This is programmed using the Boolean operator NOT which negates logical values. That is NOT TRUE is FALSE and NOT FALSE is TRUE. For example:

```
   VAR Reading: BOOLEAN;
   BEGIN
     Reading := FALSE;
     ...
     Reading := NOT Reading;  (* Reading = TRUE *)
     ...
     Reading := NOT Reading;  (* Reading = FALSE *)
```

However, more complex Boolean expressions can be used to record the result of some comparison of two values. They themselves may be compared (FALSE is defined to be less than TRUE) but it is more usual that BOOLEAN values are combined using AND or OR. The infix operator AND takes two operands, both of which must be TRUE to produce TRUE as a result. The operator OR only produces FALSE if both operands are FALSE. For example:

```
   VAR
     NumberOfErrors: CARDINAL;
     HelpNeeded: BOOLEAN;
     FoundValue: BOOLEAN;
   BEGIN
     ...
     HelpNeeded := NumberOfErrors > 30;
     ...
     FoundValue := NOT FoundValue;
```

Conceptual types

You have met literal values since Chapter 2. It is now appropriate to discuss what the type of a literal value is. To help the discussion consider the following program fragment:

```
VAR
  i : INTEGER;
  c : CARDINAL;
BEGIN
  i := 3;
  c := 3;
```

It is clear that the type of i is INTEGER, and the type of c is CARDINAL. But what is the type of 3? Does it have more than one type (in order that both assignments be valid)?

The answer to both questions is provided by defining the *value* which is *denoted* by the numeric literal 3 to belong to a conceptual type called $\mathbb{Z}$ (pronounced 'Z-Z'). $\mathbb{Z}$ is conceptual in that it is not provided in the language; it is the set of integers found in mathematics plus the associated operations of addition, subtraction, integer division, etc. $\mathbb{Z}$ contains an infinite number of whole numbers which cannot be represented in a finite computer.

The questions above, although quite reasonable to ask, were not as well-directed as they might have been. The essential question about the previous program fragment should have been: is the value (denoted by) 3 *compatible* with the INTEGER variable i *and* the CARDINAL variable c? The answer is yes: $\mathbb{Z}$ values may be assigned to either INTEGER or CARDINAL variables—as long as the $\mathbb{Z}$ value is in the range for which INTEGER or CARDINAL is implemented. All Modula-2 implementations include 3 in both INTEGER and CARDINAL and so the assignments are valid.

Now consider the same declarations but with different values assigned:

```
  i := 43300;
  c := 43300;
```

Again, 43000 is a value of $\mathbb{Z}$, but in this case it is questionable whether 43000 is implemented for the type INTEGER. This portability issue is discussed again later.

A similar situation arises for real values: they may be used with the type REAL and the type LONGREAL The conceptual type $\mathbb{R}$ (pronounced 'R-R') is defined to include all values denoted by real literal and real arithmetic (addition, multiplication, real division, etc.).

The last conceptual type is $\mathbb{S}$ (pronounced 'S-S') which is used for quoted string literals. Therefore the following are all of the type $\mathbb{S}$: 'A', ' ', "Hello world!".

By way of a summary, the following table defines the conceptual types and gives examples:

Conceptual type	Description and examples
$\mathbb{Z}$	All whole number literals (both signed and unsigned). For example: `121   +437   -892   0B      3FFH`
$\mathbb{R}$	All real number literals. For example: `0.0   -5.3452  2.3E+23      666.6666666`
$\mathbb{S}$	All string literals. For example: `'x'     "Enter a number: "`

4.5   TYPE DECLARATIONS

When subranges were introduced earlier in the chapter the following declaration was mildly criticized:

```
VAR
   NumberOfTransactions: [0..1000];
```

The reason for the disapproval is that the subrange type `[0..1000]` has not been given a name and so has been made unique to the variable `NumberOfTransactions`. To define `[0..1000]` as a named type, an identifier must be declared in a *type declaration*. Type declarations are collected together in a type declaration part which consists of the keyword `TYPE` followed by a sequence of type definitions. Each definition consists of an identifier, followed by an equals sign, followed by the definition of the type. For example, the subrange `[0..1000]` could be identified by:

```
TYPE
   TransactionRange = [0..1000];
```

This definition declares an identifier, `TransactionRange`, which denotes a type that includes the values `0..1000` in the type `CARDINAL`. The variable `NumberOfTransactions` can now be declared as a variable of type `TransactionRange`, rather than of type `CARDINAL`.

```
TYPE
   TransactionRange = [0..1000];
VAR
   NumberOfTransactions: TransactionRange;
BEGIN
   NumberOfTransactions := 0;
```

As we shall see, type declarations are used for defining a wide range of types—both simple types, like the above, and structured types (see Chapter 7). For now we shall restrict our examples to subranges. The following defines a subrange type for use with the `Balance` variable, which was used in the section on signed whole numbers:

```
TYPE
  CreditRange = [-500..20000];
VAR
  Balance : CreditRange;
```

We next look at constant declarations, which can be used in conjunction with type declarations.

4.6   CONSTANT DECLARATIONS

You have seen how literal constants are used to denote values of certain types: -325 is an INTEGER literal constant and 'X' is a character literal. Rather than use these in program statements, you can declare an identifier to represent a constant value. This is done in a constant declaration.

Simple constant declarations

A list of constant declarations starts with the keyword CONST and each declaration includes an identifier, followed by the equals sign, followed by a literal constant or a kind of expression which is made up of literal constants or constant identifiers. This kind of expression is not surprisingly called a *constant expression*. Its value is not calculated during program execution, but by the compiler as it processes your program.

Some examples of constant declarations are:

```
CONST
  LowestLevel = -200;
  TaxRate = 0.2;
  MaximumTemperature = 150.8754;
  DangerLevel = MaximumTemperature - 10.0;
  HelpKey = '?';
  MaxNumberInList = 200;
  TwiceMaxInList = 2 * MaxNumberInList;
```

The first of these constants, LowestLevel, has been defined to have a value of -200. Because the value is a negative whole number, we can tell that the type of LowestLevel is INTEGER.

The next three definitions declare three identifiers to be real numbers. TaxRate is defined to be 0.2. The constant MaximumTemperature is defined to be the value 150.8754 and DangerLevel is defined (using a constant expression) to be 10 less than whatever the value of MaximumTemperature is, making it 140.8754 in this case.

Note that these three constants were described as 'real' numbers (not REAL, or LONGREAL for that matter). Unlike the definition of LowestLevel, there is no clue as to the particular type of the constants denoted by TaxRate, MaximumTemperature, and DangerLevel. Assuming neither falls outside the range which either REAL or LONGREAL can represent, they take the conceptual type $\mathbb{R}$ and can be used in expressions which demand either REAL or LONGREAL values.

HelpKey is defined next to be the ? character.

TwiceMaxInList is related to the value which MaxNumberInList represents. In the above declarations MaxNumberInList is 200 and so TwiceMaxInList is 400. Again, these identifiers are not given concrete types but, on the assumption that they fall within the ranges of both CARDINAL and INTEGER, they are considered to be of type $\mathbb{Z}$.

In essence, a constant identifier may be used anywhere that it could be considered to be of the correct type, and you generally will not need to be concerned as to the precise type of a constant.

Constant identifiers can be useful for at least two reasons. First, by giving a value a meaningful name, you can avoid using a literal constant where its purpose is not very clear. For example:

```
Danger := Temperature > DangerLevel;
```

conveys a lot more than:

```
Danger := Temperature > 140.8754;
```

The second good reason for using constant identifiers is that they make it easier for you to change your program. If an unfortunate explosion has made you realize that the maximum temperature in a chemical reactor should actually be 20 degrees below what you thought was a safe maximum, you can easily change the program by redefining MaximumTemperature thus:

```
MaximumTemperature = 200.0000;
```

This redefinition will cause DangerLevel to be redefined and the setting of the variable Danger to work properly, assuming the explosion left a working computer!

Probably the most common occurrence of constants being changed is where subrange types are defined in terms of constants:

```
CONST
  LowestGrade = 0;
  HighestGrade = 9;
TYPE
  Grade = [LowestGrade..HighestGrade];
VAR
  Score: Grade;
```

These declarations permit the variable Score to take values between 0 and 9. Changing HighestGrade to 6 would reduce the range of values which Score can take accordingly.

Constant expression declarations

As you saw above, Modula-2 provides you with the capability to declare constants as an expression containing constant values. This facility is provided to enable programmers to make their programs more readable (i.e. self-documenting without an excessive number of comment statements).

To illustrate this facility further, let us say that you wish to declare a constant in your program which is the maximum speed of a machine, which must not be exceeded. This maximum speed may be the product of two factors, say the gear ratio and wheel size. A constant expression declaration would therefore enable you to say:

```
CONST
   GearRatio = 19.5;
   WheelSize = 5.05;   (* a comment could record units here *)
   MaxSpeed  = GearRatio * WheelSize;
```

When a programmer other than the author reads this program, he or she should be able to see easily why this particular maximum speed (98.47) was chosen. If the author subsequently decides to use a different gear ratio, the author can easily replace just the `GearRatio` constant and achieve the desired effect with just one change.

Further examples of constant expression declarations follow:

```
CONST
   Radius1 = 57.0;                      (* centimetres *)
   Area1 = Pi * Radius1 * Radius1;
   MaxLength = Radius1 + 12.0;          (* note the use of 12.0
                                          rather than just 12  *)
   MaxCard = MAX(CARDINAL);
```

Note the use of the procedure `MAX` in the last declaration. Given an ordinal type, `MAX` returns the maximum value of the type.

4.7   ORDERING OF TYPE, CONSTANT, AND VARIABLE DECLARATIONS

Modula-2 is fairly relaxed about the order in which types, constants, and variables may be declared. One main restriction is imposed: if a declaration needs to use another identifier (on the right hand side of an = or :), then the latter must have already been declared.

This means that you can place declarations close to the point in which they are used in the source code of your program or module, thus increasing readability. (Programmers familiar with Standard Pascal will recognize that this is a considerable relaxation on Pascal's strict rule on ordering of declarations.)

Modula-2 also allows as many separate type, constant, and variable declaration sections as you wish.

The following example illustrates how rules concerning the order of declarations are flexible:

```
CONST
  UpperLimit = 1000;
TYPE
  LargeArray = ARRAY [0..UpperLimit-1] OF CARDINAL;
VAR
  Large : LargeArray;
CONST
  LowerLimit = 0;
TYPE
  SmallArray = ARRAY [LowerLimit..9] OF CARDINAL;
VAR
  Small : SmallArray;
```

4.8   INTRODUCTION TO TYPE COMPATIBILITY

As we have said, Modula-2 places very strict restrictions on the mixing of different types of variables and constants. This leads us to consider the concept of *type compatibility*. The simplest form of compatibility is when two types are *identical* (also called *equivalent*). For instance, in the following example a and b share the same type. The variables c and d are of an identical type, because MyNumbers has been defined to be equivalent to the built-in type INTEGER.

```
TYPE
  MyNumbers = INTEGER;
VAR
  a, b: [0..500];
  c: INTEGER;
  d: MyNumbers;
```

Note that a and b have identical types only because they appear in the same declaration. If they had been declared separately, as shown below, they would have *different* types:

```
VAR
  a: [0..500];
  b: [0..500];
```

We criticized this style of declaration before on the grounds that the subrange was not given a name. An unnamed type is called an *anonymous type*, and all anonymous types are unique. Therefore, in this case, each [0..500] is considered unique.

The compatibility of types has to be considered in different situations. First we must know which types may be mixed in an expression, and in what way. In other words we must define *expression compatibility*.[1] For now we will define by example, and by concentrating on what may not be mixed. Consider the following declarations:

---

[1]Professor Wirth uses the term *compatible* for what is now known as *expression compatible*.

```
VAR
  Frog : INTEGER;
  Toad : CARDINAL;
  Newt : REAL;
  Salamander: LONGREAL;
```

With these declarations, the following expressions would be *illegal*:

```
Frog + Toad;
Toad * Newt;
Frog DIV Salamander;
```

In other words, you cannot mix values of fundamentally different types in an expression.

Now let us add the following constant declaration:

```
CONST
  Tadpole = 100;
```

Then consider mixing constant values with variables in an expression. Surely, it is reasonable to allow the following?

```
Frog + 10;
Toad * Tadpole;
```

The answer is yes. The values denoted by the literal 10 and the identifier are of $\mathbb{Z}$ type which is defined to be expression compatible with both of the whole number types. Similarly, real constants (whether literals or constant identifiers) are of type $\mathbb{R}$ and are expression compatible with both REAL and LONGREAL variables.

The next question of compatibility is that of *assignment compatibility*: given the type of a variable on the left hand side of an assignment statement, what are the allowable types on the right? Again we look at what is *not* permitted using our amphibious variables:

```
Toad := Newt;
Salamander := Newt;
Newt : = 3;
```

This is what you might expect from a strongly typed language: the type of the expression on the right is not the same as the type of the variable on the left, and so the assignment is not valid. However, for convenience in programming the following are allowed:

```
Toad := Frog;
Frog := Toad;
```

That is, signed and unsigned whole numbers (INTEGER and CARDINAL) may be mixed in standard Modula-2. (This is *not* the case in some implementations; see *Portability Issues*.)

Subrange types may also be mixed in assignment statements, but only if they have the same host type. Thus, a subrange of CARDINAL is not assignment compatible with a subrange of INTEGER. The following is allowed:

```
TYPE
  Small = [-5..5];
  Big = [-500..500];
VAR
  tiny: Small;
  huge: Big;
BEGIN
  tiny := 0;
  huge := tiny;
  ...
  tiny := huge;
```

Clearly, all assignments from `tiny` to `huge` will be valid, but the last assignment from `huge` to `tiny` may not be. The compiler should therefore include a check in the program to ensure that any such assignment does not result in an attempt to store values outside the `Small` range to the variable `tiny`. (This run-time compatibility check is in contrast to all other compatibility checks that are performed during compilation.)

4.9   PORTABILITY ISSUES

The portability of the simple Modula-2 data types introduced in this chapter is not as simple as it might be. There are two main reasons for this. First, the basic types of the language may be implemented differently by different compilers and for different computer systems. This immediately results in differences in the ranges of values which the basic types provide. This is a ubiquitous problem in programming languages. Second, until the standardization of the language began, many implementors interpreted the compatibility rules differently. We will outline the issues here, and explore them further in later chapters (see Chapter 16).

The first problem is that of the range of values provided by an implementor for any particular type may cause problems for another implementation. The simplest manifestation of this is an assignment such as:

```
card := 128653;
```

which would be fine for a 32-bit implementation of CARDINAL, but which would not be compiled by a compiler which uses 16 bits. The more difficult situation to avoid is *overflow* during execution. Overflow—exceeding the maximum value of a type, such as CARDINAL—is likely to occur during the evaluation of expressions that involve the multiplication or addition of large numbers. If you are lucky, the implementation will report an overflow. Unfortunately, more often than not, overflow will go unreported and an invalid value will be generated; indeed a phenomenon known as *wraparound* is likely in which the value after the maximum value of a type is the maximum, thus:

```
MAX(CARDINAL) + 1 = MIN(CARDINAL)
```

The examples in this book should not cause overflow.

The second problem is the variability of implemented compatibility rules. The rules described earlier in the chapter should be taken as an ideal, such is the disagreement between implementations. Converting expressions between implementations will only be a problem if you want to mix types in expressions and so you should avoid this.

4.10   REVIEW QUESTIONS AND EXERCISES

Q4.1   How do variable declarations start?

Q4.2   Where can variables be declared?

Q4.3   Write a single declaration which declares `Length` and `Height` as `CARDINAL` variables.

Q4.4   Consider the following assignment and explanation:
```
x := (a + b) * c;
```
The variables x, a, b, and c are all `CARDINAL` variables. The statement assigns the sum of a and b multiplied by to c to x. Explain the assignment more precisely.

Q4.5   Look at the following Modula-2 text and decide what value of z is at the end of the statements (all the variables are of type `CARDINAL`):
```
z := 33;
r :=  63 - z;
z := (r * 10) + (2 * z);
```

5 CONTROL STRUCTURES

5.1 INTRODUCTION

In this chapter we look at statements which control other statements. These statements do not have the simple form of the assignment statement; they have an internal structure which comes from the organization of the statements they control. These aspects of control and structure give the chapter its title.

These control structures break down into two sorts of statement—the selection statements and the iteration statements. Both are discussed briefly here, as both sorts are naturally suited to processing structured data, a topic which will be discussed in later chapters.

5.2 SELECTION STATEMENTS

So far the only statement to be introduced has been the assignment statement; the selection statements IF and CASE are now introduced by returning to the use of constant identifiers.

IF statement

The following program module is a variation of the hello module presented in Chapter 2. The essential difference is that the string literal used there has been replaced by the constant Greeting:

```
MODULE Greet;
FROM PortIO IMPORT WriteString, WriteLn;
CONST
  Greeting = "Hello world!";
BEGIN
  WriteString(Greeting); WriteLn
END Greet.
```

To change the program to output a less cheerful greeting now requires a change only to the definition of greeting:

```
Greeting = "Ho, hum, another day...";
```

While this is a useful facility, and a significant help when dealing with large programs, it does not allow you to select which greeting you want to make, depending on your mood. What you might want to be able to do is to write in Modula-2 something like:

If I'm happy then
    I'll say something cheerful
else
    I'll say something gloomy

Modula-2 provides an IF statement to allow just this. The simplest form of the IF statement is:

```
IF BooleanExpression THEN
    statement1;
    statement2
ELSE
    statement3
END;
```

That is, the IF keyword is followed by a Boolean expression (such as x = y). Next follows the keyword THEN and a sequence of statements which are to be executed when the expression evaluates to TRUE. Last, in this form of the statement, comes the keyword ELSE followed by the statements which are to be executed when the Boolean expression evaluates to FALSE. So, to choose between a cheerful greeting and an unhappy one you might write:

```
IF GoodDay THEN
    WriteString(HappyGreeting); WriteLn
ELSE
    WriteString(SadGreeting); WriteLn
END;
```

To complete the program module, the constants HappyGreeting and SadGreeting must be declared, and the Boolean variable GoodDay must also be declared and assigned a value. Rather than assigning it a constant, it would be better to prompt you to input a character (Y or N) in response to a question about your mood. Thus GoodDay can be assigned the value TRUE only if Y is input. If a CHAR variable called Answer is used to record input, the following will initialize GoodDay:

```
GoodDay := (Answer = 'Y');
```

(The parentheses are not strictly necessary, and so we will drop them later.)

The PortIO procedure WriteString can be used to output the question, thus:

```
WriteString (MoodQuestion) ;
```

(The actual wording of the question can be decided later.)

To input a character value from the keyboard you can use a procedure in PortIO called ReadChar. For example, if you import ReadChar from PortIO, the following will obtain a value from the keyboard and store it in Answer:

```
Answer := ReadChar();
```

(The syntax will be described fully in Chapters 8 and 9.) The words for the mood question (by defining the constant MoodQuestion) must now be decided, and the complete program is given below:

```
MODULE Greet2;
FROM PortIO IMPORT ReadChar, WriteString, WriteLn;
CONST
  HappyGreeting = "Hello world!";
  SadGreeting = "Ho, hum, another day...";
  MoodQuestion = "Are you happy?";
VAR
  Answer: CHAR;
  GoodDay: BOOLEAN;
BEGIN
  WriteString (MoodQuestion) ;
  Answer := ReadChar(); WriteLn;
  GoodDay := Answer = 'Y';
  IF GoodDay THEN
    WriteString (HappyGreeting); WriteLn
  ELSE
    WriteString (SadGreeting); WriteLn
  END;
  WriteLn
END Greet2.
```

If you compile, link, and execute this module, it will prompt you to input a character. If you input Y the happy greeting will be output; otherwise the sad one will be output. The program terminates after executing the IF statement:

```
Are you happy?Y
Hello world!
```

Note that when no statements are to be executed in the ELSE part of the IF statement, the keyword ELSE may be omitted. For example:

```
IF Count >= Maximum THEN
  Count := Count + 1
END;
```

will increment the value of Count by 1 only if Count has not already reached a Maximum value; if Count is less than Maximum, the statement after the IF statement is executed.

IF statements may be *nested* to give a powerful selection construction. For example, the following could be used to output the maximum of three integers. (The procedure WriteInt is provided by PortIO; it will print an integer value.)

```
IF a > b THEN
  IF a > c THEN
    WriteInt(a)
  ELSE
    WriteInt(c)
  END
ELSE
  IF b > c THEN
    WriteInt(b)
  ELSE
    WriteInt(c)
  END
END;
```

The occurrence of nested IF statements is so common that a special form of the statement is provided to make them easier to read (and to write). This special form uses the keyword ELSIF (note there is only one E) which combines ELSE and IF; this reduces the level of nesting. For example, the previous statement to output the maximum of three integers could be rewritten as:

```
IF a > b THEN
  IF a > c THEN
    WriteInt(a)
  ELSE
    WriteInt(c)
  END
ELSIF b > c THEN
  WriteInt(b)
ELSE
  WriteInt(c)
END;
```

Note that there are only two IF statements in this version, and hence there are only two ENDs.

This feature of the IF statement can be very effective when combined in the following way:

```
IF Condition1 THEN
  StatementSequence1
ELSIF Condition2 THEN
  StatementSequence2
ELSIF Condition3 THEN
  StatementSequence3
ELSIF Condition4 THEN
  StatementSequence4
ELSE
  StatementSequence5
END;
```

As an example of this consider how you might output messages about the weather depending on the temperature (in Celsius):

```
IF Temperature < -5.0 THEN
  WriteString("It's perishing out there!")
ELSIF Temperature < 2.0 THEN
```

```
    WriteString("It's freezing, isn't it?")
ELSIF Temperature < 12.0 THEN
    WriteString("So much for flaming June!")
ELSIF Temperature < 21.0 THEN
    WriteString("That's more like summer now.")
ELSIF Temperature < 28.0 THEN
    WriteString("Phew! What a scorcher.")
ELSE
    WriteString("My brain is addled by this heat.")
END;
```

This statement works by testing each condition (i.e. each Boolean expression) in turn until one evaluates to TRUE. Then the statement sequence which the condition is 'guarding' is executed; here it is a single string output statement.

If none of the conditions is true, the default statement sequence (the one preceded by the ELSE keyword) is executed. (If no default action is needed, the ELSE part may be omitted.)

More details of the IF statement are given in Chapter 18.

CASE statement

In many instances you will want to select between several different sequences of actions (i.e. statements) depending on the value of some expression. The CASE statement is provided for this purpose. Rather than evaluating a Boolean expression and choosing between two sets of actions, the CASE statement evaluates any ordinal expression and, depending on the value of the expression, executes one of many sequences of statements. The ordinal expression is called a *case index*. Its general form is:

```
CASE CaseIndex OF
   Constant1:
      Statement1;
      Statement2 |          These are executed when CaseIndex = Constant1
   Constant2..Constant4:
      Statement3;           These are executed when CaseIndex is in
      Statement4 |          the range Constant2..Constant4
   ELSE
      Statement5            Executed when CaseIndex is not equal to any of the labels
END;
```

The keyword CASE starts the statement. It is followed by an ordinal expression. (Remember that ordinal means a type such as the cardinal or integer or character types or subranges.) Then comes the keyword OF; between OF and the keyword END, which terminates the statement, is a list of cases which the statement selects from for execution. These cases are sequences of statements which are labelled by constant expressions. The cases are separated by a vertical bar '|' (which can be read as 'or').

When the ordinal expression, which is the case index, is evaluated, its value is compared with these labels. If it matches one of them, the statement sequence whose label includes the value is executed. (After the sequence of statements which is a particular case has been executed, the statement after the CASE statement is executed.)

If the value of the case index does not match any of the labels, the statement sequence labelled by the keyword ELSE is executed.

For example, if you wanted to output the happy greeting above if either Y or y was input, and the sad greeting if either N or n was input, and you wanted to output an error message if none of these was input, the following could be used:

```
MODULE Greet3;
FROM PortIO IMPORT
  ReadChar, WriteString, WriteLn;
CONST
  HappyGreeting = "Hello world!";
  SadGreeting = "Ho, hum, another day...";
  MoodQuestion = "Are you happy?";
  ErrorMessage = "You should have pressed either Y or N.";
VAR
  Answer: CHAR;
BEGIN
  WriteString(MoodQuestion); WriteLn;
  Answer := ReadChar();
  CASE Answer OF
    'Y': WriteString(HappyGreeting); WriteLn |
    'y': WriteString(HappyGreeting); WriteLn |
    'N': WriteString(SadGreeting); WriteLn |
    'n': WriteString(SadGreeting); WriteLn
  ELSE
    WriteString(ErrorMessage); WriteLn
  END;
  WriteLn
END Greet3.
```

In fact this can be simplified a little. You can combine the labels into lists to give the following statements in the module:

```
CASE Answer OF
  'Y', 'y': WriteString(HappyGreeting); WriteLn |
  'N', 'n': WriteString(SadGreeting); WriteLn
ELSE
  WriteString(ErrorMessage); WriteLn
END;
```

If no action needs to be taken when the case index does not match a label, then a null statement should follow the ELSE keyword. If you want an exception to be reported when case labels do not match, the ELSE part should be omitted entirely. The latter requirement arises when you believe that you have explicitly included all valid values of the case index in the case labels. For example, consider a ticket machine in a car park. The car owner pays for a ticket in advance of parking and may select either 1, 2, 5, or 12 hours. If a variable time is used for storing the number of hours, it might be declared to have the type

[1..12]. A case statement which displays the price for parking for 1, 2, 5, or 12 hours might be:

```
CASE time OF
  1: display(OneHourPrice) |
  2: display(TwoHourPrice) |
  5: display(FiveHourPrice) |
  12: display(TwelveHourPrice)
END;
```

Thus, the declaration of time allows it to take any value between 1 and 12, but the application demands that only 1, 2, 5, and 12 are valid values. If, say, time took the value 7 inadvertently, the above CASE statement should report this as an exception.

The labels of a CASE statement can include a range of values. These can be mixed in lists with single constants. For example:

```
CASE Score OF
  1..5, 10, 21..25: Weighting := 22.3 |
  26..100: Weighting := 12.5
END;
```

However, care must be taken to avoid duplicating labels. For instance, having used 25 in the first case, you cannot then have 25..100 in the second. This can be a little difficult to program if the module depends on constant definitions, rather than literals. Since the use of constants is to be encouraged, it is worth indicating how this problem can be avoided.

If you intend to parameterize a CASE statement using symbolic constants, the adjoining limits of any consecutive ranges should be specified using constant expressions. For example, if SecondRangeMax is defined to be 25, then SecondRangeMax + 1 should be used for 26:

```
CONST SecondRangeMax = 25;
...
CASE Score OF
  1..5, 10, 21..SecondRangeMax : Weighting := 22.3 |
  (SecondRangeMax + 1)..100: Weighting := 12.5
END;
```

Using this technique, changing SecondRangeMax to 35, say, would make the labels equivalent to:

```
1..5, 10, 21..35 : ...
36..100: ...
```

See Chapter 18 for further details of the CASE statement.

5.3   ITERATION STATEMENTS

An *iteration statement* is one which causes other statements to be executed repeatedly. (This type of statement is also known as a *loop*, but this can cause some confusion with the LOOP statement, so we will usually avoid it.) The way that an iteration statement starts to execute statements repeatedly, or the way in which one terminates, is different for different iteration statements. The correct use of iteration statements and the ability to choose between them often distinguishes the good programmer from the not-so-good.

In Modula-2 there are four types of iteration statements: the FOR statement, the WHILE statement, the REPEAT statement, and the LOOP statement.

FOR statement

The purpose of the FOR statement is to execute repeatedly a sequence of statements a fixed number of times. That is, the statement sequence controlled by a FOR statement is to be repeated by a number which can be calculated in advance of beginning the iteration, and which *cannot* be changed during the iteration. The general form of the FOR statement is as follows:

```
FOR Control Variable := Start TO Finish BY IncrementSize DO
    statement1;
    statement2;
    (* etc. *)
END;
```

The FOR statement is controlled by a variable of an ordinal type. It is incremented by some amount (usually by one value in its type) a fixed number of times, starting at a value and working up to a higher value. For example, Hello Hello Hello could be printed using the FOR statement thus:

```
FOR i := 1 TO 3 BY 1 DO
    WriteString("Hello ");
END;
```

The ordinal control variable need not be a number, and need not be a constant value. For example, a sequence of characters can be printed using the following:

```
FROM PortIO IMPORT ReadChar, WriteChar, WriteString, WriteLn;
VAR
    ch, Start, Finish: CHAR;
BEGIN
    WriteString('Start where?'); Start := ReadChar();
    WriteString('Finish where?'); Finish := ReadChar();
    FOR ch := Start TO Finish BY 1 DO
        WriteChar(ch);
    END;
    WriteLn;
    ...
```

In the above, the control variable, and the range of values it progresses through are of type CHAR. The Start and Finish values are obtained from the variables initialized by the ReadChar input statements. If Start is less than or equal to Finish, the character values between them will be printed; otherwise the statement after the FOR will be executed.

Notice that, despite the fact that the control variable is of type CHAR, the increment size is the whole number 1. This means that the control variable is to be incremented by one value of its type (here CHAR). The increment size *must* be a constant expression.

Normally, when the increment size is 1, the BY part of the statement is omitted. Thus it is more usual to write the following:

```
FOR ch := Start TO Finish DO
  WriteChar(ch);
END;
```

The FOR statement can also be used to proceed from a higher to lower value by specifying how much the control variable is to be changed. If this is a negative value, the statement will decrease the control variable by that number of values. So the following would print FEDCBA:

```
FOR ch := 'F' TO 'A' BY -1 DO
  WriteChar(ch);
END;
```

LOOP statement

Rather than execute a sequence of statements a fixed number of times, the other iteration statements—WHILE, REPEAT, and LOOP—allow arbitrarily complex Boolean expressions to determine when iteration should continue or terminate. This Boolean expression is known as the *termination condition* and, depending on the statement, is checked at the beginning of the iteration, the end, or somewhere inside the statements being repeated.

The most general iteration statement is the LOOP statement. Used in conjunction with the EXIT statement, you can construct very complicated iteration structures using the LOOP statement. It should be reserved for such situations which require it. (You should look at Chapter 18, Section 11 for details of the LOOP statement, and the associated EXIT statement.)

An example of a simple LOOP statement is:

```
CONST
  MaxAllowed = 20;
VAR
  Total, Number, Input : INTEGER;
BEGIN
  Total := 0;
  Number := 0;
  LOOP
    Input := ReadInt();;
    IF (Input < 5) OR (Input > 1045) THEN
      WriteString("Invalid input data. All must be corrupt.");
      EXIT
    END;
    Total := Total + Input;
    Number := Number + 1;
```

```
      IF Number = MaxAllowed THEN
         EXIT
      END
   END;
```

This `LOOP` statement inputs an integer and checks if it is in a range of valid values. If not, all the data is assumed to be invalid and the iteration is terminated. If the input is valid, then `Total` is updated and the number of inputs is incremented. If `Number` reaches the maximum allowed, the loop is terminated.

WHILE and REPEAT statements

The other two iteration statements are now considered together. The reason for doing so is that programmers often wrongly choose to use `REPEAT` statements, in preference to `WHILE`. Indeed, if you can do without any of the iteration statements, it is the `REPEAT` statement. The `WHILE` statement controls the iteration of a sequence of statements by checking the termination condition *before* the sequence is repeated; i.e. it checks before the statement sequence is executed for the first time, and before any subsequent repetitions. For example, to print the numbers 1 to 5 on separate lines using a `WHILE` statement, you could use the following:

```
VAR i: CARDINAL;
BEGIN
   i := 1;
   WHILE i <= 5 DO
     WriteInt(i); WriteLn;
     i := i + 1
   END;
   ...
```

This fragment of Modula-2 (which assumes that `WriteInt` and `WriteLn` have been imported from `PortIO`) prints 1 to 5 on separate lines. The variable i is initialized to 1 in the assignment before the `WHILE` statement. Then the condition i <= 5 is evaluated; with i = 1 this evaluates to `TRUE`. In a `WHILE` statement, the sequence of statements to be repeated are only executed if the controlling condition is true. Therefore the output statements are executed for the first time and 1, followed by a newline, is output. The value in the variable i is then incremented and execution returns to the beginning of the statement, where the condition i <= 5 is evaluated again. This pattern continues until i = 5; then i is incremented to become 6 and the subsequent test of the condition results in `FALSE`. This stops the iteration and the program proceeds to the statement after the `WHILE`.

Note that the condition i <= 5 is the condition for *continuing* the iteration, rather than for terminating it. The 'termination condition' of a `WHILE` statement is thus the negation of the condition which specifies when the iteration should continue. In spite of having to use the condition for continuing the iteration in the statement, you should determine the termination condition first, and then negate it. In the above example we wanted to print numbers from 1 to 5 and were using i to denote the number. The termination condition for this loop is i > 5. To obtain what is needed for the WHILE statement we could surround the terminating condition with parentheses and precede it by NOT to negate it, as follows:

```
NOT (i > 5)
```

However, this explicit negation can become difficult to read, hence the equivalent i <= 5 is used.

The general form of the WHILE statement is hence better expressed in terms of the negation of the termination condition:

```
WHILE NegationOfTerminationCondition DO
   statement1;
   statement2;
   (* etc. *)
END;
```

Together with the FOR statement, the WHILE statement is the most common type of iteration statement.

Whereas the WHILE statement may not allow its statement sequence to be executed even once, the REPEAT statement guarantees at least one execution. This is because the REPEAT statement evaluates a terminating condition after executing a statement sequence once, and after every subsequent execution.

Thus the statement sequence of a WHILE loop may never be executed and the statement sequence of a REPEAT loop will be executed at least once. The REPEAT statement can therefore be simulated by preceding a WHILE statement with a copy of the statement sequence!

If i is an integer the following iteration statements will print numbers from 1 to 10:

```
i := 1;
WHILE i <= 10 DO
  WriteInt(i); WriteLn;
  i := i + 1
END;

i := 0;
REPEAT
  i := i + 1;
  WriteInt(i); WriteLn
UNTIL i = 10;
```

As mentioned earlier, structured statements are most suited to processing structured data. Examples of iteration and selection statements appear throughout the rest of the book.

5.4   PORTABILITY ISSUES

There should not be many portability problems with control structures. Most implementations define some maximum level of nesting for these statements, but these rarely cause the programmer any problems. (The level of nesting of an IF statement, for example, is the number of IF statements within IF statements it contains.) These maxima do not cause problems because most programmers will structure their programs using procedures (see Chapter 8) and will avoid complex, and incomprehensible, nested control statements.

Some implementations also impose a maximum number of statements within a statement sequence, but for similar reasons these restrictions do not cause problems.

Other than encountering qualitative problems when considering the portability of structured statements, you may run up against different compatibility rules in implementation of the CASE and FOR statements. The expression in a CASE statement should be expression compatible with the type of the labels of the statement, but some compilers allow assignment compatibility in this statement. This weaker requirement allows CARDINAL (and its subranges) to match INTEGER (and it subranges). To ensure portability, assume expression compatibility.

The situation regarding the FOR statement is somewhat more complicated: originally Professor Wirth specified that the type of the control variable be assignment compatible with the types of the start and finish expression. The forthcoming standard specifies that the start expression be *expression* compatible. Some compilers may require that the type of the control variable be expression compatible with both expressions. Since this is the strongest requirement, adhering to it will avoid portability problems.

There is one significant problem with the CASE statement. Many implementations do not require that a label be matched by the case index value. That is, if there is no ELSE part to a CASE statement, and if the case index does not match a label, many implementations proceed to the next statement rather than reporting an exception.

5.5   REVIEW QUESTIONS AND EXERCISES

Q5.1   Declare a constant identifier to denote an error tolerance of 0.00001.

Q5.2   Using the constant you declared in the last exercise, write an IF statement which will print a message saying whether a real number called Measurement is within 0.00001 of a constant value called Standard.

Q5.3   Rewrite the following statements using a CASE statement and without using a variable.

```
Answer := ReadChar();
IF (Answer = 'y') OR (Answer = 'y') THEN
   WriteString("Closingdown"); WriteLn;
```

```
    ELSE
      IF(Answer = 'N') OR (Answer = 'n') THEN
      WriteString("Continuing..."); WriteLn;
    ELSE
      WriteString("Cannot understand answer!"); WriteLn;
    END;
```

Q5.4   Write an iteration statement which writes out every other character between L and Y, starting with L.

Q5.5   Rewrite the answer to Question 5.4 using a LOOP statement.

Q5.6   What would be the most appropriate iteration statement for inputting a character command over and over, only stopping when Q (for 'quit') is read?

Q5.7   Rewrite the example from the subsection of the LOOP statement using the most appropriate iteration statement.

\

6 PROGRAMMER-DEFINED TYPES

6.1 INTRODUCTION

So far the elementary data types we have encountered, CARDINAL, INTEGER, BOOLEAN, CHAR, and REAL have all been predefined by Modula-2 and as such are part of the language. One of the major advantages of Modula-2 and other similar high-level languages, such as Pascal, is the facility they give for the programmer to define new data types. Whilst a wide range of programming problems can be solved by using the predefined types there are a number of good reasons for the programmer to define new types. To a large extent the definition of program-specific types makes that program self-documenting: a choice of meaningful names for the new types, names that reflect the real world data being modelled, will make that program easier to read and understand. Also, by defining a new type, the programmer can strictly limit the range of values that variables of the new type can store. This allows compilers to check that your program does not compile invalid values.

6.2 ENUMERATION TYPES

An *enumeration type*[1] is defined by declaring an ordered list of unique names which denote constant values. These names chosen to denote the constants can then be conveniently referred to in your programs. The form for declaring an enumeration type is:

```
EnumerationTypeName = (ident1,ident2,ident3 (* etc.*));
```

---

[1]Enumeration types are sometimes called *enumerated types*, because the constants are enumerated.

In the above, `EnumerationTypeName` is the name you choose for the type and the identifiers are constant names also chosen by you to represent the set of enumeration constants. For example:

```
TYPE
   DaysOfTheWeek = (Sun, Mon, Tues, Wed, Thu, Fri, Sat);

   MicroType =
      (IBM, Compaq, Toshiba, Zenith, Olivetti, Apple,
       AMSTRAD, Acorn, Apricot);
```

In each of the examples above, a new *elementary type* has been defined. At the same time the complete range of valid values has been defined and the *ordering relationship* between the values has been specified by the order in which the constant identifiers appear. Each enumeration type declaration list associates an *ordinal value* with each *enumeration constant* with the first constant in each list having ordinal value 0 and the remainder being numbered in increments of 1. For example, `Sun` has the ordinal value 0 whilst `Sat` has the ordinal value 6.

Enumeration constants may be assigned as values to variables of an enumeration type. Referring back to the examples of type declarations above, the following variables can be declared:

```
VAR
   Day : DaysOfTheWeek;
   Micro : MicroType;
```

Values can be assigned to the variables `Day` and `Micro` as follows:

```
Day := Tue;
Micro := IBM;
```

Comparison of enumeration types

Values of enumeration constants and variables can also be compared, using the usual range of relational operators:

```
=   <>   <   >   <=   >=
```

These have the usual meaning, with the result of `<`, `>`, `<=`, and `>=` being determined by the ordering in the type declaration.

```
Tue < Fri          results in TRUE
Micro = Compaq     results in FALSE
IBM <= Apple       results in TRUE
```

Given these operators and the variables declared above we can write statements such as:

```
IF (Day > Sun) AND (Day < Sat) THEN
   WriteString("Get up and go to work!")
ELSE
   WriteString("Have a lie-in and breakfast in bed!")
END;
```

Assignment and comparison tests such as those shown above are the only operations defined for enumeration types.

Procedures for enumeration types

Enumeration types can be very useful when combined with the following built-in Modula-2 function procedures:

Procedure	Purpose
ORD(x)	returns the ordinal value of an enumeration constant or variable, x
VAL(T,x)	returns the value with ordinal number x of enumeration type T
INC(x)	sets x to be the next value in the enumeration declaration list
INC(x,n)	sets x to the nth successor to x in the enumeration declaration list
DEC(x)	sets x to the previous value in the enumeration declaration list
DEC(x,n)	reduces a by n values in the enumeration declaration list

The following examples use the type MicroType and the variables Micro.

(i)   ORD(Olivetti)   returns 4

(ii)   VAL(MicroType,2)   returns Toshiba

(iii)   Micro := IBM;
        INC(Micro);   sets Micro to Compaq
        INC(Micro,6);   sets Micro to Acorn

(iv)   Micro := Toshiba;
        DEC(Micro,2);   sets Micro to IBM

The built-in type BOOLEAN is an enumeration type which is considered to have have been declared thus:

```
TYPE BOOLEAN = (FALSE, TRUE);
```

So it can be observed that:

```
FALSE < TRUE
ORD(FALSE) = 0
ORD(TRUE)  = 1
```

(See Chapter 23 for a full explanation of Modula-2's built-in procedures. Of course, you may wish to supplement built-in procedures by procedures that you define yourself to process enumeration types; for more details see Chapter 8.)

Input/output and enumeration types

The PortIO module does not provide any input/output facilities for enumeration types. (No general-purpose module can provide such facilities.) However, this can be achieved by mapping an enumeration type to some other type value via a CASE statement.

```
MODULE enumex;
FROM PortIO IMPORT WriteCard, WriteString, WriteLn;
TYPE
  ProgrammingLanguages =
    (Algol, COBOL, FORTRAN, Modula2, Pascal);
VAR
  Prog : ProgrammingLanguages;
BEGIN
  FOR Prog := Algol TO Pascal DO
    WriteCard(ORD(Prog));
    CASE Prog OF
      Algol   : WriteString(' Algol')    |
      COBOL   : WriteString(' COBOL')     |
      FORTRAN : WriteString(' FORTRAN')   |
      Modula2 : WriteString(' Modula-2')  |
      Pascal  : WriteString(' Pascal')
    END;
    WriteLn;
  END
END enumex.
```

Within the FOR loop the program first writes to the screen the ordinal value of a variable of type ProgrammingLanguages. Next, a CASE statement selects the appropriate literal string to output using the WriteString procedure.

6.3   SUBRANGE TYPES

A *subrange type* is a type which derives from some other existing ordinal type, and consists of a restricted range of consecutive values from that existing type. The form for declaring such a subrange type is:

```
SubrangeTypeName = [StartValue .. EndValue];
```

SubrangeTypeName is the name of the type you have chosen, and the two constant expressions specify the upper and lower bounds of the subrange. The value of the lower bound must be less than or equal to the value of the upper bound.

You can declare subranges of any of Modula-2's built-in whole number types (i.e. CARDINAL or INTEGER), of the type CHAR, and also of enumeration types.

```
TYPE
  Sub1 = [0..42 ];
  Sub2 = ['A'..'Z'];
  Enum = (Mark, Rob, Tom, John, Martin, Harry);
  Sub3 = [Tom..Harry];
```

Subrange host types

Every subrange type is based on a *host type*, which is the type it is ultimately based on. In other words the values of the subrange originally 'belong' to the host type. The host type is important because it defines the set of operations for the subrange type. Hence, all operations on INTEGER values are legal on subranges of INTEGER.

A whole number literal or enumeration constant in a subrange type declaration is used by the compiler to determine the host type of the subrange (if this is not specified by the programmer).

Subrange bounds for whole number subranges must either be in the range:

    MIN(INTEGER)   to   MAX(INTEGER)
or
    MIN(CARDINAL)   to   MAX(CARDINAL)

If the lower bound of a numeric subrange is positive then the type will be CARDINAL, if the lower bound is negative then it will be INTEGER.

It is possible to specify the *range type* of a subrange by putting a type name in front of the square brackets in the declaration; a range type specification can be used for two purposes. It can be used to force the compiler to accept that a positive whole number subrange, which is normally deemed to have a CARDINAL host type, has an INTEGER host type. Also, if a range type is a subrange of an enumeration type, a compile time check can be performed to ensure that the values in the subrange being defined are within the range type's values. For example, given the following type declarations:

    TYPE PositiveNos = [1..9];

Most compilers will assume that the host type of the above subrange is CARDINAL. By putting the range type in front of the square brackets forces the compiler to set the host type to INTEGER.

    TYPE PositiveNos = INTEGER[1..9];

As an example of the second use of range types in a subrange declaration consider the definition of a subrange of DaysOfTheWeek (from Section 6.2) which represents weekdays and a definition of a subrange of the latter which represents late night shopping days:

    WeekDay = [Mon..Fri];
    LateNightShopping = WeekDay[Thu..Fri];

The second declaration, by using WeekDay, ensures that the bounds of LateNightShopping fall within Mon..Fri. While this is obvious in this example, the use of constants to specify limits often obscures relationships between subranges.

Note that the host type of LateNightShopping is the host type of its range type—i.e. DaysOfTheWeek.

The following examples give host types of subranges:

(i)   Small = [0..30];
      CapLet = ['A'..'Z'];
      WeekDay = [Mon..Fri];

In this example, Small has a host type of CARDINAL, and CapLet has a host type of CHAR. WeekDay has a host type of DaysOfTheWeek (as in Section 6.2).

(ii) MySubrange = [Lower..Upper];
      AnotherSubrange = [3 DIV LL..9 * UL];

MySubrange has a host type which depends upon the type of Upper and Lower; e.g. if they are CARDINAL then the host type is CARDINAL. AnotherSubrange has a host type which depends upon the type of LL and UL, it will either be CARDINAL or INTEGER.

Note that constant expressions have been used in the declaration of AnotherSubrange.

(iii) IntSubrange = INTEGER[0..100];

IntSubrange has a host type of INTEGER, because of the use of a range type.

Anonymous subrange types

Try to avoid anonymous subrange types; these occur when you omit a TYPE declaration and declare a subrange in a VAR declaration. For example:

```
VAR
   v : [0 .. 3];
```

This declaration creates a variable v with an anonymous type of host type CARDINAL. This would mean that you could not refer explicitly to the type of v, which you may need to do, for instance, when passing a variable as a parameter to a procedure.

Usefulness of subrange types

Subranges of enumeration types are a particularly useful way of making your programs self-documenting. Consider the following example which assumes the Microtype defined in Section 6.2:

```
TYPE
   CheapMicro = [Toshiba..AMSTRAD];
```

With these declarations, any variables of type CheapMicro will be subject to strict bounds checking—so attempts to assign IBM (for example) to a CheapMicro variable will be detected. In general 'out-of-range' values are detected during execution; during compilation a compiler inserts checking code to perform such detection. However, some compilers will report an error if a constant value is outside the subrange of a variable.

Thus, the advantage of using subranges stems from the additional safeguards that Modula-2 compilers will provide against attempts to assign a value to a subrange variable which is outside the range. The following example demonstrates how a program rejects illegal values:

```
MODULE sub;
FROM PortIO IMPORT ReadInt;
TYPE
  SmallInt  = [-15..15]; SmallCard = [0 .. 31];
VAR
  Si : SmallInt;   Sc : SmallCard;
BEGIN
  Si := -14;       (*Si := -16 should be trapped at compile time*)
  Sc := 10;        (*as would Sc := 32 *)
  Si := ReadInt ();(*input of -16 would be rejected at run-time *)
END sub.
```

6.4   PORTABILITY ISSUES

There are no significant portability problems with enumeration types, *per se.* Many compilers restrict the number of values they can contain to be something like 256. This is not a real constraint.

However, there are a number of potential problems with subrange types. The most important is that some compilers (and Topspeed Modula-2 is one of these) do not automatically check for *out-of-range values* at run-time. To ensure that the compiler generates run-time checking code, a compiler option or a source code directive must be used. Topspeed requires that (*$R+*) be included to enforce subrange checking.

A more subtle problem is caused by some compilers not permitting the range type to be specified. (Early compilers—say pre-1985—are based on older syntax rules for Modula-2 which do not allow for a range type in a subrange definition.) The inability to specify a range type will mean that some compile time checks will not be performed, and that non-negative whole number subranges are always considered to be CARDINAL.

6.5   REVIEW QUESTIONS AND EXERCISES

Q6.1   Declare an enumeration type for the months of the year.

Q6.2   What is the ordinal value of Jan?

Q6.3   Given a variable Months of type MonthNames with a value of Jun, what is the result of DEC (Months)?

Q6.4   What does VAL (MonthNames, 2) return?

Q6.5   Given a variable Months of type MonthNames with a value of Nov, what does ORD (Months) return?

Q6.6   Subrange bounds for numeric subranges must lie within two ranges. What are they?

Q6.7   Given the subrange type:
```
TYPE
  Digits = [0..9];
```
What is the host type of Digits?

Q6.8   How could you force the host type of Digits to be INTEGER?

7 STRUCTURING DATA

7.1 INTRODUCTION

In previous chapters most of the data types we have considered have been simple types (the exception being literal strings). However, it is frequently desirable to structure these simple types into more complex data structures. For example, many software systems manipulate large databases, such as stock control systems and direct sale mailing lists. A typical program to maintain a mailing list would not manipulate many variables of simple types such as integers or characters; rather it would declare a data type that would represent clients' names and addresses. This chapter considers how simple data types can be combined and structured into more complex types.

7.2 ARRAYS AND THE ITERATION STATEMENTS

When we state that only simple types have been introduced so far, we mean that individual variables have been declared and have been identified by giving them unique names. If you wanted to hold tens or thousands of related values by declaring variables in this way, life would be intolerable. In such a case it would be desirable to make just one declaration, which would give all the related values a single identifying name and then to have the ability to access individual variables by some form of index. This need is met by the *array data structure*. Modula-2 has an *array constructor* which allows you to define a type which is a collection of variables. Individual variables, termed the *components*[1] of the array,

---

[1] The term *element* is also used to describe a component of an array. We prefer component because of the potential confusion with set elements (see Section 7.4).

can then be selected, or *indexed*, and values stored in them, or extracted from them.

Array types and variables

An array consists of a fixed number of component variables which can be of any type, but which must all be of the same type, called the **component type**. Associated with these elements there is an **index type** (or **subscript**) which is used to select an individual component or element of the array. This index type must be of some ordinal type (see Chapter 6). The number of components that an array can contain is restricted by the number of values that the index type can take.

The form of an array type definition is given below. (Note that ARRAY and OF are Modula-2 keywords.)

```
ArrayTypeName = ARRAY IndexType OF ComponentType;
```

For example, the type ShortList defines an array of CARDINAL variables which is indexed by a value in the range 1..10. The variable List, which is of type Shortlist, thus contains 10 CARDINAL variables:

```
CONST
  First = 1; Last = 10;
TYPE
  ListRange = [First..Last];
  ShortList = ARRAY ListRange OF CARDINAL;
VAR
  List: ShortList;
```

To assign to a component variable within an array, the variable name is followed by the index within square brackets:

```
List[6] := 643;
```

The value within the square brackets is itself an expression, and so complex calculations may be performed to work out an index:

```
List[(Count + 1) DIV 3] := 643;
```

Of course, there is a danger, if not a likelihood, that the evaluation of the index expression will produce a value outside the range of the index.[1] In fact, the most frequent mistake that is made in processing arrays is to try to access an array with a value which is outside the index range—usually by 1.

Because the index type of an array can be any ordinal type, the following are all valid:

(i)   TYPE
            CharacterList = ARRAY CHAR OF CARDINAL;
         VAR

---

[1] This is only detected and reported as a program exception in Topspeed Modula-2 when the (*$I+*) compiler option has been used.

```
       CharList: CharacterList;
       CharList['A'] := 897;
```

Hence the index type of Characterlist is CHAR.

(ii)   TYPE
```
         Colour =
             (Black, Red, Green, Blue, Cyan, Magenta, Yellow, White);
         Intensities = ARRAY Colour OF REAL;
       VAR
         Shades: Intensities;
       BEGIN
         Shades[Black] := 0.0;
         Shade[White] := 4.5;
```

In this example the index type of Intensities is the enumeration type Colour.

It is also possible to have arrays of arrays, or other structured types, and whole array variables may be assigned to each other. Arrays of arrays can be used as *multi-dimensional* structures; details of these and other aspects of arrays can be found in Chapter 19.

Novice programmers may sometimes get confused between the index of an array and the value of a particular component. Remember that the array's index is always enclosed by square brackets and that it marks the position of a particular component within the array. In general, the index bears no relation to the value of a particular component.

The repetitive nature of the array data structure demands a processing structure to match it. In Chapter 5 you were introduced to the four iteration statements that are provided in Modula-2. To recap: the FOR statement is controlled by a variable of an ordinal type and is incremented by a set amount, a fixed number of times. Rather than execute a sequence of statements a fixed number of times, the other iteration statements—WHILE, REPEAT, and LOOP— allow arbitrarily complex Boolean expressions to determine when iteration should continue or terminate.

The FOR statement and arrays

The FOR statement is used frequently with array variables. The reason for this is that it will iterate a statement sequence a fixed number of times, which makes it eminently suitable for indexing the component variables of an array, component by component. For example, all the components of List introduced earlier can be initialized to zero using a FOR loop:

```
VAR Index: ListRange;
...
FOR Index := First TO Last DO
  List[Index] := 0
END;
```

The statement inside the FOR loop is executed 10 times: beginning with Index = 1 and working upwards, incrementing Index until the assignment has been executed with Index = 10.

The FOR statement can equally well be used with enumeration types:

```
VAR Col: Colour;
...
FOR Col := Red TO Blue DO
   Shades[Col] := 2.0
END;
```

The WHILE statement and arrays

The WHILE statement, which determines whether a statement sequence should be executed before executing it the first time, and before every subsequent execution, is the ideal control structure for assigning values to the component variables of an array. For example, in the code fragment below, a WHILE statement is used to input values into the array List—as long as the input value is not equal to zero. In other words, when the user types in zero, in response to the prompt, the loop terminates.

A variable called Index is used to step through the array; unlike the situation in the FOR statement, Index is not automatically incremented by the iteration statement and so that has to be done explicitly. Note that because of the danger that the user might attempt to input more than 10 values, the iteration condition must include a test to prevent a non-existent component being accessed by an index value of 11.

```
CONST
   First = 1; Last = 10;
TYPE
   ListRange = [First..Last];
   ShortList = ARRAY ListRange OF CARDINAL;
VAR
   List: ShortList;
   Index, Input : CARDINAL;
BEGIN
   WriteString("Input a Cardinal (zero terminates): ");
   Input := ReadCard();
   Index := First;
   WHILE (Index <= Last) AND (Input <> 0) DO
      List[Index] := Input;
      Index := Index + 1;
      WriteString("Input a Cardinal (zero terminates): ");
      Input := ReadCard()
   END;
```

After the first value has been input, the condition in the WHILE statement is evaluated. If it is TRUE, the statement sequence beginning with List[Index] := Input is executed. The condition will be true the first time only if the user has not input zero.

After each execution of the statement sequence, where the current component (as specified by `Index`) is assigned the value just input and the next value is input, the condition is again evaluated. In general the condition can be `FALSE` either when `Index` has exceeded the limit of the array (i.e. `Index <= Last` is no longer `TRUE`) or when a zero has been assigned to the variable `Input`.

One subtle point about this example is that `Index` has been declared to be of type `CARDINAL` rather than of type `ListRange`. This is because `Index` is likely to exceed the maximum value in `ListRange`, and if `Index` had been declared as being of type `ListRange` this would cause a program exception.

The REPEAT statement and arrays

Whereas the `WHILE` statement may never allow its statement sequence to be executed, the `REPEAT` statement guarantees that the statement sequence will be executed at least once. This is because the `REPEAT` statement evaluates a terminating condition after each execution of the statement sequence.

The code example given in the preceding section, which inputs values into the array `List`, could be rewritten using a `REPEAT` statement. Notice that the termination condition now evaluates:

```
(Index => Last) OR (Input = 0)
```

This is the negation of the condition tested in the `WHILE` statement, because the iteration condition of the `REPEAT` statement is a terminating condition which determines whether to stop the loop. The `WHILE` iteration condition, on the other hand, is a starting condition and determines whether the loop should be entered (or continued).

```
Index := First;
REPEAT
  WriteString("Input a Cardinal (zero terminates): ");
  Input := ReadCard();
  IF Input <> 0 THEN
    List[Index] := Input;
    Index := Index + 1
  END;
UNTIL (Index => Last) OR (Input = 0);
```

Notice that we now have to use an `IF` statement to catch one of the terminating conditions (`Input = 0`), so that it is not entered into the array.

7.3   RECORDS AND THE WITH STATEMENT

Whereas an array contains component variables which are all of the same type, *record types* contain component variables, called *fields*, which may be of a variety of types. The method of selecting a component variable is also different for records: the variable name is followed by a period and then the field's identifier.

Modula-2 provides a *record constructor* for specifying records in terms of their components. Its simplest form is as follows:

```
RECORD
  field1: type1;
  field2, field3: type2;
  (* etc. *)
END;
```

For example, the following defines a record type called `AccountRec` which contains component variables which are called `AccountNo, Balance,` and `PermittedOverdraft`:

```
AccountRec = RECORD
                AccountNo: CARDINAL;
                Balance: REAL;
                PermittedOverdraft: REAL
             END;
```

Note that the list of field identifiers may be given so as to specify a number of fields which have the same type. The foregoing declaration of `AccountRec` could just as easily be written:

```
AccountRec = RECORD
                AccountNo : CARDINAL;
                Balance, PermittedOverdraft : REAL
             END;
```

As a further example consider a type, `BoxType`, which describes how data which describes boxes is to be held. The record has to contain a part number, the dimensions of the kind of box, and the supplier's name. (The first definitions define a string type; see Chapter 10.)

```
CONST
  MaxNameLength = 40;
TYPE
  NameRange =[0..MaxNameLength-1];
  NameType = ARRAY NameRange OF CHAR;
  BoxType = RECORD
               PartNumber: CARDINAL;
               Height, Length, Width: REAL;
               SupplierName: NameType
            END;
VAR
  Box: BoxType;
```

The variable `Box` thus contains five variables (fields) which can be individually accessed:

```
Box.PartNumber := 1270056;
Box.Height := 10.5;
Box.Length := 15.0;
Box.Width := 5.75;
Box.SupplierName := "Rocky Mountain Box Company";
```

Whole records can be assigned to each other, but no other operators are permitted with them. All calculations with records must be carried out using component fields.

Records can contain fields of any type (including records) and can contain mutually exclusive groups of fields. For a fuller description of records—and how their internal structure can vary—see Chapter 20.

The WITH statement and records

The assignment statements which store values in the fields of the variable Box are somewhat cumbersome to read as well as difficult to type in correctly. Modula-2 provides the WITH statement which allows the name of a record to be omitted in the statement sequence which it contains. For example, the above statements could be written as:

```
WITH Box DO
  PartNumber := 1270056;
  Height := 10.5;
  Length := 15.0;
  Width := 5.75;
  SupplierName := "Rocky Mountain Box Company"
END;
```

This is both easier to write and easier to comprehend. Full details of the WITH statement are given in Chapter 18.

7.4 SETS

The set structure is the simplest of all data structures. A set consists of an *unordered* collection of *elements* also termed *members*, which must all be of the same ordinal type, called the *base type* of the set. Modula-2 allows the programmer to define *set types*, and a *set constructor* is provided in order to define set types. The form of a set type definition is:

```
settype = SET OF basetype;
```

For example the following defines a set type called SetOfSmallNos. The ordinal type SmallNos is a subrange of type CARDINAL.

```
TYPE
  SmallNos = [0..3];
  SetOfSmallNos = SET OF SmallNos;
```

Now that we have declared a set type called SetOfSmallNos, what set values does this type encompass? If the base type of a set type (S) has n distinct values then its set type consists of 2^n set values. The set S is said to be the *powerset* of the base type.

For example, the base type of SetOfSmallNos consists of four values, therefore the set type SetOfSmallNos consists of 2^4 sets, i.e. 16 sets. Consequently, the set values defined by the set SetOfSmallNos are as follows.

(Notice that set membership is denoted by the members being enclosed in curly brackets (braces) and that { } denotes the empty set.)

```
{}          {0}         {0,1}        {0,1,2}       {0,1,2,3}
            {1}         {0,2}        {0,1,3}
            {2}         {0,3}        {0,2,3}
            {3}         {1,2}        {1,2,3}
                        {1,3}
                        {2,3}
```

In other words variables of type SetOfSmallNos can take any of the above values.

Note that many implementations impose severe restrictions on what can be a set base type. See *Portability Issues* in the next section.

It is important to emphasize once again that a set consists of an *unordered* collection of elements, Therefore {0,2,3} is equivalent to {2,0,3}. Also, the repetition of a particular member in a set is meaningless, for example {0,0,0} is equivalent to {0}. As a further example consider a type, SetOfBoolean:

```
TYPE
   SetOfBoolean = SET OF BOOLEAN;
VAR
   BoolSet : SetOfBoolean;
```

The variable Boolset can be assigned any of the following values:

```
{}      {TRUE}      {FALSE}      {TRUE, FALSE}
```

However the strong type rules of Modula-2 require that the type of these set constants be made explicit by preceding the constant with the set type. Thus the Modula-2 assignment statements for assigning the above values to Boolset are:

```
Boolset := SetOfBoolean{};
BoolSet := SetOfBoolean{TRUE};
Boolset := SetOfBoolean{FALSE};
Boolset := SetOfBoolean{TRUE, FALSE};
```

As well as declaring set types and variables it is also possible to declare set constants. As we have seen, to denote a constant of some set type, Modula-2 requires the set type identifier to precede the members to be included, which are themselves enclosed in curly brackets. This construct is called a *set value constructor*. The form for declaring a *set constant* is as follows:

```
SetConstant = SetType{element1, element2};
```

Given the following type declarations:

```
TYPE
   Transport = (Car, Bus, Train, Plane, MotorBike, Bicycle);
   Number = [0..9];
   SetOfTransport = SET OF Transport;
   SetOfNumber = SET OF Number;
```

Then the following constant declarations can be made:

```
CONST
   TwoWheels = SetOfTransport{MotorBike, Bicycle};
   MyNumbers = SetOfNumber{0,1,2,3,4,5,6,7,8,9};
```

A set value constructor may also be used with a range specification, for example:

```
CONST
   AllTransport = SetOfTransport{Car..Bicycle};
   MyNumbers    = SetOfNumber{0..9};
```

Note that for set constants, the set elements must be constant expressions (see section 4.6).

As with all other variables, values can be assigned to set variables. The values that can be assigned to a set variable must be one of the sets defined by the set type. Given the type declarations above the following variable declarations can be made:

```
VAR
   NoTransport,
   MyTransport : SetOfTransport;
   NumberSet : SetOfNumber;
```

Values can then be assigned to a set by making use of the set value constructor.

```
NoTransport := SetOfTransport{}; (* the empty set *)
MyTransport := SetOfTransport{Car,Bicycle};
NumberSet   := SetOfNumber{1,3,4};
```

The most frequent operation that you will want to carry out involving sets is to test for set membership. This involves testing to see if a variable of the base type exists in a variable or constant of the set type. Set membership testing is accomplished by use of the asymmetric operator IN. This operator takes on its right hand side a set value and on its left hand side a value of that set's base type. The result of evaluating an expression using the IN operator is a Boolean (i.e. TRUE or FALSE).

Consider the following program module which demonstrates the usage of the operator IN and the denotation of set values:

```
MODULE IsMember;
TYPE
   Transport = (Car, Bus, Train, Plane, MotorBike, Bicycle);
   SetOfTransport = SET OF Transport;
CONST
   TwoWheels = SetOfTransport{MotorBike, Bicycle};
VAR
   IsMine, CanFly, HasTwoWheels : BOOLEAN;
   ModeOfTravel : Transport;
   MyTransport : SetOfTransport;
BEGIN
   ModeOfTravel := Bus;
   HasTwoWheels := ModeOfTravel IN TwoWheels;
   (* HasTwoWheels = FALSE *)
   ModeOfTravel := Plane;
   CanFly := ModeOfTravel IN SetOfTransport{Plane};
```

```
    (* CanFly = TRUE *)
    MyTransport := SetOfTransport{Car};
    IsMine := ModeOfTravel IN MyTransport
    (* IsMine = FALSE *)
END IsMember.
```

Sets and the operators which can be applied to them are covered in greater detail in Chapter 21.

7.5   PORTABILITY ISSUES

There are a number of portability problems associated with arrays and the iteration statements; these are explained in detail in Chapters 18 and 19. Briefly, the things to watch out for are:

- The number of dimensions allowed in array of array declarations may be limited.

- The degree to which iteration statements can be nested within each other is limited.

Records and WITH statements are relatively free of portability issues. There will, however, be limits to the number of fields allowed in records and to the depth that WITH statements can be nested in order to use the name of a field of a complex record of records. (There are some problems associated with variant records, which are discussed in Chapter 20.)

Many implementations of Modula-2 limit the elements of a set to 16 or 32 members. This is because they represent a set in memory as one or two machine words. Therefore the number of elements a set can have may be limited to the word length of the computer you are using, which will usually be 8, 16, or 32 bits. The least number of elements you can expect to be allowed is 16, therefore you may consider it prudent to keep set membership to this number in the interests of portability.

To be absolutely precise, the size of sets may be further limited, due to the fact that implementations may count the number of values in a set's base type starting from an ordinal value of zero. For example, a SET OF [9..18] would not be acceptable on implementations with a restriction of 16, even though the base type contains only 10 values. See Section 21.8 for full details.

This unfortunate restriction means that many implementations cannot represent types defined to be SET OF CHAR, or even sets of subranges of CHAR. Fortunately, more recent implementations can easily cope with SET OF CHAR and with sets of very large subranges. (Topspeed Modula-2 is one of these more useful implementations.)

You will also find that most compilers restrict INTEGER base types to non-negative subranges. This can be overcome by using type transfer functions (see Chapter 16).

Note that older compilers allow the set type to be omitted from set value constructors. The value is taken to be a bit pattern of type BITSET (see Chapter 25) which can cause problems.

7.6   REVIEW QUESTIONS AND EXERCISES

Q7.1   Of what type must the component type of an array be?

Q7.2   Of what type must the index of an array be?

Q7.3   Define an array type called Alphabet that can be used to store up to 50 letters of the alphabet in upper-case. The index of the array is to start at zero.

Q7.4   Write a program module which inputs six cardinal values into an array and then prints them out again in reverse order.

Q7.5   Define a record type called DateRec which contains three variables of suitable SHORTCARD subrange types which are to be used to store the day, the month, and the year (in the range 0–99).

Q7.6   Of what type must the base type of a set be?

Q7.7   Define a set type called SetOfColour, the element type will be an enumeration type consisting of the colours of the rainbow.

8 ORGANIZING PROGRAMS INTO MODULES AND PROCEDURES

8.1 INTRODUCTION

The programming examples you have encountered so far in this text have all been restricted to just a few lines of code. In reality, however, a commercial program could run to thousands or even hundreds of thousands of lines of code. When a program of this size is tackled, it is extremely important that the program is broken down into a number of clearly defined subprograms. The reasons for doing this are threefold:

- Each subprogram will be easier for the programmer to comprehend than the program as a whole.

- A number of programmers can work on the same program by dividing the subprograms between them.

- Not only will the resultant program be easier to read due to its clear structure, but it will be easier to maintain as the various subprograms can be updated or substituted in isolation from the program as a whole.

Modula-2 provides two program structuring tools: procedures and modules.

8.2 WHAT ARE PROCEDURES?

A procedure is a self-contained section of program which is executed by using its name as a statement which is known as a *procedure call*. What a procedure does is defined by program statements included in a *procedure declaration*. Procedure declarations may appear in program modules, implementation modules, local modules, and within other procedures. They may not appear in definition modules. Like constant, type, and variable declarations they appear before the program statements in the module or procedure which contain them. In outline, a procedure is declared in a module in this way:

```
MODULE ModuleName;
CONST
   (* constant declarations *)
TYPE
   (* type declarations *)
VAR
   (* variable declarations *)

PROCEDURE Proc1;
  BEGIN
     (* statements *)
  END Proc1;
                                    procedure declarations
PROCEDURE Proc2;
  BEGIN
     (* statements *)
  END Proc2;

BEGIN
   (* statements *)
   Proc1;            The statements in Proc1 are executed by this.
   ...
   Proc2;            This causes Proc2 to be executed.
END ModuleName.
```

The procedure Proc1 is said to be *called* by the statement Proc1; the procedure Proc2 is called by the statement Proc2. These procedure calls transfer execution to the statements declared in Proc1 and Proc2, respectively. When the statements in a procedure have completed execution, control *returns* to the point where the call was made. Note that we have indented the statements of Proc1 and Proc2 to emphasize the structure of the module. This is good programming style, but we will often not do this in order to save space.

For example, consider Init in the module below and how its statements are executed. (Each statement is labelled by a comment for description later.) The purpose of Init is to initialize three variables.

```
MODULE m;
VAR
   FirstTime : BOOLEAN;
   Count, Position : CARDINAL;
   TotalDistance : REAL;
PROCEDURE Init;
  BEGIN
     Count := 0;            (*1*)
     Position := 1;         (*2*)
     TotalDistance := 0.0   (*3*)
  END Init;
```

```
BEGIN
  FirstTime := TRUE;      (*4*)
  Init;                   (*5*)
  IF FirstTime THEN...    (*6*)
  ...
END m.
```

In module m execution begins with the statement labelled (*4*)—the first in the body of the program module. Execution proceeds to (*5*) which calls Init. Control then passes to Init and statements (*1*), (*2*), and (*3*) are executed; next control returns to the main module and statement (*6*) is executed.

You have already encountered many procedures. They have mostly been imported from the module PortIO for input and output. (For example, ReadString, WriteString, and WriteLn.) While you can get quite far by using procedures from modules supplied by other programmers, inevitably you will want to construct your own.

The primary purpose of a procedure is simply to encapsulate some task which you want the program to do. You might decide to encapsulate a number of statements in a procedure to make the task clear, or because the task is to be carried out repeatedly. Alternatively, you might want to save some space in your program. (Constructing a procedure for the latter reason often makes your program clearer.)

Statements appear inside a procedure in much the same way as in a main program module. A procedure can also include local declarations of constants, types, variables, and procedures. (Local modules are also permitted; see Chapter 13.) Procedures may also have *parameters*. These are routes for data values to pass into and out of a procedure (see below).

Parameterless procedures

The simplest form of procedure declaration has no parameters (like all those above) and has the form:

```
PROCEDURE ProcedureName;
CONST
  (* local constant declarations *)
TYPE
  (* local type declarations *)
VAR
  (* local variable declarations *)
BEGIN
  (* statements *)
END ProcedureName;
```

As an example of a procedure without parameters consider the following procedure which can be used when your program can no longer face the world. It uses the predefined procedure HALT, which stops your program (see Chapter 23).

```
PROCEDURE GiveUp;
  CONST
    FarewellMessage = "Too many values to be stored. Bye bye.";
  BEGIN
    WriteString(FarewellMessage);
    HALT
  END GiveUp;
```

What the procedure `GiveUp` will do has been defined by the above declaration: it will output the farewell message and then halt the program. To make use of `GiveUp` you simply write it as a statement. This particular procedure might be called from within an `IF` statement, for example:

```
IF NumberOfTransactions > MaximumNumber THEN
  GiveUp
END;
```

Usually parameterless procedures are used in an implementation module to manipulate variables which have been declared outside the procedure. (This is done in implementation modules in which a number of procedures may use a common variable.)

Procedures with parameters

Parameters are data routes into and out of a procedure. When a procedure is declared, parameters may be included in its heading between the procedure's name and the semicolon. The form of a procedure heading is:

```
ProcedureName(Param1: SomeType; Param2: SomeOtherType (*etc*) );
```

The parameters in the procedure heading are known as *formal parameters*. These appear similar to variable declarations and specify both the name by which the data can be identified within the procedure and specify whether the 'route' is an inward-bound or an outward-bound one. Formal parameters which allow values only to be passed into a procedure are called *value parameters*. Formal parameters which denote variables that can take values into a procedure or out from a procedure are called *variable parameters*. We will adopt the colloquial equivalent of **VAR-parameters**. (This is coined because the formal parameter identifier is preceded by the VAR keyword.)

When a procedure with parameters is called, the parameters in the call are known as *actual parameters*. If these parameters correspond to value parameters, they are either expressions which result in values to be passed into the procedure for use there, or variables in which values that the procedure needs are stored. If they correspond to VAR-parameters, they must be variables in which the procedure can access or store values.

The formal parameters (i.e. those in the heading) specify three attributes which the actual parameters must have:

- the type of the value being passed into the procedure, or the type of the variable being accessed;

- whether the parameter is a value parameter or a VAR-parameter (i.e. whether an expression or variable is required as an actual parameter);

- the left-to-right order of the parameters. The actual parameters are mapped onto the formal parameters in the order that they appear in the procedure call. Therefore, taken in order, each parameter in the actual parameter list must be of a type compatible with the parameter in the formal parameter list.

As an example of a parameter which returns a value in a variable consider the following simple procedure:

```
PROCEDURE FortyTwo(VAR CardinalNumber: CARDINAL);
  BEGIN
    CardinalNumber := 42
  END FortyTwo;
```

The VAR keyword signifies that the parameter denoted by the identifier (in this case CardinalNumber) is to be used for returning values in the variable which is the actual parameter. This works by assigning a value to the formal parameter inside the procedure. In this rather silly procedure CardinalNumber is assigned the value 42. If the procedure is called, the variable which is included as an *actual* parameter will always be changed to 42. For example, assuming that the variables x and y have been declared as CARDINAL variables, then the following statements would leave both with a value of 42.

```
FortyTwo(x);
FortyTwo(y);
```

The formal parameter of FortyTwo is a VAR-parameter (which you can see from its heading is called CardinalNumber). The *actual* parameter used in the first procedure call is x. The actual parameter in the second call of FortyTwo is y.

If the VAR keyword is omitted, the formal parameter is a value parameter and the value of the actual parameter will be copied into the procedure. (That is, the value of actual parameter is copied into a variable inside the procedure, the variables being the formal parameter.) The actual parameter which corresponds to a formal value parameter must be an expression.

Values cannot be returned to the caller of the procedure via a value parameter. Therefore, expressions may not be used to match a VAR-parameter. (Do not be confused by a variable name as an actual value parameter: it is an expression in this context.)

You probably realize that all the output procedures from PortIO that you have seen up to now take value parameters. The following procedure has one value parameter—a CARDINAL—which it outputs to the screen and follows it with a new line.

```
PROCEDURE PrintCard(CardinalValue: CARDINAL);
  BEGIN
    WriteCard(CardinalValue);
    WriteLn
  END PrintCard;
```

The following loop would print the numbers 1 to 20 on separate lines:

```
FOR c := 1 TO 20 DO
  PrintCard(c)
END;
```

Frequently, a procedure will have both value parameters and VAR-parameters: such a procedure would use the values passed in to it (via the value parameters) to calculate what should be stored in the actual VAR-parameters. For example, the following procedure takes a list of real values and returns the sum of the values, and the number of positive values which are approximately equal to zero. (With real number arithmetic, testing for equality is a problem; you must therefore check whether the value is within some range of zero.) If a number is less than the approximation to zero, it is not included in the sum. The constant and type declarations relevant to the procedure precede it:

```
CONST
  RangeMin = 0; RangeMax = 25;
  ZeroApproximation = 0.001;
TYPE
  ListRange = [RangeMin..RangeMax];
  NumberList = ARRAY ListRange OF REAL;

PROCEDURE Tally(List: NumberList; Length: ListRange;
                VAR Sum: REAL; VAR NumberOfZeros: ListRange);
  VAR
    This: ListRange;
  BEGIN
    NumberOfZeros := 0;
    Sum := 0.0;
    FOR This := RangeMin TO Length DO
      IF ABS(List[This]) < ZeroApproximation THEN
        NumberOfZeros := NumberOfZeros + 1
      ELSE
        Sum := Sum + List[This]
      END
    END
  END Tally;
```

When you have a number of formal parameters of the same kind (all value parameters or all VAR-parameters) together, you may abbreviate their declarations into a list. Thus the following declarations are equivalent:

```
PROCEDURE p(a:CARDINAL; b: CARDINAL;
            VAR x: REAL; VAR y: REAL);
```

and

```
PROCEDURE p(a, b:CARDINAL; VAR x, y: REAL);
```

Function procedures

A *function procedure* is a procedure which is used in an expression to calculate a value which is part of the expression. You have already seen examples of these used for reading values from the terminal (all but one of the input procedures in the library module PortIO are function procedures). For example, assuming that ReadCard has been imported from PortIO, the following statement inputs a real number to the CARDINAL variable Speed:

```
Speed := ReadCard();
```

ReadCard() is a call to a parameterless function procedure (hence the parentheses) which, as you can see, occurs as part of an expression and not as a statement.

A function procedure is written just as an ordinary procedure, but with a *result type* specified. The result type specifies the type of the value which is to be 'returned' by the function procedure when it is used in an expression. Unlike so-called *proper procedures*, if a function procedure has no parameters, it must include parentheses as if it had. The procedure heading for ReadCard is thus:

```
PROCEDURE ReadCard(): CARDINAL;
```

An example of a function procedure you might construct follows. This function procedure has two parameters. It takes a list of cardinal numbers, and searches it for a maximum value. This value is passed back to the expression which uses the function procedure by the RETURN statement, which also terminates execution of the function procedure.

```
CONST
  RangeMin = 0; RangeMax = 25;
TYPE
  ListRange = [RangeMin..RangeMax];
  NumberList = ARRAY ListRange OF CARDINAL;

PROCEDURE Maximum(List: NumberList;
                  Length: ListRange): CARDINAL;
  VAR
    This: ListRange;
    CurrentMax: CARDINAL;
  BEGIN
    CurrentMax := List[RangeMin];
    FOR This := RangeMin + 1 TO Length DO
      IF List[This] > CurrentMax THEN
        CurrentMax := List[This]
      END
    END;
    RETURN CurrentMax
  END Maximum;
```

Note that a function procedure *must* include a RETURN statement.

The function procedure Maximum could be used as follows:

```
WriteString("The maximum held in the list is ");
WriteCard(Maximum(List, Length));
```

(It is assumed that the variables `List` and `Length` have been declared as required.)

Together with modules, procedures are the most powerful programming constructs in Modula-2. Procedures are fully described in Chapter 14.

8.3   VARYING THE SIZE OF ARRAY PARAMETERS

Consider the situation where a program has been written that makes use of a number of arrays that have the same component type but differing index types. It is quite possible that you would want to do an identical operation on each array type, such as sorting, searching, or adding up all the elements. Clearly, it would be irritating to write a different procedure for each array that shared a common component type but differed only in their index types. Therefore, Modula-2 provides the means of declaring an array, in the formal parameter list of a procedure, as an *open array parameter*. The form of such a declaration is:

```
PROCEDURE MySort(VAR AnArray: ARRAY OF CARDINAL);
```

Note that no mention is made of the index type or its range. By declaring an open array parameter, the index range of the actual array that is passed to the procedure is mapped onto the whole numbers 0 to $n-1$ where n represents the number of elements in the actual array. In order to process an array that is passed to such a procedure it is necessary to find the high bound index of the array. This is found by using the built-in procedure `HIGH` which returns the value of the upper limit of the formal array parameter. For example:

```
UpperLimit := HIGH(AnArray);
```

A simple example should make the use of an open array parameter clearer. Consider a procedure that will sum up all the elements of an array of cardinal numbers and return the result.

```
PROCEDURE Sum(CardArray: ARRAY OF CARDINAL) : CARDINAL;
  VAR
    Result, i : CARDINAL;
  BEGIN
    Result := 0;
    FOR i := 0 TO HIGH(CardArray) DO
      Result := Result + CardArray[i]
    END;
    RETURN Result
  END Sum;
```

If in the surrounding program the following declarations were made :

```
TYPE
  SmallArray = ARRAY [0..9] OF CARDINAL;
  LargeArray = ARRAY [1..20] OF CARDINAL;
```

```
VAR
  SArray : SmallArray;
  LArray : LargeArray;
  Result1, Result2 : CARDINAL;
```

The function procedure `Sum` can be called with either `SArray` or `LArray` as its parameter.

```
Result1 := Sum(SArray);
Result2 := Sum(LArray);
```

See Chapters 14 and 19 for further details of open array parameters.

8.4   SEPARATELY COMPILED MODULES

In Chapter 2 you were introduced to the module structure of Modula-2. If you have worked through Part I to this point, you should now be able to construct Modula-2 programs which consist of a main program module which imports procedures and data types from a number of other modules (which may or may not use each other). The modules you have imported from have all been supplied by the authors. Therefore in this section you will learn how to write a program that imports procedures and data types from a definition module that has been designed and written specifically to support your program. You must imagine that you need a program which reads a calendar date, of the form 22 11 1955, checks whether it is a valid date, and, if it is valid, calculates the day of the week that the date falls on. Finally, the date must be output in the form Tuesday 22 November 1955 .

Designing the program

Modula-2 is a language which by its rules encourages good program design and discourages, or even prevents, bad designs. In Chapter 2 a number of criteria were given for deciding if the modular design of a program is a good one. One of these was the degree to which a module served a single task. Whether a module does this satisfactorily can be determined by whether the variables in the module are related to each other and if the procedures in a module only operate on those variables.

From the specification of the date problem you should be able to see that there are four main tasks to be done:

- a date must be read from the keyboard;

- the date must be validated;

- the day of the week must be calculated and added to the date;

- the modified formal date must be printed to the screen.

Although these four tasks can be identified, they all involve the same data type—a date. It would not be unreasonable therefore to encapsulate these tasks in a single module rather than separate them.

The definition module

Given the design criterion above, we program the interface to the module as a definition module. First, we shall decide on the abstract type required by the problem; here it is a date. Second, we shall define Modula-2 types and data structures to model the abstract types. The obvious choice of data structure for a date is a record (see Chapter 7). This record will need four whole number fields in order to hold the four pieces of data that will represent a date. Therefore we need to define the types of these four fields:

- `DayInWeek` (the subrange denoting week day)

- `DayNumber` (a subrange type whose value denotes days in month)

- `MonthNumber` (a subrange type whose value denotes months in a year)

- `YearNumber` (a subrange type whose value denotes the year)

Note that we do not need a type for handling the textual form of the date; we will hide the way the textual form is generated in the implementation module.

Here are the type declarations for the definition module:

```
DEFINITION MODULE Dates;
TYPE
  DayInWeek = [1..7]; (* 1 = Monday; 7 = Sunday *)
  DayNumber = [1..31];
  MonthNumber = [1..12];
  YearNumber = [1900..2010];
  DateRecord = RECORD
                 DayOfWeek : DayInWeek;
                 DayNum : DayNumber;
                 Month : MonthNumber;
                 Year : YearNumber
               END;
```

Now the data types have been defined, we can declare the procedures that will be needed to manipulate this type. We need a procedure for each of the tasks which we identified earlier:

```
PROCEDURE ReadDay(VAR d: DateRecord; VAR OK: BOOLEAN);

PROCEDURE ReadMonth(VAR d: DateRecord; VAR OK: BOOLEAN);

PROCEDURE ReadYear(VAR d: DateRecord; VAR OK: BOOLEAN);

PROCEDURE ValidDate(d: DateRecord; VAR OK: BOOLEAN);

PROCEDURE GetDayName(VAR d: DateRecord);

PROCEDURE WriteDate(d: DateRecord);

END Dates.
```

You will notice that five of these procedure headings have at least one VAR-parameter. This is because these procedures will need to change the value of a variable of type DateRecord and or a variable of type BOOLEAN. The procedures ReadDay, ReadYear, and ReadMonth alter the value of a BOOLEAN variable to indicate whether or not they have successfully read a number from the terminal and assigned it to the relevant field of a DateRecord. The procedure ValidDate alters the value of a BOOLEAN variable depending on the validity of a DateRecord.

Checking definition module design

With the definition module prepared, you can proceed to developing your main program and to checking the design. We shall want to input at least one date, and so a REPEAT statement will be appropriate. We also need to terminate the loop; arbitrarily we decide to input an exclamation mark (!) as a terminating character. Assuming this, the main program might be as follows:

```
MODULE CheckDate;
FROM Dates IMPORT
  ReadDay, ReadMonth, ReadYear, GetDayName,
  ValidDate, WriteDate, DateRecord;
FROM PortIO IMPORT ReadChar, WriteLn, WriteString;
CONST
  Quit = "!";
VAR
  Date : DateRecord;
  Control : CHAR;
  IsOk : BOOLEAN;
BEGIN
  REPEAT
    ReadDay(Date, IsOk);
    IF IsOk THEN
      ReadMonth(Date, IsOk);
      IF IsOk THEN
        ReadYear(Date, IsOk)
        IF IsOk THEN
          ValidDate(Date, IsOk)
          IF IsOk THEN
            GetDayName(Date);
            WriteDate(Date)
          END
        END
      END
    END;
    WriteString ("Type '!' to quit any key to continue :");
    Control := ReadChar();
    WriteLn
  UNTIL Control = Quit
END CheckDate.
```

Of course this program module cannot be compiled and run until the Dates implementation module has been written. However, the act of writing the program module can help you to think of the logic of the design of the definition module. In practice, you will not get this right the first time you try. It may well be that the development of the program module will throw up errors in the definition module. And often, you have to do a little bit of the program module to get to grips with the problem and hence how the definition module should be programmed.

The implementation module

Having satisfied yourself that the design of the definition module is viable (it may turn out not to be right), you must now implement the module and test your program. For added interest we will permit the client of this module to choose whether to output a prompt.

The implementation module is given below, and an explanation follows:

```
IMPLEMENTATION MODULE Dates;
FROM PortIO IMPORT
   WriteCard, ReadCard, ReadChar, WriteString,
   WriteLn, SetFieldWidth;
VAR
   GivePrompt : BOOLEAN; (* Prompt flag *)
   Response : CHAR;

PROCEDURE ReadDay(VAR d: DateRecord; VAR OK: BOOLEAN);
   VAR Input : CARDINAL;
   BEGIN
     IF GivePrompt THEN
       WriteString("Enter Day Number: ");
     END;
     Input := ReadCard();
     IF (Input >= 1) AND (Input <= 31) THEN
       d.DayNum := Input;
       OK := TRUE;
     ELSE
       WriteString('*** Day number out of range ***');
       OK := FALSE;
     END;
     WriteLn;
   END ReadDay;

PROCEDURE ReadMonth(VAR d: DateRecord; VAR OK: BOOLEAN);
   VAR Input : CARDINAL;
   BEGIN
     IF GivePrompt THEN
       WriteString("Enter Month Number: ");
     END;
     Input := ReadCard();
     IF (Input >= 1) AND (Input <= 12) THEN
       d.Month := Input;
       OK := TRUE;
     ELSE
       WriteString('*** Month number out of range ***')
```

```
        OK := FALSE;
      END;
      WriteLn;
   END ReadMonth;

PROCEDURE ReadYear(VAR d: DateRecord; VAR OK: BOOLEAN);
   VAR Input : CARDINAL;
   BEGIN
      IF GivePrompt THEN
        WriteString("Enter Year Number: ");
      END;
      Input := ReadCard();
      IF (Input >= 1900) AND (Input <= 2010) THEN
        d.Year := Input;
        OK := TRUE;
      ELSE
        WriteString('*** Month number out of range ***')
        OK := FALSE;
      END;
      WriteLn;
   END ReadYear;

PROCEDURE ValidDate(d: DateRecord OK : BOOLEAN);
   VAR NoOfDays : DayNumber;
   BEGIN
      CASE d.Month OF
        1, 3, 5, 7, 8, 10, 12:
          NoOfDays := 31 |
        4, 6, 9, 11:
          NoOfDays := 30 |
        2:
          IF (d.Year MOD 4) = 0 THEN
            NoOfDays := 29
          ELSE
            NoOfDays := 28
          END
      END;
      IF d.DayNum <= NoOfDays THEN
        OK := TRUE;
      ELSE
        WriteString('*** Date does not exist ***')
        OK := FALSE;
      END;
   END ValidDate;

PROCEDURE GetDayName(VAR d: DateRecord);
   VAR Count, DaysBetween : CARDINAL;
   BEGIN
      DaysBetween := 0;
      FOR Count := 1900 TO d.Year - 1 DO
        IF Count MOD 4 = 0 THEN
          DaysBetween := DaysBetween + 366
        ELSE
          DaysBetween := DaysBetween + 365
        END
```

```
    END;
    FOR Count := 1 TO d.Month - 1 DO
      CASE Count OF
        2:
          IF d.Year MOD 4 = 0 THEN
            DaysBetween := DaysBetween + 29
          ELSE
            DaysBetween := DaysBetween + 28
          END|
        1, 3, 5, 7, 8, 10, 12:
          DaysBetween := DaysBetween + 31 |
        4, 6, 9, 11:
          DaysBetween := DaysBetween + 30
      END
    END;
    DaysBetween := DaysBetween + d.DayNum;
    d.DayOfWeek := (DaysBetween - 2) MOD 7
  END GetDayName;

PROCEDURE WriteDate(d: DateRecord);
  BEGIN
    WriteString(' The date input was :');
    CASE d.DayOfWeek OF
      1 : WriteString('Monday')|
      2 : WriteString('Tuesday')|
      3 : WriteString('Wednesday')|
      4 : WriteString('Thursday')|
      5 : WriteString('Friday')|
      6 : WriteString('Saturday')|
      7 : WriteString('Sunday')
    END;
    SetFieldWidth(3);
    WriteCard(d.DayNum);
    CASE d.Month OF
      1 : WriteString(' January')|
      2 : WriteString(' February')|
      3 : WriteString(' March')|
      4 : WriteString(' April')|
      5 : WriteString(' May')|
      6 : WriteString(' June')|
      7 : WriteString(' July')|
      8 : WriteString(' August')|
      9 : WriteString(' September')|
      10 : WriteString(' October')|
      11 : WriteString(' November')|
      12 : WriteString(' December')
    END;
    WriteCard(d.Year);
    WriteLn
  END WriteDate;

BEGIN (*Dates*)
  WriteString("Do you wish a date GivePrompt? ");
  WriteLn;
  WriteString("Type 'y' for yes, any other key for no: ");
```

```
    Response := ReadChar();
    WriteLn;
    GivePrompt := Response = 'y';
END Dates.
```

The implementation of `ReadDay`, `ReadMonth`, and `ReadYear` are quite straightforward; they all make use of a procedure from `PortIO` to read a cardinal number from the terminal. Only if the numbers are within the appropriate range are the numbers assigned to the date. These procedures also alter the value of a `BOOLEAN` variable to indicate whether or not a number has been assigned to the appropriate field of a `DateRecord` variable.

The procedure `ValidDate` checks that the day number is a valid one according to the month of the year and whether the year is a leap year or not. If the date is valid it alters the value of the `BOOLEAN` variable `OK` to indicate that this is the case.

The procedure `GetDayName` is a little more complex, it calculates the number of days that have passed since 1 January 1900 up until the value of the date variable. The result of this calculation (which is held in `DaysBetween`) is then used to calculate the day of the week. This is achieved by taking the modulus of the calculation `DaysBetween` divided by 7. As 1 January 1900 was a Sunday rather than a Monday we need to subtract 1 to arrive at the correct result.

The final procedure `WriteDate` needs little explanation as it simply writes the date back to the screen, mapping from values of the subrange types `DayInWeek` and `MonthNumber` to literal string constants.

Finally, and most importantly, the *module initialization* (actually, the initialization of module variables) must be explained. The variables `GivePrompt` and `Response` are said to be not *visible* outside the implementation module, and so cannot possibly be accessed. This is as it should be. They are necessary because their values alter the behaviour of the procedures `ReadDay`, `ReadMonth`, and `ReadYear` (whether they display a prompt). Therefore it is the responsibility of the implementation module to initialize these variables, or indeed any others.

Modula-2 recognizes that module initialization is a common requirement when designing programs in a modular way. Thus statements may be placed between the `BEGIN` keyword and the keyword `END` which always terminates an implementation module. These statements are executed before the statements in the main program begin execution.

Details of separate modules and local modules can be found in Chapter 13.

8.5   THE SCOPE OF IDENTIFIERS

Where an identifier is declared in a Modula-2 program affects where it can be used—this is termed the *scope* of an identifier. Identifiers that are declared in the declaration part of a program module, or are imported into the program module with an import statement, are said to be *global* to the program. This is because they pervade throughout any procedures that are also declared in the program module.

Declaring a procedure builds a wall around all the identifiers declared within the procedure, making them inaccessible to the surrounding program. The identifiers declared in the procedure are said to be *out of scope* to the surrounding module.

However, the identifiers in a module which encloses a procedure, plus those in any enveloping procedures (if the procedure is nested), can permeate this wall and are accessible by the procedure. These identifiers are said to be *in scope* to the procedure. The wall surrounding the procedure therefore has a number of holes, corresponding to every identifier in the surrounding program, allowing them to be accessed by the procedure. However, these holes in the wall can be patched by declaring an identifier in the procedure which has the same name as an identifier in the surrounding program.

Consider the diagram below. In the diagram there are three identifiers declared in the module M. These are v and w, which have been declared as CARDINAL variables, and P, which has been declared as a procedure. There are also two identifiers x and y which have been imported into the module M from a separate module MyLib. By default all of these identifiers are accessible by the procedure P. However, you will note that the identifier y is unable to permeate through the wall of the procedure P. This is because the identifier y has been redeclared inside the procedure P, blocking off that hole in the procedure wall which would have allowed the identifier y (declared in the surrounding module M) to pass into the procedure P.

```
MODULE M;
```

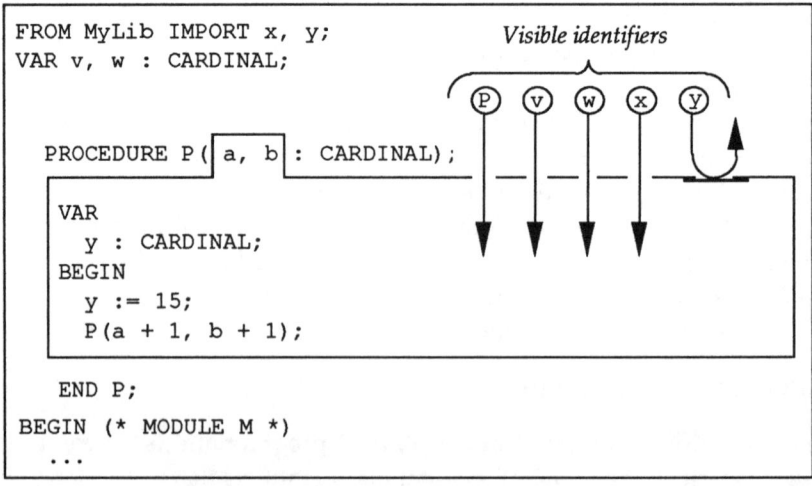

```
FROM MyLib IMPORT x, y;            Visible identifiers
VAR v, w : CARDINAL;

                                    P  v  w  x  y

    PROCEDURE P ( a, b : CARDINAL);

    VAR
       y : CARDINAL;
    BEGIN
       y := 15;
       P(a + 1, b + 1);

    END P;
BEGIN (* MODULE M *)
    ...
END M.
```

Note that none of the identifiers declared in the procedure P is accessible by the surrounding module. The holes in the procedure wall only allow identifiers to pass through in one direction, inwards, into the procedure.

8.6   THE VISIBILITY OF IDENTIFIERS

The *visibility* of identifiers concerns modules. A module (no matter its type) provides a solid wall around all of its identifiers. Identifiers from other modules cannot permeate through this wall unless they are explicitly imported or exported. This is true of all identifiers except the built-in pervasive identifiers such as INTEGER, CARDINAL, ABS, HIGH, etc.

The diagram below shows a *local module*, L, which has been declared inside the program module, M. Local modules provide the means by which procedures and data declarations can be collected together and access to them controlled. We discuss them here to complete the discussion of scope and visibility. (They are described in detail in Chapter 13.)

```
MODULE M;
```

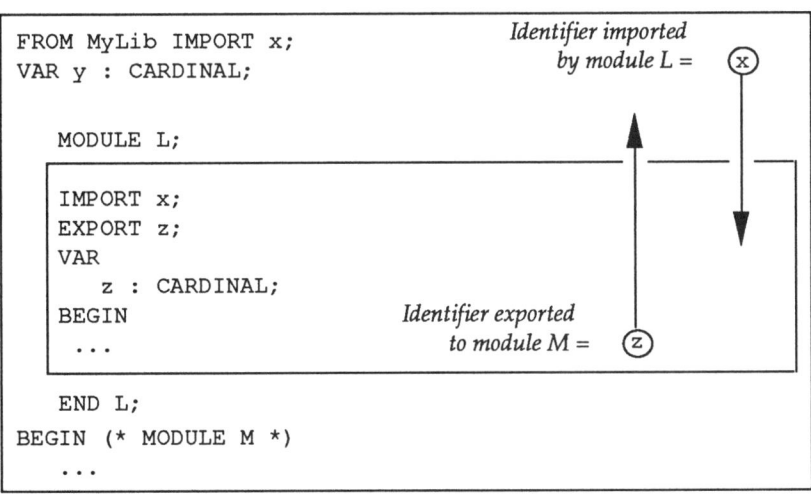

```
FROM MyLib IMPORT x;              Identifier imported
VAR y : CARDINAL;                   by module L =    (x)

   MODULE L;

   IMPORT x;
   EXPORT z;
   VAR
      z : CARDINAL;
   BEGIN            Identifier exported
   ...                to module M =   (z)

   END L;
BEGIN (* MODULE M *)
   ...
```

```
END M.
```

The identifiers that are visible in module M are x, y, and z. The identifier x is declared in the separate module MyLib and is only visible to module M because it has been explicitly imported by the module M. The identifier z is declared in the local module L and is only visible to module M because it has been explicitly exported by the module L.

The identifiers that are visible in module L are z and x. The identifier x is imported by the module M and is only visible to the local module L because it has also been explicitly imported by the module L.

8.7   THE LIFETIME OF VARIABLES

When you declare variables in a procedure or module, storage is allocated for them at run-time in an area of memory set aside for a program's variables.[1] Exactly when these variables are allocated storage will depend on whether they have been declared in a procedure or in a module.

Procedures

A variable declared in a procedure exists for as long as that procedure is being executed. Therefore the lifetime of a variable and the procedure that declares it are one and the same. A procedure comes into existence as soon as it is called, the storage for any variables it declares is therefore allocated on the call of the procedure. The lifetime of a procedure (and so any variables it declares) comes to an end as soon as the end of the procedure is reached or when a RETURN statement is encountered, whereupon storage associated with any of its variables is deallocated. A consequence of this is that variables that are declared locally to a procedure do not retain their values between subsequent calls of a procedure. If a program needs to save the value of a variable between calls of a procedure, that variable must be declared globally at the module level, or declared as a parameter to a procedure.

Modules

A variable declared in a module exists for as long as that module exists, which is the lifetime of the program that uses that module either directly or indirectly. For example, when you run a program, all the variables declared in the program module, all the variables declared in any of the modules it imports, all the variables declared in any of the modules they import etc., will have storage allocated for them as soon as the program starts. This storage only being deallocated when the program ends.

The only exception to this is the special case of local modules. The lifetime of a local module (and so its variables) is the lifetime of the program unit that immediately surrounds it. For example, if a local module were declared within a procedure, storage for its variables would be allocated when the procedure was called and deallocated when the procedure was left. (See Chapter 13 for full details.)

8.8   RECURSION

Procedures are not passive structures. As well as being the subject of procedure calls, they can call other procedures that are in scope. The one procedure that is

---

[1]A Modula-2 program can declare two types of variables: static or dynamic variables. In this context we are referring to static variables. The allocation of memory for dynamic variables, and hence their lifetime, is a separate issue which is covered in Chapter 11.

always in scope to a procedure is the procedure itself, therefore it is quite permissible for a procedure to call itself. This phenomenon of self-activation is termed *recursion*. Recursion is easier to grasp if a common everyday occurrence is defined recursively.

Consider an algorithm for reading a book, the outline for which is expressed in incomplete Modula-2:

```
PROCEDURE ReadABook;
  BEGIN
    ReadAPage;
    IF Book <> Finished THEN
      ReadABook
    END
  END ReadABook;
```

In the algorithm above the problem of reading a book is broken down into a succession of smaller problems. When the procedure is first entered, a single page of the book is read. What to do next? The original problem of reading a book still remains, only this time it is a smaller book. The solution is for the procedure to call itself. The procedure continues to call itself with an ever-decreasing problem, until the book is finished.

Note that every recursive procedure should place its recursive call within a selection statement, otherwise the chain of recursive calls would never terminate! Consider this example of a recursive procedure:

```
PROCEDURE ReverseAList;
  VAR
    Atom : CHAR;
  BEGIN
    Atom := ReadChar();
    IF Atom <> '!' THEN
      ReverseAList;
      WriteChar(Atom)
    END
  END ReverseAList;
```

The effect of this procedure is to read in a list of characters from the keyboard. When the list is terminated by an exclamation mark, the list is written back to the screen in reverse order.

At first glance it would seem that there is only one instance of the variable `Atom`, so where is the list stored before it is written out in reverse order? The answer is, of course, that every time a procedure is invoked its local variables are created anew and are only disposed of when the procedure ends. Consequently, when the recursive chain halts, there will be as many instances of the variable `Atom` as there are characters in the list.

It is always possible to write recursive procedures in an iterative manner. In fact in many cases an iterative solution will be preferable due to speed considerations. In some cases iteration will be the only possibility, as some algorithms do not lend themselves readily to recursive solutions.

There are, however, many instances where a recursive solution is the most 'natural' option, especially if the problem is to process a recursive data structure such as a tree (see Chapter 11).

8.9 PORTABILITY ISSUES

There are many portability issues (both simple and complex) associated with organizing programs into modules and procedures. These are dealt with in detail in Chapters 13 and 14, so only an overview will be given here.

The compatibility rules concerning VAR-parameters have changed during the lifetime of the language and do differ between compilers. In the second edition of *Programming in Modula-2*, Professor Wirth's position was that an actual parameter had to be expression compatible with a formal parameter that was also a VAR-parameter. By the third edition of this book Professor Wirth's stance had changed: he now stated that the type of an actual parameter had to be identical with a formal parameter that was a VAR-parameter. One of the consequences of this is that those compilers that comply with the third edition of *Programming in Modula-2* will not allow you to have an actual parameter which is the subrange of the formal parameter's type, if that formal parameter is a VAR-parameter. The position for value parameters has remained unchanged, they only have to be assignment compatible.

With modules, a problem arises with the importation of enumeration types. With certain implementations, if you import a subrange of an enumeration type and assign to a variable of this type a value which is outside the subrange but part of the host type, this will not be picked up at compile-time but will cause a run-time error.

Some compilers allow you to write definition modules that have no corresponding implementation part. This is quite a useful facility when you wish simply to isolate constant declarations from your program module (thus no implementation part is needed). However, not all compilers allow this, but if necessary it is quite easy to comply with such a restriction, by writing a corresponding implementation module that is empty, consisting of only the module name and the keyword END.

Finally not all compilers require the definition module to be compiled (e.g. Topspeed Modula-2). In such cases it is only necessary to compile the implementation module.

8.10 REVIEW QUESTIONS AND EXERCISES

Q8.1 Which kind of parameters take values out from a procedure? Can an actual parameter corresponding to this kind of parameter be an expression?

Q8.2 Write a procedure which swaps the two values in two CARDINAL variables.

Q8.3   A function procedure terminates when it reaches the END of the procedure. True or false?

Q8.4   Write a function procedure that returns the sum of two cardinal parameters.

Q8.5   Consider the following definition module which is used to store birthdays, and then to print them (in the order stored):

```
DEFINITION MODULE Birthdays;
FROM Dates IMPORT DateRecord;

PROCEDURE SaveBirthday(d: DateRecord);

PROCEDURE PrintBirthdays;

END Birthdays.
```

Write the corresponding implementation module.

Hints: (i) Store the dates in an array. (ii) The procedure SaveBirthday should update a variable in order that Birthdays can keep track of how many dates have been stored. (iii) The procedure GetDate uses the value Index to access the appropriate component of the array.

Q8.6   Modify the program module CheckDate so that it saves a number of dates using the procedure SaveBirthday. The program should not print out any dates until the user decides to quit the program. Whereupon the program will recover each date with PrintBirthdays and print it to the screen.

9 SIMPLE TERMINAL INPUT AND OUTPUT

9.1 INTRODUCTION

Input and output routines are not provided as part of the Modula-2 *language* and consequently there is a great deal of variation both in the power and the semantics of the input and output (I/O for short) facilities provided by different implementations. (Many claim to have provided 'standard' I/O facilities, but these vary in their operation; see *Portability Issues*.) We have therefore devised a minimal set of I/O functions in a module called `PortIO`. When compiling and executing examples in this book, you can either use `PortIO` directly, as we have,[1] or you can approximate its facilities by substituting the I/O facilities offered by the implementation you are using.

9.2 THE PortIO MODULE

`PortIO` provides serial text I/O to the terminal only. (It does not allow you to manipulate disk files.) As a module written in Modula-2 it has to conform to the language. This has a number of implications:

- To use `PortIO` you have to import it explicitly. (A Modula-2 compiler would not provide built-in keywords such as 'INPUT' or 'OUTPUT'.)

- Each procedure provided by `PortIO` reads or writes a fixed number of values (one value, as we have defined it).

- Each type catered for by `PortIO` has a different procedure associated with the input and the output of values of that type.

---

[1]An implementation of `PortIO` is provided in Appendix 3.

110

Since I/O facilities are not part of the language you usually have to write more explicit procedure calls to do I/O than in other languages.

PortIO allows you to read or write values of the types CHAR, INTEGER, CARDINAL, and values of subranges of these types. It also provides procedures for reading and writing 'string' values. (In Modula-2, character arrays can be used for representing strings. The use of character arrays as strings is fully explained in Chapter 10.)

In order to use PortIO you have to import it, thus:

```
IMPORT PortIO;
```

If you use this form of import clause, the procedures provided by PortIO must be qualified by PortIO (e.g. PortIO.WriteLn). If you do not want to have to qualify procedure names imported from PortIO, you can use the 'FROM' form of import and name each identifier you intend to use, for example:

```
FROM PortIO IMPORT ReadChar, WriteChar, WriteString, WriteLn;
```

Throughout the rest of this chapter we will assume that all the procedures from the module PortIO have been individually imported using the 'FROM' form of IMPORT and so do not need to be explicitly qualified.

The goal of providing a portable I/O module has influenced the way in which the I/O operations have been specified. Their meaning in other chapters should be clear from their names (ReadCard does indeed expect a CARDINAL value to be input). However, the detailed semantics of the main operations should be understood so as to allow full use of the module.

The definition module of PortIO is given below:

```
DEFINITION MODULE PortIO;

(* Input procedures *)
PROCEDURE ReadChar(): CHAR;
PROCEDURE ReadCard(): CARDINAL;
PROCEDURE ReadInt(): INTEGER;
PROCEDURE ReadString(VAR str: ARRAY OF CHAR);
PROCEDURE ReadLn;
PROCEDURE SetPrompt(prompt: ARRAY OF CHAR);

(* Indicates whether last input was successful *)
PROCEDURE Done(): BOOLEAN;

(* Output procedures *)
PROCEDURE WriteChar(ch: CHAR);
PROCEDURE WriteCard(c: CARDINAL);
PROCEDURE WriteInt(i: INTEGER);
PROCEDURE WriteString(str: ARRAY OF CHAR);
PROCEDURE WriteLn;

(* Set the default field width for whole number output *)
PROCEDURE SetFieldWidth(W: CARDINAL);
PROCEDURE FieldWidth(): CARDINAL;
```

```
(* Returns next of any pending characters *)
PROCEDURE NextChar(): CHAR;

(* Returns logical end of line character *)
PROCEDURE EolChar(): CHAR;

END PortIO.
```

PortIO implements line-oriented I/O.[1] That is to say, input values are only passed to the program which calls an input procedure when the terminal ENTER key is pressed. (This is true even when single character values are being input.) This strategy does not preclude the input of several values on a line; the first would be consumed if the ENTER key was pressed while any others input would remain available for use by subsequent calls to input procedures. (Pending values may be discarded, as described below.)

When the ENTER key is pressed, the keyboard may generate a single character, or a sequence of characters. In order to deal with this in a portable fashion, a single end-of-line character is assumed to exist. This character is chosen when PortIO is implemented and should not be changed; its value may be obtained using the function procedure EolChar. Note that the value chosen for an implementation need not be the same as any of the character value(s) generated when an ENTER key is pressed.

There is one aspect of PortIO which cannot be fully defined, and that is the way individual characters are generated by a terminal and are interpreted by the operating system. For example, if the character set is the ASCII set, the CR (carriage return) character will almost certainly be the code generated by the ENTER key, but the effect of other codes is less predictable. Also, such keys as those for deleting characters cannot be defined independently of an operating system. Appendix 3 provides an example of how this is handled for Topspeed Modula-2.

Finally, you should be aware that input from and output to a terminal is concerned with character processing. When procedures are used to read or write numeric types, a type conversion is being performed between the characters and the whole number values. In such situations it is likely that invalid representations of whole number values will be encountered. Exceptions of this type may be detected using the function procedure Done , as described below.

9.3   I/O PROCEDURES

This section describes the operation of the PortIO procedures. Not all the procedures described below are used in examples in the book, but were felt to be necessary for a portable I/O module.

---

[1]Line-oriented I/O was chosen because it is easier to implement across the widest range of computer architectures. Many operating systems provide line-oriented I/O as the usual method of I/O, and make character-oriented input, in particular, difficult to provide.

Detecting exceptions

`PortIO` provides a function procedure `Done`, which can be used to detect when an error has occurred during input. `Done` takes no parameters, but requires empty parentheses when invoked in order to conform to the Modula-2 syntax for function procedures. Its general form is:

```
BooleanVariable := Done();
```

`Done` returns `TRUE` if the previous read operation was successful and `FALSE` otherwise. Success is defined for each individual input procedure below.

Procedures for line-oriented I/O

The procedures `WriteLn`, `ReadLn`, `EolChar`, and `NextChar` are all relevant to line-oriented I/O:

```
WriteLn;
```

This causes the printing position on the screen to move to the next line. Colloquially, we say that it outputs a *new line* to the terminal.

```
ReadLn;
```

The `ReadLn` procedure causes all the data pending on the current input line to be discarded.

```
CharacterVariable := EolChar();
```

The function procedure `EolChar` returns the implementation defined character value which is used to indicate the end of an input line.

```
ch := NextChar();
```

This function returns the next character pending in the input line.

The last two procedures can be used together to test for pending data, and if necessary discard it. For example:

```
c := ReadCard();                    (* read a cardinal value *)
IF NextChar() <> EolChar() THEN     (* was there extra input? *)
  ReadLn;                           (* discard pending input *)
END;
```

String I/O

Literal strings, string constants, or values of character arrays may be output using `WriteString`:

```
WriteString(StringExpression);
```

writes a string to the terminal. For example:

```
WriteString("I'm pink, therefore I'm spam");
```

would write `I'm pink, therefore I'm spam` to the screen, starting at whatever the current screen position is.

```
ReadString(StringVariable);
```

ReadString reads a sequence of characters from a line into StringVariable. A 'string' variable is one whose type is a character array with a zero-based index type. For example:

```
TYPE String = ARRAY [0 ..9] OF CHAR;
VAR
  Name: String;
  ...
  WriteString("What's your Name?");
  ReadString(Name);
```

If there are more characters on the line than can be stored in StringVariable, then only those characters that can be stored are read. Otherwise the whole line is read into StringVariable with the end-of-line character replaced with the string terminator (see Chapter 10). ReadString is considered to be successful if the string read is not empty. For example, the following program reads in an initial line of text, and then reads successive input lines whilst checking for a match with the initial line. If a match is found, then a simple message is output. It is terminated by entering a null string (i.e. by just pressing ENTER).

```
MODULE In1;
FROM PortIO IMPORT
  WriteString, WriteLn, ReadString, ReadLn, Done;
FROM PortString IMPORT Compare, equal;
CONST
  MaxLine = 255;           (* maximum line length *)
VAR
  LookFor, Line : ARRAY [0..MaxLine] OF CHAR;
BEGIN
  WriteString('Input Line to be searched for');
  WriteLn;
  ReadString(LookFor);
  ReadLn;                  (* discard any left over data*)
  LOOP
    ReadString(Line);      (* read a line into Line *)
    ReadLn;                (* discard rest of line *)
    IF Done() THEN         (* check if the string was ok *)
      EXIT                 (* exit when no more lines *)
    END;
    IF Compare(LookFor,Line) = equal THEN
      (* The string is found so output the message and quit *)
      WriteString('string found');
      EXIT
    END
  END
END In1.
```

The procedure function Done was used to check that ReadString has been successful.

`ReadLn` is used to consume extra characters which could not fit into the string, `Line`, if any exist. This ensures that partial lines are not read by accident.

Whole number I/O

`PortIO` provides for whole number input by two function procedures: `ReadCard` and `ReadInt`.

```
CardinalVariable := ReadCard();
IntegerVariable := ReadInt();
```

The above function procedures return a `CARDINAL` or `INTEGER` value read from the terminal. These procedures ignore leading white space (including end-of-lines). The number is read and if it is well formed and terminated by white space the operation is considered to be successful. Function procedures were chosen, in preference to proper procedures, because it was felt to be simpler (and in a sense more natural) to use just one procedure for inputting values to variables of a built-in type and to variables whose types are subranges of built-in types. (The proper procedures demand that actual VAR-parameters be of *identical* type to the corresponding formal parameters and so the use of proper procedures would have entailed reading with a temporary `CARDINAL` or `INTEGER` variable, and then assigning it to the subrange variable whose value you wanted to read.)

Two output procedures are provided, for output of either a `CARDINAL` or `INTEGER` (or subrange) value to the terminal.

```
WriteCard(CardinalExpression);
WriteInt(IntegerExpression);
```

A printing field is assumed for outputting the number. If the width of the field has not been set (using `SetFieldWidth`, described below), it is assumed to be, by default, one greater than the number of digits in the maximum value of `INTEGER,` in this case 6.

Setting the printing field width

`PortIO` provides *formatted output* of whole number types; they may be output in a *print field*—a sequence of output character positions. The size of the field may be examined or changed.

```
SetFieldWidth(CardinalExpression);
```

This procedure specifies an amount of blank space in which the `INTEGER` or `CARDINAL` value to be printed is to be placed. For example:

```
SetFieldWidth(5);
WriteCard(7);
WriteInt(-34);
```

will output the value 7 in a field width of 5, followed by the value –34 in a field width of 5. The number 7 requires only one character so it will be preceded by four spaces; the integer −34 requires three characters and so will only be preceded by two spaces:

```
   7   -34
^^^^^^^^^^
```

```
CardinalVariable := FieldWidth();
```

You can determine the current value of the field width using the parameterless function `FieldWidth`. (This function is useful if the current width has to be found and saved while some other width is used temporarily.)

The following example alternately reads CARDINALs and INTEGERs and prints them in two columns to the screen. (By way of a change from our usual style, the individual procedures are not imported from PortIO; hence all are qualified by the module name.)

```
MODULE PrintColumns;
FROM PortIO IMPORT SetFieldWidth, WriteString, WriteLn,
  ReadInt, Done, ReadCard, WriteInt, WriteCard;
VAR
  Int : INTEGER;
  Card : CARDINAL;
BEGIN
  SetFieldWidth(15);       (* width in which to print values *)
  WriteString('INTEGER CARDINAL'); WriteLn;
  LOOP
    Int := ReadInt();      (* read values *)
    IF Done() THEN
      Card:= ReadCard();
      IF Done() THEN       (* write a row *)
        WriteInt(Int);
        WriteCard(Card);
        WriteLn;
      ELSE
          EXIT  (* because the CARDINAL was not well-formed *)
      END
    ELSE
      EXIT     (* because the INTEGER was not well-formed *)
    END
  END
END PrintColumns.
```

Character I/O

ReadChar and WriteChar are provided for character input and output:

```
CharacterVariable := ReadChar();
```

This function procedure reads a character.

```
WriteChar(CharacterExpression);
```

This procedure writes a character to the screen at the current position. WriteChar is not affected by the field width.

The string and whole number procedures shown above do not provide full control over what is read. If you want to read an individual character or a sequence of characters exactly as they were typed in you should use ReadChar. It returns the next character that was typed or an end-of-line character. It is considered successful (as reported by Done) if it returns a character other than the end-of-line character.

For example, the following program reads from the keyboard and echoes to the terminal, replacing all the occurrences of multiple spaces by a single space.

```
MODULE RemovePadding;
FROM PortIO IMPORT ReadChar, EolChar, WriteChar;
CONST
  Space = ' ';
VAR
  ch : CHAR;
  LastWasSpace : BOOLEAN;          (* has a space been read? *)
BEGIN
  LastWasSpace := FALSE;
  LOOP
    ch := ReadChar();              (* read a char into ch *)
    IF ch = EolChar() THEN
      EXIT
    END;                           (* exit when end of line *)
    IF ch = SPACE THEN             (* char is a space *)
      IF NOT LastWasSpace THEN
        WriteChar(Ch);             (* last char was not a space *)
        LastWasSpace := TRUE       (* set flag for next read *)
      END
    ELSE
      LastWasSpace := FALSE;       (* current char isn't a space *)
      WriteChar(ch)
    END
  END
END RemovePadding.
```

Prompting

A prompt may be specified which will be written to the terminal prior to all subsequent input operations until it is called again. Its general form is:

```
SetPrompt(StringValue);
```

The parameter StringValue is typically a string literal, but it could be a value of a character array (as described in Chapter 10). SetPrompt is particularly useful when a sequence of identical prompts is required, as in the following example:

```
SetPrompt('Input a positive Number:');
FOR i := 1 TO 5 DO
  List[i] := ReadCard()
END;
```

The string `Input a positive number:` will be output before each of the five inputs.

In most modern line-oriented I/O systems, editing a line as it is input (e.g. using a DELETE key) causes the erroneous input to disappear as if it had not been typed. However, some systems do not do this, but interpret a particular control key as a request to reprint the input without the errors. The prompt which proceeded the input is often not reprinted by such an operation unless it is known by the operating system. `PortIO` can be implemented to mimic this—if it 'knows' about a prompt through the use of `SetPrompt`. Appendix 3 gives an implementation which outputs a prompt, if it has been set using `SetPrompt`.

9.4   PORTABILITY ISSUES

Many Modula-2 implementors provide an I/O module called `InOut` which they describe as 'standard'. This is an inaccurate description because the semantics of `InOut` implementations vary enormously. It is this variation (ranging from subtle to major differences) that prompted us to develop `PortIO`. The `PortIO` module is intended to be a useful, but restricted, I/O implementation. There are a few issues which arise from its use:

- Different Modula-2 implementations use different strategies for implementing I/O facilities. Calling an operating system function to write a character will not necessarily mean that it will be output immediately.

- `PortIO` does not contain procedures for REAL I/O. This is because REAL I/O cannot be done efficiently, accurately, *and* portably. Portable programs will inevitably have to deal with the accuracy and precision problems inherent in real arithmetic.

The decision to put all input and output facilities of Modula-2 in library modules (rather than in the language) is both a strength and a weakness. The usefulness of the separate approach is illustrated by the use of `PortIO` in this book; the approach is flexible, modular, and extensible. However, the provision of I/O is often tied to an operating system, and this makes portability a problem.

Appendix 3 gives an implementation of `PortIO` and Chapter 24 gives guidance for overcoming portability problems. If it is not convenient for you to implement this module, you should be able to approximate its facilities, using the I/O module provided by your implementation. The following table lists the main I/O procedures provided by `PortIO` together with their rough equivalents provided by Topspeed Modula-2's `IO` module and by a typical example of `InOut`. (Note that parentheses after a procedure name implies it is a function procedure. Also note that `IO.OK` and `InOut.Done` are variables.)

PortIO	Topspeed IO	Typical InOut
ReadChar()	RdChar()	Read
ReadCard()	RdCard()	ReadCard
ReadInt()	RdInt()	ReadInt
ReadString	RdStr	ReadString
ReadLn	RdLn	-
Done()	OK	Done
WriteChar	WrChar	Write
WriteCard	WrCard	WriteCard
WriteInt	WrInt	WriteInt
WriteString	WrStr	WriteString
WriteLn	WriteLn	WriteLn

Note that input facilities for the simple types are provided in PortIO by function procedures. (Recall that this strategy was adopted because of the need to allow values to be input to variables of subrange types.) The availability of function procedures may tempt you to combine them in expressions; this is not portable, since you cannot predict which function procedure call will execute first. (See Section 16.3 for full details on the evaluation of expressions.)

9.5 REVIEW QUESTIONS AND EXERCISES

Q9.1 Write two versions of a program to read in a line of text from the terminal and convert all lower-case characters to upper-case. One version should use string I/O and the other character I/O.

Q9.2 Consider the following program :

```
MODULE Tst;
FROM PortIO;
IMPORT WriteString, WriteLn, WriteChar, ReadChar;
VAR ch : CHAR;
BEGIN
  WriteString('input characters');
  WriteLn;
  REPEAT
    WriteChar('?');              (* output prompt *)
    ch := ReadChar();
  UNTIL (ch = 'x');
END Tst.
```

What would be the output of the above program if its input were the following three lines:

```
ab
b
x
```

Q9.3 Write a function procedure, ReadOct, to read an octal number into a cardinal variable, and a procedure WriteOct to output the decimal equivalent in a printing field width of 20.

10 STRINGS

10.1 INTRODUCTION

Previously our use of character strings has been limited to string constants, both literal strings and those denoted by identifiers. Up to now, no mention has been made of string variables. The reason for this is that unlike BASIC and certain dialects of Pascal, Modula-2 does not support variables of type string. However, there is a need for string variables: people communicate with each other in natural language, not in CARDINAL or INTEGER expressions! Therefore it is not unreasonable to expect to write programs that interact with the user with a subset of natural language defined within a program.

In fact Modula-2 does allow the programmer to define variables that are compatible with string constants by allowing special rules for character arrays. However, in order to program in a consistent manner we will need to define what we mean by a string and the operations we might wish to carry out on them. In other words we need to lay our own structure on top of the primitive facilities offered. To do this we will start by looking at strings in the abstract.

10.2 ABSTRACT STRINGS

We shall define our abstract string in terms of sequences. In particular we will define a string as a sequence of characters. A *sequence* is a finite, *ordered* collection of zero or more items. Sequences are collections of objects, like sets (see Chapter 11) but differ from them in that they incorporate the ideas of order and repetition. Sequences are represented in a similar manner to sets, by separating the items with commas, but the entire sequence is enclosed with square brackets, [ ], rather than the curly brackets, { }, used with sets. Also, unlike sets, the order in which the items appear in a sequence is important. For example, the sequence of characters a, b, c is denoted in the following mathematical (*not* Modula-2) notation:

[a, b, c]

Thus, because order and repetition matter in a sequence, the following sequences which are comprised of the same set of characters {a, b, c} are not the same:

[a, b, c]   [a, c, b]   [a, a, c, b]

A sequence is said to comprise of a **head** and a **tail**. The head is the first item in a sequence. The tail is the sequence which is left when the head item has been removed. For example, given the sequence [a, b, c, d, e], a is the head of the sequence and [b, c, d, e] is the tail. We shall use this property of sequences in specifying the *LENGTH* function in Section 10.3.

We shall call our abstract string type, type $\mathbb{S}$ (pronounced 'S-S'). $\mathbb{S}$ is a conceptual, fundamental type which comprises of the set of all possible sequences of characters plus all the operations which we will define as being associated with strings.

$\mathbb{S}$ = Sequence of Characters

Examples of valid strings of type $\mathbb{S}$ would be:

[ ], [a], [a, b], [x, y, z]

This mathematical notation for sequences can be applied to sequences of any abstract type. However, it is conventional to bracket character sequences using quotation marks. Thus the first four sequences may be equivalently written as follows:

'', 'a', 'ab', 'xyz'

(We will use both forms below.)

Note that the first example '', (the empty sequence) is a valid sequence, therefore empty strings of type $\mathbb{S}$ are valid strings.

10.3   STRING OPERATIONS

You will remember that in Chapter 4 the operators that can be applied to numbers in Modula-2 were given and described. As Modula-2 does not provide a string data type, it obviously does not provide operators to manipulate strings. Given our description of an abstract data type called String, we need to define operations that can be applied to strings. In order to represent these operations on strings, we need to define three abstract operators: $\leftarrow$, ::, and $\frown$. These are defined thus:

$s[x :: y]$ is used to denote the sequence of characters of s from the position x to the position y, with the first position numbered 1. (x and y must both be between 1 and the length of s, and $x \leq y$.)

s1 ← *s2* means the assignment of string *s2* to *s1*.

s1 ⁀ *s2* is the concatenation of the strings or substrings, *s1* and *s2*.[1]

A few examples will clarify the semantics of these operators:

(i)   *String1* ← [p, q, r, s, t, u, v]
        String2 ← [a, b, c, d, e]

        results in:

        String2[1 :: 3] = [a, b, c]
        String1[6 :: 6] = [u]

(ii)   *String3* ← *String2*[1 :: 3]

        results in:

        String3 = [a, b, c] = 'abc'

(iii)   *String2* ← *String1*[2 :: 4] ⁀ 'xyz'

        results in:

        String2 = [q, r, s, x, y, z] = 'qrsxyz'

By using and combining these operators we can explicitly define the operations that we wish to specify for strings. We shall define these abstract operations in terms of functions, rather than procedures. Note that both the declarations of these abstract functions and these examples will be enclosed in boxes so that they cannot be confused with Modula-2 code. In the examples given with these abstract definitions, we will use quotation marks (rather than brackets) since the sequences we are concerned with are strings.

LENGTH

Probably the most useful and important operation to define for strings is the *LENGTH* function, which we shall define using a recursive technique (see Chapter 8). As stated above, all sequences are comprised of a head and a tail. Therefore, defining *LENGTH*, we can say that the length of a sequence is 1 + *LENGTH* of its tail. Although the meaning of *LENGTH* is probably obvious to most people, the simple recursive definition is:

        LENGTH(s) ≜   *if s* = "
                        then 0
                        else 1 + *LENGTH*(tail of *s*)

---

[1]The notation is based on a set of operators suggested by Barry Cornelius of Durham University, whom we gratefully acknowledge.

An example should make this clearer. We will apply *LENGTH* to the character sequence [a,b,c]. *LENGTH* will be recursively called until the tail of the sequence is the empty sequence which has zero length:

$$LENGTH('abc') = 1 +$$
$$LENGTH('bc') = 1 +$$
$$(1 + LENGTH('c')) = 1 +$$
$$(1 + (1 + LENGTH(''))) = 3$$

LENGTH(s1)
Example:
s1 ← 'pqrstuv'
s2 ← 'ABCDE'
LENGTH(s1) returns 7
LENGTH(s2) returns 5

ASSIGN

The purpose of the *ASSIGN* function is to return all the characters of a string *s1*.

ASSIGN(s1) returns s1
Example:
s1 ← 'pqrstuv'
ASSIGN(s1) returns 'pqrstuv'

EXTRACT

This is similar to *ASSIGN*; however, in this case the function returns just part of *s1*, consisting of a sequence of *y* characters starting from position *x*.

EXTRACT(s1, x, y) returns s1[x :: x + y - 1]
Example:
s1 ← 'pqrstuv'
EXTRACT(s1, 3, 4) returns 'rstu'

DELETE

The purpose of the *DELETE* operation is to return the characters of the string *s1*, minus a sequence of *y* characters starting from position *x* in *s1*.

DELETE(s1, x, y) returns s1[1 :: x-1] ˜ s1[x + y :: LENGTH(s1)]
Example: s1 ← 'pqrstuv'
DELETE(s1, 3, 2) returns 'pqtuv'

INSERT

The *INSERT* function returns the characters of a string *s1* expanded at position *x* by the characters of a string *s2*. That is, the character at position *x* of *s1* and all those that follow it are 'moved along' to make room for *s2*.

INSERT(s1, s2, x) returns s1[1 :: x-1] ˜ s2 ˜ s1[x :: LENGTH(s1)]
Examples: s1 ← 'pqrstuv' s2 ← 'ABCDE'
INSERT(s1, s2, 3) returns 'pqABCDErstuv' INSERT(s1, s2, 1) returns 'ABCDEpqrstuv' INSERT(s1, s2, 8) returns 'pqrstuvABCDE'

APPEND

The purpose of the *APPEND* operation is to return a string consisting of the characters of a string *s1* concatenated with the characters of a string *s2*.

APPEND (s1, s2) returns s1 ˜s2
Example: s1 ← 'pqrstuv' s2 ← 'ABCDE'
APPEND(s1, s2) returns 'qrstuvABCDE'

REPLACE

The *REPLACE* function returns a string consisting of the characters of *s1* where *s1* has been overwritten from a position *x* in *s1* with the string *s2*.

REPLACE(s1, s2, x) returns s1[1 :: x - 1] ˜ s2 ˜ s1[x + LENGTH(s2) :: LENGTH(s1)]
Example: s1 ← 'pqrstuv' s2 ← 'ABC'
REPLACE(s1, s2, 3) returns 'pqABCuv'

FIND

The function *FIND* returns the Boolean value *true* if a substring *s1* is present in a string *s2*, otherwise the function will return the value *false*.

FIND(s1, s2) returns *true* or *false*
Examples:
s1 ← 'rst'
s2 ← 'pqrstuv'
FIND(s1, s2) returns *true*
s1 ← 'abc'
s2 ← 'pqrstuv'
FIND(s1, s2) returns *false*

COMPARE

The purpose of the *COMPARE* function is to compare lexicographically two strings *s1* and *s2*. If *s1* is less than *s2* the value *less* is returned. If *s1* is greater than *s2* the value *greater* is returned. If *s1* is equal to *s2* the value *equal* is returned.

COMPARE(s1, s2) returns *less, equal , or greater*
Examples:
s1 ← 'aaa'
s2 ← 'aaa'
COMPARE(s1, s2) returns *equal*
s1 ← 'aaa'
s2 ← 'bbb'
COMPARE(s1, s2) returns *less*
s1 ← 'bbb'
s2 ← 'aaa'
COMPARE(s1, s2) returns *greater*

10.4 CHARACTER ARRAYS AS STRINGS

String constants, both literals and those denoted by identifiers, have been used freely in these introductory chapters. To refresh your memory here is an example to demonstrate their use:

```
CONST
  Greeting = "Hello World";
BEGIN
  WriteString(Greeting);
  WriteString('Fred');
```

In the above examples `Greeting` is a string constant identifier, whereas `"Hello World"` and `'Fred'` are literal string constants. Note how a literal string constant is denoted, by either bounding it with double quotes or single quotes. It is important that you do not become confused between these *concrete strings* and the abstract strings which we introduced in Section 10.2. Remember that a character sequence is commonly called a string and can be represented by:

[F,r,e,d] or 'Fred'

A Modula-2 string value will appear thus:

'Fred'

As we mentioned in the introduction to this chapter, there is no built-in string type in Modula-2 and there are no variables of a string type; instead there are some special rules for character arrays. These character arrays are called *concrete string types.* [1]

Two of the rules for concrete string types which ensure portability are:

* They have components which are of the type CHAR (and not a CHAR subrange).

* Their index is a CARDINAL subrange which starts at 0.

Thus following these rules we can make the declarations necessary for a type called `String` and a variable called `Str`:

```
CONST
   MaxStringIndex = 4;
TYPE
   String = ARRAY [0..MaxStringIndex] OF CHAR;
VAR
   Str: String;
```

These declarations identify a variable `Str` which can hold up to five characters, representing items in a string. The number of characters a string variable can hold is called its *capacity* (e.g. the capacity of `Str` is five).

Note that constant strings are not of a particular concrete string type, but are of the conceptual type $\mathfrak{S}$. This type is assignment compatible with all concrete string types (see below).

Assigning string constants to character arrays

Now that we have a variable called `Str` of type `String`, what can we assign to it? Well we can assign string constants, so long as they have no more characters than there are elements in the array. Therefore the largest string constant we can assign to our variable `Str` has a length of `MaxStringIndex + 1`. For example:

```
Str := 'ABCDE';
```

or

---

[1] For brevity, concrete string types are often referred to as *string types*. Similarly variables of a concrete string type are often referred to as *string variables.*

```
CONST
  StrConst = 'ABCDE';
BEGIN
  Str := StrConst;
```

Both of these examples are equivalent to making the following statements:

```
Str[0] := 'A';
Str[1] := 'B';
Str[2] := 'C';
Str[3] := 'D';
Str[4] := 'E';
```

Modula-2 also allows 'shorter' string constants (and only constants) to be assigned to 'longer' string variables, thus:

```
Str := 'ABC';
```

As before, the components indexed by 0, 1, 2 are assigned 'A', 'B', and 'C'. However, we now come to the third special rule for character arrays:

- If the number of characters in the string constant is less than the capacity of the string variable, then a special CHAR, known as the *string terminator*, is placed in the string variable immediately after the last character in the constant.

Therefore, following this rule, the fourth component of Str is assigned the string terminator. This marks the 'end' of string held in the character array. (You can think of this as being analogous to terminating a list of real numbers held in an array by including an infrequently used value.)

We shall denote the string terminating character by a constant identifier called StringTerminator. This constant is not commonly provided by implementations of Modula-2. We have therefore declared it in the definition module of PortStrings (see Appendix 3). To maintain portability this constant *must* be defined to be the value of the string terminating character used by your implementation in the assignment statement. In Topspeed Modula-2, in common with many other implementations, this string terminating character is the value 0C (sometimes called the NULL character).

The convention of marking the end of a string held in a character array is observed by the library modules PortIO and PortStrings. The procedure WriteString only outputs values in a character array up to the string terminator. Similarly, ReadString includes the string terminator if you input fewer characters to a character array variable than there are components in the array. (In particular, if you simply press the ENTER key, the first character will be set to the string terminator.)

Assigning character arrays to character arrays

String variables can only be assigned to variables of an *identical* type, for example:

```
 VAR
   Str1,Str2 : String;
 BEGIN
   Str1 := 'ABC';
   Str2 := Str1;
```

However, given the following declarations:

```
 TYPE
   String1 = ARRAY [0..4] OF CHAR;
   String2 = ARRAY [0..4] OF CHAR;
 VAR
   Str1 : String1;
   Str2 : String2;
```

Str1 cannot be assigned to Str2 or vice versa, as although they have the same number of components, they have been declared as different types.

Assigning CHAR variables to character arrays

Variables of type CHAR are not compatible with character arrays; however, variables of type CHAR are compatible with the individual components of character arrays as they are also of type CHAR. Therefore you can make assignments to individual components of a string variable:

```
 TYPE
   String1 = ARRAY [0..4] OF CHAR;
 VAR
   Str1, Str2 : String1;
   ch : CHAR;
 BEGIN
   Str1 := 'ABC';
   ch := 'z';
   Str1[1] := ch;
```

The value of Str1 is now 'AzC'. However, extreme care must be taken when assigning variables of type CHAR to components of character arrays. Problems arise in two cases. The first is when you assign a value in a CHAR variable to a component of a character array that is preceded by a component holding the string terminator value. The second is when you assign a value in a CHAR variable to a component that actually holds the string terminator value. For example:

```
 Str1 := 'ABC';
 ch := 'z';
 Str1[4] := ch;
```

The value of Str1 will appear to be unaffected by this last assignment statement as the component Str1[3] holds the constant value StringTerminator. The three assignment statements result in:

```
 Str1[0] has the value 'A'
 Str1[1] has the value 'B'
```

```
Str1[2] has the value 'C'
Str1[3] has the value StringTerminator
Str1[4] has the value 'z'
```

Consider this next example:

```
Str2 := 'ABC';
ch := 'z';
Str2[3] := ch;
```

By making this last assignment statement we have overwritten the string terminator. What is the value of Str2 now? Components 1–3 have been initialized, but Str2[4] is undefined. Any characters from the position after the overwritten string terminator will be garbage. The three assignment statements result in:

```
Str2[0] has the value 'A'
Str2[1] has the value 'B'
Str2[2] has the value 'C'
Str2[3] has the value 'z'
Str2[4] has the value ?
```

10.5 DESIGNING A PORTABLE STRINGS MODULE

So far in this chapter we have defined abstract strings and their associated operations and we have described how strings can be represented in the concrete by the use of character arrays. Therefore we are now in the position to design a strings module which will implement the abstract operations defined in Section 10.3.

Our goal is to design our implementation to be as close to the abstract specification as possible. However, certain implementation constraints will inevitably mean that certain features of the abstract specification will need to be changed. The most obvious is that of range. In the abstract specification, positions in the character sequence were indexed from position 1 to position n, where n represents the length of the sequence. In implementing strings as character arrays, however, positions in the strings will be indexed from 0 to $n-1$. This is because one of the special rules for character arrays states that the index type must be a CARDINAL subrange which starts at 0.

In the definitions below we will assume the following declarations:

```
TYPE
   LargeString = ARRAY [0..25] OF CHAR;
   SmallString = ARRAY [0..4] OF CHAR;
VAR
   ch : CHAR;
   Large : LargeString;
   Small : SmallString;
```

Length procedure

The Length procedure will have the following heading.

```
PROCEDURE Length(String : ARRAY OF CHAR): CARDINAL;
```

The Length function procedure returns the number of characters in String, up to, but not including, the string terminator character, if present.

Examples

(i)   Large := 'ABCD';   (ii)   Small := 'Frodo';

Length(Large)   **returns 4**   Length(Small)   **returns 5**

Assign procedure

The operation will be implemented as a procedure rather than a function procedure as we have made the decision that the operation should alter the value of a second VAR-parameter rather than returning the characters of a string value parameter. We can implement this specification quite easily by declaring a procedure with two character array parameters.

```
PROCEDURE Assign
    (Source : ARRAY OF CHAR; VAR Destination : ARRAY OF CHAR);
```

The string value in Source is copied, character by character, to Destination starting at the lowest index of Destination and ending when the capacity of Destination has been filled or the last character in the string held in Source has been copied to Destination. If the length of the string in Source is shorter than the capacity of Destination, then the StringTerminator will be appended to the string in Destination.

Examples

(i)   Assign('ABC', Small);

results in:

```
Small[0] has the value 'A'
Small[1] has the value 'B'
Small[2] has the value 'C'
Small[3] has the value StringTerminator
```

(ii)   Small := 'ABCDE';

Assign(Small, Large);

results in:

```
Large[0] has the value 'A'
Large[1] has the value 'B'
Large[2] has the value 'C'
```

```
Large[3]  has the value  'D'
Large[4]  has the value  'E'
Large[5]  has the value  StringTerminator
```

(iii)   `Assign('Hello!', Small);`

results in:

```
Small[0]  has the value  'H'
Small[1]  has the value  'e'
Small[2]  has the value  'l'
Small[3]  has the value  'l'
Small[4]  has the value  'o'
```

(iv)   `Assign('', Small);`

results in:

```
Small[0] = StringTerminator
```

AssignChar procedure

We need to be able to assign variables of type CHAR to a string. The Assign procedure cannot be used, as the source parameter is an open array parameter which is incompatible with variables of type CHAR. Therefore we will need to implement a procedure called AssignChar. The specification will be the same as that for Assign except that instead of a string value parameter in the heading we shall have a CHAR parameter.

```
PROCEDURE AssignChar
   (SourceChar : ARRAY OF CHAR; VAR Destination : ARRAY OF CHAR);
```

The character SourceChar is assigned to Destination[0]; if the capacity of Destination is greater than 1 then Destination[1] is assigned StringTerminator.

Example

```
Small := 'ABCDE';
ch := 'z';
AssignChar(ch, Small);
```

results in:

```
Small[0]  has the value  'z'
Small[1]  has the value  StringTerminator
```

Extract procedure

Our implementation of the *EXTRACT* specification will need four parameters as we will implement this function as a procedure. The first parameter will be the source string. The second and third parameters will be the index to the first character that is to be assigned to destination, and the number of characters we wish to assign. These two parameters will be used to specify which characters from the source string are to be assigned to the final parameter, the destination string.

```
PROCEDURE Extract
  (Source: ARRAY OF CHAR;
   StartIndex: CARDINAL; NumberToExtract: CARDINAL;
   VAR Destination: ARRAY OF CHAR);
```

Starting with `StartIndex`, `NumberToExtract` characters, or if there are not enough in `Source`, as many characters as are left, are copied to `Destination`. This copying stops if the capacity of `Destination` is reached before `NumberToExtract` are copied. If the `NumberToExtract` is less than the capacity of `Destination`, then the value of `StringTerminator` will be appended to the string in `Destination`.

Examples

(i)
```
Large := 'ABCDE';
Extract(Large, 2, 3, Small);
```

results in:

```
Small[0] has the value 'C'
Small[1] has the value 'D'
Small[2] has the value 'E'
Small[3] has the value StringTerminator
```

(ii)
```
Large := 'ABCDE';
Extract(Large, 1, 2, Small);
```

results in:

```
Small[0] has the value 'B'
Small[1] has the value 'C'
Small[2] has the value StringTerminator
```

Delete procedure

The operation will be implemented as a procedure rather than a function procedure as we have made the decision that the operation should alter the value of an input parameter rather than return a second string. Our implementation will need three parameters in order to meet the specification: the source string, the index of the first character to delete, and the number of characters to delete. The reader at first glance may consider that our implementation does not match the specification, as no mention is made of the concatenation of the two substrings of the source. However, we have implicitly defined the two substrings by defining the substring that is to be deleted.

```
PROCEDURE Delete
  (VAR Source : ARRAY OF CHAR;
   StartIndex : CARDINAL; NumberToDelete : CARDINAL);
```

The characters from the index (`StartIndex + NumberToDelete`) to the index `Length(Source)-1` are shifted down the array a number of positions determined by `NumberToDelete`. The string terminator is then appended to the new string at the position `Length(Source)` - `NumberToDelete`.

Examples

(i)
```
Small := 'ABCDE';
Delete(Small, 2, 2);
```

results in:

`Small[0]` has the value `'A'`
`Small[1]` has the value `'B'`
`Small[2]` has the value `'E'`
`Small[3]` has the value `StringTerminator`

(ii)
```
Small := 'ABC';
Delete(Small, 2, 2);
```

results in:

`Small[0]` has the value `'A'`
`Small[1]` has the value `'B'`
`Small[2]` has the value `StringTerminator`

Insert procedure

The operation will be implemented as a procedure rather than a function procedure as we have made the decision that the operation should alter the value of one of the input strings rather than return a third string. We will need three parameters to implement this specification. Two of these will be the source string and the destination string. The two substrings will be determined by an index to a position in the destination that will mark the insertion point.

```
PROCEDURE Insert(Source: ARRAY OF CHAR; StartIndex: CARDINAL;
                 VAR Destination: ARRAY OF CHAR);
```

Characters in `Destination` at indices greater than or equal to `StartIndex` are shifted up the array by a number determined by `Length(Source)`, or if this would exceed the capacity of `Destination`, by a number that would exhaust the capacity of `Destination`. Then a number of characters from `Source`, equal to the number of characters that have been shifted up, are copied from `Source` to `Destination`, starting in `Destination` at `StartIndex`.

Examples

(i)
```
Small := 'ABCD';
Insert('XYZ', 2, Small);
```

results in:

`Small[0]` has the value `'A'`
`Small[1]` has the value `'B'`
`Small[2]` has the value `'X'`
`Small[3]` has the value `'C'`
`Small[4]` has the value `'D'`

(ii)
```
Large := 'ABCD';
Insert('XYZ', 2, Large);
```

results in:

`Large[0]` has the value `'A'`
`Large[1]` has the value `'B'`
`Large[2]` has the value `'X'`
`Large[3]` has the value `'Y'`
`Large[4]` has the value `'Z'`
`Large[5]` has the value `'C'`
`Large[6]` has the value `'D'`
`Large[7]` has the value `StringTerminator`

InsertChar procedure

We need to be able to insert variables of type CHAR into a string. The `Insert` procedure cannot be used, as the source parameter is an open array parameter which is incompatible with variables of type CHAR. Therefore we will need to implement a procedure called `InsertChar`. The specification will be the same as that for *INSERT* except that instead of a string value parameter in the specification we shall have a CHAR parameter.

Thus three parameters are needed to implement this specification. Two of these will be the source character and the destination string. The two substrings in the abstract specification will be replaced by an index to a position in the destination that will mark the insertion point.

```
PROCEDURE InsertChar
    (SourceChar: CHAR;
     StartIndex: CARDINAL; VAR Destination: ARRAY OF CHAR);
```

Characters in `Destination` at indices greater than or equal to `StartIndex` are shifted up the array by one character. Then the character `SourceChar` is inserted into the destination string at position `StartIndex`.

Example

```
Small := 'ABCD';
ch := 'z';
InsertChar(Small, 2, ch);
```

results in:

`Small[0]` has the value `'A'`
`Small[1]` has the value `'B'`
`Small[2]` has the value `'z'`
`Small[3]` has the value `'C'`
`Small[4]` has the value `'D'`

Append procedure

The operation will be implemented as a procedure rather than a function procedure as we have made the decision that the operation should alter the value of one of the input strings rather than return a third string. We will need just two parameters for the implementation: the source string and the destination string.

```
PROCEDURE Append
    (Source: ARRAY OF CHAR; VAR Destination: ARRAY OF CHAR);
```

Characters in `Source` are copied to `Destination` starting at index `Length(Destination)`. Thus `Append` is equivalent to:

```
Insert(Source, Length(Destination), Destination);
```

Examples

(i)
```
Small := 'pqr';
Append('XYZ', Small);
```

results in:

`Small[0]` has the value `'p'`
`Small[1]` has the value `'q'`
`Small[2]` has the value `'r'`
`Small[3]` has the value `'X'`
`Small[4]` has the value `'Y'`

(ii)
```
Small := 'pqr';
Append('s', Small);
```

results in:

```
Small[0] has the value 'p'
Small[1] has the value 'q'
Small[2] has the value 'r'
Small[3] has the value 's'
Small[4] has the value StringTerminator
```

AppendChar procedure

We need to be able to append variables of type CHAR to a string. The Append procedure cannot be used, as the source parameter is an open array parameter which is incompatible with variables of type CHAR. Therefore we will need to implement a procedure called AppendChar. The specification will be the same as that for *APPEND* except that instead of a string input parameter in the specification we shall have a CHAR parameter:

```
PROCEDURE AppendChar
   (SourceChar : CHAR; VAR Destination : ARRAY OF CHAR);
```

The character SourceChar is copied into Destination at index Length(Destination). Thus AppendChar is equivalent to:

```
InsertChar(Source, Length(Destination), Destination);
```

Example

```
Small := 'pqr';
ch := z;
AppendChar(ch, Small);
```

results in:

```
Small[0] has the value 'p'
Small[1] has the value 'q'
Small[2] has the value 'r'
Small[3] has the value 'z'
Small[4] has the value StringTerminator
```

Replace procedure

The operation will be implemented as a procedure rather than a function procedure as we have made the decision that the operation should alter the value of one of the input strings rather than return a third string. The implementation will require three parameters: the source string, the destination string, and an index to a position in the destination that will mark the point in it where replacement will start.

```
PROCEDURE Replace
   (Source : ARRAY OF CHAR;
    StartIndex: CARDINAL; VAR Destination: ARRAY OF CHAR);
```

The string value in Source is copied character by character to Destination, starting at the StartIndex of Destination. Copying stops either when all of the characters in Source have been copied, or when the last character in Destination has been replaced, whichever happens first.

Examples

(i)   Small := 'ABCD';
         Replace('XYZ', 2, Small);

results in:

Small[0] has the value 'A'
Small[1] has the value 'B'
Small[2] has the value 'X'
Small[3] has the value 'Y'
Small[4] has the value 'Z'

(ii)   Large := 'ABCDEFG';
         Replace('XYZ', 2, Large);

results in:

Large[0] has the value 'A'
Large[1] has the value 'B'
Large[2] has the value 'X'
Large[3] has the value 'Y'
Large[4] has the value 'Z'
Large[5] has the value 'F'
Large[6] has the value 'G'
Large[7] has the value StringTerminator

Find procedure

We shall alter the abstract specification slightly so that the procedure will also return the starting index of any pattern found. Therefore, as we wish two values to be altered, we will implement the operation as a procedure rather than as a function procedure.

```
PROCEDURE Find
   (Pattern : ARRAY OF CHAR; String : ARRAY OF CHAR;
    VAR PosOfPattern : CARDINAL; VAR Found : BOOLEAN);
```

If Length(Pattern) is greater than Length(String), Found is returned as FALSE and PosOfPattern is left unchanged. If Pattern is found in String then Found is returned as TRUE and PosOfPattern is returned as the index of the first occurrence of Pattern in String. If neither of these conditions is met, Found is returned as FALSE, and PosOfPattern is left unchanged.

Examples

```
VAR
   ok : BOOLEAN;
   pos : CARDINAL;
```

(i)
```
Large := 'Hello hello hello';
Find('ll', Large, pos, ok);
```

results in:

ok has the value TRUE
pos has the value 2

(ii)
```
Large := 'abcdefghijklmnopqrstuvwxyz';
Find('x', Large, pos, ok);
```

results in:

ok has the value TRUE
pos has the value 23

FindChar procedure

We need to be able to find variables of type CHAR in a string. The Find procedure cannot be used, as the parameter for the pattern that is to be searched for is an open array parameter which is incompatible with variables of type CHAR. Therefore we will need to implement a procedure called FindChar. The specification will be the same as that for *FIND* except that instead of a string pattern we shall have a CHAR pattern.

```
PROCEDURE FindChar
   (Char : CHAR; String : ARRAY OF CHAR;
   VAR PosOfPattern : CARDINAL; VAR Found : BOOLEAN);
```

If Char is found in String then Found is returned as TRUE and PosOfChar is returned as the index of the first occurrence of Char in String. If this condition is not met, then Found is returned as FALSE, and PosOfPattern is undefined.

Example

```
Small := 'Hello';
ch := 'l';
FindChar(ch, Small, pos, ok);
```

results in:

ok has the value TRUE
pos has the value 2

Compare function procedure

In order to implement the `Compare` procedure it is also necessary to define the type of its result.

```
TYPE CompareResult = (less, equal, greater);
```

`CompareResult` is an enumeration type (see Chapter 6).

```
PROCEDURE Compare (String1 : ARRAY OF CHAR;
                   String2 : ARRAY OF CHAR) : CompareResult;
```

`String1` and `String2` are compared lexicographically (i.e. the procedure compares characters from left to right until a difference is found).

Examples

(i)   `Compare('', '')` results in `equal`

(ii)   `Compare('', 'abc')` results in `less`

(iii)   `Compare('abc', '')` results in `greater`

(iv)   `Compare('pqr', 'pqr')` results in `equal`

(v)   `Compare('pqr', 'pqrstuv')` results in `less`

(vi)   `Compare('pqrstuv', 'pqr')` results in `greater`

(vii)   `Compare('abc', 'pqr')` results in `less`

(viii)   `Compare('pqr', 'abc')` results in `greater`

(ix)   `Compare('abcdef', 'p')` results in `less`

(x)   `Compare('p', 'abcdef')` results in `greater`

Predicates for strings module

In this context a predicate is a precondition that must evaluate to TRUE before an operation can be successfully carried out. Before any of the procedures defined above are called (except for the procedures `Length`, `Compare`, and `Find`) you are advised to call an associated procedure from `PortStrings` that acts as a predicate. These procedures are called `CanAssign`, `CanExtract`, `CanDelete`, `CanInsert`, `CanReplace`, `CanAppend`. These procedures all check that the associated operation can be carried out successfully.

For example, before you call the `Assign` procedure you should first test that the destination string has a capacity large enough to take the source string. The procedure `CanAssign` therefore checks the following precondition:

```
Length(Source) <= HIGH(Destination)
```

Similarly the procedure `CanDelete` checks this precondition:

```
(StartIndex < Length(String)) AND
(StartIndex + NumberToDelete <= Length(String))
```

If one of these predicate procedures (such as `CanAssign`) returns `FALSE` and you go on to call the associated operation (such as `Assign`), the procedure will carry out the operation 'to the best of its ability'; in reality, until the upper limit of the destination string is reached, whereupon the procedure will terminate the operation. For example:

```
TYPE
  LargeString : ARRAY [0..23] OF CHAR;
  SmallString : ARRAY [0..3] OF CHAR;
VAR
  LString : LargeString;
  SString : SmallString;
  Result : BOOLEAN;
BEGIN
  LString := "Hello World";
  Result := CanAssign(LString, SString);
  Assign(LString, SString);
```

The result of calling `CanAssign` will be `FALSE` and the statement `Assign(LString, SString)` will result in `SString` being assigned the value `"Hell"`.

10.6 STRING INPUT/OUTPUT

By making use of procedures in the library module `PortIO`, simple input and output of strings can be achieved. This enables a program to read strings typed in at the terminal and also to write strings to the terminal.

The procedure `WriteString` is used for output and takes as its parameter a string literal, a string constant, or a string variable. For example:

```
TYPE
  String = ARRAY [0..23] OF CHAR;
VAR
  Prompt: String;
...
Prompt := "Please enter a string : ";
WriteString(Prompt);
```

The procedure `ReadString` is used to read strings that are either typed in at the terminal or are contained in a file and takes as its parameter a string variable. For example :

```
ReadString(AString);
```

See Chapter 9 for details of all I/O procedures.

Example

```
MODULE Frighten;
FROM PortStrings IMPORT Compare, CompareResult;
```

```
FROM PortIO IMPORT ReadString, WriteString, WriteLn;
CONST
  BString = "yes"; CString = "no";
VAR
  AString : ARRAY [0..4] OF CHAR;
  End : BOOLEAN;
BEGIN
  End := FALSE;
  WHILE NOT End DO
    WriteString("Type yes to frighten, or no to quit: ");
    ReadString(AString);
    IF Compare(AString, BString) = equal THEN
      WriteString("Boo!"); WriteLn
    ELSIF Compare(AString,CString) = equal THEN
      End := TRUE
    ELSE
      WriteString("You have mis-keyed"); WriteLn
    END
  END
END Frighten.
```

10.7 PORTABILITY ISSUES

There are few portability issues to consider here, as we have demonstrated how a portable abstract string type can be added to any implementation of Modula-2. However, there are three potential problems which you might encounter—the definition of the string terminator character, the compatibility rules for ARRAY OF CHAR, and restrictions on accessing characters within character arrays.

Most implementations use 0C for the string terminator value but this is not universally true. You should therefore check the value that your implementation uses as the string terminator and if necessary alter the value of the constant StringTerminator (to be found in the definition module of PortStrings— see Appendix 3).

Some implementations allow CHAR values to be assignment compatible with ARRAY OF CHAR value parameters. If this was universally true, InsertChar, AssignChar, etc. would not be needed. Do not use this extension if provided.

Regarding restrictions on accessing components of a character array, you may find that an implementation does not allow a component of a character array to be an actual VAR-parameter. Many implementations economize on storage of concrete string types by 'packing' CHAR values into storage units smaller than that used for a CHAR. Poor implementations then prevent an element of a 'packed' concrete string type from being an actual VAR-parameter.

Finally, some implementations allow any ordinal type to be the index type of a concrete string type. Thus the following is often legal:

```
VAR
  s1: ARRAY BOOLEAN OF CHAR;
  s2: ARRAY [10..20] OF CHAR;
BEGIN
```

```
s1 := 'AB';
s2 := 'Hello';
```

Not all implementations allow this and so, for portability, you should only use zero based CARDINAL arrays.

10.8   REVIEW QUESTIONS AND EXERCISES

Q10.1   Of what type are the components of character arrays?

Q10.2   Of what type must the index of a character array be to be used as a string?

Q10.3   If characters are assigned to an array in such a manner that the array is not filled, what character marks the end of the string?

Q10.4   Given the constants Low = 1 and High = 14 declare an array type which will store 14 characters.

Q10.5   Using the array type defined in the last exercise, write a program module which will input characters one by one to all the 14 component variables of such an array. (Use ReadChar from the library module PortIO.)

Q10.6   Write the precondition for the procedure CanExtract.

Q10.7   Write the precondition for the procedure CanAppend.

Q10.8   Write a procedure that reverses the order of the characters in a character array.

11 DYNAMIC VARIABLES

11.1 INTRODUCTION

This chapter introduces the reader to the subject of dynamic variables: how to create them, how to dispose of them, and how, through their use, data structures that are not part of the Modula-2 language can be created. Dynamic variables and the pointer variables that refer to them are not easy concepts to grasp and the reader is advised to study this chapter carefully before attempting to use them.

11.2 STATIC AND DYNAMIC VARIABLES

The variables that have been encountered so far in this text have all been what are termed static variables. They have to be declared with a VAR declaration. Whether or not these variables are actually used in the execution of a procedure, these variables come into existence as soon as the procedure is entered and their lifetime is the lifetime of the procedure within which they are declared.

In this chapter we shall be discussing *dynamic variables*. These variables are not declared with a VAR declaration, although a pointer which refers to them must be. Dynamic variables are brought into existence in an explicit manner, where and when they are needed in a program. They are also explicitly disposed of when they are no longer needed. This ability to create and dispose of dynamic variables as and when the execution of a program demands, can lead to highly efficient use of the computer's memory. However, there are pitfalls for the unwary.

If a dynamic variable is not disposed of before the end of a procedure, it will still exist in the computer's memory; however, the pointer that refers to it may have disappeared if it has been declared as a local variable. The storage that is associated with a dynamic variable that has been allowed to survive past the lifetime of its procedure can never be reused, as it has been 'lost forever'.

Therefore, a programmer should take care to dispose of a dynamic variable before the end of a procedure in which it was created. Failure to do so can cause severe memory problems.

11.3 POINTER VARIABLES

A *pointer variable* is a static variable that is used to refer to a dynamic variable, it does this by pointing to (or referring to) the location of the dynamic variable, hence the name. To access a dynamic variable the pointer variable must be dereferenced (see below).

Declaring pointers

When a pointer is declared, a type has to be specified which will be the type of the pointer's associated dynamic variable. This dynamic variable can be any named type. A pointer variable can then only be used to refer to objects of that type. The form of such a pointer type declaration is:

```
PointerTypeName = POINTER TO type;
```

POINTER and TO are Modula-2 reserved words.

In a program a pointer type and a variable of that type would be declared in the following manner:

```
TYPE
  PointerToCardinal = POINTER TO CARDINAL;
VAR
  CardPtr : PointerToCardinal;
```

In the above example, although the declaration of CardPtr brings into existence a static variable of type PointerToCardinal, no dynamic variable has been created, nor has any storage for such a dynamic variable been set aside in memory. The creation of a dynamic variable is achieved through the use of the procedure NEW (see Section 11.4 below).

Dereferencing pointers

Gaining access to the variable pointed to by a pointer is termed *dereferencing*. This is achieved by following the pointer identifier with the dereferencing operator, which is represented by the circumflex (^). It is used in much the same way as the field selector is used in records. Compare the following :

```
CardPtr^
```

which is the dynamic variable pointed to by CardPtr, and

```
CardPtr
```

which is the pointer to a dynamic variable.

11.4 NEW AND DISPOSE

As stated above, the declaration of a pointer variable merely brings into existence a static variable to which the location of a dynamic variable can be assigned; it does not bring into existence a dynamic variable or any storage for that variable. The creation and disposal of dynamic variables is provided for by two procedures called ALLOCATE and DEALLOCATE which are exported from a module called Storage, supplied as part of a Modula-2 implementation. However, these procedures are difficult to use, and to simplify matters Modula-2 provides two built-in procedures called NEW and DISPOSE.

NEW and DISPOSE do not have to be imported before use, as they are part of the Modula-2 language. However, they do make use of ALLOCATE and DEALLOCATE, which must be imported from the supplied module Storage (see Chapter 22 for details of Storage). Therefore any module that makes use of NEW and DISPOSE must include the following import statement:

```
FROM Storage IMPORT ALLOCATE, DEALLOCATE;
```

NEW takes as its parameter a variable whose type is pointer type, allocates storage for a dynamic variable, and assigns to the pointer the location of that dynamic variable in the computer's memory.

```
NEW(CardPtr);
```

This new dynamic variable pointed to by CardPtr will have no name of its own, but may be referenced by dereferencing the pointer variable thus:

```
CardPtr^
```

Similarly, when a dynamic variable has been finished with, it is good programming practice to dispose of that variable, and thereby to make it inaccessible. This is achieved by the use of the built-in procedure DISPOSE which takes as its parameter a variable of type POINTER. On machines with limited memory, it is quite easy to exhaust available memory by using pointers to large arrays and records. In recognition of this, many implementations of DISPOSE not only make the dynamic variable inaccessible, but also reallocate the storage occupied by that variable. Consider the following example in which a list, which is held in a dynamic variable (TempList^) is sorted. TempList^ is a relatively large dynamic variable created using NEW. Without a corresponding call to DISPOSE to deallocate TempList^, its storage would remain unusable after SortList has finished (and so after TempList has disappeared).

```
PROCEDURE SortList;
  CONST ListMax = 200;
  TYPE
    String = ARRAY [0..79] OF CHAR;
    List = ARRAY [1..ListMax] OF String;
    ListPtr = POINTER TO List;
```

```
VAR
  TempList : ListPtr; n: [1..ListMax];
  BEGIN
    NEW(TempList); (* typically allocates 16000 bytes *)
    FOR n := 1 TO ListMax DO
      WriteString('Name: '); ReadString(TempList^[n]);
    END;
    Sort(TempList^);
    FOR n := 1 TO ListMax DO
      WriteString(TempList^[n]); WriteLn
    END;
    DISPOSE(TempList) (* recovers 16000 bytes *)
  END SortList;
```

Extreme care must be taken when using DISPOSE. If any other pointer variable refers to the same dynamic variable, the value of that pointer would become undefined. A pointer in such a state is referred to as a *dangling pointer* and is considered a serious programming error, as it is often very difficult to detect. For example:

```
VAR
  CardPtr1, CardPtr2 : PointerToCardinal;
BEGIN
  NEW(CardPtr1);
  ...
  CardPtr2 := CardPtr1;
  DISPOSE(CardPtr1);
  ...
```

The call of the procedure NEW creates a new dynamic variable and sets CardPtr1 to point to it. The assignment statement CardPtr2 := CardPtr1; sets CardPtr2 to point to the same variable as CardPtr1. The call to DISPOSE with CardPtr1 as its parameter does two things: it instructs the compiler to make the dynamic variable inaccessible to CardPtr1 and it also marks the storage associated with the dynamic variable as free for reallocation. The state of CardPtr2 is now undefined. What does it point to? It still points to the same location in memory that CardPtr1 used to point to, but now this area of memory may have been reallocated.

Initializing pointers

During the execution of a program a pointer variable may point to many different dynamic variables and at times may point to nothing at all. Therefore it is sensible to indicate explicitly when a pointer variable points at nothing. This will usually be immediately after a call of NEW or DISPOSE (see above). Initialization of a pointer is achieved by the use of the constant identifier NIL, which is assignment compatible with any pointer variable. NIL is used without any prior declaration, as it is one of the three pervasive identifiers provided by

Modula-2 that denote standard constant values. (The other two are TRUE and FALSE.)

The reason we initialize pointers with the value NIL is that before a call of NEW or after a call of DISPOSE, a pointer variable is likely to point to somewhere unexpected. Therefore, by initializing a pointer to NIL you can program in a defensive fashion by checking the value of the pointer variable before use; if it has the value NIL you will know that you can only set it to point to an existing dynamic variable, or set it to point to a new dynamic variable by a call of NEW with the pointer variable as its parameter. This next program fragment demonstrates the use of NIL:

```
TYPE
  PointerToCardinal = POINTER TO CARDINAL;
VAR
  CardPtr : PointerToCardinal;
  BEGIN
    CardPtr := NIL;              (* initialize pointer to NIL *)
    ...
    IF CardPtr = NIL THEN    (* check value of pointer *)
      NEW(CardPtr);
      CardPtr^ := SomeNumber
    ELSE
      CardPtr^ := SomeNumber
    END;
    ...
    (* dispose of dynamic variable associated with CardPtr *)
    DISPOSE(CardPtr);
    CardPtr := NIL;      (* initialize pointer to NIL *)
```

11.5   ASSIGNMENT WITH POINTERS

Having declared a pointer variable we need to be able to assign two types of values to it. Remember that a pointer variable is a composite object, and depending on whether the dereferencing operator is present or absent either the location of a dynamic variable or the dynamic variable itself can be assigned to it. If we add a CARDINAL variable MyCard to the declaration given in the last example, then the following assignment statements can be made:

```
NEW(CardPtr1);
CardPtr1^ := 42;
```

The meaning of the above assignment statement is that the value 42 is assigned to the variable pointed to by CardPtr1.

```
MyCard := 60;
CardPtr1^ := MyCard;
```

The last statement means assign to the variable pointed to by CardPtr1, the value held by the cardinal variable MyCard.

Now consider the following assignment (and notice the absence of the dereferencing operator):

```
CardPtr2 := CardPtr1;
```

The meaning of this statement is that the location of the variable pointed to by CardPtr1 is assigned to CardPtr2. This means that CardPtr1 and CardPtr2 now point to the same variable. Note that NEW has not been called with CardPtr2 as its parameter as we do not wish to create a new dynamic variable, we just want CardPtr2 to point to the same variable as CardPtr1.

To create a new variable with CardPtr2 we would use:

```
NEW(CardPtr2);
```

By calling NEW with CardPtr2 as its parameter a new dynamic variable has been created and CardPtr2 has been set to point to it. Now, CardPtr1 and CardPtr2 no longer point to the same variable.

Finally, take a look at this next example and think about what is wrong:

```
CardPtr1 := CardPtr2^; (* illegal statement *)
```

It is an illegal statement because the two arguments are of different types! The left hand side of the assignment is a pointer variable whereas the right hand side refers to a (dynamic) cardinal variable.

11.6   DYNAMIC DATA STRUCTURES

In Chapter 7 you were introduced to record and array data structures. These data structures are said to be static as their size is predetermined in the program text. For example, if an array is declared as having 20 components, storage is set aside for 20 variables of the component type when the procedure declaring the array is invoked. This storage stays constant throughout the execution of that procedure and is released when that procedure is left. How many of those 20 elements are used during execution will probably vary in different calls of the procedure. There are quite simple programs for which it is not known in advance how much data will be input into a data structure. Dynamic data structures, on the other hand, are 'elastic' and can change size whilst the program is running, storage being allocated and deallocated on demand.

Dynamic data structures are created by using pointers. If a dynamic variable is a record (a dynamic variable can be of any type), one of that record's fields can itself be a pointer to another record. The term *node* is often used to describe a record containing a data variable and one or more pointers. In this way, by using nodes as 'building blocks', a variety of data structures can be created, with each node in the structure pointing to one or more other nodes. Examples of such data structures are linked lists, queues, stacks, trees, and graphs.

Sequences

One of the most commonly used abstract data types in computer science is the notion of the *sequence*. A sequence is defined as: zero or more items of data placed one after each other, in an order that is determined by some predefined relationship.

Graphically we could represent a sequence like this:

The ordering of the sequence could be based on the order of entry into the sequence or on some alphabetic or numerical key. Examples of such a sequence could be the list of products sold by a supermarket chain, or the list of spare parts held by a motor manufacturer. Such a sequence could either be implemented by an array or by the use of dynamic variables to construct the concrete data structure.

Using an array to represent a sequence has a number of disadvantages. If you want to delete the second component in array representation of a sequence, so that the third component becomes the second and the fourth components becomes the third, this can only be achieved by moving the third and successive components up by one position. Similarly, in order to insert a new component, all the components from the point of insertion onwards would have to be moved down to make room for the insertion. As the sequence becomes longer the number of components that would have to be shifted for an insertion or deletion would probably increase, causing the program to run slower and slower. Furthermore, if the programmer has underestimated the number of components which have to be stored in the array-sequence, there is no way of increasing the size of the array at runtime.

Using dynamic variables to implement a sequence enables the programmer to construct a far more flexible data structure, one that can consist of any number of items, limited only by the size of the computer's memory. As the data items are not stored in contiguous locations in memory, deletions and additions are simply a matter of pointer manipulation.

Constructing a sequence from dynamic variables is enabled by the declaration of a pointer variable which points to a record that has at least two fields. One of these fields is for data; the other is a pointer to the next record in the sequence. Such a record is termed a node and its pointer field is termed a *link field,* so called because it 'links' the node to the next node in the sequence. A sequence constructed from dynamic variables can be represented graphically, as in the diagram below. In this diagram an arrow represents a pointer, the link to the next node in the sequence.

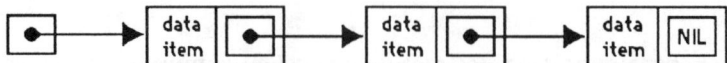

Notice the arrow emerging from a small box to the far left in the above diagram. This pointer variable is not part of the sequence, but is needed to point to the very first node in the sequence. Note also that the pointer in the link field of the last node has been assigned the value NIL. This is done in order to mark the end of the sequence.

Sequences implemented by pointers in this way are termed *linked lists* and represent the simplest of data structures that can be constructed from a number of nodes (records that include at least one link field). A linked list of cardinal numbers can be represented as in the diagram below.

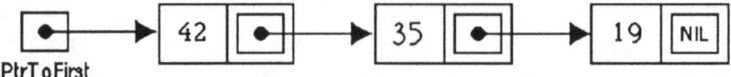

In order to delete the second node (containing the cardinal value 35), all that needs to be done is to redirect the pointer in the link field of the node that contains the value 42 to refer to the node that contains the value 19. This is done by assigning the link field of the second node to the link field of the node that precedes it.

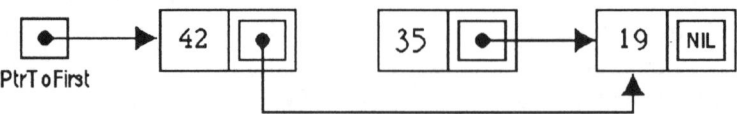

The second node is now the node that contains the cardinal value 19. In order to complete the deletion, a call of DISPOSE should be made with a pointer to the redundant node. The resultant list would now look like this:

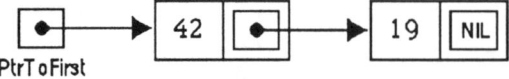

A new addition to the list can be added at any point in the list. The method is first to create a new dynamic variable and to assign to its link field the value of the link field of the node that will precede it. Next the link field of the node that will precede it is assigned the location of the new node. The diagram below shows how a node containing the value 58 could be inserted between those containing 42 and 19.

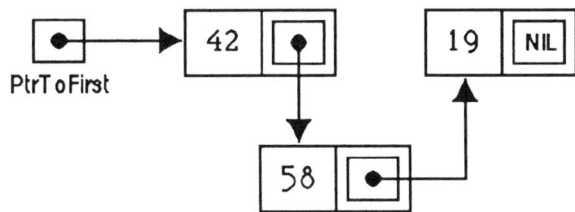

Implementing a linked list

The program below illustrates how a simple linked list can be constructed in order to represent an ordered sequence of cardinal values. Each node consists of a pointer field and a cardinal data field.

```
MODULE List;
FROM Storage IMPORT ALLOCATE, DEALLOCATE;
TYPE
  NodePtr = POINTER TO Node;
  Node = RECORD
           Data : CARDINAL;
           Link : NodePtr;
         END;
VAR
  PtrToFirst : NodePtr;
```

Notice the declaration of the global variable PtrToFirst. This variable will be used to maintain a pointer to the first node in the linked list and will be used for all access to the sequence. If this pointer is not maintained it would become impossible to access or alter the linked list .

The first operation to carry out is to initialize PtrToFirst to NIL. We do not need to allocate storage for the first node (with a call of NEW) as it does not point to anything at this stage.

```
PROCEDURE InitializeList;
  BEGIN
    PtrToFirst := NIL
  END InitializeList;
```

Now the list has been initialized, nodes can be added to the list. Because we maintain a pointer to the first item in the list, the easiest place to add a new node is to the front of the list. The parameter to the following procedure is the CARDINAL value we wish to add to the list.

```
PROCEDURE AddToList1(CardVal: CARDINAL);
  VAR
    NewNode : NodePtr;
  BEGIN
    NEW(NewNode);
    NewNode^.Data := CardVal;
    NewNode^.Link := PtrToFirst;
    PtrToFirst := NewNode
  END AddToList1;
```

The first operation is to create storage for the new node with a call of NEW. Next, the fields of the new node are assigned values. The data field is assigned the cardinal value we wish to add to the list and the link field is assigned the value of PtrToFirst. The link field of the new node will now point to whatever PtrToFirst referenced. Finally, PtrToFirst is set to refer to the new node by assigning NewNode to PtrToFirst.

Being able to add elements only to the beginning of a list is obviously rather limiting. The list may need to be maintained according to some ordering system, for example on the ascending value of a node's data field. To enable the addition of a new node at a position in the list that will maintain the order, it is necessary to search the list from PtrToFirst onwards until the first node that has a data field of a greater value than the new value is found.

```
PROCEDURE AddToList2(CardVal: CARDINAL);
  VAR
    LookAheadPtr, PreviousPtr, NewNode : NodePtr;
  BEGIN
    PreviousPtr := NIL; LookAheadPtr := PtrToFirst;
    WHILE (LookAheadPtr <> NIL) AND
          (CardVal < LookAheadPtr^.Data) DO
      PreviousPtr := LookAheadPtr;
      LookAheadPtr := LookAheadPtr^.Link
    END;
    NEW(NewNode);
    NewNode^.Data := CardVal;
    NewNode^.Link := LookAheadPtr;
    IF PreviousPtr = NIL THEN
      PtrToFirst := NewNode
    ELSE
      PreviousPtr^.Link := NewNode
    END
  END AddToList2;
```

Consider the VAR declarations in the above procedure. LookAheadPtr is used to find the position of the first node that has a cardinal value greater than the value that is to be inserted in the list. PreviousPtr is used to keep track of the position in the list immediately before LookAheadPtr, as the link field of PreviousPtr will be needed to latch onto the new node. At the start of the procedure LookAheadPtr is assigned the value of PtrToFirst so that it points to the beginning of the list. The WHILE loop constitutes a search operation, the loop terminating when either the end of the list is found, or a value that is greater than the value to be inserted in the list. Following the WHILE loop a new node is created, its data field is assigned the CARDINAL value that is to be added to the list, and the link field is set to point at whatever LookAheadPtr refers to. This will either be NIL (if the new value is larger than any other in the list) or the location of a node that contains a value greater than the value to be inserted. The IF statement checks to see if the list was empty prior to insertion, in which case PtrToFirst is set to point to the first node in the list, i.e. the new node. If the list is not empty, then the link field of the node referenced by `PreviousPtr` is set to point at the new node.

The next procedure will enable deletion from the list. First of all, a search through the list must be made until the node that contains the value we wish to delete is found. The `WHILE` loop iterates until either the value is found, or until `TargetPtr` is `NIL`; the latter condition would indicate that the search value is not present in the list. Notice once again the use of the pointer `PreviousPtr`. Deletion of a node in a linked list is achieved by assigning the pointer that precedes the target node with the pointer value held by the target node. Therefore we must keep track of which node precedes the target node.

```
PROCEDURE Delete(CardVal : CARDINAL);
  VAR
    PreviousPtr,TargetPtr : NodePtr;
  BEGIN
    PreviousPtr := NIL; TargetPtr := PtrToFirst;
    WHILE(TargetPtr <> NIL) AND (TargetPtr^.Data <> CardVal) DO
      PreviousPtr := TargetPtr;
      TargetPtr := TargetPtr^.Link
    END;
    IF TargetPtr <> NIL THEN
      IF PreviousPtr <> NIL THEN
        PreviousPtr^.Link := TargetPtr^.Link
      ELSE
        PtrToFirst := TargetPtr^.Link
      END;
      DISPOSE(TargetPtr)
    END
  END Delete;
```

If, after the `WHILE` loop, the value of `TargetPtr` is `NIL`, then the search has failed and there is no node to delete. The next `IF` statement checks the value of `PreviousPtr`. If it is equal to `NIL`, the node to be deleted is the first node in the list and we simply need to update `PtrToFirst` so that it points to the node which follows the node we wish to delete. If `PreviousPtr` is not equal to `NIL`, then we assign to its link field the value of the link field of `TargetPtr`. Finally `DISPOSE` is called to deallocate the variable which implemented the deleted node.

Implementing a queue

A variation on the idea of the linked list is the queue. Queues are familiar to us all, as we come across them in everyday life, e.g. queues for buses or the cinema. The basic properties of queues are that items are added at the end or tail of the list and are removed from the front or head of the list. Because of these properties, queues are often described as a *FIFO* (first in, first out) or *LILO* (last in, last out) data structure.

The operations that are needed to be defined for a queue are `InitializeQueue`, `AddToQueue`, and `RemoveFromQueue`.

```
MODULE QueueHandler;
FROM Storage IMPORT ALLOCATE, DEALLOCATE;
TYPE
  NodePtr = POINTER TO Node;
  Node = RECORD
            Data : CARDINAL;
            Link : NodePtr
         END;
VAR
  PtrToFirst, PtrToLast: NodePtr;
```

You will remember that in our example implementation of a linked list in the previous subsection, we maintained a marker to the front of the list, using a pointer variable called PtrToFirst. In our implementation of a queue we will also maintain a pointer to the last node in the queue. The reason for this is that nodes are added to the end of a queue. This additional pointer is not strictly necessary; however, if such a marker is not maintained an extra procedure would have to be written to search for the end of the list, using the pointer to the first node as its starting point.

The first operation that must be carried out is to initialize the queue. This is achieved by assigning the value NIL to the pointers that mark the front and end of the queue. Notice that we do not allocate storage with a call of NEW as they do not point to anything at this stage.

```
PROCEDURE InitializeQueue;
  BEGIN
    PtrToFirst := NIL;
    PtrToLast := NIL
  END InitializeQueue;
```

Now that the queue has been initialized we can add nodes to the queue. First, storage for the new node is allocated with a call of the NEW procedure. Next, values are assigned to the fields of the node. The data field of the node is assigned with a value that has been passed as the parameter of the AddToQueue procedure. The link field (Link) is assigned the value NIL. This is because the new node is destined to become the last item in the queue and will therefore point at nothing. The IF statement checks for the case of PtrToFirst being equal to NIL as this would signify an empty queue. If the queue is empty, then the address of the new node can simply be assigned to PtrToFirst. If it is not an empty queue, then the node which was the last item has its link field assigned with the location of the new node. Finally PtrToLast is updated to point to the new node.

```
PROCEDURE AddToQueue(CardVal : CARDINAL);
  VAR
    NewNode : NodePtr;
  BEGIN
    NEW(NewNode);
    NewNode^.Data := CardVal;
    NewNode^.Link := NIL;
```

```
        IF PtrToFirst = NIL THEN
          PtrToFirst := NewNode
        ELSE
          PtrToLast^.Link := NewNode
        END;
        PtrToLast := NewNode
      END AddToQueue;
```

We also need to be able to remove nodes from the front of the queue. Once again a check is made for an empty queue, in which case there would be nothing to remove. Note the use of additional pointer called ToBeRemoved. This pointer is assigned the location of the first node in the queue which is held by PtrToFirst. Next, PtrToFirst is set to point to the second node in the queue. This 'leap frogging' of the first node effectively unlinks it from the queue, and makes the second node the new first node. Finally the storage associated with the old first node is disposed of with a call to DISPOSE.

```
      PROCEDURE RemoveFromQueue;
        VAR
          ToBeRemoved : NodePtr;
        BEGIN
          IF PtrToFirst <> NIL THEN
            ToBeRemoved := PtrToFirst;
            PtrToFirst := PtrToFirst^.Link;
            DISPOSE (ToBeRemoved)
          END
        END RemoveFromQueue;
```

11.7   TREES

In Section 11.6 we considered two types of sequences—linked lists and queues. These are classed as linear data structures as each node in the sequence points to either zero or one other node in the sequence. Trees, however, belong to a class of data structures that are classed as non-linear and they are constructed from nodes that have two or more link fields. That is to say, each node can point to zero, one, or more other nodes in the structure.

A tree has one special node called the *root* which is the first node in the tree. Nodes that do not point to other nodes are called *leaf nodes* or *terminal nodes*. The links between nodes are called *branches*.

A tree is defined as a data structure which has zero or more nodes organized in a hierarchical manner, such that:

- except where the tree is empty, there is one node called the root, at the highest level;

- every node, except the root, is joined by a branch to just one node at the next higher level;

- one item of data of a predefined type is associated with each node;

- a predefined relationship exists between the data on adjacent levels.

In this section, discussion will be confined to trees that are constructed from nodes having two link fields: these are known as **binary trees**. The tree data structure is represented graphically as an upside-down botanical tree, with the root at the top and the leaves at the bottom.

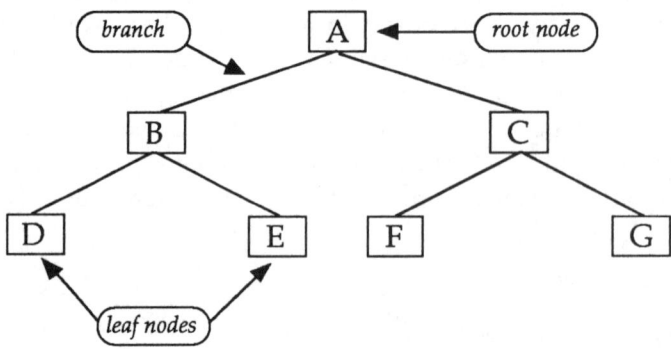

The above diagram is useful as a guide for defining the terminology associated with trees.

The node labelled A is the root of the tree; however, any node that has at least one branch (i.e. points to at least one node) can be considered the root of a *subtree*. In the above diagram there are two subtrees that have as their roots, nodes A and B. If a new node was added to the diagram after node D then node D would become the root of a new subtree. A tree can therefore be defined in terms of its subtrees, therefore a tree is an example of a *recursive data structure*, i.e. a data structure can be defined in terms of itself.

In the above diagram, node A, as well as being the root of the tree, is also termed the *parent* of nodes B and C, which are in turn termed the *children* of A. Similarly B is the parent of D and E, which have no children and are therefore termed leaf or terminal nodes.

One of the main uses of a binary tree is to maintain an ordered list in a manner that is easy to update. In the last section it was pointed out that in order to insert a node in an ordered linked list, a linear search had to be made to find the insertion point. This type of search can be quite slow, particularly if the list is long and the node is to be inserted towards the end of the list. By using a binary tree to maintain an ordered list, locating a node in the list is usually much more efficient.

The diagram below represents a binary tree that has been created from dynamic variables.

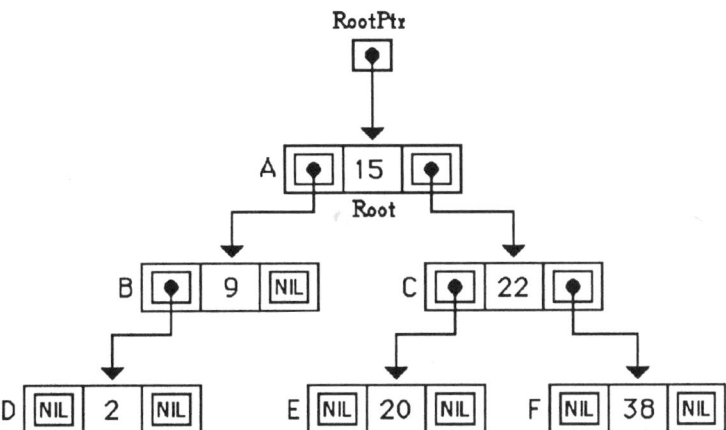

The node containing the data value 15 was the first item to be added to the tree and it is the root node. As the value 9 is less than 15, node B has been added to the tree as the left child of node A. As the value 22 is greater than 15, C has been added to the tree as the right child of node A. Similarly the value 2 is less than 15 and therefore it belongs in the left subtree of node A. As 2 is less than 9 it is added to the tree as the left child of node B. 38 is greater than 15 and therefore it belongs in A's right hand subtree. 38 is also greater than 22, and so is added to the tree as the right hand child of node C. Finally the value 20 is added to the tree, it is greater than 15 and so must go in A's right hand subtree. It is less than 22 and so is inserted into the tree as C's left hand child.

The tree represented above represents somewhat of an ideal as it is a *balanced tree*, which means that the heights of the two subtrees of any particular node differ at the most by only one node. For example, in the above tree the node that holds the value 9 has only one subtree hanging from it; however, as that subtree only consists of one node the tree is still balanced. If a new node was added to this subtree, the tree would then become unbalanced.

Whether a tree is balanced or unbalanced is not simply a matter of aesthetics but a factor which determines the efficiency of searching the tree. The nearer a node is to the root of the tree the quicker it can be found. Consider this next diagram which represents the worst case of an unbalanced tree.

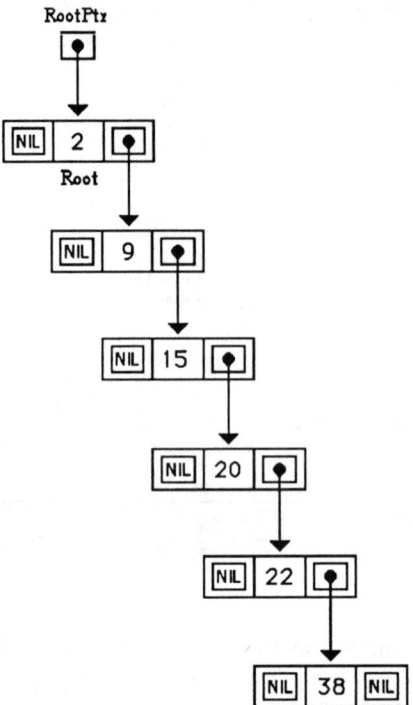

The degenerate tree above has been constructed by entering the values in sorted order! In order to search for the value 38 it would be necessary to visit six nodes, whereas in the previous diagram of a balanced tree, only a maximum of three nodes would need to be visited to find any value. The techniques for programming balanced trees is not the subject of this book; there are many good texts on the subject.

Implementing a tree

We now develop a module for a tree in a similar fashion to the module for linked lists.

```
MODULE TreeHandler;
FROM Storage IMPORT ALLOCATE, DEALLOCATE;
TYPE
  NodePtr = POINTER TO Node;
  Node = RECORD
            Data : CARDINAL;
            LeftChild, RightChild : NodePtr
         END;
VAR
  RootPtr : NodePtr;

PROCEDURE InitializeTree;
  BEGIN
```

```
      RootPtr := NIL
  END InitializeTree;
```

First, we define a procedure to add a node to the tree. Because of the recursive nature of the tree data structure, we shall make use of a programming technique called recursion which you encountered in Chapter 8.

```
PROCEDURE AddToTree(VAR TreePtr: NodePtr; CardVal:CARDINAL);
  BEGIN
    IF TreePtr = NIL THEN
      NEW(TreePtr);
      TreePtr^.Data := CardVal;
      TreePtr^.RightChild := NIL;
      TreePtr^.LeftChild := NIL;
    ELSIF CardVal < TreePtr^.Data THEN
      AddToTree(TreePtr^.LeftChild,CardVal)
    ELSE
      AddToTree(TreePtr^.RightChild,CardVal)
    END
  END AddToTree;
```

In order to add a new node to a binary tree, in a manner that will maintain the ordering of the tree, two rules must be followed:

- All data values in the left subtree of a node must be less than or equal to the data value in the node.

- All data values in the right subtree of a node must be greater than the data value in the node.

This procedure would be activated with the following call

```
AddToTree(RootPtr,15);
```

TreePtr will initially be the pointer to the root of the whole tree. If TreePtr has the value NIL, then the tree is empty and dynamic storage can be allocated for TreePtr with a call of NEW. However, if TreePtr does not equal NIL, then the procedure must be recursively called with the pointer argument being either the .LeftChild or RightChild link field of the node pointed to by TreePtr. This link field is itself, of course, the root of a subtree. Which subtree is used in the recursive call is dependent on whether the value to be added to the tree is less than or equal to, or greater than the value held in the node pointed to by TreePtr, in accordance with the rules given above. The procedure will continue to be recursively called until a subtree denoted by a NIL value is found (TreePtr has the value NIL), whereupon dynamic storage can be allocated for TreePtr and the new value can be assigned to the data field of the node.

If the following calls to AddToTree were made:

```
AddToTree(15);
AddToTree(9);
AddToTree(22);
AddToTree(2);
```

```
AddToTree(20);
AddToTree(38);
```

Then a balanced binary tree would be constructed.

Having constructed the tree it is useful to be able to query the tree in order to ascertain whether a particular value exists.

```
PROCEDURE SearchTree
  (TreePtr: NodePtr; CardVal: CARDINAL): BOOLEAN;
  BEGIN
    IF TreePtr = NIL THEN
      RETURN FALSE
    ELSIF CardVal < TreePtr^.Data THEN
      RETURN SearchTree(TreePtr^.LeftChild, CardVal)
    ELSIF CardVal > TreePtr^.Data THEN
      RETURN SearchTree(TreePtr^.RightChild, CardVal)
    ELSE
      RETURN TRUE
    END
  END SearchTree;
```

The above procedure is somewhat similar to the AddToTree procedure in that it is of a recursive construction. The procedure is first called with RootPtr as the actual pointer parameter:

```
IsPresent := SearchTree(RootPtr, 22);
```

If the tree is empty, the search fails. If the search value is less than the data field of TreePtr then the procedure is recursively called with the LeftChild link field as the root of the subtree to be searched. If the search value is greater than the data field of TreePtr then the procedure is recursively called with the RightChild link field as the root of the subtree to be searched. Repeated recursive calls of SearchTree are made until either the data field of TreePtr is equal to the search value or until TreePtr has the value NIL.

11.8   PORTABILITY ISSUES

The biggest problem concerning the programming of dynamic variables is the potential absence of NEW and DISPOSE. Professor Wirth dropped them in the third edition of *Programming in Modula-2*, and some, but not all, implementors followed his lead. The forthcoming standard reinstates them. If they are not present, you must program using ALLOCATE and DEALLOCATE directly. See Chapter 22 for details. (Topspeed Modula-2 does implement NEW and DISPOSE.) Because some implementations do not provide the built-in procedures NEW and DISPOSE, the use instead of the procedures ALLOCATE and DEALLOCATE (which all implementations provide) will obviously lead to portable code. However, ALLOCATE and DEALLOCATE are unwieldy to use, and therefore we have chosen to use NEW and DISPOSE. (Translating calls of NEW and DISPOSE to calls of ALLOCATE and DEALLOCATE is relatively straightforward; see Chapter 22 for details).

It is important to consider what the value of a pointer variable is after a call to DISPOSE. Some Modula-2 compilers will assign to the pointer the constant value NIL, in order to indicate that the pointer points to nothing. However, with some compilers, the value of a pointer after a call to DISPOSE is undefined. Therefore it is sensible and good programming practice to follow a call to DISPOSE with an assignment statement, setting the value of the pointer to NIL.

```
DISPOSE(CardPtr1); CardPtr1 := NIL;
```

Hopefully, after a call of DISPOSE, the storage associated with a dynamic variable should be freed for other use. It would not be unreasonable to expect that after a call of DISPOSE with a pointer that has a dynamic variable 4 bytes in size, that the amount of free memory would be increased by 4 bytes. However, this is not always the case, and it is quite likely that a call of DISPOSE will simply make what was pointed at inaccessible, with the storage associated with the redundant dynamic variable being reallocated (maybe) at some later stage. If the amount of free memory is critical to a program, you would be advised to override the DISPOSE procedure and to maintain your own free list of redundant dynamic variables that you can reuse at some later stage in your program. In other words you should keep a queue of free dynamic variables which would be added to instead of calling the DISPOSE procedure. Then whenever a new dynamic variable is needed you would first check to see if there was any in the queue that could be reused before calling the procedure NEW.

Finally, it should be noted that some Modula-2 compilers do not require the importation of ALLOCATE and DEALLOCATE before NEW and DISPOSE can be used.

11.9 REVIEW QUESTIONS AND EXERCISES

Q11.1 Of what type can a pointer's dynamic variable be?

Q11.2 Does the declaration of a pointer variable bring into existence a dynamic variable of the pointer's bound type?

Q11.3 How is a pointer variable initialized?

Q11.4 How is a dynamic variable disposed of?

Q11.5 What is the value of a pointer variable after its dynamic variable has been disposed?

Q11.6 What are nodes and what are they used for?

Q11.7 How do dynamic data structures differ from static data structures?

Q11.8 A stack is a data structure that is described as LIFO (last in, first out). Write a module to manipulate a stack; include the procedures: InitializeStack, AddToStack, and RemoveFromStack.

PART II—MODULA-2 REFERENCE

12 SYNTACTIC NOTATION

12.1 INTRODUCTION

This chapter describes the notation which is used to define formally the lexical and syntactic rules of Modula-2. The lexical rules are concerned with how sequences of characters form the words, or *tokens* of the language. In a programming language, sequences of tokens can be combined to form sentences: in Modula-2 these are program modules, definition modules and implementation modules. The rules which determine whether a module is well formed are called the *syntax* of the language. (The *semantic* rules, which assign a meaning to a program, are given informally in the book.)

12.2 TERMINOLOGY

The notation used to specify formally the syntax of Modula-2 in this part and later in the book is the Backus-Naur Formalism, called *BNF* for short. We have chosen the variant of BNF which is being used to define the syntax in the draft Modula-2 standard. The variant is the British Standards Institution's (BSI) syntactic metalanguage.[1]

The syntax of a programming language consists of the following:

* A set of *terminal symbols*, which are the symbols or words used in the language. These are enclosed in quotation marks, e.g. "2", "MODULE", "END" etc.

---

[1]The BSI metalanguage is defined by BS 6154 Standard Syntactic Metalanguage, 1981.

- A set of *non-terminal symbols* which are place holders, used only in the definition of the syntax of the language. The names of non-terminals are usually chosen to reflect constructs in the programming language, e.g. definition module, repeat statement, etc.

- A set of *production rules* which are the rules by which non-terminals are replaced by other non-terminals and terminals. To make them easily distinguishable, BNF syntax rules will be given in a sans-serif font enclosed in a box; for example:

```
vowel = "a" | "e" | "i" | "o" | "u";
```

means that when the non-terminal vowel is encountered it can be replaced by either "a", "e", "i", "o", or "u".

The symbols '=' and '|' in the above example are not part of the language which is being defined, but part of the production rules. They are called *meta-symbols*. A full list of meta-symbols and their meanings is contained in the table below. Every production is ultimately reduced to terminal symbols which are not defined further.

Meta-symbol	Meaning
A	the non-terminal, A
'E' or "E"	the terminal E
=	is defined as
,	followed by
A | B	either A or B but not both
{A}	0 or more occurrences of A
[A]	0 or 1 occurrences of A
( )	delimits groups of symbols
–	excludes the symbols which follow it
; or .	end of the rule
(* *)	encloses comments
? ?	encloses special sequences

12.3   WORKED EXAMPLES OF SYNTAX PRODUCTION RULES

The following table includes some simple production rules (not from programming languages):

Production	Generates
X = A | B;	A and B
X = Z, {A | B};	Z and ZAAAAA and ZABBBA and ZA and ZB...
X = Z, [A | B];	Z and ZA and ZB
X = [ST | C], UPID;	UPID and STUPID and CUPID
X = A, B, {CD} | E ;	AB and ABCD and ABE and ABCDCDCD....
Y = P | Q | R;	P and Q and R
X = A, (P | R);	AP and AR

An example of the use of BS 6154 in defining syntax rules of Modula-2 is:

```
numeric literal = real number literal | whole number literal;
whole number literal = digit, {digit};
real number literal = whole number literal, ".", {digit}, [scale factor];
scale factor = "E", ["+" | "-"], whole number literal;
digit =  "0" |"1" | "2" | "3" | "4" | "5" | "6" | "7" | "8" | "9" ;
```

The above set of productions define the syntax for numeric literals used in Modula-2. We can assign meanings to the productions, using the table in Section 12.2, in a step-by-step fashion

Step 1: numeric literal is defined to be either a real number literal or a whole number literal ;

Step 2: whole number literal is defined to be a digit followed by zero or more occurrences of a digit;

Step 3: real number literal is defined as whole number literal followed by a decimal point followed by zero or more occurrences of digit followed by zero or one occurrences of scale factor;

Step 4: scale factor is defined as E followed by zero or one occurrence of either a plus or a minus sign followed by a whole number literal;

Step 5: digit is defined to be either 0 or 1 or 2 or 3 or 4 or 5 or 6 or 7 or 8 or 9.

At this point, we have processed all the special meta-symbols and have only to choose from terminals.

The rules can be used to produce any numeric literal. To produce the number 9.6 we expand the production of numeric literal as summarized in the table below:

Action	Produces
expand numeric literal	real number literal
expand real number literal	whole number literal.digit
expand whole number literal	digit.digit
expand digit twice	9.6

In this way BNF syntax rules can be used to determine the required form of Modula-2 source code (e.g. the format of a real number literal). Alternatively BNF rules can be used to check if a number, such as 9 . 6, is valid.

12.4 PORTABILITY ISSUES

There are two portability issues concerning syntax. The first is the syntactic notation. A number of notations are used and this can confuse the programmer wishing to determine what the syntax of the language is. The second is to do with implementation-defined aspects of syntax.

Syntactic notation

The BSI standard syntactic metalanguage is more or less equivalent to other metalanguages that could be used for defining Modula-2, but has the advantage of being the notation used in the forthcoming Modula-2 standard.

Note that the choice of non-terminal names and ordering of production rules can have a significant effect on the comprehensibility of a fragment of syntax. Also note that brackets may be used at different levels but define equivalent syntax. To illustrate this, consider the following rules which are *equivalent* to those given for numeric literal above:

```
numeric literal = pZq | brillig;
dot = ".";
brillig = n, {n};
n = "0"|"1"|"2"|"3"|"4"|"5"|"6"|"7"|"8"|"9";
spuzzm = ["E", ["+"|"-"], brillig];
pZq = brillig, dot, {n}, spuzzm;
```

The syntax of a numeric literal given at the beginning of Section 12.3 would have been rewritten as follows in the syntactic notation used in the original definition of Modula-2.[1]

```
numeric Literal = realNumberLiteral | wholeNumberLiteral.
wholeNumberLiteral = digit {digit}.
realNumberLiteral = whole NumberLiteral "." {digit} [scaleFactor].
```

---

[1]Programming in Modula-2 (3rd Ed.) N. Wirth, Springer Verlag, New York, 1985.

scaleFactor = "E" ["+" | "-"] wholeNumberLiteral.
digit = "0" |"1" | "2" | "3" | "4" | "5" | "6" | "7" | "8" | "9" .

As you can see, this is very similar to the BSI syntactic notation; the meta-symbols are mostly the same—|, [,], (,), {, and } all have the same meaning. However, in the above a period has been used to terminate production rules. (This is allowed in the BSI notation but we prefer to use semicolons to terminate rules.) Note that no explicit concatenation symbol (such as the comma in the BSI notation) is used, and so non-terminal symbols must be single words (e.g. 'realNumberLiteral' must be used rather than 'real number literal').

It is usually not difficult to translate between variations of BNF syntactic notations. For example to translate from the notation used to define syntax in Topspeed manuals means replacing the symbol '::=' by '=', adding commas between symbols, including keywords in quotation marks, and terminating each rule with a semicolon. It may also be helpful to split up unwieldy non-terminal symbols. Thus,

LoopStatement ::= LOOP StatementSequence END

becomes:

Loop Statement = "LOOP", Statement Sequence, "END";

You should also note that graphical syntactic languages are common. So much so that we have provided a set of syntax diagrams in Appendix 1.2. These are exactly equivalent to the collected BNF syntax rules in Appendix 1.1. To a large extent they are self-explanatory.

Implementation defined syntax

Finally, the main portability issue relevant to syntax is that non-portable extensions to the language are often to be found in the syntax supplied by an implementation. For example, the memory address of a variable may be specified in its declaration. The syntax for an address is implementation defined (and so potentially non-portable). It is given in Appendix 1, thus:

```
address =
    ? Implementation defined.  For Topspeed Modula-2  address is
       cardinal constant expression, ":", cardinal constant expression?;
```

Since Topspeed Modula-2 runs on Intel segmented architecture computers (which require a segment and an offset for an address), the Topspeed syntax for address is (with suitable translation) as follows:

```
address = "[", segment number, ":", offset number, "]";
segment number = constant expression;
offset number = constant expression;
```

12.5   REVIEW QUESTIONS

Q12.1   What variant of BNF is used as the syntactic notation in this book?

Q12.2   What is the difference between a terminal symbol and a non-terminal symbol?

Q12.3   What does the following production rule mean?
```
household = person, {person | pet};
```

Q12.4   When is the meta-symbol ? used?

Q12.5   Given the following production rules:
```
identifier = letter, {letter | digit};
digit = "0" |"1" | "2" | "3" | "4" | "5" | "6" | "7" | "8" | "9";
letter = ? "a".."z" | "A" .."Z" | "—"?;
```
are the following valid identifiers?

(i) abc (ii) 2Count (iii) Distance_between_town

(iv) _ _ _   (v) 2 - x

13 MODULES

13.1 INTRODUCTION

Modula-2 is a language designed to encourage a modular approach to programming. The module concept is central to both the language, and to the way in which Modula-2 programs can and should be constructed. Modules facilitate the structuring of program code—whether it be for small projects where there is only one programmer, or for large complex projects employing many programmers. This chapter describes program, separate, and local modules in detail. Library modules are described briefly in Section 13.9 and discussion of system modules is deferred to Chapter 25.

13.2 COMPILATION UNITS

Not all types of modules can be separately compiled in Modula-2. There are five different types of modules in Modula-2:

- program module;
- separate modules, split into definition and implementation parts;
- local modules;
- library modules;
- system modules.

Under normal circumstances, only the first three types of module will be written by a programmer. Only program modules and separate modules can be separately compiled.

Library modules and system modules are used as if they are separately compiled Modula-2 modules, but they may be implemented differently. (Also, system modules have special properties which cannot be specified in Modula-2.)

Syntax

```
compilation unit =
    definition module | implementation module | program module;
```

13.3   PROGRAM MODULES

The program module is that part of a program where execution is initiated. As described below, this does not imply that the first statement of the program module is the first statement to be executed. Rather, the program module controls what happens throughout the program. Normally, it is at the top of a hierarchy of modules, and by accessing data and procedures in subordinate modules, it controls their processing.

Syntax

```
program module =
    "MODULE", module identifier, [priority], ";",
    {import}, block, module identifier, ".";

import = ["FROM", module identifier], "IMPORT", identifier list, ";";

priority = "[", constant expression, "]";

block = {declaration}, ["BEGIN", statement sequence], "END";
```

The module identifier at the end of a program module must be the same as that used after the MODULE keyword at the beginning of the module.

The priority of a program module is a value which determines how a concurrent program reacts to interrupt. It is described in Chapter 26 but also see *Portability Issues* at end of this chapter.

Description of execution

Any modules which a program module imports are initialized *before* execution of the main program block. The statement sequence of the main block is then executed. On reaching the end of the block, the program terminates. The program module may be also be terminated by a RETURN statement in the body of the program module.

There may be no statement sequence (and therefore no BEGIN) in the program module's block. If this is the case, the program may still perform a useful function, but only by initiating execution in the initialization part of a separate or local module. (This obscures the design and is generally not good practice.)

In complex programs, the initialization order of imported modules may not be straightforward. Essentially, if one module imports another, then the imported module will be initialized first. If the set of modules imported by the main program modules contains mutual (i.e. circular) references, then there is no proper initialization order. Different compilers will have their own solutions to this problem (see *Portability Issues*).

Examples

(i)
```
MODULE NoImports;
CONST
  Factor = 2;
TYPE
  Number = CARDINAL;
VAR
  x: Number;
BEGIN
  x := 44 * Factor
END NoImports.
```

Without importing and using output procedures from a suitable module, the effect of executing this program module cannot be observed.

(ii)
```
MODULE GoodGolly;
FROM PortIO IMPORT WriteString, WriteLn;
TYPE
  onetofour = [1..4];
VAR
  c : onetofour;
BEGIN
  FOR c := 1 TO 4 DO
    WriteString ("Good Golly Miss Molly!"); WriteLn
  END
END GoodGolly.
```

Two procedures WriteString and WriteLn have been imported from the module PortIO in order to write Good Golly Miss Molly! to the screen four times.

13.4 SEPARATE MODULES

The main program module controls the use of facilities defined and implemented in separate modules (or library modules, or system modules). These separate modules may themselves control the use of facilities from other separate modules, and so on. It is generally held that a modular program design can be improved by restricting the interface between modules. This is achieved in

Modula-2 by limiting the visibility of information in a module. By this method, the services provided by one module to another can be strictly controlled, to ensure that they are used as their designer intended.

Modula-2 makes provision for both of these concepts with separate modules. (Separate modules also provide the mechanism for Modula-2 library modules, which provide the basic services—such as input/output—which are not built into the language itself.) Generally, Modula-2 compilers are supplied with the Modula-2 source code of the definition part of separate library modules (so that the facilities are visible) but only the executable code of the implementation part. Thus, the method of implementation (the algorithms used, for example) remains hidden.[1]

The provision of facilities like I/O gives rise to some convenient terminology: a module which uses the 'services' provided by another is called a *client* of the service module.

Separately compiled modules are essentially split into two parts: the public part, called the definition module, and the private part, called the implementation module. Despite the names, the definition and implementation modules are two aspects of the *same* conceptual module, and they share the same identifying name to create this association. The definition and implementation modules must always match: any change to the definition module will require a change to the implementation module. On the other hand, the implementation module may be changed without any change being required by the definition module.

In all implementations known to the authors, the definition and implementation modules are held in separate files. While this is not required, it is convenient for most implementors. Therefore, in the description below we describe definition and implementation modules as if they were separate files, but we do not imply that they need to be implemented as such.

Note also that most implementations require definition modules to be compiled before they can be used (i.e. before a client module which imports then can be compiled), but this is not necessary in Topspeed Modula-2.

Definition modules

One module uses constants, types, variables, procedures, and modules declared in another by 'importing' from the public part of the module, the definition module. Everything that is declared in a definition module is implicitly exportable, therefore any client module is free to import any of the identifiers declared in a definition module.

---

[1]The source text of implementation modules in the Topspeed Modula-2 library are provided with the implementation in order to help programmers understand how their facilities are provided. Close examination of these should not be necessary for most programming tasks.

Syntax

```
definition module =
  "DEFINITION", "MODULE", module identifier, ";",
  {import},
  {definition},
  "END", module identifier, "." ;

module identifier = identifier;

definition =
  "CONST", {constant declaration, ";"} |
  "TYPE", {(type declaration | opaque type), ";"} |
  "VAR", {variable declaration, ";"} |
  procedure heading, ";";

opaque type = identifier;
```

A definition module may contain CONST, TYPE, and VAR declarations and procedure headings. A definition module may not contain module declarations, or procedure bodies. Since a definition module cannot contain a module body (unlike a program module), a definition module may not contain the word BEGIN or any statements.

The module identifier following the END must be the same as the identifier following the keywords DEFINITION MODULE.

Example

```
DEFINITION MODULE Days;
TYPE DaysOfTheWeek = (Sun, Mon, Tue, Wed, Thu, Fri, Sat);

PROCEDURE NextDay(a : DaysOfTheWeek) : DaysOfTheWeek;
  (* returns an incremented value of the parameter *)

PROCEDURE WriteDay(a : DaysOfTheWeek);
  (* outputs to the screen *)

END Days.
```

In the example, all identifiers (i.e. Days, DaysOfTheWeek, Sun, Mon, Tue, Wed, Thu, Fri, Sat, NextDay, WriteDay) may be imported by a client. Such an import statement would look like this:

```
FROM Days IMPORT DaysOfTheWeek, NextDay, WriteDay;
```

Implementation modules

An implementation module provides the implementation of all procedures declared in the corresponding definition module. An implementation module may use any identifiers declared in that definition module without declaring them and it may also declare local types, variables, constants, procedures, and modules. These locally declared identifiers will not be visible to any clients of the definition module.

Syntax

```
implementation module =
  "IMPLEMENTATION", "MODULE", module identifier, [priority], ";",
  {import}, block, module identifier, ".";

block = {declaration}, ["BEGIN", statement sequence], "END";

import = ["FROM", module identifier], "IMPORT", identifier list, ";";

priority = "[", cardinal constant expression, "]";
```

Note that the term *block* is used to refer to the declarations and statements of a module (or procedure). The term *body* refers to the statement part of a block.

Examples

```
(i)      IMPLEMENTATION MODULE Days;
         FROM PortIO IMPORT WriteString;

         PROCEDURE NextDay(a : DaysOfTheWeek) : DaysOfTheWeek;
           VAR b : DaysOfTheWeek;
           BEGIN
             b := a;
             IF b = Sat THEN
               b := Sun
             ELSE
               INC(b)
             END;
             RETURN b
           END NextDay;

         PROCEDURE WriteDay(a : DaysOfTheWeek);
           BEGIN
             CASE a OF
               Sun : WriteString('Sunday') |
               Mon : WriteString('Monday') |
               Tue : WriteString('Tuesday') |
               Wed : WriteString('Wednesday') |
               Thu : WriteString('Thursday') |
               Fri : WriteString('Friday') |
               Sat : WriteString('Saturday')
             END
           END WriteDay;

         END Days.
```

The foregoing example is an implementation of the module whose public part was given earlier. It shows that an implementation module need not have a body; when it does, the body is used to initialize the module when it is first imported by a client. The following example illustrates the use of initialization code in an implementation module.

```
(ii)      IMPLEMENTATION MODULE Days;
          FROM PortIO IMPORT WriteString, WriteLn, ReadChar;
          VAR
            Underline : BOOLEAN;
            Ch : CHAR;

          PROCEDURE NextDay(a : DaysOfTheWeek) : DaysOfTheWeek;
            (* As in Example (i) *)
            END NextDay;

          PROCEDURE WriteDay(a : DaysOfTheWeek);
            BEGIN
              CASE a OF
                Sun : WriteString('Sunday') |
                Mon : WriteString('Monday') |
                Tue : WriteString('Tuesday') |
                Wed : WriteString('Wednesday') |
                Thu : WriteString('Thursday') |
                Fri : WriteString('Friday') |
                Sat : WriteString('Saturday')
              END;
              WriteLn;
              WriteString('_____')
            END WriteDay;

          BEGIN
            Underline := FALSE;
            WriteString('Type the letter y to set underline to ON:');
            Ch := ReadChar();
            Underline := CAP(ch) = 'y'
          END Days.
```

The effect of the added module body will be to write a prompt to the screen. The response of the user will alter the execution of the procedure WriteDay.

The IMPORT statement

In order for a client module to use the types, constants, variables, and procedures that have been declared in definition modules, it is necessary for the client module to import them explicitly. This is achieved by using the IMPORT statement.

Syntax

```
import = ["FROM", module identifier], "IMPORT", identifier list, ";";
```

There are two syntax forms, which we will refer to as *unqualified import* and *qualified import*. Unqualified import will be described first; in this form the optional FROM part of the syntax is used.

The identifier list in an unqualified import can include the names of several identifiers which denote constants, types, variables, or procedures from an imported module. The client module must have separate unqualified import statements for each module that it wishes to import from. However, unqualified import statements can easily lead to clashes in identifier names (where the imported module, constant, type, variable, or procedure name is the same as one already declared in or imported by the client module). Such name clashes are not allowed.

In other words, when an identifier is imported using a unqualified import statement into a client module, it cannot be globally redefined in that client module. If there is some reason for redefining an identifier name, then this would have to be done in a separate inner block—by using a procedure or local module (see later). Unqualified import allows simple reference to the names of the imported identifiers in the client module.

The second form of import omits the FROM part. The identifier list is then a list of names of other definition modules. This form, referred to as qualified import, means that access to constants, types, variables, or procedures in the imported module is gained by preceding their name by the name of the module and a period. For example:

```
IMPORT PortIO;
...
BEGIN
  PortIO.WriteString('Wenhame Haaneti');
```

The name clash problem is less acute with qualified import, but in this case the name clash rule applies only to the names of modules. Thus, imported module names must not clash with global identifiers in the client module.

If there is a name clash outside the client module (e.g. when two server modules both provide a procedure with the same name), qualified import can be used to distinguish between them. This method can also be combined with unqualified import. (See Example (i) below.)

Note that identifiers which are imported into a definition module (which can only be for declaring other identifiers) are not automatically available to an implementation module. If an implementation module requires identifiers which have been imported into its definition module, it must explicitly import them. Identifiers which are declared in a definition module are automatically available in the implementation module. Indeed they must not be redeclared globally in the implementation module.

Examples

(i)   FROM PortIO IMPORT WriteString;
         IMPORT DoubleIO;
         IMPORT TrebleIO;
         ...
         BEGIN
           WriteString('One');
           DoubleIO.WriteString('Two', 'Two');
           TrebleIO.WriteString ('*', '*', '*');

In this example three modules, PortIO, DoubleIO, and TrebleIO, each export a procedure called WriteString. The procedure from PortIO is imported in unqualified mode. To avoid name clashes the others are imported in qualified mode.

(ii)   DEFINITION MODULE MyModule;
         IMPORT AnotherMod;
         FROM YetAnotherMod IMPORT Limit;
         CONST
           Last = Limit;
         TYPE
           Loco = AnotherMod.Train;
         ...

Although identifiers like Limit become visible in this example of a definition module, the visibility is not passed on to the implementation module.

(iii)   IMPLEMENTATION MODULE MyModule;
         FROM YetAnotherMod IMPORT Limit;
         TYPE
           Range = [1..Limit];
         VAR
           Engine: Loco;

In any implementation of MyModule defined in Example (ii), only the identifiers declared in the definition module are accessible. Thus to use Limit from YetAnotherMod, it has to be reimported. However, this is not necessary: the constant Last could have been used, in the same way as Loco can be used without importing AnotherMod again.

Implementation module initialization

The importation of a module causes the imported module to be initialized as a program begins to execute. Initialization means that (if it exists) the body of a module is executed; this only occurs once, even if a module is imported a number of times. Since many different modules may be imported by many others (in a large program, for example), it is necessary to give an ordering for the initialization of modules. The defined order is the one in which they are (textually) listed in the import statement, so it is usually possible for the compiler to work this out (essentially by examining the main program module and working backwards). If there is found to be a circularity in the initialization order (i.e. two modules importing from each other) then strictly speaking the order is undefined—but again compilers may be able to resolve the problem (see *Portability Issues* below).

Opaque types

One of the main advantages of Modula-2 over other high-level languages is the ability that it gives to programmers to hide away the details of how particular data structures are implemented. However, if types are declared in a definition module, an element of insecurity is introduced into this notion of information hiding. The problem is that any type that is declared in a definition module is said to be *transparent*. This term was coined because a type so declared has all its structure visible and thus accessible to any client modules ('visible' is being used in a different way than we have previously used it. Here it means physically in vision). For example, if a record type is declared, any client module that imports that record type will automatically import the fields of the record. This does not usually present a problem, as the client module should also import those procedures that have been defined to operate on that type. Nevertheless problems do arise when a client module attempts to use the imported type in ways other than those defined by the procedures provided to manipulate that type.

To provide for a more secure hiding of type structure, Modula-2 allows a definition module to contain type declarations which do not specify the details of a type. In such cases only the type identifier is declared in the definition module. Types declared in such a manner are known as *opaque* types. Types so declared *must* have their full declaration specified in the corresponding implementation module (some implementations relax this rule, see *Portability Issues*). As opaque types have their implementation details hidden away in the implementation module, the type is known to client modules by name only. Since only the type name is known, the only way in which data structures of this type can be manipulated is via procedures that are also made visible by the definition module. Therefore, the implementation module should define all the procedures that are necessary to manipulate the opaque types.

Modula-2 requires that opaque types be restricted to pointer types only. However, this is not a restriction on the type of abstraction, only the way that it will be implemented. This small restriction is helpful to the compiler (since it can easily allocate storage for a pointer at compile time) and should not seriously affect programming style. Indeed, there is a pleasing consequence to the requirement that an opaque type be implemented as a pointer: almost no operations will be defined on it and procedures to manipulate the opaque type must be supplied in the definition module containing the opaque type declaration. Thus the security of the interface is increased. (See Chapter 25 for use of opaque types in implementing an opaque data structure.)

Example

```
DEFINITION MODULE Opaque;
TYPE
  String = ARRAY [0..23] OF CHAR;
  Name;
PROCEDURE AssignToName
  (VAR NewName: Name; SecondName: String;
   FirstName: String);

PROCEDURE WriteName(AName: Name);

END Opaque.
```

```
IMPLEMENTATION MODULE Opaque;
FROM PortIO IMPORT WriteString, WriteLn;
FROM Storage IMPORT ALLOCATE;
TYPE
  Name = POINTER TO NameRecord;
  NameRecord = RECORD
                 Surname, Forename: String
               END;

PROCEDURE AssignToName
  (VAR NewName : Name; SecondName : String;
   FirstName : String);
  BEGIN
    NEW(NewName);
    NewName^.Surname := SecondName;
    NewName^.Forename := FirstName;
  END AssignToName;
PROCEDURE WriteName(AName : Name);
  BEGIN
    WriteString(AName^.Surname);
    WriteString(' ');
    WriteString(AName^.Forename);
    WriteLn
  END WriteName;
END Opaque.
```

Note how the declaration of the structure of the type Name is postponed until the implementation module, where it is redeclared in full. By using this mechanism, the structure of the type Name is hidden from any importing module. The procedure AssignToName provides the mechanism to store two values of type String in a variable of opaque type Name. The procedure WriteName allows the values stored in this manner to be printed.

It should be noted that in reality, such a separate module, would provide a data structure such as a tree or a linked list to store a number of variables of the opaque type, and procedures to manipulate such a data structure.

A fragment of a program module which uses the `Opaque` module is given below. Note that the internal structure of the `Name` data type cannot be accessed in the program module.

(iii)
```
        MODULE names;
        FROM Opaque IMPORT Name, String, AddName, WriteName;
        VAR
          MyName: Name;
          Surname, Forename: String;
        BEGIN
          ...
          AddName(MyName, Surname, Forename);
          ...
          WriteName(MyName)
        END names.
```

13.5   LOCAL MODULES

The third kind of module provided by Modula-2 is called the local module. Local modules get their name from the fact that they are nested (i.e. embedded) inside other modules or (less frequently) procedures. Local modules provide a form of information hiding which is somewhere between that provided by separate modules and procedures. The difference between local modules and procedures (in terms of information hiding) comes from the fact that local modules have import and export lists rather than parameters to control their interface with the surrounding block. Also, a local module provides a secure boundary between any locally declared identifiers and those in scope in the block surrounding it, whereas a procedure may access variables which are visible in its surrounding block. For a full explanation of scope, see Section 13.6.

Local modules are best viewed as a way of encapsulating variables and the procedures that manipulate them, so as to hide the inner workings from inadvertent access. Although local modules cannot be compiled separately, a local module can be viewed as conceptually complete—and can therefore be used to assist with the design of a complex program.

Local module declarations

A local module can be declared anywhere a procedure may be declared. This means that local modules can appear in the declaration part of both implementation and program modules, and they can also be nested within the declaration parts of procedures or other local modules. Such nesting can be arbitrarily deep, but in practice deep nesting is best avoided.

Syntax

```
module declaration =
   "MODULE", module identifier, [priority], ";", {IMPORT}, [export],
   block, module identifier;
```

The syntax for a local module resembles that of an implementation module; the minor differences are: the absence of the word IMPLEMENTATION and that the syntax is terminated with a semi-colon (;) rather than a period (.). The main difference is that a local module must explicitly export identifiers it wants to make available outside itself. (See Appendix 1 for the full syntax rules.)

Example

```
IMPLEMENTATION MODULE IMod;
VAR
   Identifier1: CARDINAL;

MODULE OtherLocalModule;
EXPORT Identifier2, Identifier3;
VAR
   Identifier2, Identifier3: CARDINAL;
BEGIN
...
END OtherLocalModule;

MODULE Local;
IMPORT Identifier2, Identifier3;
IMPORT Identifier1;
EXPORT Identifier4;
VAR
   Identifier4: CARDINAL;
BEGIN
   Identifier4 := Identifier1 * Identifier2 + Identifier3
END Local;

BEGIN
...
END IMod.
```

This example illustrates the importation of two identifiers (Identifier2 and Identifier3) from another local module (which must first export them to the surrounding block) and one (Identifier1) which has been declared in the enclosing block. A local variable (Identifier4) is declared within Local and exported, after it has been initialized using the values of the imported identifiers.

Local modules and IMPORT

Although the syntax is the same for importing from separate modules and for importing into local modules from the enclosing block, the meaning of the different forms is subtly different. Whereas importing from a separate module can be clearly divided into two forms—unqualified and qualified, with and without the FROM part respectively—the absence of the FROM part in a local module import does not necessarily mean that imported identifiers must be qualified by the name of their declaring block. IMPORT on its own, can apply to objects which are not modules and which are in scope in the surrounding block.

If a global variable g is imported into a local module by the statement IMPORT g; it can be accessed inside the module as g. However, importing another local module makes its identifiers accessible when qualified (see Example (i) below).

Examples

(i)
```
MODULE Outer;
FROM PortIO IMPORT WriteString;
CONST
  min = 0;
  max = 23;
TYPE
  SmallNos = [min..max];
  String = ARRAY SmallNos OF CHAR;

PROCEDURE Blank(VAR AString : String);
  VAR i : SmallNos;
  BEGIN
    FOR i := min TO max DO
      AString [i] := ' ';
    END
  END Blank;

MODULE Local1;
EXPORT Example;
TYPE
  Example = ....(* some local definition *);
BEGIN
  ...
END Local1;

MODULE Local2;
IMPORT String, Blank; (* visible in Outer *)
IMPORT Local1;
FROM PortIO IMPORT WriteString;
(* import from separate module*)
VAR
  NewEx : Local1.Example;
BEGIN
  ...
END Local2;

END Outer.
```

The above example illustrates all three kinds of import, although the last case relies on the IMPORT statement at the head of the module Outer—which may not be portable (see *Portability Issues*).

```
(ii)        MODULE Outer2;
            TYPE REC = RECORD
                            day: [1..31];
                            month:[1..12];
                            year: [1900..1999]
                        END;
                MODULE Inner;
                IMPORT REC;
                VAR date : REC;
                BEGIN
                  date.day    := 30;
                  date.month := 7;
                  date.year   := 1952
                END Inner;
            ...
            END Outer2.
```

The importation of a record type also (implicitly) imports the record type field identifiers, so that these will be accessible within the local module.

```
(iii)       MODULE Outer3;
            TYPE Media = (LP, Cassette, CD, DAT, Video);
                MODULE Inner;
                IMPORT Media;
                VAR Album: Media;
                BEGIN
                  Album := CD
                END Inner;
            END Outer3.
```

The importation of an enumeration type also (implicitly) imports the enumeration constants, so that these will be accessible within the local module. Hence, importing `Media` imports its enumerated constants.

Local modules and EXPORT

In Example (i) in the previous subsection, the `EXPORT` statement is used in module `Local1`. EXPORT statements are unique to local modules, and control the access from the outer block to any local identifiers declared within the local module.

Syntax

```
export = "EXPORT", ["QUALIFIED"], identifier list, ";";
```

As can be seen from the syntax, the `EXPORT` statement has two forms: *qualified* and *unqualified*. This is to provide as much symmetry as possible with `IMPORT`, so that there is a consistent control interface in both directions through the local module boundary.

The unqualified form of EXPORT is the more usual form, since normally only one programmer will be involved in the production of all the local modules contained within a given compilation unit. The unqualified form could give rise to name clashes in the block surrounding a local module, but these can be prevented more easily than is the case for separately compiled modules.

Identifiers exported from a local module via an unqualified export list become visible in the surrounding block as if they had been declared there.

Examples

(i)
```
        MODULE Outer4;
          MODULE Local;
          EXPORT LocalArray;
          TYPE
             LocalArray = ARRAY [0..23] OF CHAR;
          END Local;
        VAR
          AnArray : LocalArray;
          ...
```

This example shows how LocalArray may be accessed outside the module in which it was declared (and from which it was exported) as if it had been declared in the outer block.

(ii)
```
        MODULE Outer5;
        MODULE Local;
        EXPORT QUALIFIED LocalArray;
        TYPE
           LocalArray = ARRAY [0..23] OF CHAR;
        END Local;
        VAR
          AnArray : Local.LocalArray;
          ...
```

The second, qualified form of EXPORT applies an additional control to the visibility of the exported identifiers in the surrounding block. Such identifiers must be prefixed (using the dot notation) with the local module name that exports them. (See Section 13.6 for a full discussion of visibility.)

Nested modules can perform successive imports and exports through several levels, but the only way that this can be done is by repetition of the import and export statements thus:

```
MODULE One;
TYPE A = ...;

  MODULE Two;
  EXPORT B;
  IMPORT A;

    MODULE Three;
    EXPORT B;
    IMPORT A;
```

```
      TYPE B = ...;
      BEGIN
        (*A and B are visible here*)
      END Three;

    (* A and B are visible here*)
    END Two;

  (* A and B are visible here*)
  END One;
```

A local module may contain both an EXPORT and an EXPORT QUALIFIED list.

Local module initialization

Local modules may contain a module body, which is used for initialization. If a local module is embedded within a procedure, then every time the procedure is called the local module body will be executed first. If several local modules are embedded in a procedure, their module bodies will be executed in textual order prior to execution of the procedure body. If several local modules are embedded in a nested form within a procedure, the local module bodies will be executed in the order of most deeply nested first (outwards). Textual order takes precedence over nesting if there is a combination of multiple nested and non-nested local modules.

If a local module is declared in a main program module or implementation module (but not inside a procedure), its module body will be executed once, just prior to the execution of the main program body or initialization of the implementation body. If there are several local modules (nested or at the same level) in a main program module or implementation module, their module body execution order will be as described for local modules inside procedures.

The module bodies of local modules in implementation modules will be executed prior to the module bodies of local modules in the main program module.

Example

```
MODULE TestOrder;
FROM PortIO
  IMPORT WriteString, WriteLn, WriteInt, SetFieldWidth;
PROCEDURE P;
  MODULE TestM1;
  (* local module nested inside procedure P *)
  IMPORT WriteLn, WriteString;
  EXPORT I;
  VAR I : INTEGER;
  BEGIN
    I := 712; (* unlikely value for an uninitialized variable*)
    WriteString('  Local module M1 initialized '); WriteLn
  END TestM1;
BEGIN
  I := I + 1;
```

```
    WriteString(' Procedure P executed '); WriteLn;
    WriteString(' The value of I is  ');
    SetFieldWidth(3);
    WriteInt(I); WriteLn;
  END P;
  BEGIN
    WriteString('Starting to execute program TestOrder'); WriteLn;
    P;
    WriteString('Program TestOrder now finished.'); WriteLn
  END TestOrder.
```

When executed, the above program outputs the following:

```
Starting to execute program TestOrder
  Local module M1 initialized
 Procedure P executed
  The value of I is  713
Program TestOrder now finished.
```

Local module initialization enables all identifiers exported by the module to be given an initial value (for example) which ensures that a common source of programming errors (use of an uninitialized value) is avoided.

13.6   SCOPE, VISIBILITY, LIFETIME AND BLOCKS

This section covers both scope and the related notions of visibility and lifetime. Scope has an impact on both modules and procedures; visibility applies to all identifiers used in a program, but is most relevant to modules; lifetime applies to modules and procedures.

To discuss these issues, we need to understand what constitutes a block. Block is used in syntax descriptions throughout this book, and it is important that Modula-2 (like Pascal) is often described as a block-structured language.

A block is defined to be a declaration and a sequence of statements. From the following syntax it can be seen that both modules and procedures contain a block. Therefore, it can be seen that any declaration that is possible in a module is also possible in a procedure.

```
block = {declaration}, ["BEGIN", statement sequence], "END";

program module =
  "MODULE", module identifier, [priority], ";",
  {import}, block, module identifier, ".";

procedure declaration =
  procedure heading, ";", block, procedure identifier;
```

Typically a program module declaration part will include constant, type, variable, procedure, and module declarations. These procedure declarations are also likely to have their own declaration parts, which can also include procedure and module declarations. A procedure which is declared in another procedure is said to be *local* to that procedure or *nested* within that procedure.

Scope

The scope of an identifier is the span of program text in which the identifier can be used. The scope of an identifier includes the block in which it was declared or into which it was imported. (The term scope is sometimes used as a synonym for the declaring, or importing block. However, this practice omits important aspects of scope and is misleading).

By default, the scope of an identifier extends to procedure blocks which the declaring/importing block contains, either directly or indirectly. If a previously declared identifier is redeclared in an enclosing procedure block, the original identifier becomes inaccessible; i.e. the scope of the original identifier becomes bounded by the procedure which redeclares the identifier.

Also by default, the scope of an identifier is bounded by any local module which is declared in the block in which the identifier has been declared or imported. Unlike the case for procedures, the scope of an identifier only extends into a local module if the module imports it.

The idea of scope, and the facility to declare identifiers to be local to a particular block, allows the possibility of using the *same* identifying name to denote different *objects*—types, constants, procedures, etc.—that are within different blocks.

Because of this separation of scopes, programmers are at liberty to choose identifying names for particular modules and procedures, without having to worry about name clashes with other identifiers which already exist in different blocks. This is extremely important when developing large programs, which can involve many programmers.

There are a number of rules which define the scope of an identifier, these are given below.

General scope rule

The most basic concept of scope is that identifiers declared in a block can be referenced throughout that block. Those identifiers are said to be global to that block. So the general rule is that the scope of an identifier is the block in which its declaration occurs, including all procedures that the block may enclose.

The main exception to the general scope rule concerns redeclaration of an identifier within an enclosed block. Consider the following example:

```
MODULE Global;
VAR
  GlobVar1, GlobVar2, GlobVar3 : CARDINAL;
PROCEDURE Add;
  BEGIN
    GlobVar3 := GlobVar1 + GlobVar2
```

```
    END Add;
BEGIN
  Add
END Global.
```

`GlobVar1`, `GlobVar2`, and `GlobVar3` are global to the module. Therefore as the procedure `Add` has been declared within the same block, it can access those global variables. The disadvantage of this is that the procedure `Add` is dependent on the rest of the module. If the names of the global variables were changed in the main program, then the procedure would have to be changed to reflect this. It would be much better to write `Add` as a function procedure with value parameters, in this way:

```
PROCEDURE Add(a, b : CARDINAL) : CARDINAL;
  BEGIN
    RETURN a + b
  END Add;
```

A call to the procedure from the module would then look like:

```
GlobVar3 := Add(GlobVar1, GlobVar);
```

Procedure `Add` now has complete independence from the calling module. It would not be affected if the names of the variables in the module were changed.

Although the procedure `Add` has full access to variables declared in the surrounding module, the inverse is not true.

Consider this example:

```
MODULE Main;
TYPE
  IndexRange = [0..23];
  MyArray = ARRAY IndexRange OF CHAR;
VAR
  CharArray : MyArray;

PROCEDURE Simple;
  VAR
    x, y, z : CHAR;
  BEGIN
    ...
    CharArray [0] := x
  END Simple;

BEGIN (*Main*)
  ...
END Main.
```

Whilst the procedure `Simple` has full access to both the types `MyArray` and `IndexRange` and the variable `CharArray`, the surrounding module has no access to the variables x, y, z (which are local to `Simple`).

The following diagram illustrates the concept of scope for nested procedures.

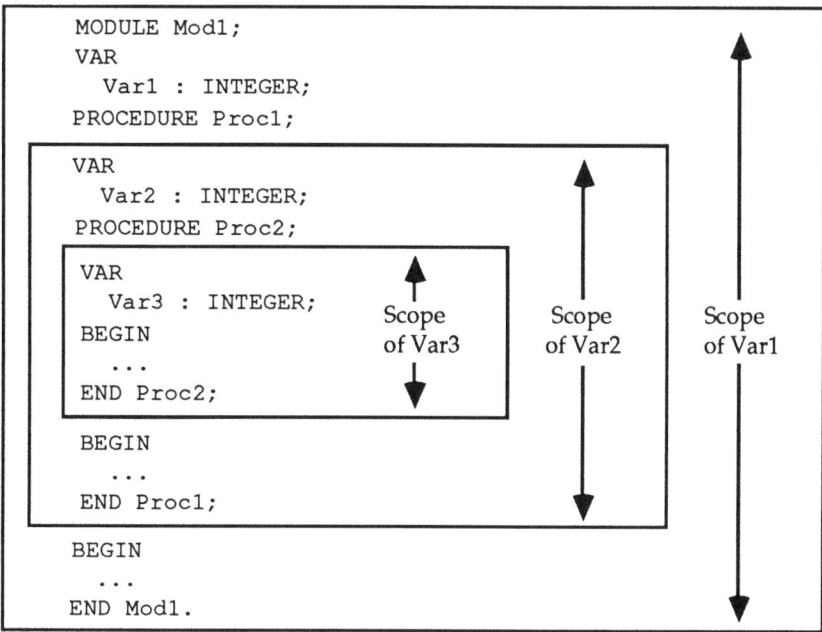

Redeclaration scope rule

When an identifier id is declared in a block X, and is redeclared in some inner procedure block Y, which is enclosed by X, then block Y and any blocks enclosed by Y are excluded from the scope of id declared in X. Block Y is the scope of the redeclared id.

This rule is illustrated by the following example:

```
PROCEDURE Outer;
   VAR
     id : INTEGER;
   PROCEDURE Inner;
     VAR
       id : ARRAY [0..5] OF CHAR;
     BEGIN
       ...   (* id denotes a character array here *)
     END Inner;
   BEGIN
     ...   (* id denotes an integer variable here *)
   END Outer;
```

Procedure Inner has declared a variable with the same name as a variable in procedure Outer. Therefore, procedure Inner is unable to access the variable id in the procedure Outer. Variable id in procedure Outer is said to be out of scope for procedure Inner. Note that the two variables can have different types, as in the example.

Restriction on redeclaration

Two objects cannot have the same name if they are declared in the same block. Therefore, a declaration of the following kind is not allowed:

```
VAR
    a : CARDINAL;
    b : INTEGER;
    a : BOOLEAN;
```

since the type of a would be ambiguous.

Scope of predefined identifiers

The predefined identifiers of Modula-2 which denote the built-in constants, types, and procedures are considered to be declared in an imaginary block enclosing the program. Therefore these standard identifiers are always accessible, unless they are redeclared—in which case the identifier names are subject to the rules previously described. However, built-in procedures, types, etc., are not just used at the global level of a program module or separate module; they must be available within local modules. They are therefore treated differently: they do not need to be imported by a local module, but pervade its boundary with impunity. This is why they are described as *pervasive*.

The redeclaration rule does work on pervasive identifiers: they lose their pervasive characteristics when redeclared.

Visibility

The term *visibility* is used to capture the way in which scope is affected by module import/export rules. The visibility of an identifier is determined by its scope and also by module import/export rules. One of the strengths of Modula-2 is the provision for restricting scope. Procedures are not adequate because of the way in which an identifier's scope will extend into a procedure block unless the identifier is redeclared, although a procedure may have local variables that are only visible within it. All identifiers visible immediately outside a procedure are also visible within (they are said to be non-local to the procedure).

Modules provide extra protection, which is valuable to the encapsulation of data types (to prevent name clashes, inadvertent access, etc.). We can view this protection as a wall around modules; this 'wall' can only be breached by explicitly importing or exporting identifiers. Therefore, scope is a one-way protection (i.e. from reference outwards), whereas modularity provides full two-way protection.

Consider the following example:

```
MODULE Outer;
VAR Ido;
    MODULE Inner;
    VAR Idi;
    ...
```

```
  END Inner;
...
END Outer;
```

The variable Idi is not visible in the module Outer; it is protected by the 'wall' around Inner and is not exported by Inner. Similarly, Ido is not visible in Inner (since it is not imported)—although it would have been if Inner was a procedure rather than a local module.

So far, we have only considered local modules, but the visibility concept applies equally well to separate (implementation) modules. Here, we do not have the same confusion with scope, since scope does not extend beyond the implementation module boundary.

Consider this example:

```
DEFINITION MODULE Thing;
CONST Rogue = 'Black Adder';
END Thing.

IMPLEMENTATION MODULE Thing;
FROM PortIO IMPORT WriteString;
VAR int : INTEGER;
BEGIN
   WriteString(Rogue);
END Thing.
```

The constant Rogue is visible in the implementation module and also available (i.e. visible) for import by any other module. The variable int is only visible in the implementation module and is not available for import anywhere outside of Thing.

Now let us consider scope and visibility acting together:

```
DEFINITION MODULE Adder;
CONST num = -42;
PROCEDURE Add (a, b : INTEGER) : INTEGER;
END Adder.

IMPLEMENTATION MODULE Adder;
VAR
  anum : INTEGER;
PROCEDURE Add (a, b : INTEGER) : INTEGER;
  VAR temp : INTEGER;
    MODULE Protect;
    CONST newnum = -41;
    END Protect;
  BEGIN
    temp:= num;
    RETURN (a + b);
  END Add;

BEGIN (* body of Adder*)
  anum := Add(num, num);
END Adder.
```

The new block established by Add makes the local variables and formal parameters invisible to Adder. The wall around Protect (which has no import/export statements) makes all identifiers except the locally declared newnum invisible.

The following table shows what identifiers are visible from a given block:

Visible identifiers			
From inside Add	From inside Adder	From inside Protect	From outside Adder
num	num	newnum	num
temp	anum		Add
a	Add		
b			
anum			

Here is a summary of the visibility rules:

1. Pervasive identifiers (e.g. denoting built-in types such as CHAR and INTEGER and built-in procedures such as ORD, HIGH, etc.) are visible everywhere, except where they have been redeclared in a local block.

2. A local module creates a wall around all of the identifiers within it; such identifiers are only visible outside the module if they are explicitly exported. Similarly, all identifiers whose scope surrounds the local module are invisible within it unless explicitly imported. The only exceptions to these rules are for enumeration and record types; see Rule 5 in the *Scope of identifiers in local modules* section below.

3. The name of a local module is always visible in the block surrounding it.

Lifetime

The lifetime of the variables of a local module (i.e. the duration during which access to them is possible) is determined by the lifetime of the surrounding block. If a local module is declared within a procedure, the lifetime will be restricted to the duration of each procedure call.

If the local module is declared in an implementation or program module (but not inside a procedure), the lifetime of the local module variables will be the duration of the implementation or program module—i.e. the duration of the program.

The lifetime of a procedure, and hence any identifiers declared within its block, is from the time it is called, until the time the procedure is exited, which will be when an END or RETURN statement is encountered.

Example

```
MODULE Life1; (* demonstrates 'lifetime' and initialization *)
IMPORT T;
```

```
FROM PortIO IMPORT WriteString, WriteLn;

  PROCEDURE P;
  BEGIN
    WriteString(' Procedure P executed '); WriteLn;
  END P;

  MODULE TestM1;
  (* first module nested inside Life1 *)
  IMPORT WriteLn, WriteString;
  BEGIN
    WriteLn;
    WriteString(' Local module TestM1 in Life1 initialized ');
  END TestM1;

  MODULE TestM2;
  (* second module nested inside Life1 *)
  IMPORT WriteLn, WriteString;
  BEGIN
    WriteLn;
    WriteString(' Local module TestM2 in Life1 initialized ');
  END TestM2;

BEGIN (* Life1 *)
  WriteLn;
  WriteString('Starting to execute program Life1 '); WriteLn;
  P;
  WriteString('Program Life1 now finished. '); WriteLn;
END Life1.

DEFINITION MODULE T;
END T.

IMPLEMENTATION MODULE T;
FROM PortIO IMPORT WriteString, WriteLn;
PROCEDURE Q;
  MODULE TM1;
  IMPORT WriteLn, WriteString;
  BEGIN
    WriteString(' Local module TM1 in Q initialized ');
    WriteLn;
  END TM1;

  MODULE TM2;
  IMPORT WriteLn, WriteString;
  BEGIN
    WriteString(' Local module TM2 in Q initialized '); WriteLn;
  END TM2;
BEGIN (* procedure Q *)
  WriteString(' Procedure Q executed '); WriteLn;
END Q;

BEGIN (* main body of T *)
  WriteString('Starting to initialize T, and calling Q twice ');
  WriteLn;
  Q; Q;
  WriteString('Implementation module T is now initialized ');
```

```
    WriteLn;
  END T.
```

When executed, Life1 will produce the following output, which shows the order of initialization of modules and the lifetime of modules:

```
Starting to initialize T, and calling Q twice
  Local module TM1 in Q initialized
  Local module TM2 in Q initialized
 Procedure Q executed
  Local module TM1 in Q initialized
  Local module TM2 in Q initialized
 Procedure Q executed
Implementation module T is now initialized
  Local module TestM1 in Life1 initialized
  Local module TestM2 in Life1 initialized
Starting to execute program Life1
 Procedure P executed
Program Life1 now finished.
```

Scope of identifiers in local modules

The visibility of any identifiers declared in local modules is controlled by a set of scope rules. Some of these rules have already been covered, but for clarity a full set is now given here.

1. The scope of any identifier imported into a local module or declared in a local module is the local module itself. A consequence of this rule is that the redeclaration of any predefined (pervasive) identifier within a local module excludes that identifier from the scope of any nested local module (i.e. it takes on the redeclared meaning in the inner block).

2. The scope of any identifier (other than another local module) which is exported qualified or unqualified from a local module, is as follows:

    (a) the local module itself;

    (b) the immediately surrounding block, and any procedure or procedures that contain that block;

    (c) any further surrounding block, established by further explicit export of the identifier (or by export as part of whole module export—see Rule 4).

    In the surrounding block covered by cases (b) and (c), any identifier which is exported in qualified mode *must* be dot qualified by the exporting module name, whereas any identifier which is exported in unqualified mode may have to be dot qualified (but see *Portability Issues*).

3. The scope of any local module identifier, A, exported by a local module, B, is the same as for Rule 2. In addition, any identifiers in the export list(s) of

the exported local module also becomes visible in the surrounding scope, subject to the following two rules:

(a)   for identifiers exported in qualified mode, reference to them must be of the form:

```
A.identifier or B.A.identifier
```

(b)   for identifiers exported in unqualified mode, reference to them may be of the form:

```
A.identifier, B.A.identifier or identifier
```

4.   The export of an enumeration or record type from a local module also exports the associated enumeration constants and record field names. As for Rules 2(b) and (c), these must be qualified (with the module name) if the type name was exported in qualified mode.

5.   A general rule applies, which prevents two objects with the same name being in the same block. Therefore, it is not legal to export an identifier into a surrounding block where one of the same name is visible. Similarly it is not legal to import an identifier (in unqualified mode) into a local module, and then to declare an identifier of the same name.

These rules can be made a good deal simpler in practice by avoiding the temptation to nest local modules within each other. Nesting of local modules does not serve a particularly useful purpose, and the avoidance of it also prevents the export of module identifiers (which has considerably complicated the foregoing).

13.7   VERSION CONTROL

Although Modula-2 could be implemented without a separate compilation facility, in practice this is one of the key attractions of virtually all Modula-2 implementations. In this discussion of version control, we assume that separate modules (i.e. program, definition, and implementation modules) exist as distinct files that may be compiled separately.

It should be clear that a program module must be compiled last, but what about the others—especially as they are designed/edited/debugged? In general, the definition module of a separate module must be compiled before the corresponding implementation module can be compiled. However, some compilers (and Topspeed Modula-2 is an example) do not require definition modules to be compiled at all—they are simply examined during compilation of implementation modules (to facilitate the necessary checks).

If an implementation module of M is compiled and then the corresponding definition module of M is modified in any way, the implementation module of M must always be recompiled. Such a change and recompilation also triggers the need for recompilation of all other definition and implementation modules which import or import from the modified module.

As a program designer or author, you could organize the recompilation of all affected modules yourself—after each change to any particular module. However, most Modula-2 compilers will do this for you, by way of a program building facility. The compilers are usually assisted by a time and date stamp of files used for the file definition and implementation modules, but other methods of version control are possible. The benefit of these program building facilities is that they do not simply recompile everything (which could be very time consuming); they only recompile the exact set of modules that are affected by a modification (as determined by the import lists).

13.8   A MODULE FUNCTIONALITY GUIDE

Modularity is the most powerful structuring mechanism in Modula-2. With this power comes considerable flexibility and the temptation to over-elaborate the design of Modula-2 programs. However, Modula-2 (as with all high-level languages) contains considerable redundancy, so a simple functionality guide to modules and their components may prove helpful.

The following guide considers the purpose of the four principal components of modules: export lists, import lists, declarations, and module body. (Procedures are not considered as a distinct section—only the declaration of them is—but procedures are the basic building blocks of Modula-2 programs.)

Program modules

Export lists	These are not permitted as Modula-2 does not define an interface to an underlying system this way. (Access to the operating system must be done through operating system library functions.)
Import list(s)	These provide the mechanism for access to external modules, procedures, types and constants needed for: 1. local modules in the program module; 2. main program declarations; 3. main program body.
Declarations	These are essentially global, so declarations here establish global objects (which data hiding design techniques aim too minimize).
Module body	This controls the main execution sequence and can be used for initialization.

Definition modules

Export list	Not permitted, all visible identifiers are implicitly available for export (at the behest of other modules). See Section 13.10 for a related portability issue.
Import list(s)	These *only* provide access to any identifiers that are needed in the definition module declarations. Note: they do not serve to import to the implementation module.
Declarations	This is the mechanism for making identifiers implicitly available for export. Note: procedure headers and opaque types are introduced in definition modules.
Module body	Not permitted, all code must be in the implementation module.

Implementation modules

Export list	Not permitted, handled by the definition module.
Import list(s)	These provide access to any identifiers that are needed in the implementation module, and identifiers imported in the definition module may have to be reimported—since the import list(s) in the definition module of the same name do not serve this purpose.
Declarations	These are used in several ways: 1. to provide encapsulated local objects for the implementation module body, procedures and local modules; 2. to declare fully any procedures and opaque types redefined in the definition module; 3. to declare local modules.
Module body	This is used for module initialization code only; a typical use will be the initialization of variables which are global to the module. Note: any local modules are initialized before the implementation module body.

Local modules

Export list(s)	These control the interface to the surrounding block, making internally declared identifiers visible externally. Note: the qualified mode of EXPORT can be used to overcome potential name clashes.
Import list(s)	These control the interface to the surrounding block, making objects which are visible in the surrounding block visible inside the module.
Declarations	These establish local objects and procedures.
Module body	This only provides for initialization of a local module. If it is nested within a procedure then it is executed every time the procedure is called, otherwise just once.

13.9 LIBRARY MODULES

Modula-2 is quite a small programming language, but the power and ease of expression of the language is not compromised by its size. One of the fundamental reasons for this is the provision of a set of library modules to provide input/output and other vital facilities. We have already introduced two of these modules (`PortIO` and `PortStrings`) in Part I of this book. This section is designed to give a brief overview of the library modules that are provided with Modula-2 implementations.

In the design of Modula-2, Professor Wirth deliberately allowed for flexibility of approach in the implementation of library modules, so that library modules could provide facilities appropriate to specific classes of users or to complement the attributes of the computer hardware on which they are based. Although this approach has many advantages, it has led to diversity in implementations. This is best illustrated by considering input/output. Appendix 2 of the third edition of Wirth's book lists nine input/output modules, some of which are arranged in a hierarchy—according to how the user wishes to control high-resolution displays. In practice, almost no Modula-2 implementations provide an identical set of such library modules, which is why we have implemented a portable subset of their facilities in `PortIO`.

In addition to input/output, it will be common to find at least two or three additional library modules, as follows:

- `Storage`. This module provides ALLOCATE and DEALLOCATE; for details see Chapter 22.

- `MathLib`. This provides mathematical functions like sin, cos, log, etc. (For obscure reasons, this is usually called `MathLib0`.) We do not attempt to explain this library module in the book, since both the syntax and semantics (and even the data types supported) are heavily implementation dependent.

- `Strings`. This library module provides string handling procedures in many implementations, but is not mentioned in Wirth's book. We have implemented `PortStrings` for this book, see Chapter 10.

Topspeed Modula-2 provides FIO, IO and `Window` for input/output, `Storage` for ALLOCATE and DEALLOCATE, MATHLIB for maths library functions, and `Str` for string handling facilities. Topspeed Modula-2 also provides additional library and system modules; see the Topspeed user manual for details.

13.10 PORTABILITY ISSUES

As we have observed, modules are the most powerful structuring device in Modula-2. Unfortunately this means that they are necessarily affected by any weaknesses in the definition of the language. They have therefore been implemented in a variety of ways, with resulting portability problems.

Export from definition modules

The very earliest version of the Modula-2 language required an EXPORT QUALIFIED statement to be used in definition modules to make identifiers visible outside. Although this approach has long been dropped (and export statements are neither needed nor legal in definition modules), some older compilers may still require this. Under these circumstances, much of what we have said about definition modules will not be relevant—so great attention must be given to the compiler manual (so as to work out the differences). Such compilers are becoming rarer, so this is unlikely to be a problem in practice.

Declare before use

All identifiers in Modula-2 programs must be declared. However, the declaration can textually follow the usage of the identifier. Consider the following:

```
MODULE Poor;

  MODULE What;
    IMPORT where;
  BEGIN
  END What;

TYPE where = CARDINAL;
BEGIN
END Poor.
```

The type where is declared in a position that textually follows the import statement in which it is used, but the local module What is still legal. This is because the scope of where spans the whole of the module Poor.

Unfortunately, 'single pass' compilers cannot process this code correctly (they will report a compile time error), therefore the practice should be avoided to ensure portability of programs. We strongly urge the use of a strict 'declare before use, by textual ordering' policy for maximum portability.

It should be noted that there are other, more complex problems of this kind (e.g. mutually importing local modules), and that all resultant portability problems will be avoided if you adopt our proposed policy. This issue is revisited in the *Portability Issues* section of Chapter 14 as it also applies to procedures.

Import from non-surrounding blocks into local modules

The rules concerning importation of identifiers from non-surrounding blocks into local modules will vary from compiler to compiler. Consider the following example:

```
IMPLEMENTATION MODULE A;
FROM PortIO IMPORT WriteCard;
IMPORT PortStrings;
CONST B = 42;
  MODULE Outer;
    (* first import list here*)
```

```
    MODULE Inner;
       (*second import list here*)
    END Inner;

  END Outer;
END A.
```

The positions of two import lists for the two (nested) local modules are illustrated by comments. Some compilers will allow statements of the form

```
FROM PortIO IMPORT WriteLn;
```

at either of these usual positions. Such an import reaches over module 'walls', whereas it is more normal for local module import statements simply to access identifiers visible in the immediately surrounding block. Under these circumstances, the module Outer could import the constant B, where the 'wall' created by Outer would prevent the module Inner from importing B. It is possible to produce code that certainly will not be portable by using nested local modules and import statements in the manner illustrated. We therefore recommend that you do not use nested local modules and confine imports to those identifiers available in the surrounding block.

Export closure rules

Export closure is a term coined[1] to cover the set of names of identifiers that are exported from a local module by any given statements. Some compilers permit several names (using dot qualification) to be used for the same exported identifier outside a local module. Consider the following examples:

(i)
```
MODULE M1;

   MODULE M2;
   EXPORT A;
   CONST A = 42;
   END M2;

   (* what names can be used here ? *)
END M1;
```

In this example, some compilers will allow reference to M2.A. For portability, it would be better to refer only to the more obviously legal name, A.

(ii)
```
MODULE M1;

   MODULE M2;
   EXPORT B;

      MODULE M3;
      EXPORT B;
      CONST B = 42;
      END M3;

   END M2;
```

---

[1]By Chuck Bilbe of Oregon Software, whom we gratefully acknowledge.

```
    . . .
    (* what names can be used here ? *)
    END M1;
```

In this example, some compilers will allow the following names to be used at the point indicated in M1:

```
B, M2.B, M2.M3.B
```

It is even possible that some compilers will allow reference to M3.B, but for portability we recommend that you only refer to B.

Topspeed Modula-2 does not allow reference to either M2.B or M3.B.

(iii)
```
    MODULE M1;

       MODULE M2;
       EXPORT M3;

          MODULE M3;
          EXPORT C;
          CONST C = 42;
          END M3;

       END M2;
       . . .
       (* what names can be used here ? *)
    END M1;
```

This example is similar to Example (ii), except that M2 exports the module name M3. We do not recommend the export of module names in portable programs, so we cannot recommend the best way to refer to C at the point indicated in M1.

Circular import lists

It is quite easy to construct circular import lists (where, for example, A imports B, which imports C, which imports A). This happens particularly with larger programs, and may give rise to portability problems. As was said earlier, compilers may be able to work out a valid order, but Professor Wirth's original language definition states:

> 'If circular references occur among modules, their order of intitialization is not defined.'

This has allowed compilers to produce different solutions, so every effort should be made to avoid circular reference in portable programs. It is not easy to propose alternative implementation strategies, particularly in large programs— but a reduction in program complexity (and a high degree of data encapsulation) will usually be needed.

Topspeed Modula-2 can resolve circular import lists: it initializes in an order starting with the last module in the circular reference list (before repetition occurs). Therefore, in the case of A importing B, B importing C, and C importing A, the initialization order would be C, then B, then A.

Initialization of modules

Although the initialization order of modules is well defined, there is one (rare) case when compilers can produce different initialization orders for the same program. This occurs when a module is imported into a definition module but is then not used in the corresponding implementation module. Some compilers do not initialize the imported module in such cases, but it is quite easy to check this by inserting a suitable output message in the body of the relevant module. For portability, and if initialization is needed (which will probably be rare), then this can be forced by adding suitable code to the implementation module that uses the imported module.

Nesting of procedure bodies in local modules

If a procedure is declared in a definition module, then the procedure body must be defined in the corresponding implementation module. Some compilers will permit this procedure body to be nested within a local module declared within the implementation module. This is obscure programming practice and should be avoided in portable programs.

Depth of nesting of local modules

The depth to which local modules can be nested is undoubtedly a portability issue, but we do not recommend that you do this at all.

Compilation of definition modules

Some compilers do not require that definition modules be compiled. Topspeed Modula-2 (and others) work this way: it is only necessary to compile implementation modules on such systems. This has no effect on the portability of programs, but obviously does affect how you develop programs when using such compilers.

Absent implementation modules

As mentioned in Chapter 8, some compilers allow you to write definition modules that have no corresponding implementation part. This is quite a useful facility when you wish simply to isolate constant declarations from your program module (thus no implementation part is needed). However, not all compilers allow this, but if necessary it is quite easy to comply with such a restriction, by writing a corresponding implementation module that is empty, consisting of only the module name and the key word END.

Topspeed Modula-2 does not allow absent implementation modules.

Implementing opaque types

Most implementations require that opaque types be fully declared in the implementation module corresponding to the definition module in which they were introduced. This unnecessarily precludes an implementation of an opaque type being in terms of an opaque type from another module. For example you might want to define a stack module using a general purpose sequence module:

```
DEFINITION MODULE SeqMod;
...
TYPE sequence;
PROCEDURE CreateSeq(VAR s: sequence);
...
END SeqMod.

DEFINITION MODULE StackMod;
...
TYPE stack;
...
END StackMod.

IMPLEMENTATION MODULE StackMod;
FROM SeqMod IMPORT sequence, CreateSeq ...
TYPE stack = sequence;
...
```

For the sake of portability it is best to avoid these designs.

13.11 REVIEW QUESTIONS AND EXERCISES

Q13.1 When are modules that are imported by a program module initialized?

Q13.2 How is a program terminated?

Q13.3 What are the terms for the two forms of the IMPORT statement?

Q13.4 Give examples of how to use these two types of import in a separate or program module; and show how they affect the use of imported identifiers in the importing module.

Q13.5 In what way is the use of the IMPORT statement different for local modules?

Q13.6 What is an opaque type and why would one be declared?

Q13.7 Of what types can opaque types be declared?

Q13.8 What type of modules make use of the EXPORT statement?

Q13.9 What is an EXPORT statement used for?

Q13.10 What is the lifetime of any module imported by a program module?

Q13.11 What is the lifetime of a local module?

Q13.12 Consider the situation where three programmers are working on the same program. Each programmer is working on a different module. Programmer John is working on module A, Programmer Martin is working on module B, which will be used by module A. Programmer Rob is working on module C, which makes use of module A—how can you stop programmer Rob seeing and having access to module B?

Q13.13 If the array value constructor is available in your implementation of Modula-2, how could you reduce the number of exportable procedures in the module PortStrings? (See Chapter 10 and Appendix 3 for details of the module PortStrings.)

Q13.14 Study the following program and its modules and predict its output when executed. Then test your prediction by compiling and executing it.

```
MODULE Life2;
IMPORT ST;
FROM PortIO IMPORT WriteString, WriteLn;
BEGIN
  WriteLn;
  WriteString('Starting to execute program Life2 ');
  WriteLn;
  WriteString('Calling procedure ST.Q '); WriteLn;
  ST.Q;
  WriteString('Program Life2 now finished. '); WriteLn;
END Life2.

DEFINITION MODULE ST;
PROCEDURE Q;
END ST.

IMPLEMENTATION MODULE ST;
FROM PortIO IMPORT
  WriteString, WriteLn, WriteInt, SetFieldWidth;
PROCEDURE Q;
  MODULE STM1;
  IMPORT WriteLn, WriteString;
  EXPORT I;
  VAR I : INTEGER;
  BEGIN
    WriteString('  Local module STM1 initialized ');
    WriteLn;
    I := 42;
  END STM1;
BEGIN (* procedure Q *)
  WriteString(' Procedure Q executed '); WriteLn;
  I := I + 1;
  WriteString(' The value of I is  ');
  SetFieldWidth(3);
  WriteInt(I); WriteLn;
END Q;
BEGIN (* main body of ST *)
  WriteString
    ('Starting to initialize ST, and calling Q twice');
  WriteLn;
  Q; Q;
  WriteString
    ('Implementation module ST is now initialized ');
  WriteLn;
END ST.
```

14 PROCEDURES

14.1 INTRODUCTION

A fundamental concept in the design of Modula-2 programs is the avoidance of unwieldy, monolithic programs, by subdividing a program into a number of smaller units. This is achieved by use of procedures and modules. This chapter deals with procedures; Chapter 13 deals with modules.

A procedure allows implementation of a section of code, which when invoked either returns a result or results, or causes some action to take place.

14.2 PROCEDURE DECLARATIONS

The complete syntax for procedure declarations is as follows (note: we will not need all of this yet, but the parts we do not need now will be explained later).

Syntax

procedure declaration = procedure heading, ";", block, procedure identifier;

procedure heading =
    "PROCEDURE", procedure identifier, [formal parameter list];

procedure identifier = identifier;

formal parameter list = "(", [formal parameters], ")", [function result];

formal parameters =
    formal parameter section, {";", formal parameter section};

formal parameter section = ["VAR"], identifier list, ":", formal type;

block = {declaration}, ["BEGIN", statement sequence], "END";

Declarations within a program module

A program module has two distinct sections, the first being the declaration part and the second being the main body of the module, which consists of a sequence of statements.

Procedure declarations are like all other declarations in that they precede the main body of the module in which they occur (denoted by the reserved word BEGIN), along with the data declarations.

Example

```
MODULE Calculations;
FROM PortIO IMPORT ReadCard, WriteCard;
VAR
  p, q, r : CARDINAL;

PROCEDURE Add(VAR a : CARDINAL; b, c : CARDINAL);
  BEGIN
    a := b + c
  END Add;

PROCEDURE Multiply(VAR a : CARDINAL; b, c : CARDINAL);
  BEGIN
    a := b * c
  END Multiply;

BEGIN (* main body *)
  p := ReadCard();
  q := ReadCard();
  Add(r, p, q);
  WriteCard(r);
  Multiply(r, p, q);
  WriteCard(r)
END Calculations.
```

The fact that the procedure declarations follow the VAR declaration in the above example is purely a matter of style. If the syntax for declarations is studied, it can be seen that the order of declarations is unimportant. Thus the order in which the two procedures Add and Multiply are declared in the above example is also unimportant. The procedure Multiply could have been declared prior to Add without affecting the compilation or execution of the program. The sequences of statements defined by the procedures Add and Multiply are only executed when the procedures are called from the main body of the program module. (See Chapter 15 on fine detail data declarations.)

Procedure activation

A procedure call has the status of a complete statement. When calling a procedure, the actual parameters are substituted for the formal parameters and the body of the procedure is executed. When the end of the procedure is reached, execution of the program is resumed from the statement immediately following the calling statement. The execution of a procedure body is terminated if a RETURN statement is encountered. Although this is only normally done in function procedures (see Section 14.4), RETURN statements can be used to provide multiple exit points from procedure bodies.

In the above examples, the actual parameter names are different from the formal parameter names given in the procedure declarations. In fact the actual parameters can be complex expressions or literal constants (in the case of parameters which take values into a procedure). What is important is that the actual parameters are of types which are parameter compatible with the formal parameters and that the parameter lists have the same number of parameters in the same order (see Section 14.3).

Declarations within procedures

Any declaration that is possible in a module is also possible in a procedure. Therefore identifiers may be declared within a procedure using the familiar CONST, TYPE, and VAR declarations. Similarly a procedure or a module may be declared from within a procedure. The objects denoted by these identifiers are said to be *local* to the procedure. An object that is local to a procedure is not visible to enclosing blocks, and therefore cannot be accessed from outside the procedure.

Examples

(i)
```
      PROCEDURE Swap(VAR a, b : CARDINAL);
        VAR
          Temp : CARDINAL;
        BEGIN
          Temp := a;
          a := b;
          b := Temp
        END Swap;
```

The variable Temp is an example of a local variable. It is invisible to the surrounding program module; its scope is said to be local to the procedure. (Further details of scope are given in Chapter 13.)

(ii)
```
      PROCEDURE Greater(VAR x, y : CARDINAL);
        PROCEDURE Swap(VAR a, b : CARDINAL);
          VAR
            Temp : CARDINAL;
          BEGIN
            Temp := a;
            a := b;
            b := Temp
          END Swap;
        BEGIN (* procedure body of Greater *)
          IF x > y THEN
            Swap(x, y)
```

```
      END
   END Greater;
```

The procedure `Swap` is said to be local to the procedure `Greater` and therefore invisible to the surrounding program module.

14.3   PROCEDURE PARAMETERS

When calling a procedure it is often necessary to pass data to that procedure in order that it might use that data to perform the task which it is designed to execute. Similarly a procedure may need to pass data back to the main program that represents the result of some task. The requirement for procedure input and output in this sense is met by passing values and variables as actual parameters to a procedure.

Consider the procedure `Add`:

```
PROCEDURE Add(VAR a : CARDINAL; b, c : CARDINAL);
   BEGIN
      a := b + c
   END add;
```

The formal input parameters to the procedure are b and c. These parameters are used to pass values to the procedure that it can use in its computation. The variable a is the output parameter which is assigned the result of adding the values b and c together.

Formal and actual parameters

The syntax for specifying formal parameters is:

> formal parameter list = "(", [formal parameters], ")", [function result];
>
> formal parameters =
>   formal parameter section, {";", formal parameter section};
>
> formal parameter section = ["VAR"], identifier list, ":", formal type;

Note that when specifying a formal parameter its type must also be given. This is to enable the compiler to check whether an associated actual parameter is of the correct type. The formal type part of the parameter section can only be a type name or an open array parameter. (Open array parameters are explained in Section 14.6.)

It is possible to have many parameter sections; separate parameter sections must be separated by semicolons. However, when calling a procedure, all actual parameters are separated by commas. Actual parameters may be identifiers, constants, or expressions (see below for the rules). Identifiers and expressions used as actual parameters must be evaluated at the point where the procedure call is made. The order in which this is done, when the actual parameter list contains more than one section, is implementation dependent. This is therefore a portability issue and is dealt with in Section 14.8. Despite this uncertainty about order, potential problems can be avoided by ensuring that actual parameter expression evaluation does not give rise to side-effects that modify other actual parameters.

VAR and value parameters

Names introduced in the formal parameter list of a procedure define new identifiers whose scope is local to the procedure body. When a procedure is called, the actual parameters are substituted for these formal parameters. However, Modula-2 provides two mechanisms for parameter substitution: which mechanism is used is dependent on whether the formal parameter has been declared as a *variable parameter* or a *value parameter*.

A variable parameter, or **VAR-parameter**, is one which must be used with a variable to take values into a procedure and to take values back from a procedure to its caller. In order to declare a parameter as a variable parameter, the reserved word VAR must precede the parameter's identifier.

When calling a procedure which has a VAR-parameter, the corresponding actual parameter must be a variable. Constants or expressions are not allowed.

Any parameter not declared using the VAR keyword is automatically a value parameter. There is no special keyword to denote a value parameter.

When calling a procedure that has value parameters, the corresponding actual parameters must be expressions (which can include variables, constants, or complex expressions).

When calling a procedure with value parameters, storage is allocated for the formal parameter, the actual parameter is evaluated, and a *copy* of the current value is assigned to the formal parameter, which is then regarded as a local variable. New values can be assigned to the formal parameter without affecting the value of the actual parameter, because the formal parameter holds only a *copy* of the actual parameter.

Formal and actual parameter compatibility

The formal parameter list of a procedure declaration constitutes a set of restrictions on the actual parameters that can be used when calling that procedure. These restrictions comprise a set of procedure compatibility rules:

* The number of actual parameters in a procedure call must match the number of parameters in the formal parameter list.

* Actual parameters are mapped onto formal parameters in the order they appear in the procedure call. Therefore, taken in sequence, each parameter in the actual parameter list must be of a type which is compatible with the parameter in the formal parameter section (see next two rules).

- If a formal parameter is declared as a VAR-parameter, then the associated actual parameter must be a variable of the same type (i.e. their types must be identical, see Chapter 16).

- If a formal parameter is declared as a value parameter, then the associated actual parameter must be an expression which is assignment compatible with that of the formal parameter (see Chapter 16).

When to use VAR and value parameters

Care must be taken when using parameters, in order that you avoid some unexpected results. Consider the following example:

```
MODULE Main;
VAR
  p, q : CARDINAL;
PROCEDURE Swap(a, b : CARDINAL);
  VAR
    Temp : CARDINAL;
  BEGIN
    Temp := a;
    a := b;
    b := Temp
  END Swap;
BEGIN
  p := 3;
  q := 6;
  Swap(p, q)
END Main.
```

Clearly, the procedure Swap does not carry out the required task.

Before the call to Swap, we know that p = 3 and q = 6. After calling Swap, three new storage locations are created for a, b, and Temp. Parameter a is assigned the current value of p, and b is assigned the current value of q. The procedure then swaps the values of a and b by making use of the variable Temp. However, when the procedure terminates, the storage locations associated with a, b, and Temp are lost, and since all association between the formal parameters and actual parameters is lost once the procedure call has completed, the variables p and q retain their original values.

If a parameter is to serve as both an input and output parameter, it must be declared as a VAR-parameter. A parameter that is only for output, must be a VAR-parameter. However, if a parameter is for input to a procedure only, then it should be declared as a value parameter. This is to ensure that the execution of the procedure does not unintentionally affect the values of objects in the main program.

When using value parameters, it must be kept in mind that since the formal parameter represents a local variable, storage will be needed for that variable. This could cause problems if the parameter type is a large array, due to the amount of storage that would be needed. Also, the time taken to copy a large array might not be justified, especially if not all the array is used or if the array is used infrequently inside the procedure. In cases like these it is recommended that the parameter is declared as a VAR-parameter, even if the parameter is used for input only. The need to do this should only occur rarely, when available storage is limited.

14.4 FUNCTION PROCEDURES

The previous sections have shown how a procedure can communicate the results of its computations to the outside program, either by the use of VAR-parameters or by altering the values of global variables (the latter is considered to be bad programming practice in most cases). A third method of communicating the result of a procedure call to the calling program is provided in Modula-2, in the form of function procedures. Function procedures are used in situations where it is necessary to process a number of values of a variety of types and to return a single value of a particular type.

Function procedure declarations

The syntax for function procedure declarations differs from that of proper procedures only in requiring a function result (shown as optional in the rules given in Section 14.2).

It is important to note that unlike normal procedures, function procedures must have a parameter section, even if the parameter section is empty and consists only of opening and closing brackets. The function results may be any qualified identifier. This means that both built-in simple types such as CHAR, BOOLEAN etc. and structured types such as arrays and records are allowed. This, however, is a portability issue (see Section 14.8).

One or more of the statements within the body of a function procedure must consist of a RETURN statement. This is frequently the last statement before the end of a procedure; its action is to cause the expression following RETURN to be evaluated and the resulting value to be passed back to the calling expression as the procedure's result.

Example

```
PROCEDURE AddUp(a, b : CARDINAL) : CARDINAL;
  BEGIN
    RETURN a + b
  END AddUp;
```

The type of the return expression must be assignment compatible with the function result (see Chapter 16).

The RETURN statement also serves to terminate the execution of a procedure (either a function procedure or a proper procedure).

Function procedures normally only take input parameters, which are therefore naturally programmed as value parameters. A function procedure should not access any variable that is outside the procedure. If a function procedure refrains from reading or writing to global variables and also refrains from making use of VAR-parameters, then the programmer can be confident that the function procedure will produce one, and only one, result. Failure to comply with these guidelines will produce what are known as side-effects (see below *Function procedures and side-effects*), the behaviour of programs with side-effects can be difficult to predict.

Calling function procedures

Function procedures do not have the status of a statement, they must appear as part of an expression.

Example

(using the declaration of AddUp in the last example)

```
VAR
  Answer, x, y : CARDINAL;
  ...
Answer := AddUp(5 * 2, 20 DIV 4);
```

When the assignment statement is executed, the values 10 (the result of evaluating 5 * 2) and 5 (the result of evaluating 20 DIV 4) are passed to the function procedure AddUp. Calling the AddUp function procedure returns the value 15, which is then assigned to the variable Answer.

Other acceptable function procedure calls would be:

```
Answer := AddUp(x, y);
Answer := AddUp(5, 6);
```

The result of a function procedure can be passed directly to another procedure if that procedure's corresponding formal parameter is a value parameter.

Function procedures and side-effects

A procedure can also access and modify variables which are not local to it. This is considered to be bad programming practice. A function should be designed to return a single value, via the RETURN statement; therefore there should be no need to alter the value of a non-local variable. Similarly any input to a function procedure should be by the means of value parameters and not non-local variables.

If the purpose of a procedure is to return more than one result, then a proper procedure should be written, using the mechanism of VAR-parameters, rather than writing a function procedure that accesses global variables.

Consider this function procedure, which contains a side-effect:

```
VAR Count, Answer, MyNumber : CARDINAL;

PROCEDURE BadDouble(ParamNum : CARDINAL) : CARDINAL;
  BEGIN
    Count := Count + 1;
    RETURN ParamNum + ParamNum
  END BadDouble;
```

The variable Count is not local to BadDouble and is being used to count how many times the procedure is used. However, given the following variable declarations, would the result of the following expressions be the same?

```
Answer := BadDouble(MyNumber) + Count;

Answer := Count + BadDouble(MyNumber);
```

The problem to address is what part of the right hand side of the assignment statement is evaluated first? Will operands be evaluated left to right or right to left? In the first statement, if the right hand side is evaluated left to right then the variable Count will have been incremented by one. In the second statement, if the evaluation of the operands is left to right, then Count will not have been incremented by one.

Although the order of evaluation is usually left to right in Modula-2 implementations, this is implementation dependent. Any program that relies on an implementation dependent aspect to guarantee a result would not be portable.

Similar side-effect problems arise if a function procedure is declared with VAR-parameters, in order to communicate more than one result to the calling program.

Consider this function procedure:

```
VAR Answer, MyNumber : CARDINAL;

PROCEDURE BadTwice(VAR Number : CARDINAL) : CARDINAL;
  VAR
    Temp : CARDINAL;
  BEGIN
    Temp := Number;
    Number := Number + 1;
    RETURN Temp + Temp
  END BadTwice;
```

Again, we can see that the following two statements will yield different values in answer if the order of evaluation of the expressions remains constant.

```
Answer := BadTwice(MyNumber) + MyNumber;

Answer := MyNumber + BadTwice(MyNumber);
```

14.5   PROCEDURE TYPES

In previous sections procedures have been regarded as being a convenient method of structuring a program into a number of definable subtasks that encapsulate part of an algorithm. The procedure declarations used so far in the book are actually constants of unique, anonymous procedure types. Modula-2 also provides a construct that allows the programmer to define explicitly procedure types and variables.

Procedure type and variable declarations

A procedure type may be declared wherever any other type may be declared. The declaration of a procedure type is very similar to that of procedure headings, the difference being that procedure and parameter identifiers are omitted (the parameter types are required).

Syntax

```
procedure type = "PROCEDURE", [formal parameter type list];
```

The procedure type declaration specifies the number and type of parameters and if the procedure type is to be of a function procedure type (in which case the type of the result must also be specified).

Examples

```
ProcType1 = PROCEDURE (REAL, REAL);
ProcType2 = PROCEDURE (VAR BOOLEAN, INTEGER);
ProcType3 = PROCEDURE (CARDINAL, CARDINAL) : CARDINAL;
ProcType4 = PROCEDURE (VAR ARRAY OF CHAR);
```

Modula-2 also provides one built-in procedure type, PROC, which is used for defining parameterless procedure types. PROC is predefined as:

```
TYPE PROC = PROCEDURE;
```

An example of a procedure type declaration using PROC:

```
TYPE
   ProcType5 = PROC;
```

The set of values defined by a procedure type are those procedures declared in scope which are *structurally compatible* with the procedure type. For a procedure to be compatible with a procedure type it must comply with set of procedure compatibility rules:

- The number of parameters a procedure has must match the number of parameters declared for the procedure type.

- If a parameter is declared in the procedure heading as a VAR-parameter, then the associated parameter of the procedure type must be a VAR-parameter of an identical type (see Chapter 16).

- If a parameter is declared in the procedure heading as a value parameter, then the associated parameter of the procedure type must be a value parameter of the same type.

- If a procedure is a function procedure with result type X, then the procedure type must also define a function procedure with result type X.

The procedure types declared above would be structurally compatible with the following procedure headings.

```
PROCEDURE Math1(a, b : REAL);                   (* ProcType1 *)
PROCEDURE Math2(a : REAL; b : REAL);            (* ProcType1 *)
PROCEDURE IsEven(VAR Res: BOOLEAN; a: INTEGER); (* ProcType2 *)
PROCEDURE Math3(a, b : CARDINAL).: CARDINAL;    (* ProcType3 *)
PROCEDURE Math4(a: CARDINAL;
                      b: CARDINAL) : CARDINAL;  (* ProcType3 *)
PROCEDURE GetString(VAR Str: ARRAY OF CHAR);    (* ProcType4 *)
```

Using procedure types and variables

The use of procedure types and variables is best illustrated with examples. First, a simple case:

```
TYPE
  ProcType = PROCEDURE(VAR CARDINAL, CARDINAL);
VAR
  ProcVar : ProcType;
  x, y : CARDINAL;

PROCEDURE Swap(VAR a, b : CARDINAL);
  VAR
    Temp : CARDINAL;
  BEGIN
    Temp := a;
    a := b;
    b := Temp
  END Swap;
```

Given the above declarations, the procedure Swap can be assigned to the procedure variable ProcVar, in the following manner:

```
ProcVar := Swap;
```

Note that no parameter lists are included when assigning a procedure to a procedure type.

The procedure variable which now contains the procedure Swap can be used to call Swap using the variable identifier.

```
ProcVar(x, y);
```

The same kind of thing can be done with function procedure types:

```
TYPE
  FuncProcType = PROCEDURE(CARDINAL, CARDINAL) : BOOLEAN;
VAR
```

```
Appraise : FuncProcType;
Answer : BOOLEAN;
x,y : CARDINAL;

PROCEDURE IsGreater(p, q : CARDINAL) : CARDINAL;
  BEGIN
    RETURN p > q
  END IsGreater;
```

Given the above declarations, the function procedure `IsGreater` can be assigned to the procedure variable `FuncProcVar`, in the following manner:

```
Appraise := IsGreater;
```

The procedure variable which now contains the function procedure `IsGreater` can be called in the normal manner:

```
Answer := Appraise(x, y);
```

Procedure types can be used in any situation where other types can be used. Therefore it is possible to use a procedure type as a formal parameter to a procedure.

Procedure types are commonly used to parameterize mathematical functions which are to be used by a procedure. The various functions can be written as Modula-2 function procedures and passed as a parameter when required.

Another important use is the encapsulation of different comparison criteria. For example, a sort procedure may be programmed to take a different comparison procedure for different ordering criteria. (See Example (ii), below.)

Examples

```
(i)     MODULE HappyDays;
        FROM PortIO IMPORT WriteString, WriteLn;
        TYPE
          DaysOfTheWeek = (Sun, Mon, Tue, Wed, Thu, Fri, Sat);
          Greeting = PROC;
          ArrayOfGreetings = ARRAY DaysOfTheWeek OF Greeting;
        VAR
          Day : DaysOfTheWeek;
          Platitudes : ArrayOfGreetings;
        PROCEDURE HelloSun;
          BEGIN
            WriteString("Good morning it's Sunday"); WriteLn
          END HelloSun;
        PROCEDURE HelloMon;
          BEGIN
            WriteString("Good morning it's Monday"); WriteLn
          END HelloMon;
        PROCEDURE HelloTue;
          BEGIN
            WriteString("Good morning it's Tuesday"); WriteLn
          END HelloTue;
        PROCEDURE HelloWed;
          BEGIN
```

```
      WriteString("Good morning it's Wednesday"); WriteLn
    END HelloWed;
PROCEDURE HelloThu;
    BEGIN
      WriteString("Good morning it's Thursday"); WriteLn
    END HelloThu;
PROCEDURE HelloFri;
    BEGIN
      WriteString("Good morning it's Friday"); WriteLn
    END HelloFri;
PROCEDURE HelloSat;
    BEGIN
      WriteString("Good morning it's Saturday"); WriteLn
    END HelloSat;
BEGIN
    Platitudes[Sun] := HelloSun;
    Platitudes[Mon] := HelloMon;
    Platitudes[Tue] := HelloTue;
    Platitudes[Wed] := HelloWed;
    Platitudes[Thu] := HelloThu;
    Platitudes[Fri] := HelloFri;
    Platitudes[Sat] := HelloSat;
    FOR Day := MIN(DaysOfTheWeek) TO MAX(DaysOfTheWeek) DO
      Platitudes[Day]
    END
END HappyDays.
```

This example illustrates the use of the built-in procedure PROC. A greeting is defined to be a type PROC: it has no parameters or result type. The array variable Platitudes is used to store the values of the procedure type Greeting.

The FOR statement in the body of HappyDays will call each procedure variable stored in the array named MyArray. The outcome of this will be a list of good-humoured messages.

```
(ii)     CONST
           MaxNameLength = 40;
           MaxProducts = 500;
         TYPES
           NameType = ARRAY [0..MaxNameLength-1] OF CHAR;
           ProductType = RECORD
                           Code: CARDINAL;
                           Name: NameType;
                           Price: REAL;
                           StockLevel: CARDINAL
                         END;
           ProductList = ARRAY [1..MaxProducts] OF ProductType;
           LessThan = PROCEDURE (ProductType, ProductType) : BOOLEAN;
         VAR
           List: ProductList;
         PROCEDURE Sort(VAR L: ProductList; Comparison: LessThan);
             (* not given here *)
           END Sort;
         PROCEDURE CodeLessThan(r1, r2: ProductType) : BOOLEAN;
           BEGIN
             RETURN r1.Code < r2.Code
```

```
            END CodeLessThan;
        PROCEDURE NameLessThan(r1, r2: ProductType) : BOOLEAN;
            BEGIN
                RETURN (PortStrings.Compare(r1.Name, r2.Name) =
                        PortStrings.less)
            END NameLessThan;
        PROCEDURE PriceLessThan(r1, r2: ProductType) : BOOLEAN;
            BEGIN
                RETURN r1.Price < r2.Price
            END PriceLessThan;
        PROCEDURE StockLessThan(r1, r2: ProductType): BOOLEAN;
            BEGIN
                RETURN r1.StockLevel < r2.StockLevel
            END StockLessThan;
        BEGIN
            WriteString('Sort by Code, Name, Price or Stock level? ');
            WriteLn;
            WriteString('Type C N P or S:');
            CASE
                'C': Sort(List, CodeLessThan)  |
                'N': Sort(List, NameLessThan)  |
                'P': Sort(List, PriceLessThan) |
                'S': Sort(List, StockLessThan)
            END;
            ...
```

The above example outlines how a single sort procedure can be used to sort an array of records using different fields for the purpose of ordering the values in the array. Thus, for example, the procedure PriceLessThan can be used to sort the product List according to price.

14.6   OPEN ARRAY PARAMETERS

Modula-2 does not have dynamically sizeable arrays (which feature in some other languages), but compensates with a method of passing different sized arrays of the same component types to common (or generic) procedures. This method uses open array parameters.

Syntax

```
formal parameter section = ["VAR"], identifier list, ":", formal type;
formal type = {"ARRAY", "OF"}, qualified identifier;
```

The important point about this syntax is that the formal parameter does not specify either an array index type, or the range of values that such an index type is constrained to. The component type of the array *is* specified, and it is this that allows a match to be made with actual parameters (which must be ordinary arrays, declared normally elsewhere in the program).

Example

```
PROCEDURE SendMessage(VAR in: ARRAY OF CHAR);
  VAR temp: CARDINAL;
  BEGIN
    FOR temp := 0 TO HIGH(in) DO
      WriteChar(in[temp]); WriteLn
    END
  END SendMessage;
```

This procedure accepts varying length arrays of characters as the open array parameter, then uses a local variable to index the array up to its maximum length (found using HIGH) whilst outputting it a character at a time. Open array indexing is described in Section 19.6.

Varying length arrays would be pretty useless if we could not find out how long they are. The built-in function procedure HIGH is provided to determine the length of open array parameters; it is more formally described in Section 23.10.

Actual open array parameters

An actual open array parameter must have a component type that is identical to the component type of the formal parameter. There is an exception to this rule, concerning open arrays of BYTE (and/or WORD, if one or the other is provided). This is dealt with in Chapter 25.

Example

```
TYPE
  charraytype = ARRAY [0..72] OF CHAR;
VAR
  Charray : charraytype;
BEGIN
  Charray := 'hello';
  SendMessage(Charray);
  ...
```

The above program fragment illustrates the use of an open array parameter to output an arbitrary message.

Use of open array parameters

Open array parameters are a powerful feature of Modula-2 which encourage the production of generic, reusable array processing procedures. However, there are no whole array operations defined for open arrays. Hence entire open arrays cannot be used in assignment statements (they must be assigned component by component). Further examples are given in Section 19.5.

14.7 PORTABILITY ISSUES

Regrettably, there are a great many portability issues concerning the use of procedures. This is due to a number of factors:

- changes in the language during its evolution;

- the difference between single-pass and multi-pass compilers;

- gaps in the original language definition (when compared with Pascal, for example);

- the level of error checking provided by different compilers (this is essentially a quality issue).

Forward declaration of procedures

Modula-2 is essentially a *multi-pass* language—from a compiler design standpoint. Usually a Modula-2 compiler must make multiple 'passes' over the source-code before it is translated into machine-code. However, some Modula-2 compilers (and Topspeed is an example of the type) manage to translate source-code in just one pass, by restricting the rules of the language in certain ways. Chief amongst these restrictions is a requirement to declare identifiers before use, and this has an impact on the use of procedures. Although the genuine need for it does not occur very often, Modula-2 allows two or more procedures to be mutually recursive—as illustrated by the following example:

```
PROCEDURE A;
  BEGIN
    B
  END A;
PROCEDURE B;
  BEGIN
    A
  END B;
```

As you can see, procedure B is called in procedure A, but B has not been declared at the point when a compiler first encounters its use. The solution that is commonly adopted by single-pass compilers is borrowed from Pascal: procedures such as B in the foregoing example must be declared using a *forward declaration*.

This results in the normal syntax for a procedure declaration being extended by a forward declaration option, as follows:

```
procedure declaration =
    procedure heading, ';', block, procedure identifier |
    forward declaration;
forward declaration = procedure heading, 'FORWARD';
```

The foregoing example would then be coded as follows:

```
PROCEDURE B; FORWARD;
PROCEDURE A;
  BEGIN
    B
  END A;
PROCEDURE B;
  BEGIN
    A
  END B;
```

If a procedure which has been declared using FORWARD has a parameter list (and/or a function result), these are given in the initial declaration (before the word FORWARD) and must be repeated in the heading where the procedure body is eventually defined.

The FORWARD directive is usually not supported by multi-pass Modula-2 compilers (it is not needed), and its use (and necessity) can be avoided with single-pass compilers if you do not use mutually recursive procedures, whose procedure headers do not appear in a definition module. There are other areas of the language where declare before use is a portability issue, these are dealt with in Chapters 13 and 15.

Parameter naming across definition and implementation modules

When a procedure is declared in a definition module (i.e. making it available for export to other modules) the corresponding implementation module must contain the definition of the body of the procedure. This body must be identified by a procedure header, so that the compiler can match and check the two components.

However, some Modula-2 compilers allow you to change the parameter list in the implementation module, and some programmers have taken advantage of this for various reasons. (The most often quoted of which is the use of two different natural languages, so that the definition module and actual parameter are in English, whereas the implementation module might use the natural spoken language of the programmer.)

If an implementation allows parameter names to change, the parameter name used in the definition module will not be known in the body of the procedure in the implementation module. Consider the following example:

```
DEFINITION MODULE Example;
PROCEDURE myproc(VAR inpar: INTEGER) : REAL;
END Example.

IMPLEMENTATION MODULE Example;
PROCEDURE myproc(VAR newname: INTEGER) : REAL;
  BEGIN
    RETURN FLOAT(newname);
  END myproc;
...
END Example.
```

The change of name (from inpar to newname) has no effect on the meaning of myproc, but some compilers will reject this renaming. These issues get more complex when the ordering (but not the names) of the parameter lists is altered, or when the form of parameter specification changes, as in the following examples:

```
PROCEDURE aproc(tom: INTEGER: dick: INTEGER; harry: INTEGER);
PROCEDURE aproc(tom, dick, harry: INTEGER);
```

It is very likely that the last two examples, if used in corresponding definition and implementation parts, would be rejected by most Modula-2 compilers.

Therefore, for maximum portability repeat parameter lists *exactly*.

Topspeed Modula-2 does not object to the renaming of formal parameters across definition and implementation modules.

Number of parameters allowed in procedure parameter lists

This is a quality issue; the number of parameters allowed in procedure parameter lists is implementation dependent, and will probably have a fixed upper limit in most Modula-2 compilers. Experiments have shown that most reasonable quality compilers will allow at least 15 parameters, the need for more than this is rare in practice.

Topspeed Modula-2 accepts test programs with 26 formal parameters in a procedure parameter list.

Failure to return a function result

Some Modula-2 compilers do not regard the failure to return the function's result within a function procedure as an error. This can arise in two ways: either no RETURN statement is called at all, or the RETURN is protected by some conditional statement that is never satisfied, as is possible in the following example if flag is FALSE:

```
PROCEDURE myfunc() : REAL;
  BEGIN
    IF flag = TRUE THEN RETURN 0.1;
  END myfunc;
```

This is only a portability issue in the sense that a false sense of security can be obtained if you believe that Modula-2 compilers always check this for you. Without the check, an undefined value will probably be returned from an unassigned function result—with unpredictable consequences.

Topspeed Modula-2 reports a run-time exception when no function result is returned, and also gives a compile-time error if no RETURN statement is used to produce a function result.

Use of bad actual VAR-parameters

It is possible to supply an actual VAR-parameter in a procedure call statement that is syntactically correct but nevertheless a bad thing to do. The worst case is the use of an inactive field of a variant record as an actual parameter, as in the following example:

```
TYPE
   GENDER = (Male, Female);
VAR
   myrec : RECORD
              CASE Sex : Gender OF
                 Male :
                    Name : NameType; |
                 Female :
                    Name : NameType;
                    HasChildren: BOOLEAN;
              END;
           END;
BEGIN
   myrec.Sex := Male;
   myproc(myrec.HasChildren);
```

If the procedure myproc has a formal parameter of type BOOLEAN, then the foregoing is syntactically legal—but meaningless. Most Modula-2 compilers will not check for this error at either compile-time or run-time.

Topspeed Modula-2 does not catch this use of bad actual VAR-parameters.

Multi-dimensional open array parameters

Whilst all Modula-2 compilers will accept single-dimension open array parameters, since these are fundamental, not all will accept multi-dimensional open array parameters. Multi-dimensional open array parameters have appeared in implementations as a language extension. It is not clear whether they will become a part of the official Modula-2 standard; therefore, to maximize portability of code do not use them, even if they are provided by your implementation.

Topspeed Modula-2 does not allow multi-dimensional open array parameters.

The use of HIGH on formal parameters

The intended use for HIGH is with formal open array parameters only. However, some compilers allow HIGH to be used on ordinary formal array parameters—although this does not add great functionality (since their maximum index is declared and static). For maximum portability use of this feature should be avoided.

A further problem arises with the result type of HIGH. Where compilers have provided extended data types (such as LONGINT and LONGCARD), they have found it necessary to change the result type of HIGH to the largest whole number data type available. However, if this gives rise to type compatibility problems, at least they will be reported at compile-time. (See Chapter 23 for more details.)

VAR-parameter compatibility rules

Professor Wirth changed his mind about VAR-parameter compatibility rules between editions 2 and 3 of *Programming in Modula-2*. Originally, only expression compatibility was required, but the newer rule is tougher and requires formal and actual VAR-parameters to have identical types. Older compilers may implement the older, less strict rule. The following example illustrates the point:

```
TYPE
  range = [0..42];
VAR
  a1 : range;
PROCEDURE test(VAR formal : CARDINAL);
...
  test(a1);   (* OK before, now illegal *)
```

Order of evaluation of actual parameter lists

The order of evaluation of actual parameter lists at the point of a procedure call is implementation dependent, and could therefore occur in any order. You cannot even rely on a particular compiler consistently employing an order; it could vary for the same compiler for similar looking procedure calls. Problems arise when the same identifier appears in expressions used as an actual parameter in the same parameter list, as in the following example:

```
myproc(x, fiddle(x));
```

If the function fiddle modifies the value of x as a side-effect, then the order in which x and fiddle(x) are evaluated could make a difference to the value of the parameters that are passed to myproc.

The best way of preventing such potential problems is to avoid the use of functions with side-effects, and—where possible—avoid the use of the same identifier in several positions in the same actual parameter list.

Topspeed Modula-2 may evaluate parameter lists in any order, depending upon circumstances.

Relational operators on procedure types

Some compilers allow relational operators, such as = (equals) and <> (not equal) to be applied to procedure types. This language extension has not yet become sufficiently common to be recommended for portable programs.

Nesting of procedures

The depth to which procedures may be nested within one another is implementation dependent. Modula-2 compilers will normally allow procedures to be nested at least 15 deep; the need for a greater depth of nesting than this rarely arises.

Structured types as function results

Some compilers will not allow function procedures to return structured types such as arrays and records. Therefore, in the interests of portability, if your compiler does allow this facility, do not use it; instead have your function procedure return a pointer to a structured type, which all compilers allow.

14.8 REVIEW QUESTIONS AND EXERCISES

Q14.1 How is a procedure terminated?

Q14.2 What is the scope of a procedure's formal parameters?

Q14.3 What are the compatibility rules for formal and actual parameters?

Q14.4 Write the declaration for a procedure type that will search an array of cardinal numbers for a particular value and will return a Boolean value depending on the result of the search.

Q14.5 Consider the following program.

```
MODULE Main;
VAR
  p, q: CARDINAL;
PROCEDURE Add(a, b: CARDINAL);
  BEGIN
    a := a + b
  END Add;
BEGIN
  p := 2;
  q := 4;
  Add(p, q)
END Main.
```

What is the value of p, after the call of Add? Explain why p has this value. How should the procedure Add be declared?

Q14.6 Why would a single-pass compiler not accept the following procedure declarations?

```
MODULE Fickle;
FROM PortIO IMPORT WriteString,WriteLn;
CONST
  NoOfPetals = 11;
PROCEDURE LovesMe(I : CARDINAL);
  BEGIN
    WHILE I <> DO
      WriteString('She Loves Me'); WriteLn;
      LovesMeNot(I-1); (* Call before procedure is declared *)
    END;
  END LoveMe;
```

```
PROCEDURE LovesMeNot(I : CARDINAL);
  BEGIN
    WHILE I <> DO
      WriteString('She Loves Me Not'); WriteLn;
      LovesMe(I-1);
    END;
  END LovesMeNot;
BEGIN
  LovesMe(NoOfPetals);
END Fickle.
```

How could the above procedure declarations be altered for a single-pass compiler?

15 DATA DECLARATIONS

15.1 INTRODUCTION

Modula-2 requires all identifiers to be declared in order that they may be used in programs, modules, or procedures. While this is mostly straightforward, there are aspects of declaring identifiers relating to data constants, types, and variables which warrant a short chapter. This chapter formally describes the declaration of types, variables, and constants. The declaration of modules and procedures is dealt with in Chapters 13 and 14, respectively.

15.2 TYPES

Modula-2 is said to be a strongly typed language, since all variables and values must have a type. The type of a variable establishes the set of values that it may take; the type of a constant establishes the context within which it can be used within a program. A type identifier can be declared independently of any variables or constants, as a basic building block for the declaration of other type identifiers. Note that for two identifiers to denote an identical type, they must be defined in terms of a common identifier (see Chapter 16).

Syntax

```
type declaration = identifier, "=", type;
type =
    qualified identifier | enumeration | subrange type | array type |
    record type | set type | pointer type | procedure type;
```

In general, an identifier must be declared textually before it is used on the right hand side of a type declaration. The main exception to this rule is pointer types, but there is also a portability aspect of the declare-before-use rule—see *Portability Issues* at the end of this chapter.

Example

```
TYPE
   doubleword = [0..31];
   anarraytype = ARRAY [0..255] OF doubleword;
   anotherarray = ARRAY [0..255] OF doubleword;
   zarray = anarraytype;
   ptrtype = POINTER TO node;
   node = RECORD
            data: doubleword;
            next: ptrtype;
          END;
```

The last two declarations illustrate the relaxation of the declare-before-use rule in the case of pointers, which are dealt with more fully in Chapter 22. The other declarations are conventional ones, although the three array declarations are given to illustrate the dangers of confusing structural equivalence with type equivalence. The types anarraytype and zarray are identical, but anotherarray is not identical (nor compatible) with the other two, despite having the same index and component types (see Chapter 16).

Declaring subrange types

Subrange types are said to have a *host* type. For whole number subranges, the host type is either INTEGER or CARDINAL, depending upon the range of values declared. Therefore, in the following example:

```
TYPE
   Intrangetype = [-7..+7];
   Cardrangetype = [0..15];
```

we can say that the host type of Intrangetype is INTEGER and the host type of Cardrangetype is CARDINAL.

It is possible to declare a subrange of a subrange, and we must use the notion of *range types* to cover this.

Example

```
TYPE
   rtype = [0..alpha];
   srtype = rtype[0..beta];
```

In this example, rtype is the range type of srtype and CARDINAL is the host type of both types. The use of the rtype type identifier on the right hand side of the srtype declaration enforces a compile-time check that beta is less than or equal to alpha (it is assumed that alpha and beta are declared elsewhere). The use of range types is also a portability issue (see Section 15.5).

The range type syntax may also be used to force the host type of a whole number subrange to be of type INTEGER, when it would otherwise default to CARDINAL, as in the following example:

```
TYPE myint = INTEGER[1..99];
```

This use of a range type identifier in the declaration of a subrange ensures that myint is a subrange of INTEGER and so expression compatible with INTEGER. Hence variables of type myint and of type INTEGER may be combined in an expression.

15.3 VARIABLES

Variables are storage locations whose values change during the execution of the program. A variable is defined by declaring an identifier which denotes it. Variables must have an associated type, which determines the values they may take, what operators and built-in procedures apply, and the size of storage required for them.

Syntax

```
variable declaration = variable identifier list, ":", type ;
variable identifier list =
    identifier, ["[", address,"]"], {",", identifier, "[", [address], "]" };
address =
    ? Implementation defined..
    For Topspeed Modula-2  address is defined as:
    cardinal constant expression, ":", cardinal constant expression?;
```

On non-virtual memory systems, it can sometimes be convenient to specify the storage location of a variable and so the (non-portable) address constructor may be provided by the compiler. (See *Portability Issues* at the end of this chapter.)

Examples of variable declarations are:

```
VAR
  myint : INTEGER;
  myarray : ARRAY [0..7] OF [0..7];
```

The first example is a straightforward declaration of an INTEGER variable, but the second (although perfectly legal) illustrates the poor programming practice of using anonymous types. Neither the index range nor the array component type have a type name, and, as we shall see later, this can cause problems. It would be only slightly better to declare the latter example as follows:

```
TYPE
  smallrange = [0..7];
VAR
  myarray : ARRAY smallrange OF smallrange;
```

However, it still would not be possible to pass `myarray` as an actual VAR-parameter, unless it corresponded to a formal parameter of type `ARRAY OF Smallrange`. This is because no type name would have been available to use as the type of a formal parameter. Declaring an identifier to denote the array type is by far the best approach.

Anonymously typed variables may only be used as actual VAR-parameters if the corresponding formal parameter is an open array parameter (or is of either of the types `BYTE` or `WORD`), since no type name is available to use as the formal parameter in the procedure declaration.

Just as with type declarations, it is possible to use a range type qualifier on the right hand side of a variable declaration.

Examples

(i)
```
FROM somemod IMPORT limit;
TYPE
   smallsub = [0..31];
VAR
   newsub : smallsub[0..limit];
```

(ii)
```
VAR
   smallrange : INTEGER[0..99];
```

The first example causes a check to be done in the VAR declaration, that the limit is less than or equal to 31. The second example shows how to ensure that `smallrange` is of type `INTEGER` (rather than defaulting to `CARDINAL`).

15.4 CONSTANTS

A constant is an identifier whose value does not change during the execution of a program. Constant identifiers are used to simplify reference to such unchanging values.

Syntax

```
constant declaration = "CONST" , { constant declaration list } ;
constant declaration list = constant name, "=", constant, ";" ;
```

This simple form of syntax just associates a value with an identifier. The value associated can be a literal constant (e.g. `42`, `5.0`, etc.) or another constant identifier that has already been declared. The full syntax is given in the next subsection.

Example

```
CONST
   Pi = 3.14595;
   DefaultMessage = 'Hello World';
```

Constant expression declarations

There is one additional refinement of constant declarations: the ability to declare constants as an expression of constant values. This facility is provided to enable programmers to make their programs more readable (i.e. self-documenting and without an excessive number of comment statements) and to allow the compiler to generate and store the values at compile time.

Syntax

```
constant declaration =
   identifier, "=", (constant expression | constant identifier);
constant expression = expression;
expression = simple expression, [relation, simple expression];
```

In this syntax, the term *relation* is any of the permitted relational or mathematical operators of Modula-2 (see Chapter 16). The use of the non-terminal *simple expression* also permits the use of built-in functions (see Chapter 23) and theoretically also permits the use of imported functions—but this is a portability issue (see Section 15.5).

Example

```
FROM AMod IMPORT BigArray;
CONST
   SafeLimit = MAX(CARDINAL) - 1;
   SpaceNeeded = SIZE(BigArray);
```

Literal constants

Nearly all literal constants are of the conceptual types $\mathbb{Z}$, $\mathbb{R}$, and $\mathbb{S}$ (see Chapter 16). The declaration of identifiers as literal constants allows them to be used in a natural manner without worrying too much about whether literal 5 is of type CARDINAL or INTEGER. The type compatibility rules for the conceptual types $\mathbb{Z}$, $\mathbb{R}$, and $\mathbb{S}$ are given in Section 16.2.

Note that one form of literal does not belong to a conceptual type: the character number literal (consisting of an octal number followed by a C) denotes values of the type CHAR. Thus 101C and 'A' both denote the same value in the type CHAR,[1] but the former may not be assigned to a string variable.

Structured constants

One form of structured constant declaration is permitted in Modula-2, to cover the construction of constants of a set type (see Chapter 21). With the possible exception of BITSET (which is either pervasive or can be imported from SYSTEM), all set constant declarations must be preceded by an appropriate set type declaration.

The following examples illustrate the use of set constant declaration:

(i)
```
CONST
   SetVal1 = BITSET{0, 1, 2, 3, 4};
```

(ii)
```
TYPE
   Small = [0..3];
   MySet = SET OF Small;
CONST
   SetVal2 = Myset{0, 1, 2, 3};
```

The first example uses the fact that BITSET is predefined (or imported), the second utilizes the previous type declarations.

15.5   PORTABILITY ISSUES

There are a number of portability issues concerning data declarations. The most severe of these is the forward declaration restriction (see below).

Forward declaration

As we have said, there is a portability issue associated with the general declare-before-use rule. Some Modula-2 compilers are constructed such that they process the source code of a module in just one pass. These single-pass compilers do not allow the use of identifiers which have not been declared in the preceding text.

Consider the following example:

```
MODULE Multipass;
(* could declare globaltype here*)
PROCEDURE myproc;
  VAR local : globaltype;
  BEGIN
    local := ...
  END myproc;

TYPE
  globaltype = [1..99];
...
```

---

[1]This equivalence is true when CHAR is implemented as the ASCII set, but may not be true for other implementations of CHAR.

In this case, the type `globaltype` is in the block surrounding the procedure `myproc`, and so the `local` variable in `myproc` can be declared as of that type. A single-pass compiler will not be able to process this code properly, and it will usually fail to compile it. The text could be reordered to declare `globaltype` at the earlier point indicated in the example. This strict textual ordering of the declare-before-use rule is strongly recommended for portable programs.

Topspeed Modula-2 is a single-pass compiler, and will reject the foregoing example.

Structured value constructors

Some Modula-2 compilers have extended the structured constant syntax available for sets to include arrays and records. This extended syntax allows the assignment of initial values to some or all of the elements of an array variable or the fields of a record variable, in the declaration. Although an attractive feature and one which foreshadows structured value constructors for standard Modula-2, it is not yet implemented sufficiently widely to be recommended for portable programs. There are variations in the syntax and other rules for this extension. (See Sections 19.8 and 20.5 for examples.)

Topspeed Modula-2 does not implement this extension fully, but does provide structured constant constructors for arrays and records (called 'aggregates').

Address constructors

Some Modula-2 compilers provide a facility to specify the address of a variable in its declaration. This can be used in a system-specific manner to fix the location of a variable, or to associate a variable with a particular system address (that perhaps has meaning outside the scope of a Modula-2 program). As this facility is system specific, it cannot be used in portable programs. Topspeed Modula-2 does provide this facility. See Chapter 25 for an example.

Range types in subrange declarations

Not all compilers allow the specification of a range type in a subrange declaration, so the examples given at the end of Section 15.2 could be rejected at compile-time by some implementations. Since this is a compile-time issue, it is usually possible to get around the problem fairly easily, so we do not recommend the abandonment of the use of range types. Some compilers allow a half-way house—only permitting pervasive types as range types (e.g. `INTEGER`, or `CARDINAL`) but not permitting programmer-defined types as range types.

Topspeed Modula-2 does allow range types in a subrange declaration.

The use of functions in constant expression declarations

Declarations involving constant expressions can contain functions whose arguments are themselves constant expressions, as in the following example:

```
CONST aval = ORD('A');
```

However, most implementations restrict the use of functions in data declarations to the built-in function procedures (e.g. ORD, CHR, CAP) but not all of these will be permitted. It is possible that an implementation would allow functions exported from system modules (e.g. TSIZE) to be in data declarations; this facility can only be regarded as an unportable extension.

15.6   REVIEW QUESTIONS AND EXERCISES

Q15.1 A rectangle has length 5 inches and width 2 inches. Declare a constant named Area to denote the area of the rectangle. Declare any other constants that you might need.

Q15.2 Although the following declaration is syntactically and semantically correct, what is wrong with it stylistically? How could the declaration be improved?

```
VAR time : RECORD
                 Hours   : [0..24];
                 Minutes : [0..60];
                 Seconds : [0..60]
              END;
```

Q15.3 In what way are the following declarations incorrect? How should the declarations be written?

```
TYPE
   ArrayType = ARRAY Index OF CARDINAL;
   Index = [0..99];
```

Q15.4 Are the following declarations incorrect?

```
TYPE
   VolPtr = POINTER TO VolRec;
   VolRec = RECORD
                 Height, Width, Depth: REAL;
              END;
```

16 EXPRESSIONS, TYPES, AND TYPE COMPATIBILITY

16.1 INTRODUCTION

Modula-2 is a strongly typed language. It can thus assist the programmer by checking the validity of using certain values (of some type) in particular contexts. Modula-2 requires the programmer to specify the type of each variable, and from context can determine the type of each value; with this knowledge, Modula-2 can check for valid type usage. For the most part, the occurrence of mixed types (for which checks on valid usage are required) is most evident in expressions. This is the reason for dealing with expressions, types, and type compatibility in the same chapter.

16.2 CLASSIFICATION OF TYPES

When discussing type compatibility it is helpful to have a vocabulary which adequately describes the essential differences between types. The classification which follows has been devised specifically for describing types in Modula-2, and is not generally applicable.

The first division of types is between the structured types (array and record types) and the elementary types. The *structured types* permit component values to be selected. The elementary types are mostly single-valued; the exception—set types—do not allow the selection of individual component values, and hence they are not classed as structured types. The following diagram summarizes the type classification.

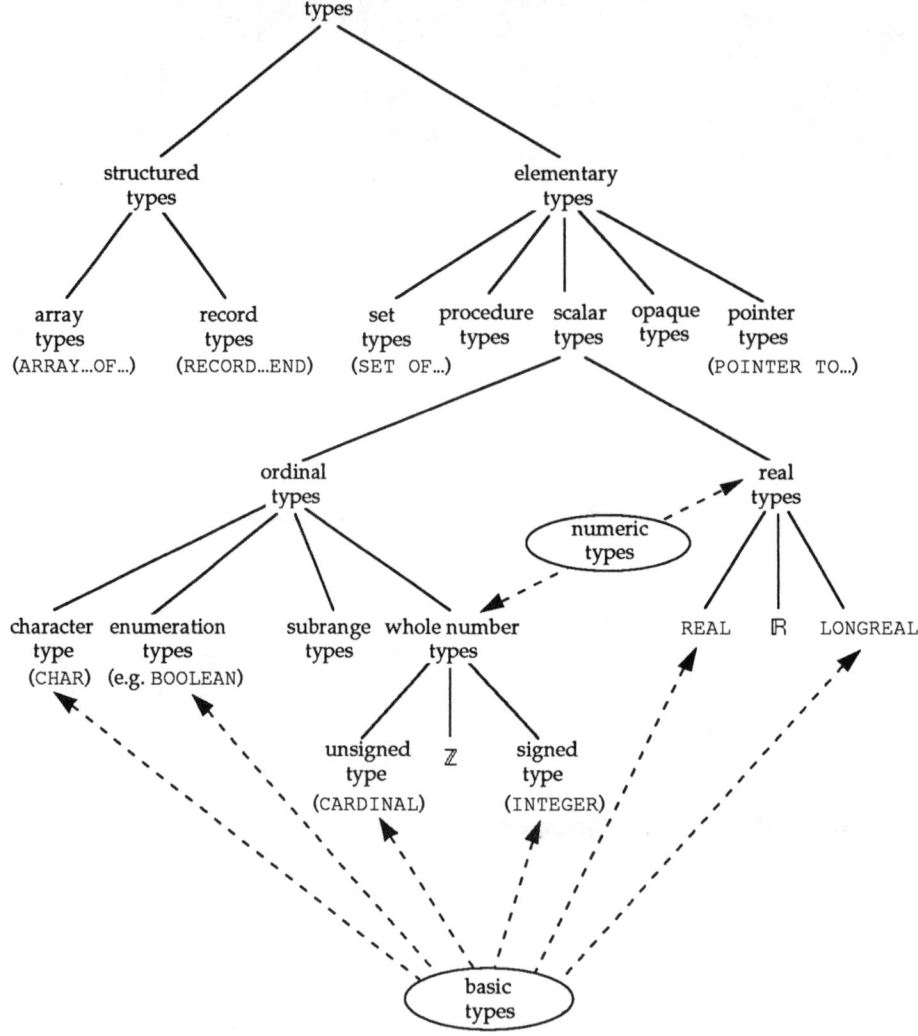

The *elementary types* comprise the pointer types, opaque types, procedure types, set types, and scalar types. The latter contains the real types and those which map to the whole numbers—the ordinal types.

The *real types* are REAL, LONGREAL, and the conceptual type ℝ.

The *ordinal types* include the whole number types (CARDINAL, INTEGER, and the conceptual type ℤ), the character type (CHAR), enumeration types, and subranges of all of these.

Note that the *conceptual type* 𝕊 is not shown in the diagram since it represents character sequences which must be realized with single CHAR variables or arrays of CHAR.

The conceptual types have been devised in order to regularize the type compatibility rules as follows:

- $\mathbb{Z}$ allows constant values (or the result of some built-in procedures) to be expression compatible with INTEGER and CARDINAL;

- $\mathbb{R}$ allows constant values to be expression compatible with REAL and LONGREAL;

- $\mathbb{S}$ allows single-character constants to be expression compatible with CHAR and all string constants to be assignment compatible with concrete string types (as defined in Chapter 10).

The classification serves to summarize certain properties of types (e.g. if component values may be selected) and to indicate logical relationships between types. The latter aspect is exemplified by the ordinal type: these types are ordered and map onto the mathematical set of integers; they can all be used with ORD, INC, DEC, MIN, and MAX. However, the relationships do not form a strict hierarchy. The numeric types, for example, are *scalar types*, but real types are not ordinal. Also, a subrange type need only be ordinal, and is not necessarily numeric.

The term *basic type* is used to describe the types BOOLEAN, CHAR, CARDINAL, INTEGER, REAL, and LONGREAL.

Note that a type does not need to be explicitly identified (although it is generally held to be good practice to do so). Thus, the type of the variable Coordinates in the example below belongs to the class of record types. The actual type given in the variable declaration has no name, and so is termed an anonymous type.

```
VAR
   Coordinates: RECORD
                   x, y: INTEGER
                END;
```

Anonymous types are considered to be unique, and so variables may only share an anonymous type if they appear in the same declaration. (See example of identical types, below.)

Four other relationships between types are relevant. The first is between types which are identical. Two types t1 and t2 are said to be *identical* only if one of the following statements is true.

- within the scope of t1, t2 has been defined as t2 = t1;

- within the scope of t2, t1 has been defined as t1 = t2;

- within the scope of another type t3, t1 is identical to t3 *and* t2 is identical to t3.

For example, in the following, Sequence, InputList, and ListType are identical. However, Stream is *not* identical to any of the others; it just happens to have the same structure.

```
TYPE
  ListType = ARRAY [0..500] OF item;
...
TYPE
  Sequence = ListType;
  InputList = ListType;
  Stream = ARRAY [0..500] OF item;
```

The second relationship is that which relates a subrange type to a *host type*.[1] The host type of a subrange type is the (ordinal) type on which it is ultimately based. Thus, for numeric subrange types their host types will be either the unsigned whole number type (i.e. CARDINAL) or the signed whole number type (i.e. INTEGER). For character subranges the host type will be CHAR; the host type of an enumeration subrange is the enumeration type.

An ordinal type which is not a subrange is its own host type. Note that if a subrange is preceded by a range type identifier (see Example (iii) below) the host type of the subrange is the host type of the range type. (There is a temptation to think that the range type is the host type, but a host type cannot be a subrange type.)

The third relationship between types is that which associates a set type with its *base type*. The base type of a set is the ordinal type (often a subrange) from which the set type is constructed. A set type defines the powerset of the values of its base type (see Chapter 21).

Base types are often restricted by Modula-2 implementations: either the number of values in a base type may be constrained by a small maximum (e.g. 16) and/or the minimum ordinal value of the base type may have to be zero. (This is a portability issue; see Chapter 21.)

(The base type of a set is relevant to the compatibility rules concerning the set type IN operator and the built-in procedures INCL and EXCL; see Chapter 21.)

The final relationship is between procedure types and is known as *structural equivalence*. At a crude level, this means that the types of the formal parameters of one procedure match those of another, and that they both be proper procedures, or both be function procedures. However, structural equivalence does not simply mean that the parameter lists of two procedures are the same: there may be a different number of parameter sections in each, with the procedure which has the fewer sections declaring more than one formal parameter per section. Thus, for example, p and q are structurally equivalent:

```
PROCEDURE p(a: REAL; b: REAL; VAR c, d: LONGREAL);
...
PROCEDURE q (x, y: REAL; VAR s: LONGREAL; VAR t: LONGREAL);
...
```

---

[1] In his books Professor Wirth uses 'base type' for what we describe as a 'host type'. Not only does this cause confusion with the type from which set types are constructed, but it is out of keeping with the terminology established for standard Pascal. Hence, we use 'host type'.

In essence, to decide if two procedures are structurally equivalent, you should rewrite the parameter sections of the procedures in full. For the above example, this would result in two REAL value parameters followed by two LONGREAL VAR-parameters. See Section 14.6 for full details of procedure types.

Examples

(i)
```
TYPE
    Grade = [1..5];
    MenuChoices = ['A'..'E'];
    SettingRange = [-10..15];
```

In the above the host type of Grade is CARDINAL, the host type of MenuChoices is CHAR, and the host type of SettingRange is INTEGER. (See Chapter 15 on how the host type of whole number subranges is decided.)

(ii)
```
TYPE
    BloodGroup = (OPos,ONeg,APos,ANeg,BPos,BNeg,ABPos,ABNeg);
    ABGroup = [APos..ABNeg];
CONST
    first = APos; last = ANeg;
TYPE
    AGroup = ABGroup [first..last];
```

In this example, the range type ABGroup is used to ensure (during compilation) that the limits of AGroup are in the range [APos..ANeg]. The host type of AGroup is the host type of ABGroup—i.e. BloodGroup.

(iii)
```
TYPE
    AlphaSet = SET OF ['A'..'Z'];
    LetterSet = SET OF ['A'..'Z'];
```

Although both AlphaSet and LetterSet are sets which may contain the same values of the same base type (the subrange ['A'..'Z']), they are not identical and so values of these different types cannot, for example, be directly compared (see *Expression compatibility*, below).

16.3 EXPRESSIONS

An expression is a specification of a computation which generates a value of a given type. The computation is expressed in terms of combining values, called **operands**, with **operators** which produce new values. Operands may themselves be expressions, constants, or references to values stored in variables, as shown by the syntax rules for expressions.

Syntax

```
expression = simple expression, [relation, simple expression];
simple expression = ["+" | "-"], term, {add operator, term};

term = factor, {multiply operator, factor};
factor =
    numeric literal | string literal | "(", expression, ")" | not operator, factor |
    designator, [actual parameters] | value constructor;
```

The above syntax rules do not exclude many illegal combinations of operands and operator; for information on applicability see *Operators* subsection below, and the rules of expression compatibility that determine allowable combinations of operands.

Operands

The *factors* in the syntax rules for expressions are usually known as operands. Their syntax is given here, followed by a discussion on the more complex operands.

Syntax

```
numeric literal = whole number literal | real number literal;

whole number literal =
    digit, {digit} | octal digit, {octal digit}, "B" | digit, {hex digit}, "H";

real number literal = digit, {digit}, ".", {digit}, [scale factor];
scale factor = "E", ["+" | "-"], digit, {digit};

string literal =
    ' " ', {character -' " '}, ' " ' | " ' ", {character - " ' "}," ' " |
    character number literal;
character number literal = octal digit, {octal digit}, "C";

designator =
    qualified identifier, {".", identifier | "[", expression list, "]" | "^" };

value constructor =
    array constructor | record constructor | set constructor;
```

The most complex expressions are often those which include a designator which specifies the value of a structured variable's component. Consider the following expression:

```
a[i] + 1
```

This specifies a whole number value which is 1 greater than the value of the ith component of the array a. The 1 is a whole number literal; the a[i] is a designator. Another example of a complex designator value is:

```
ModName.RecName.Field^(b[0])
```

If ModName is a module identifier and if RecName is a record identifier, then ModName.RecName is a qualified identifier and Field is the name of a field in RecName. Also, Field must be a pointer variable which points to a dynamic variable of a procedure type: the ^ dereferences the field and the parentheses indicate that the value of the referenced variable is a procedure. The latter's parameter is the value b[0]. Fortunately, such complex designators are not too common. Literal values are however, common. The following table gives some examples, and includes their syntactic class and type.

Syntactic class	Examples	Type
whole number literal	0, 64, 3726	$\mathbb{Z}$
whole number literal (octal)	177B, 266B	$\mathbb{Z}$
whole number literal(hex)	077FH, 0HFFH	$\mathbb{Z}$
real number literal	1.236784219	$\mathbb{R}$
real number literal (scale factor +3.0)	0.2666E+3.0	$\mathbb{R}$
string literal	"Gone away"	$\mathbb{S}$
character number literal	0C	CHAR

Note that all literal values, except character number literals, belong to one of the conceptual types—$\mathbb{Z}$, $\mathbb{R}$, or $\mathbb{S}$. This is in order to ease the compatibility rules, which are given below.

Finally, it is worth pointing out that the forthcoming Modula-2 standard has proposed three classes of value constructors. These are: array value constructors, record value constructors, and set value constructors. (See Chapters 19, 20, and 21, respectively.) Most compilers currently provide only the set value constructor. However, if the array constructor is provided, it should be noted that its syntax demands that the array type be specified; this means that concrete string values may be constructed which are *not* of the type $\mathbb{S}$ but which are of a specified array type. Consequently, assignment compatibility of these values demands that they be of an identical type to a variable or formal parameter.

Operators

The syntax for the relational and other operators referred to in the syntax of expressions is given below.

Syntax

```
add operator = "+" | "-" | "OR";
multiply operator = "*" | "/" | "DIV" | "MOD" | "REM"| and operator;
not operator = "NOT" | "~" ;
and operator =  "AND" | "&" ;
not equal = "<>" | "#" ;
relation = "=" | not equal  | "<" | "<= " | ">" | ">=" | "IN";
```

The table below lists the Modula-2 operators. Note that many symbols are used as several *different* operators. For example, + is used for the addition operator in both the real and whole number types, and is also used as the union operator if its operands are set types. Thus the meaning of the symbol denoting an operator is determined by the types of its operands.

With the exception of the *unary operators* NOT, +, and –, all operators in the table are *binary operators* which require two operands. (The unary operators precede their operands; the binary operators are placed between their operands.)

Symbol	Operator	Operand types	Result type	Examples
=	equals	2 real numbers[1]	Boolean	`r = 4.32E-6`
		2 whole numbers		`i = -5`
				`c = 32G`
		2 characters		`ch = 'A'`
		2 Booleans		`flag = TRUE`
		2 sets		`Letters =`
				`  SetOfChar{'a'..'c'}`
		2 enumerations		`today = Tue`
		2 pointers		`EntryPtd = Last`
		2 procedures		
<>	not equal	2 real numbers	Boolean	`year <> 1989`
#		2 whole numbers		`c <> MAX(CARDINAL)`
		2 characters		`ch <> 'A'`
		2 Booleans		`EndOfInput # TRUE`
		2 sets		`Letters <> LetterSet{}`
		2 enumerations		`Today # Mon`
		2 pointers		`PlaceHolder <> NIL`
		2 procedures		

---

[1]Because of approximation errors, real number equality is rarely useful in practice.

Symbol	Operator	Operand types	Result type	Examples

>	greater than	2 real numbers
		2 whole numbers
		2 characters
		2 Booleans
		2 enumerations
			Boolean	`TOTALTAX > 32.85`
				`index > 10`
				`ch > 'Z'`
				`HouseHolder > FALSE`
				`today > Fri`

<	less than	2 real numbers
		2 whole numbers
		2 characters
		2 Booleans
		2 enumerations
			Boolean	`r < 4.26E10`
				`Hoursleft < 8`
				`InputChar < 'a'`
				`Drive < TRUE`
				`IBM < COMPAQ`

>=	greater than or equal to
	
	or is a superset of (⊇)
		2 real numbers
		2 whole numbers
		2 characters
		2 Booleans
		2 enumerations
		
		2 sets
			Boolean	`x >= 16.E-5`
				`Count >= 56`
				`Letter >= 'A'`
				`NoTime >= FALSE`
				`Today >= Mon`
				
				`MonthsOfYear >=`
				`    HolidayMonths`

<=	less than or equal to
	
	or is a subset of (⊆)
		2 real numbers
		2 whole numbers
		2 characters
		2 Booleans
		2 enumerations
		
		2 sets
			Boolean	`3.1 <= P`
				`NoOfFiles <= 255`
				`Input <= TRUE`
				`DrugTest <= TRUE`
				`red <= ColourChoice`
				
				`QualityMicros <=`
				`    AllMicros`

IN	member of	first operand is ordinal value of set's base type; second operand is a set	Boolean	`Letter IN` `    LetterSet{'A'..'Z'}`
AND &	conjunction	2 Booleans	Boolean	`(x > 1.0) AND` `    (x <= 6.0)`
OR	disjunction	2 Booleans	Boolean	`FirstTime OR(n > 21)`

Symbol	Operator	Operand types	Result type	Examples

NOT
~
	negation	1 Boolean	Boolean	`NOT FirstTime`
				`NOT (A OR B )`
				`~ (y < 5.6E-3)`

+	identity	precedes a real value or an INTEGER or subrange	type of operand	`+ x` `+ (5.0 + 8.0)`

+	addition
	
	or
	union
		2 whole numbers
		
		2 real numbers
		or
		2 sets
			whole number
			or
			real number
			or
			set
				`5 + y`
				
				`1 + 0.00001`
				
				`LetterSet{"E"} +`
				`    Letters`

−	negation	precedes a real value or an INTEGER or subrange	type of operand	`-33` `-(x * y)`

−	subtraction
	
	or
	
	set difference
		2 whole numbers
		
		or
		2 real numbers
		or
		2 sets
			whole number
			or
			real number
			or
			
			set
				`54 - C`
				
				`34.92 - r`
				
				`Letters -`
				`    LetterSet{'A'..'Z'}`

*	multipli-cation
	
	or
	set inter-section
		2 whole numbers
		
		or
		2 real numbers
		or
		2 sets
			whole number
			or
			real number
			or
			set
				`2 * n`
				
				`2.0 * Distance`
				
				`Letters *`
				`    LetterSet{'a','e'}`

Symbol	Operator	Operand types	Result type	Examples
/	division or symmetric set difference	2 whole numbers[1] or 2 real numbers or 2 sets	whole number or real number or set	n/- 2 Distance/2.0 Letters/ LetterSet{x..y}

DIV	whole
	number
	division
		first is whole
		   number
		second is positive
		   whole number
			whole
			number
				64 DIV 7

REM	remainder[2]	2 whole numbers	whole number	69 REM - 8

MOD	modulus	first is whole
		   number
		second is positive
		   whole number
			whole
			number
				44 MOD 6

In addition to the operators, the following built-in function procedures may be used in expressions (see Chapter 23 for full details):

ABS, CAP, CHR, FLOAT, HIGH, LFLOAT, MAX, MIN, ODD, ORD, SIZE, TRUNC, VAL

Operator precedence

In evaluating an expression, the order in which operands are combined with an operator to generate a value is significant. This order of operator application is particularly relevant to portability when there is a danger that a value will be generated which is illegal in a particular context. For example, on the right of the expression in the following assignment statement, the value 65710 is generated as the result of the addition, before 180 is subtracted to give 65530:

```
card := 210 + 65500 - 180;
```

If this statement is executed on an implementation for which the maximum CARDINAL value is 65535, the intermediate value generated is an exception. (Many implementations will not report this, however, and an invalid result will

---

[1] / for whole number division is not yet common in implementations.

[2] REM is the remainder whole number division and is not yet common in implementations.

occur.) Rewriting the assignment in either of the following ways avoids the problem:

```
card := 210 - 180 + 65500;
card := 210 + (65500 -180);
```

In all these assignment statements, the operators have the same precedence and so their application is defined to be from left to right. The operators + and – have the same precedence: consequently left-to-right evaluation causes the problem in the first assignment and resolves it in the second.

The third statement creates a subexpression as an operand on the right hand side of the last statement (65500-180). This forces the subtraction to take place before the addition. (See *Evaluation of expressions*, below.)

The precedence of an operator is the ranking it has when determining the order of how operators shall be applied. The following list gives the precedence of operators, from highest to lowest:

Highest precedence:	not operator	(NOT, ~)
↓	multiplication operators	(*, /, DIV, MOD, REM, AND, &)
	addition operators	(+, -, OR)
Lowest precedence:	relational operators	(=, <>, #, <, <=, >=, >, IN)

Parentheses can be used to introduce new subexpressions as operands and thus to override precedence.

Examples

(i)	2 * 7 * 8	returns 112
(ii)	2 * 7 DIV 8	returns 1
(iii)	2 + 7 DIV 8	returns 2
(iv)	(2 + 7) DIV 8	returns 1

Evaluation of expressions

In evaluating an expression the value of the operands must be evaluated and the values must be combined according to the meaning of the operators. The order of operator evaluation and the precedence rules are discussed above; the order of operand evaluation is equally important. According to the forthcoming standard for Modula-2, the operands may be evaluated in any order and the operators should be applied from left to right. This lack of prescription simply reflects the variety of methods used in current implementations.

Generally the order, or lack of it, should not matter as, for example, in the following assignment statements:

```
a := 6;
b := -2;
```

```
c := 1;
x := a + b + c;
```

The first three statements are straightforward. The fourth *could* be evaluated as follows:

1. evaluate a to 6

2. evaluate b to –2

3. evaluate c to 1

4. add 6 to –2 to obtain 4

5. add 4 to 1 to obtain 5

6. assign 5 to x

Alternatively it could as well be evaluated thus:

1. evaluate c to 1

2. evaluate b to –2

3. evaluate a to 6

4. add 6 to –2 to obtain 4

5. add 4 to 1 to obtain 5

6. assign 5 to x

However, if an operand is a function procedure invocation, there is a danger that its evaluation will have a side-effect which changes the value of another operand. Consider the following function procedure, which returns twice the value of its argument and which also adds the value to a global variable `Global`.

```
VAR Global: CARDINAL;
PROCEDURE f(local : CARDINAL) : CARDINAL;
  BEGIN
    Global := Global + local ;
    RETURN 2 * local
  END f;
```

Now consider the following pair of assignments:

```
Global := 0;
x := Global + f(2);
```

The first statement is no problem; the second will result in 4 if the operands are evaluated left-to-right, and in 6 if they are evaluated right-to-left.

Programs which include expressions with side-effects are not portable and should be avoided. (The *Portability Issues* section of Chapter 14 discusses this problem in greater depth.)

Short-circuit evaluation of Boolean expressions

There is one exception to the uncertainty of the order of evaluating operands in an expression. If the expression is BOOLEAN, then the operands are evaluated left-to-right in a *short-circuit* fashion. This means that the whole expression is not evaluated if the answer can be determined by partial evaluation. For example, if the BOOLEAN expression is of the form:

```
Condition1 OR Condition2
```

then if Condition1 is found to be TRUE, the result of the whole expression will always be TRUE, no matter what value Condition2 has. The converse of this is with BOOLEAN expressions of the form:

```
Condition3 AND Condition4
```

With this form, if Condition3 is FALSE, the whole expression will be FALSE, no matter what the value of Condition4.

From this you can see that it is not necessary to evaluate Condition2 or Condition4 in all circumstances, and Modula-2 compilers can generate more efficient code as a result.

16.4 TYPE COMPATIBILITY RULES

In a strongly typed programming language like Modula-2, it is generally the rule that types should not be mixed. That is, the type of a value to be stored in a variable should be identical to the type of the variable, the values in expressions should be of identical types, and actual parameters should have identical types to the formal parameters to which they correspond. However, this general rule is too simple: it does not take into consideration the mathematical relationship between the values of the numeric types, nor does it allow for the complex interactions in the real world which a program must model. The notion of type compatibility is, therefore, useful for allowing types to be 'mixed' in certain circumstances.

Very often compatibility rules are determined by common implementation strategies which compiler writers employ, rather than by any logical relationship between the values of different types. This fact is clearly seen when the numeric types are considered. In mathematics the non-negative whole numbers (offered in Modula-2 as the type CARDINAL) are a subset of the integers (INTEGER) which are a subset of the real numbers (REAL and LONGREAL in Modula-2). Unfortunately, this is not reflected by many languages, and Modula-2 is no exception. The compatibility rules at least allow some mixing of CARDINAL and INTEGER (and built-in functions are provided for converting between whole number types and the real types, as described below).

Type compatibility is defined by three sets of rules which cover the situations in which it is convenient to mix types. These are:

- in expressions;

- when assigning a value to a variable;

- when matching actual parameters to formal parameters.

The rules for standard Modula-2 are given below. Note, however, that the compatibility rules for Modula-2 vary widely among implementations; see Section 16.5.

Expression compatibility

The rules for expression compatibility[1] allow operands of different elementary types to be mixed in expressions. (They apply only to elementary types since only elementary values may be combined in an expression using operators.)

If two types t1 and t2 are the types of operands in an expression, they are expression compatible if any of the following statements are true:

1. t1 and t2 are identical types (see Section 16.2);

2. t1 is $\mathbb{Z}$ type and t2 is a whole number type, or vice versa;

3. t1 is of $\mathbb{R}$ type and t2 is a real type, or vice versa;

4. t1 and t2 have the same host type (which includes the case where t1 is a subrange of t2 or vice versa);

5. the host types of t1 and t2 are expression compatible;

6. t1 is a pointer type and t2 is the type of the value NIL, or vice versa;

7. t1 is a procedure type and t2 is a procedure type of the same structure.[2]

Note that INTEGER and CARDINAL are not expression compatible, and so subranges of these are not expression compatible. Thus, the following is illegal:

```
VAR
   i : [0..5];
   j : [-5..5];
...
   IF i > j THEN...
```

Similarly, REAL and LONGREAL are not expression compatible.

Examples

(i)
```
VAR a, b, c : INTEGER;
...
a := a + b + c;
```

By Rule 1, a, b, and c are expression compatible.

(ii)
```
TYPE
   Seabird = (gull, pelican, puffin, guillemot, albatross);
```

---

[1]The term *compatible* used to be used for what is now called *expression compatible*.

[2]The only operators which an implementation might provide for procedure types are = and <>. If these are not supplied, Rule 7 will only be relevant to assignment compatibility.

```
VAR
   b1 : [gull..puffin];
   b2 : [puffin..guillemot];
   ...
   IF b1 = b2 ...
```

b1 and b2 are expression compatible by Rule 4.

(iii)
```
CONST MaxDistance = 298.4;
VAR
   NumberOfTrucks : CARDINAL;
   Distance : LONGREAL;
   ...
   NumberOfTrucks := NumberOfTrucks + 1;
   IF Distance >= MaxDistance...
```

In this example NumberOfTrucks and 1 are expression compatible by Rule 2, and Distance and MaxDistance are expression compatible by Rule 3.

Assignment compatibility

This form of compatibility permits the values of certain types to be assigned to variables which are not of the identical type of the values. If tv is the type of the variable into which a value is to be placed and te is the type of the value resulting from the expression (which will compute the value), then te is assignment compatible with tv if any of the following statements are true:

1. tv and te are expression compatible (which includes the case of them being identical);

2. tv and te are whole number types, either CARDINAL, INTEGER, or $\mathbb{Z}$ (e.g. one may be CARDINAL and the other INTEGER);

3. tv is a concrete string type, say ARRAY[0..n −1] OF CHAR, and te is of $\mathbb{S}$ type with a length $\leq$ n.

Note that although the mathematical relationships of INTEGER, CARDINAL, and $\mathbb{Z}$ are recognized by making them assignment compatible, REAL and LONGREAL are not assignment compatible with each other, but each is with $\mathbb{R}$.

Also note that if a concrete string value is constructed with an array value constructor, it cannot be of $\mathbb{S}$ type (because the type of a value constructor must be given and $\mathbb{S}$ is reserved for literals) and so Rule 3 will not apply.

Examples

(i)
```
VAR
   Count : INTEGER;
   Number : [0..255];
   ...
   Number := 1;
   Count := Number;
```

The first assignment is legal because Number and 1 are expression compatible as in Rule 1: the former is a subset of CARDINAL, and the later is of type $\mathbb{Z}$. The second assignment is legal because of Rule 2.

(ii)   VAR Message : ARRAY [0..39] OF CHAR;
        ...
          Message := '?';

The assignment is valid through Rule 3. (The '?' is of type $\mathbb{S}$ and not of type CHAR; if it were of the latter type, the assignment would be illegal.)

Parameter compatibility

Parameter compatibility rules deal with the two classes of parameters in Modula-2 —value parameters and VAR-parameters. The need to relax the ideal goal of requiring that the type of an actual parameter be identical to the type of the corresponding formal parameter arises largely from the similarity of parameter passing to assignment.

If tf is the type of a formal parameter, and ta is the type of the corresponding actual parameter, then ta is parameter compatible with tf if one of the following statements is true:

1.   ta is identical to tf;

2.   tf is a value parameter and ta is assignment compatible with tf;

3.   tf is an open array parameter and ta is an array of the same number of dimensions as tf and whose component type is identical to that of tf;

4.   tf is a procedure type and ta has the same structure as tf;

5.   tf is of the smallest addressable unit[1] type (e.g. BYTE or WORD) and ta is any type whose size is that of the smallest addressable unit (i.e. SIZE(ta) = 1);

6.   tf is an array of smallest addressable units, as defined by
     tf = ARRAY[0..n-1] OF WORD; and ta is any type for which
     SIZE(ta) = n;

7.   tf is an open array parameter of smallest addressable units (e.g. ARRAY OF BYTE or ARRAY OF WORD) and ta is any type;

8.   tf is an open array of arrays of smallest addressable units, as
     ARRAY OF Chunk when Chunk = ARRAY[0..m-1] OF WORD, and ta
     is any type whose size (given by SIZE) is a multiple of m.

Note that because the type of an actual VAR-parameter must be identical to the type of the formal parameter, a subrange of the type of a formal VAR-parameter is not parameter compatible with it.

---

[1]We use the term smallest addressable unit to generalize the concept of BYTE or WORD. See Chapter 25 for more details.

Examples

(i)
```
        VAR V1 : T1;   V2 : T2;

        PROCEDURE p (VAR f1 : T1; f2 : T2);
        ...
        p(V1, V2);
```

The call to p is legal because of Rule 1.

(ii)
```
        VAR Small : [0..56];
        PROCEDURE print (value : CARDINAL);
        ...
        Print(small);
```

The type, small, is the anonymous CARDINAL subrange type [0..56]. This is assignment compatible with the type of the formal parameter, value, and so is parameter compatible with it, according to Rule 2.

(iii)
```
        TYPE
          Range  = [0..700];
          Person =  RECORD
                       Name : ARRAY [0..49] OF CHAR;
                       Code : CARDINAL
                    END;
        VAR
          NumberOfPeople : Range;
          PersonList : ARRAY Range OF Person;
          ShortList : ARRAY [1..10] OF Person;
        PROCEDURE CurrentNumber (List : ARRAY OF Person) : CARDINAL;
        ...
          NumberOfPeople := CurrentNumber(PersonList);
          NumberOfPeople := CurrentNumber(ShortList);
```

Both of the types of PersonList and ShortList are parameter compatible with List by Rule 3. (Note that the use of a function procedure, whose result type needs only to be assignment compatible with the types of NumberOfPeople, overcomes the difficulty of not being able to match a subrange type, such as Range, with a CARDINAL VAR-parameter which would have been the mechanism for returning a value from a proper procedure.)

(iv)
```
        TYPE Operation = PROCEDURE(INTEGER,INTEGER,VAR CARDINAL);
        VAR C : CARDINAL;
        ...
        PROCEDURE PosMult(x, y : INTEGER; VAR result: CARDINAL);
        ...
        PROCEDURE Change(a, b : INTEGER; Op: Operation) : CARDINAL;
          VAR Temp : CARDINAL;
          BEGIN
            Op(a, b, Temp);
            RETURN Temp
          END Change;
        ...
        C := Change (5, 10, PosMult);
```

Rule 4 means that `PosMult` is procedure compatible with the type `Operation`.

16.5 PORTABILITY ISSUES

The portability issues which effect expressions and types are the type compatibility rules that determine what types may be mixed in an expression, and how the expression determines its use in statements, and the availability and semantics of some operations.

Diversity of compatibility rules

The compatibility rules which a Modula-2 implementation applies depend, in large measure, on what stage in the history of the Modula-2 language the compiler was written. Early compilers (roughly, those whose development started before 1985) enforce the rules which Wirth described in the second edition of *Programming in Modula-2* (1983). Later compilers (or updated versions of early ones) enforce the rules given in the third edition of *Programming in Modula-2* .

However, there are not just two compatibility classes of Modula-2 compiler. Many compilers have stricter rules than those of the third edition of *Programming in Modula-2* some are more lax. The following list outlines the main differences between existing compilers and the rules given above.

* `CARDINAL` and `INTEGER` may not be assignment compatible.

* `CARDINAL` and `INTEGER` may be expression compatible.

* The type of actual `VAR`-parameters may need to be only expression compatible with the type of the formal parameter.

In order to avoid problems due to the diversity of compatibility rules and to make code portable, you must use either or both the following techniques to ensure types are compatible by being identical:

1. Avoid mixed arithmetic and the use of subrange types.

2. Use the type conversion function, `VAL`.

Unfortunately, both these strategies have drawbacks. Mixed arithmetic is often unavoidable, and subrange types are to be encouraged rather than deprecated. Moreover, the type transfer `VAL` presents portability problems itself, as described below.

Compatibility and statements

The diversity of compatibility rules clearly affects the portability of assignment statements and procedure calls. It also affects all other statements which include expressions in their syntax, namely the `IF`, `CASE`, `WHILE`, `REPEAT`, `FOR`, and `RETURN` statements. The two which show most diversity are the `FOR` and `CASE` statements.

According to the forthcoming Modula-2 standard the type of the start value in a FOR statement must be assignment compatible with the type of the control variable, and the type of the final value must be expression compatible with the type of the control variable. Early compilers (as defined above) enforce assignment compatibility of both values with the type of the control variable; later compilers require that *both* values be expression compatible. The latter variation is the next-strictest type requirement to demanding identical types and so is to be recommended for portability.

The CASE statement can be the source of portability problems because some implementations demand only that the type of the case labels be assignment compatible with the case selector expression. They should always be expression compatible for portability.

Type transfer and conversion

It is often necessary to move values between types. This is quite natural between the numeric types, INTEGER, CARDINAL, REAL, and LONGREAL: in mathematics the number denoted by 7 and by 7.0 are indistinguishable; in Modula-2, 7 must be explicitly converted to 7.0 because the numeric types use different representations from each other. The changing of a value of one type into a value which in some sense corresponds to the original is called *type conversion*. Ideally it should include a check for valid type changes. For example, an implementation (such as Topspeed Modula-2) implements both CARDINAL and INTEGER values in 16 bits; however, you will not be able to convert the CARDINAL value 64000 to the corresponding INTEGER value. (Strictly speaking, attempting such a conversion is an exception which should cause a runtime error.)

Also, in systems programming (see Chapter 25), it is not unusual to need to manipulate the binary representation of values. Changing the type of a value while simply maintaining a bit pattern is called a *type transfer*. Transferring a 16-bit CARDINAL value of 64000 to a 16-bit INTEGER would result in the INTEGER having the value −1536.

In the forthcoming standard the built-in procedure VAL (see Chapter 23) is proposed as the type conversion function, while a procedure called CAST is to be provided in the module SYSTEM (see Chapter 25 for type transfer). Unfortunately, in many implementations, VAL is used for type *transfer*, as well as for type *conversion*. (Topspeed Modula-2's VAL does both.) Many implementations allow the pervasive identifiers INTEGER and CARDINAL to be used as functions for type transfer, but this is not universal. Some implementations (including Topspeed Modula-2) extend this notion by permitting any type identifier to be used as a type conversion/transfer function, thereby making VAL redundant.[1]

---

[1]A type transfer function is sometimes called a *coercion* or a *cast* (see Chapter 25).

All implementations provide the type conversion functions TRUNC and FLOAT; few yet provide LFLOAT.

Provision of operators

Not all compilers implement the whole number operators / and REM (e.g. Topspeed Modula-2 provides neither). Some implementations do not object to a negative right hand operand for DIV and MOD. The semantics for these operators when the second operand is negative is unpredictable in these implementations. If you need these mathematical operations to be portable, you may have to implement them as function procedures (see Chapter 17).

The equality and inequality operation for procedure types may not be universally available. If they are not available, then type transfer must be used to test the values of a procedure type. (Similarly, you may not always be able to use set operators—not because of their absence, but because of the limitations of set size. See Chapter 21.)

16.6   REVIEW QUESTIONS AND EXERCISES

Q16.1   What is wrong with the following code?
```
TYPE
  a1 = ARRAY [1..5] OF INTEGER;
  a2 = ARRAY [1..5] OF INTEGER;
VAR
  x : a1;
  y : a2;
  ...
  y : = x;
```

Q16.2   How would you fix the erroneous code in Q16.1?

Q16.3   Write a program to implement equality checking between two procedure variables of type:
```
PROCEDURE (INTEGER, INTEGER, VAR CARDINAL);
```
You should assume that the equality and inequality operators have not been implemented for procedure types.

Q16.4   Write a function procedure SCompare to compare the value of two different set types. The set types and the enumeration type which is to be used as the result type of the function are defined below:
```
TYPE
  SmallSet = SET OF [0..7];
  LittleSet = SET OF [0..7];
  Comparison = (NotEqual, Equal, StrictSubset);
```
The values of the type Comparison correspond to (1) different values being held in the two sets, (2) all the elements in the first being found in the second (and no others being present in the second), and (3) all elements of the first being found in the second, but the latter having some extra.

17 BASIC TYPES

17.1 INTRODUCTION

The basic types in Modula-2 are:

- signed whole numbers (INTEGER and its subranges)

- unsigned whole numbers (CARDINAL and its subranges)

- real numbers (REAL and LONGREAL)

- characters (CHAR and its subranges)

- truth values (BOOLEAN)

In this chapter the details of each type are given: its typical range of values (the values implemented in Topspeed Modula-2), its operators, and the built-in functions which apply to them. (The representation of basic types is discussed in Chapter 25.) For the BOOLEAN type, a set of truth tables is provided. The problems of processing values of numerical types are also outlined.

17.2 CONCEPTUAL TYPES $\mathbb{Z}$, $\mathbb{R}$, AND $\mathbb{S}$

To simplify the rules of expression compatibility (see Section 16.4) and to allow *mixed arithmetic* (i.e. mixing CARDINAL and INTEGER values) the forthcoming Modula-2 standard has devised the type $\mathbb{Z}$. (This is the usual symbol used in mathematics for denoting the infinite set of integers.) $\mathbb{Z}$ is defined to be the type of whole number literals (or constant expressions comprising them) or of symbolic whole number constants. Thus the following are of type $\mathbb{Z}$:

```
1, 2, 4625, 65535, -32760, 64 DIV 7, 777B, 0FFAH
```

$\mathbb{Z}$ is expression compatible with both CARDINAL and INTEGER and subranges of these (see Section 16.4).

Similarly ℝ is provided to allow literals to be compatible with both REAL and LONGREAL. The following are of type ℝ:

```
3.562E10, -5.0, 54.2/26
```

𝕊 is the abstraction for string literals—both single character literals (which may denote values of type CHAR) and multi-character literals. The following are of type 𝕊:

```
'A', "What have we here?"
```

However, note that character number literals (e.g. 0C) are of type CHAR, and not 𝕊.

17.3 CARDINAL

The data type CARDINAL represents the non-negative whole number values; typically the range of values is determined by the range of ones-complement arithmetic provided by a computer's word. On 16-bit machines the range of CARDINAL is typically 0..65535.

CARDINAL operators

CARDINALs can be operated on by seven mathematical binary operators:

Operation	Operator	Operation	Operator
addition	+	division	/
subtraction	−	remainder (after division)	REM
multiplication	*	whole number division	DIV
modulus	MOD		

These operators give the expected mathematical result when used in CARDINAL expressions, unless the result of the calculation (or intermediate result, if it is a complicated expression) goes out of the implemented range. (See *Overflow and underflow* in Section 17.9.)

Remember that these seven operators can only apply to expressions made up of CARDINAL values, and values which are expression compatible with CARDINAL.

Modula-2 CARDINAL division is performed by truncation (because the result must always be a CARDINAL). So the expression 9 DIV 4 yields 2 and the expression 9 MOD 4 yields 1. You can see from these examples that the operator DIV gives the result of division truncated to the nearest whole CARDINAL, and MOD gives the remainder after DIV.

The relationships between / and REM, and DIV and MOD are expressed by the following formulae:

```
a = (a / b) * b + (a REM b)
a = (a DIV b) * b + (a MOD b)
```

Examples

```
53 / 10 returns 5
65 DIV 4 returns 18
53 REM 10 returns 3
75 MOD 4 returns 3
```

Unlike the first three operators discussed, /, MOD, REM, and DIV cannot themselves cause expressions using them to go out of range.

In addition to the mathematical operators, it is also possible to apply relational operators to CARDINAL values in expressions (but note that such expressions will return BOOLEAN values).

The available relational operators are: =, <, >, <=, >=, <>.

Built-in procedures

It is also possible to apply a large number of built-in procedures for CARDINAL variables and constants. These will not be covered here (see Chapter 23 for full details) but the following list shows which ones can apply to CARDINAL types:

```
ABS, DEC, FLOAT, INC, LFLOAT, MAX, MIN, ODD, ORD, VAL
```

Note that FLOAT and LFLOAT provide the means by which CARDINAL values can be converted to REAL or LONGREAL values. Also, VAL can be used to convert a CARDINAL value to an INTEGER and vice versa.

17.4 INTEGER

The data type INTEGER represents a set of whole number values that can either be positive or negative; typically, the range of values is determined by the range which can be represented by twos-complement arithmetic in a computer word. On machines which have a 16-bit word size the range of values in INTEGER is typically -32768..32767.

INTEGER operators

INTEGER values and values from INTEGER subranges can be operated on by the same seven mathematical operators as for CARDINAL. However, there are also two unary operators defined for INTEGER:

Operation	Operator	Operation	Operator
identity	+	division	/
negation	-	remainder (after division)	REM
addition	+	whole number division	DIV
subtraction	−	modulus	MOD
multiplication	*		

As with CARDINAL, these operators give the expected mathematical result when used in INTEGER expressions, unless the result of the calculation (or partial result, when evaluating a part of a complicated expression) goes out of the range implemented for the INTEGER type. This can happen by the result being either too large a positive INTEGER (e.g. greater than 32767) or too large a negative INTEGER (e.g. less than –32768). Therefore you need to take care when you design your programs, because incorrect results will occur if an INTEGER expression attempts to return a value outside the legal range of INTEGER.

MOD presents some problems when used with integers. The right hand operand will give unpredictable results if it is negative. If the left hand operand is negative the result returned will be negative (unlike the mathematical definition of modulus which only returns positive values). Therefore:

-31 MOD 10 returns -1 not 9, as in mathematics

This distinction should be noted when copying algorithms.

In addition to the mathematical operators, it is also possible to apply relational operators to CARDINAL values in expressions (but note that such expressions will return BOOLEAN values).

The available relational operators are: =, <, >, <=, >=, <>.

Built-in procedures

It is also possible to apply a large number of built-in procedures to INTEGER variables and constants. These will not be covered here (see Chapter 23 for full details) but the following list shows which ones can apply to INTEGER types:

ABS, DEC, FLOAT, INC, LFLOAT, MAX, MIN, ODD, ORD, VAL

Note that FLOAT and LFLOAT provide the means by which INTEGER values can be converted to REAL or LONGREAL values. Also, VAL can be used to convert an INTEGER value to a CARDINAL and vice versa.

17.5 REAL

The type REAL is used in Modula-2 to give an approximate representation of the real numbers in mathematics. In Topspeed Modula-2, REAL values are implemented as floating point values. REAL numbers are said to give an approximate representation because computers can only represent a limited number of decimal places—so rounding and truncation of values can (and does) occur.

REAL numbers are represented by a pair of values, called the *mantissa* and the *exponent*, although using the exponent part in constant values of type REAL is optional.

In Topspeed Modula-2, REALs have the range:

-3.4028234663852884E+38 to +3.4028234663852884E+38

REAL operators

REAL values can be operated on by four binary operators and two unary operators:

Operation	Operator	Operation	Operator
identity	+	subtraction	–
negation	-	multiplication	*
addition	+	division	/

All these operators have the familiar, mathematical meanings, but remember that the result when used in REAL expressions will only be an approximation to the actual result of calculating them exactly.

Note that these operators can only be applied to expressions made up of REALs; you cannot mix REAL values in expressions using LONGREAL values, or Modula-2 whole number values.

The available relational operators are the same as those for CARDINALs and INTEGERs (see Sections 17.3 and 17.4). However, special care is needed with the equality relational operator. It is bad programming practice to use equality with REAL types and REAL expressions; using this operator will rarely evaluate to TRUE.

Built-in procedures

It is possible to apply a slightly smaller number of built-in procedures to REAL variables and constants than those available for whole number types. These will not be covered here (see Chapter 23 for full details), the following list shows which ones can apply to the REAL type:

ABS, TRUNC

(Neither trigonometric nor hyperbolic functions are built-in Modula-2. They are usually provided by an implementation in a library of mathematical modules.) Note that TRUNC allows REAL values to be converted to CARDINAL values. For those implementations which conform to the forthcoming standard, TRUNC may be used to convert a LONGREAL to a REAL value.

17.6 LONGREAL

LONGREAL behaves just like REAL, but LONGREAL and REAL are neither expression compatible nor assignment compatible.

Topspeed Modula-2 provides a typical LONGREAL implementation; in this implementation LONGREALs range from:

$-1.7976931348623158E+308$ to $+1.7976931348623158E+308$

All of the operators and built-in procedures that can be applied to type REAL can also be applied to type LONGREAL.

17.7   CHAR

The data type CHAR represents the set of single characters that can be represented in a Modula-2 implementation.

Topspeed Modula-2 supports a set of 256 characters, made up of letters (a to z and A to Z, digits, and special characters such as punctuation symbols, accents, graphic symbols, and non-printable characters (usually interpreted as control characters).

These characters are ordered according to their ordinal value. This value can be obtained by looking up the symbol (or mnemonic, in the case of non-printing characters) in the character set table of your computer manual. For most American and British machines, the ordering of the first 128 characters is based on the ASCII character code standard, the remaining 128 character ordering is determined by the hardware.

Operations on type CHAR

Only two operations are defined for type CHAR: the assignment of a value and comparison with other variables or constants of type CHAR.

There are no arithmetic operations defined for type CHAR, although arithmetic operations can be performed on the ordinal values of CHAR types, by first using a type conversion function.

Comparison of CHAR types is performed using the familiar relational operators: =, <, >, <=, >=, <>.

The result of comparison of CHAR values is defined by the ordinal value, and so for the ASCII set:

```
'A'  <  'a'
```

because the ordinal value of A is 65 and the ordinal value of a is 97.

Built-in procedures

A number of Modula-2's built-in procedures apply to type CHAR:

```
CAP, CHR, DEC, INC, MAX, MIN, ORD, VAL
```

These are explained in full in Chapter 23.

17.8   BOOLEAN

The logic data type BOOLEAN is an enumeration type containing two (ordered) values defined by:

```
BOOLEAN = (FALSE, TRUE);
```

TRUE and FALSE are thus standard identifiers in Modula-2. BOOLEAN variables allow you to store truth values, such as the results of relational operations.

BOOLEAN is also special in that it is the automatic result type of relational operations for expressions involving all elementary types. As an example, the following statement assigns the result of an expression comparing the value of a CARDINAL variable with a fixed value:

```
MyBooleanValue := NumberOfThings < 3;
```

Logical operators

BOOLEAN values can be operated on by three logical operators:

Operation type	Operator	Alternative symbol
negation	NOT	~
conjunction	AND	&
disjunction	OR	

Note: OR does not have an alternative one-character symbol, but the alternative symbols for AND and NOT can be used interchangeably with the three-character names.

These operators only apply to BOOLEAN operands and produce BOOLEAN results. The following truth tables show the effect of the logical operators. Note that, because of short-circuit evaluation, the BOOLEAN operators cannot be considered to be commutative, as in classical two-valued logic. This is because in Modula-2 the operators are defined to work in certain cases where an operand is undefined. The symbol ? is used to denote undefined:

Truth table for NOT:

B1	NOT B1
FALSE	TRUE
TRUE	FALSE

Truth table for AND:

B1	B2	B1 AND B2
FALSE	FALSE	FALSE
FALSE	TRUE	FALSE
TRUE	FALSE	FALSE
TRUE	TRUE	TRUE
?	FALSE	?
?	TRUE	?
FALSE	?	FALSE
TRUE	?	?

Truth table for OR:

B1	B2	B1 OR B2
FALSE	FALSE	FALSE
FALSE	TRUE	TRUE
TRUE	FALSE	TRUE
TRUE	TRUE	TRUE
?	FALSE	?
?	TRUE	?
FALSE	?	?
TRUE	?	TRUE

The precedence of logical operators is from highest to lowest: NOT, AND, OR. Therefore, the expression:

```
NOT Bool1 AND Bool2 OR Bool3
```

is interpreted as:

```
((NOT Bool1) AND Bool2) OR Bool3
```

Note that operands in a Boolean expression are always evaluated from left to right. This allows the evaluation of the expression to be terminated if the result becomes known from a single operand.

17.9 PORTABILITY ISSUES

When using the data types of a programming language, the finite capacity of computers is often encountered. This is particularly the case with the basic types of a language: since they are primitive building blocks, they are often constrained by low-level aspects of the host system—both the machine and the operating system. Modula-2 is no exception. Indeed, some of the portability problems that users of the language now encounter are due to a desire to keep the language, in some sense, close to the machine.

Because the values of basic types are usually implemented in a small number of addressable units (e.g. bytes or words), the range of values is often considered to be inadequate by an implementor or by his or her programming customers. Therefore, many implementations provide extra basic numeric types. (Topspeed Modula-2 is one of these implementations and its extensions are described below.)

The provision of some operators or the meaning of some operators and built-in procedures also varies from implementation to implementation; this is particularly the case with operations for numeric types. Also the basic type identifiers can sometimes be used as type transfer functions in Topspeed Modula-2. Finally, the character type CHAR is theoretically implementation defined and could present portability problems, see below.

Extensions to the basic numeric types

Because of a desire to economize on the storage of variables, many implementations provide other basic types. Usually these are variants of the whole number and real types. Some whole number extensions provide for smaller numbers than the standard type; some provide for larger. Different implementations use different compatibility rules for these types and for their use with the standard types.

As an example of these extensions, consider those provided by Topspeed Modula-2.

The type SHORTCARD contains non-negative whole number values in the more limited range than CARDINAL: 0..255.

The main reason for using this type is that variables of type SHORTCARD occupy half the space that CARDINAL variables do. You will probably only use SHORTCARD when you are very concerned about economizing on storage. (This might be the case when storing a very large number of small numbers in an array, see below.) SHORTCARD and CARDINAL are different types and values of one cannot simply be assigned to a variable of another. The same is true of SHORTCARD and the subrange CARDINAL[0..255] (which you might think are the same).

Like CARDINAL and SHORTCARD, the type LONGCARD also contains non-negative whole number values. However, a variable of type LONGCARD can take values in a much greater range than a CARDINAL variable: 0..4294967295.

You would use LONGCARD for non-negative whole numbers greater than 65535. LONGCARD variables occupy twice the space that CARDINAL variables do. LONGCARD and CARDINAL are different types and values of one cannot simply be assigned to a variable of another. The same is true of CARDINAL and LONGCARD[0..65535].

The type SHORTINT also contains negative and non-negative whole number values. A variable of type SHORTINT can take values in the more limited range: -128 to 127. SHORTINT variables occupy half the space that INTEGER variables do.

SHORTINT and INTEGER are different types and values of one cannot simply be assigned to a variable of another. The same is true of SHORTINT and INTEGER [-128..127].

Like INTEGER and SHORTINT, the type LONGINT also contains negative and non-negative whole number values. However, a variable of type LONGINT can take values which are in a much greater range than an INTEGER variable: -214783648..214783647.
LONGINT variables occupy twice the space that INTEGER variables do.

LONGINT and INTEGER are different types and values of one cannot simply be assigned to a variable of another. The same is true of INTEGER and LONGINT[-32768..32767].

In general, the use of extended whole number types limits the portability of the program. Whilst many implementations provide 'long' integer or cardinal types, few support 'short' whole number types. The type compatibility rules governing these types vary considerably.

Overflow and underflow

Overflow and underflow are conditions that arise when evaluation of an expression (or a partial expression, since it can apply to an intermediate result) results in a value that is outside the range that can be represented by the result type.

Overflow is the easier of the two to understand, and applies to all the numeric types (CARDINAL, INTEGER, REAL, and LONGREAL). Underflow occurs with division or subtraction and means that a computed value has become so small that it is not representable; underflow with whole numbers occurs only with subtraction and means a whole number value is out-of-range.

Strictly speaking, overflow and underflow are exceptions (i.e. run-time errors) but not all compilers generate code to enable them to be detected. The treatment of overflow and underflow is therefore a portability issue, since the value returned when either of them is not detected is usually undefined. Great care should be taken to avoid these conditions in portable programs.

Topspeed Modula-2 does not detect REAL or LONGREAL overflow or underflow. Topspeed does detect whole number overflow and underflow when the compiler directive (*$O+*) is set. This is not the default (although it can be made so by reconfiguring the compiler environment). Topspeed is unusual in that this detection extends to subexpressions and intermediate results (as opposed to assignment and parameter passing). When the (*$O-*) directive is set, Topspeed generates code with predictable semantics (i.e. whole number values wrap around, REAL underflow results in zero and REAL overflow results in 9999999E+2).

Provision of operators and procedures

As noted above, the whole number operators / and REM have not been implemented by many compilers yet.

For CARDINAL values (and positive INTEGER values) this is not a problem: DIV is equivalent to / and MOD is equivalent to REM.

A more serious problem is the variety of semantics ascribed to DIV and MOD. Mathematically they are only defined for positive divisors (right hand operands). However, many Modula-2 implementations return values when the right hand operand is negative.

These problems can be overcome by writing mathematically correct operations using function procedures. (However, this forces an awkward style when writing numeric expressions.)

The built-in procedures for basic numeric types also vary; see *Portability Issues* in Chapter 23.

Type identifiers as type transfer functions

For a period during the development of Modula-2, the built-in procedure `VAL` became deprecated (with some implementations relegating it to the module `SYSTEM`). It was considered to be an 'unsafe' type transfer function; i.e. a means of transferring a bit-pattern representing a value of a type to another type without checking if the bit-pattern was a value of the destination types. 'Safe' type conversion was required, this was often provided by permitting the identifiers `INTEGER` and `CARDINAL` to be used to force a value to become a value of the named type. In such implementations `INTEGER` and `CARDINAL` are not assignment compatible. To allow 'mixed arithmetic' the type identifier is used, for example:

```
VAR
  i : INTEGER; c : CARDINAL;
...
  i := INTEGER(c);
```

These type transfer functions should be avoided and `VAL` used where assignment compatibility demands it.

```
i := VAL(INTEGER, c);
```

Character sets

Most American computers include the ASCII set, which includes 128 values. When ASCII or a national equivalent is used a further 128 values are often defined, but you will need to check just what these are for your computer. However, it is not sensible to assume that ASCII is the character set used for the type `CHAR`. Nor is it sensible to assume the ordering of the values in `CHAR`.

17.10 REVIEW QUESTIONS AND EXERCISES

Q17.1 Name the built-in simple data types provided by Modula-2.

Q17.2 What whole number operators are often not defined properly?

Q17.3 Implement a function procedure to implement the mathematical modulus (`MOD`) function.

Q17.4 Why does Modula-2's type `REAL` only give an approximate representation of the real numbers in mathematics?

Q17.5 If your implementation of Modula-2 includes the type `SHORTCARD`, what would the advantage be in using it preface to the subrange `CARDINAL` `[0..255]`?

Q17.6 Given the following variables:

```
VAR
  R: REAL;
  B, C: CARDINAL;
  I: INTEGER;
```

write the statement that would assign to B the result of multiplying R, C, and I. Remember, Modula-2 does not allow mixed arithmetic.

18 STATEMENTS

18.1 INTRODUCTION

In this chapter the formal syntax of each statement is given, together with short examples and a detailed description of their execution.

18.2 STATEMENT SEQUENCE

In Modula-2 statements may occur in any block—in a program module, implementation module, local module, or procedure. They may not appear in a definition module. The IF, CASE, WHILE, REPEAT, LOOP, FOR, and WITH statements all permit a sequence of statements to be executed. Such a sequence is just a list of statements separated by semicolons.

Syntax

```
statement sequence = statement, {";", statement};
statement =
  null statement |
  assignment |
  procedure call
  if statement |
  case statement |
  while statement
  repeat statement |
  loop statement |
  for statement |
  with statement |
  exit statement |
  return statement ;
```

18.3   NULL STATEMENT

The null statement has no purpose except to relax the syntax rule which would otherwise prevent the use of a semicolon before an END, ELSE, ELSIF, or UNTIL reserved word. A semicolon may be used in any context where a statement would be permitted.

Syntax

```
null statement = ;
```

Description of execution

No execution is performed!

Examples

(i)   a := 55; ; b := 66;

There is a null statement between the two assignment statements above.

(ii)   REPEAT
             x[this] := 0;
             this := this + 1;
         UNTIL this > 300;

There is a null statement just before the UNTIL reserved word.

18.4   ASSIGNMENT STATEMENT

The assignment statement is the means by which the result of evaluating an expression (see Chapter 16) is stored in a variable. The variable may be of *any* type: it may be declared as an elementary type (such as a CARDINAL, REAL, or pointer) or may be declared as a structured type (such as a RECORD or ARRAY).

Syntax

```
assignment = designator, ":=", expression;
designator =
   qualified identifier, {".", identifier | "[", expression list, "]" | "^" };
```

The term *designator* is used to indicate that the variable may be the field of a record (see Chapter 20), the element of an array (see Chapter 19), or a pointer dereference (see Chapter 22). Indeed the designator may be some combination of these.

The type of the expression must be assignment compatible with the variable designated on the left hand side of the assignment (see Chapter 16 on type compatibility).

Description of execution

The order in which the left and right hand sides of an assignment statement are evaluated (and thus the way an assignment statement is executed) is implementation defined. For most situations, the order is immaterial and so we describe left-to-right evaluation. (The problems of order of evaluation are discussed fully in the *Portability Issues* section below.)

The assignment statement works as follows. The designator on the left hand side of the : = operator is evaluated first (to obtain a variable). Then the expression on the right hand side of the : = operator is evaluated, from left to right (as described in Chapter 16). The resulting value is then stored in the variable on the left hand side of the : =. The value replaces any value previously stored in the variable.

If an expression appears on the left hand side of the assignment operator : =, such as when an array is indexed in order to assign a value to a component, then the order of evaluation of the two expressions is unpredictable. (A compiler may choose a different order in an attempt to optimize the executable code.) (See Chapter 16 about expressions and Chapter 19 about array indexing.) You should not rely on any particular order of evaluation, instead you should simplify the assignment by using a temporary variable.

There is a special rule for string (e.g. ARRAY [0..n] OF CHAR) variables: they may be assigned a string literal of length m where m <= n + 1. If the length of the literal is less than the possible length of the variable, a string terminating character is placed in the variable after the literal. See Example (iv) below (and Chapter 10 for further details).

Examples

(i)
```
Count := 0;
Speed := Distance / Time;
Message := Uppercase(Copy(String, 1, X));
```

These are simple examples of the assignment statement, involving a literal value, a simple expression, and function evaluation, respectively.

(ii)
```
ErrorModule.UserProfile.Expertise := Novice;
```

Here ErrorModule.UserProfile is a qualified identifier and refers to a record declared in the ErrorModule definition module. Expertise is a field of UserProfile, and is being assigned the value Novice (which is probably a constant of an enumeration type).

(iii)   `Dialog.UseMenu :=`
          `Answer('Use menu (Y for menus, N for commands) ?');`

In the above example `UseMenu` is a Boolean flag which determines the type of dialogue the `Dialog` module uses. `Answer` is a function procedure with a Boolean result type. It prompts the user with the question which is its parameter, and returns TRUE or FALSE.

(iv)   `VAR str: ARRAY [0..19] OF CHAR;`
         `...`
         `str := 'ABCD';`

This assignment results in:

`str[0]` contains `'A'`
`str[1]` contains `'B'`
`str[2]` contains `'C'`
`str[3]` contains `'D'`
`str[4]` contains the implementation defined string terminator.

(v)   `Array[index] := HasSideEffect(index);`

If the function procedure `HasSideEffect` alters the value of `index` (because it is a VAR-parameter, for example) then the variable designated by `Array[index]` may not be what you intend. Safer code would be:

```
temp := index;
Array[temp] := HasSideEffect(index);
```

Even better would be to try to avoid function procedures with side-effects .

18.5   PROCEDURE CALL

A procedure call invokes a procedure which has been declared previously (see Chapter 14) or which has been imported from another module (see Chapter 13).

Syntax

```
procedure call = designator, [actual parameters];
actual parameters = "(", [expression list], ")";
expression list = expression, {",", expression};
```

When a procedure is declared, any values it uses or returns are indicated by means of formal parameters in the procedure's heading (see Chapter 14). When a procedure is called the actual values which it needs, or the variables for storing its results, are passed as actual parameters. Any actual parameters are matched to the formal parameters in the procedure's heading; they are matched by order, by whether they are VAR- or value parameters, and by type (see below).

Description of execution

A procedure call involves a transfer of execution from the point of the call to the main body of the called procedure. When the body of the procedure has been executed (i.e. the END has been reached or a RETURN statement executed), control returns to the point just after the call.

The call also causes the actual parameters to be substituted in place of any formal parameters declared in the procedure's heading (see Chapter 14). Parameters are matched left to right according to type rules given below.

If a formal parameter is a value parameter, i.e. its declaration is not preceded by a VAR, then a copy of the actual parameter is made, and the procedure accesses it through the corresponding formal parameter. If the formal parameter is a VAR-parameter, the procedure is supplied with the location of the actual parameter, and it accesses the actual parameter and its values directly. For a further discussion of parameters see Chapter 14.

Note that if a procedure does not have any parameters then an empty parameter list may be given in the procedure call (e.g. p(); instead of simply p;).

Procedure variables (see Chapter 14) are called in exactly the same way as other procedures.

Examples

(i)
```
      PROCEDURE Initialize;
        ...
        END Initialize;
      BEGIN
        ...
        Initialize;
        ...
```

This is an example of a parameterless procedure.

(ii)
```
      TYPE
        ListRange = [0..500];
        ListType = ARRAY ListRange OF ItemType;
      VAR
        StockList : ListType;
        NumberInStock : ListRange;
        StockItem : ItemType;

      PROCEDURE InsertInList(VAR List: ListType;
                                 NumInList: ListRange;
                                 Item: ItemType);
        ...
        InsertInList (StockList, NumberInStock, StockItem);
```

To specify an array as a formal parameter its type name must be used. Thus ListType must appear in the parameter list, not ARRAY [0..500] OF ItemType.

(iii)   TYPE
    ErrorCondition =
      (DeviceError, InvalidData, EndOfFile, Overflow);

    PROCEDURE ReportError(ErrorValue: ErrorCondition);
    ...
    ReportError(Overflow);
    HALT;

In this example the parameter (ReportError) is of an enumeration type. HALT is a call to a built-in procedure which terminates a program (see Chapter 23).

18.6   IF STATEMENT

The IF statement provides a means of choosing between which of two different sequences of statements to execute, depending on some condition, which is a Boolean expression. In other words, the IF statement allows a program to select between two execution paths. If the Boolean expression evaluates to TRUE, one path is taken, and if FALSE, the other.

Syntax

```
if statement =
   "IF", boolean expression, "THEN", statement sequence,
   {"ELSIF", boolean expression, "THEN", statement sequence},
   ["ELSE", statement sequence], "END";
```

Description of execution

IF...THEN: This is the simplest form of the statement. When the condition is TRUE, the path taken is the sequence of statements after the THEN; after the THEN sequence of statements, the statement which follows the IF statement is executed. When the condition is FALSE, there is no alternative path and the statement after the IF is executed. Thus the following are equivalent:

```
IF condition THEN          IF condition THEN
  path1                      path1
END;                       ELSE
                           END;
```

IF...THEN...ELSE: This is the more general form of the statement in which each path is specified. A statement sequence following the THEN must be executed when the condition is TRUE. A statement sequence following the ELSE must be executed if the condition is FALSE:

```
IF condition THEN
  path1
ELSE
  path2
END;
```

IF...THEN...ELSIF: It is a common programming requirement to evaluate a sequence of conditions, and to perform some actions as soon as one condition evaluates to TRUE. That is, a condition is evaluated and if the result is TRUE a sequence of statements is executed; if FALSE, another condition is evaluated and if this is TRUE another sequence of statements is executed. The condition evaluation continues while all conditions are FALSE. Eventually a TRUE condition is evaluated (and its THEN-path taken), or there are no more conditions to be evaluated. In this last case, an ELSE-path must be supplied or execution continues at the statement following the IF.

It is fairly easy to write program code to do this with nested IF...THEN...ELSE statements: each ELSE branch includes another IF statement. For example:

```
IF condition1 THEN
  path1
ELSE
  IF condition2 THEN
    path2
  ELSE
    IF condition3 THEN
      path3
    ELSE path4
    END
  END
END
```

This is cumbersome to write and, what is worse, difficult to understand. Modula-2 therefore provides the ELSIF reserved word which combines the ELSE-path and a condition evaluation. Thus each IF or ELSIF reserved word has an associated Boolean expression which determines whether a statement sequence will be executed or not; if none are executed then if an ELSE part exists, the statement sequence following the ELSE is executed.

The above set of three nested IF statements can be rewritten much more clearly as follows:

```
IF condition1 THEN
  path1
ELSIF condition2 THEN
  path2
ELSIF condition3 THEN
  path3
ELSE
  path4
END;
```

Execution proceeds as follows: if the IF expression condition1 evaluates to TRUE, then the statement sequence of the matching THEN path1 is executed. If the IF expression evaluates to FALSE, the expression of the first ELSIF, condition2, is evaluated; if TRUE then path2 is executed. If condition2, is FALSE then the next ELSIF condition, condition3, is evaluated, and so on. IF neither `condition1, condition2,` nor `condition3` is `TRUE`, then `path4` will be executed.

If there had been no `ELSE` part, the statement after the `END` of the `IF` statement would be executed.

Notes

1. The evaluation of Boolean expressions is short-circuited if the value can be determined without evaluating all terms in the expression (see Chapter 16). This means that function procedures which have side-effects may not be executed, which may in turn affect the outcome of later expression evaluations.

2. The `IF...THEN...ELSIF...ELSE` structure generalizes the `CASE` statement which tests an ordinal expression against a set of constant expressions (see below).

3. If the conditions of an `IF...THEN...ELSIF...ELSE` structure are tests of equality between a single ordinal expression and a set of values, then probably a `CASE` statement should be used.

Examples

(i)   `IF Answer = 'Y' THEN ShutDownSystem END;`

The simplest case, easily expressed as one line of code.

(ii)
```
IF FileExists(OldName) AND (NOT FileExists(NewName))
THEN
    ChangeName(OldName, NewName, Result);
    ReportResult(Result)
END;
```

In this case, a more complex Boolean expression is evaluated, and a statement sequence (rather than just one statement) is executed if the expression is true.

(iii)
```
IF (Temperature > Critical) THEN
  IF SystemOnManual THEN
    SoundWarning('Tank temperature > critical')
  ELSE
    MessageToDutyOfficer('Tank temperature > critical');
    MessageToDutyOfficer('Shutting down system.');
    ShutDownSystem
  END
ELSIF TemperatureRise(Temperature) > 0.5 THEN
  TestingFrequency := TestingFrequency * 2
ELSIF TemperatureRise(Temperature) <= 0.5 THEN
  TestingFrequency := TestingFrequency / 2
END;
```

This example illustrates the full power of IF statements, with nesting and the use of both ELSE and ELSIF. The example also shows that multiple ELSIF parts can be used.

18.7 CASE STATEMENT

The CASE statement provides a mechanism for selecting between a number of paths of statement sequences depending on the value of an ordinal expression. In other words, the value of an expression can be used to choose between a number of mutually exclusive statement sequences.

Syntax

```
case statement =
   "CASE", expression, "OF", case, {"|", case},
   ["ELSE", statement sequence], "END";
case = [case label list, ":", statement sequence]
```

The values of the case labels should be expression compatible with the type of the ordinal expression. (See Chapter 16 for further details of type compatibility.)

A range of *consecutive* case labels in a case label list may be specified using '. .' between two constant expressions. (Duplicate values in a case list should be avoided; see *Portability Issues*.)

Description of execution

The ordinal expression following the CASE is evaluated first. It is called the case index. Its value is then used to index the list of statement sequences. (It is as if the list of statement sequences is an array which is indexed by the value of the case expression.) The statement sequence corresponding to the value of the expression is executed. If the value of the expression is not equal to one of those specified in the case labels and is not within any of the range of values specified using '. .', then an exception should occur. (However, see *Portability Issues*.) If you need to know that the value of the expression did not cause a labelled path within the case statement to be selected, you must use the CASE statement's ELSE case.

If an ELSE is included just prior to the end of the case statement, and if the expression's value does not match any values covered by the labels, the statement sequence following the ELSE will be executed. (Of course, this statement sequence may simply consist of the null statement; some argue that always including it is good programming style.)

The CASE statement corresponds closely to the structure of variant records, whose declaration uses a similar syntax. Variant record variables are often processed with a CASE statement whose labels match the labels of the variant or variants (see Example (iii) below).

Because no general-purpose I/O module can provide a means to input values
of an enumeration type, the CASE statement is often used to map character input
to values of an enumeration type and enumerated constants to character strings.

Examples

(i)
```
TYPE
  Month = (Jan, Feb, Mar, Apr, May, Jun,
           Jul, Aug, Sep, Oct, Nov, Dec);
  DayRange = [1..31];
VAR
  ThisMonth: Month;
  MonthNumber: CARDINAL;
  NumberOfDays: DayRange;
BEGIN
  WriteString('Which month (1..12) ?');
  MonthNumber := ReadCard();
  CASE MonthNumber OF
     1: ThisMonth := Jan;
        NumberOfDays := 30 |
     2: ThisMonth := Feb;
        IF ThisYear MOD 4 = 0 THEN
           NumberOfDays := 29
        ELSE
           NumberOfDays := 28
        END |
     3: ThisMonth := Mar;
        NumberOfDays := 31 |
     4: ThisMonth := Apr;
        NumberOfDays := 30 |
     5: ThisMonth := May;
        NumberOfDays := 31 |
     6: ThisMonth := Jun;
        NumberOfDays := 30 |
     7: ThisMonth := Jul;
        NumberOfDays := 31 |
     8: ThisMonth := Aug;
        NumberOfDays := 31 |
     9: ThisMonth := Sep;
        NumberOfDays := 30 |
    10: ThisMonth := Oct;
        NumberOfDays := 31 |
    11: ThisMonth := Nov;
        NumberOfDays := 30 |
    12: ThisMonth := Dec;
        NumberOfDays := 31
  ELSE
    WriteString ('Number input not a valid month')
  END;
  ...
```

This example shows the use of a CASE statement to assign enumeration constants
to the ThisMonth variable (and also to set the appropriate number for
NumberOfDays). Although verbose, this shows how Modula-2 code can be

constructed to be self-documenting and maintainable. Hereafter, meaningful names (like Jan, Feb, etc.) will be used in the code—rather than CARDINAL values.

```
(ii)    GetNextChar(ch);
        CASE ch OF
          ':': GetNextChar(ch);
              IF ch = '=' THEN
                 Symbol := AssignmentOp;
                 GetNextChar(ch);
              ELSE
                 Symbol := Colon
              END |
          '<': GetNextChar(ch);
              CASE ch OF
                '>': Symbol := NotEquals;
                    GetNextChar(ch); |
                '=': Symbol := LessOrEqual;
                    GetNextChar(ch)
              ELSE
                 Symbol := LessThan
                 (* leave character for next time into CASE *)
              END
          ...
        END;
```

This example illustrates the use of a CASE statement with non-alphabetic case label lists, and also the use of nested CASE statements and the ELSE part. This type of code would typically be found in a compiler; its purpose is to change character sequences into tokens of the language.

```
(iii)   TYPE
        ValidCode = [1..9999];
        ProductType = RECORD
                        ProductName: ARRAY [0..19] OF CHAR;
                        CASE ProductCode: ValidCode OF
                          1..3999: (* own brand *)
                            Department: DeptType |
                          4000..5999: (* outside supplier *)
                            Supplier: String;
                            Address: AccountNumber;
                            SalesRep: RepRecord |
                          6000..9999: (* imported product *)
                            Country: CountryName;
                            LocalOffice: OfficeRec
                        END
                      END;
        VAR
          Product: ProductType;
        BEGIN
          WITH Product DO
            ReadString(ProductName);
            ProductCode := Lookup(ProductName);
            CASE ProductCode OF
              1..3999: InputDept(Department) |
```

```
    4000..5999:
       InputSupplierDetails(Supplier, Address, SalesRep) |
    6000..9999: InputImportDetails(Country, LocalOffice)
  END
END;
  ...
```

This example illustrates the use of the CASE statement for processing a variant record.

18.8   WHILE STATEMENT

The WHILE statement allows a statement sequence to be repeatedly executed *zero* or more times, depending on the value of a Boolean expression.

Syntax

```
while statement =
   "WHILE", boolean expression, "DO", statement sequence, "END";
```

Description of execution

The Boolean expression is evaluated, and, if true, the statement sequence is then executed. If false, the statement after the WHILE statement is executed.

After each execution of the statement sequence, the expression is evaluated. If true, the statement sequence is repeated; if false, the repetition finishes.

The evaluation of the Boolean expression is short-circuited if the value can be determined without evaluating all terms in the expression (see Chapter 16). This allows succinct loop conditions to be written. In particular, when processing arrays, Boolean variables do not have to be introduced as flags in order to avoid evaluating indices beyond the array bounds.

The WHILE statement implements a loop which has its continuation condition before the sequence of statements to be repeated (it is a pre-condition loop). This type of loop occurs frequently in software development, but is often avoided because of the way in which the condition specifies when the loop is to continue. These types of conditions are awkward to express in English, but do not be put off by this.

Examples

```
(i)     List[0] := Target;
        Index := NumberInList;
        WHILE List[Index] <> Target DO DEC(Index) END;
        IF Index = 0 THEN
          WriteString('Value not found')
        END;
```

The simplest case with the WHILE statement easily expressed as one line of code.

```
(ii)      WritePrompt; ReadCommand(Command);
          WHILE NOT Command IN ValidCommands DO
            WriteString('Error - invalid command'); WriteLn;
            WriteString('Please re-enter.'); WritePrompt;
            ReadCommand(Command)
          END;
```

This example shows a more complex Boolean expression being used to control the execution of a statement sequence with a WHILE loop.

18.9   REPEAT STATEMENT

The REPEAT statement allows a statement sequence to be repeatedly executed *at least once*; the repetition continues until the value of a Boolean expression becomes true.

Syntax

```
repeat statement =
    "REPEAT", statement sequence, "UNTIL", boolean expression;
```

Description of execution

The statement sequence bracketed by the REPEAT and UNTIL reserved words is executed. Then the Boolean expression is evaluated, and, if false, the statement sequence is executed again. If true, the statement after the REPEAT statement is executed.

After each execution of the sequence, the Boolean expression is re-evaluated to determine whether the loop should continue.

Just as with the WHILE statement, the evaluation of the Boolean expression is short-circuited if the value can be determined without evaluating all terms in the expression (see Chapter 16).

The REPEAT statement implements a loop which has its termination condition after the sequence of statements to be repeated (it is a post-condition loop). This type of condition tends to be easy to express in English, and this can tempt the programmer to use it when a WHILE should be used. This is most obvious when the negation of the terminating condition appears just after the REPEAT in the form of an IF statement whose THEN contains the statements to be repeated. In this case a WHILE should be used (with half as many condition tests!). For example:

```
REPEAT
  IF NOT EndIt THEN
    StatementSequence
```

```
    END
UNTIL EndIt;
```

should be:

```
WHILE NOT EndIt DO
   StatementSequence
END;
```

Example

```
REPEAT
   InputCommand(Command);
   CASE Command OF
     Stop: CleanUp |
     SpreadSheet: SwitchToSpreadSheet |
     WordProcessor: SwitchToWP
   END
UNTIL Command = Stop;
```

This example shows a REPEAT loop which controls task switching, and provides the opportunity for cleaning up prior to termination.

18.10 FOR STATEMENT

The FOR statement is used to repeat a statement sequence a fixed number of times, that number being computed in advance of executing the statement sequence.

Syntax

```
for statement =
    "FOR", identifier, ":= ", expression, "TO", expression,
    ["BY", constant expression], "DO", statement sequence, "END";
```

The identifier must denote a loop control variable of an ordinal type. The FOR loop control variable must not be imported or exported or used as a parameter to a procedure.

The start expression (the first in the statement) must be assignment compatible (see Chapter 16) with the control variable. The end expression should be expression compatible with the control variable. (But see *Portability Issues.*)

The constant expression used to increment or decrement the loop control variable must be of type CARDINAL or INTEGER. If the BY and the constant expression is omitted, an increment of 1 is assumed.

FOR loop control variables

To *threaten* the control variable means to change its value within the loop, or to produce a set of circumstances where the value could be changed, in a way that is likely to cause logic errors in the program. In Standard Pascal there is a rigorous set of rules to prevent threatening of the FOR loop control variable. Modula-2 (as originally defined by Wirth) did not require compilers to implement threatening checks and the majority do not. The forthcoming standard fully defines threatening and what checks should ideally be implemented. The threatening programming problem can be avoided by sensible practices. Therefore the existence or otherwise of threatening checks is a portability issue.

It is sensible to adopt the practice of only using control variables declared locally to the block containing the loop and *never* to assign values to them within loops.

Topspeed Modula-2, in common with most implementations, does not prevent access to the value of the control variable after execution of the FOR loop. However, after execution of a FOR statement, the value of variable used to control the loop is theoretically no longer defined and so should not be used until assigned a new value.

Description of execution

The start expression and end expression are evaluated first. The order with which the start and end expressions themselves are evaluated is implementation dependent (see *Portability Issues*). If the value of the end expression is greater than the start expression (with positive increments) by at least the number of values indicated by the increment, then the statement sequence is executed at least once. Similarly, if the value of the end expression is less than the start expression (with negative increments) by at least the number of values of the increment, then the statement sequence is executed at least once. Otherwise the statement after the FOR statement is executed.

The number of repetitions is given by the formula:

```
(((end expression) - (start expression)) DIV increment) + 1
```

provided that the end expression is greater than the start expression and the increment is positive.

Examples

```
(i)      Total := 0;
         FOR Index := 1 TO NumberInList DO
           Total := Total + List[Index]
         END;
```

Here, the FOR loop is being used to compute the total of all of the elements of the array named List. Note that this will only work if List was indexed from 1 to the value in NumberInList.

```
(ii)     TYPE
            Substance = (a, b, c, d, e);
         VAR
```

```
     Compound: Substance;
...
FOR Compound := a TO e BY -1 DO
   Monitor (Compound)
END;
```

This example shows that the FOR loop control values can be enumeration constants. It also demonstrates how to decrement the control variable : the BY -1 will cause compound to take the values e, d, c, b, a in that order.

18.11 LOOP STATEMENT

The LOOP statement provides for the infinite repetition of a statement sequence. It may also be used in combination with the EXIT statement as a general iteration construct with the possibility of multiple termination points.

Syntax

```
loop statement = "LOOP", statement sequence, "END";
```

Description of execution

The statement sequence is executed repeatedly. If an EXIT statement is executed then the loop is terminated and the statement after the LOOP statement is executed. If LOOP statements are nested (i.e. one LOOP statement inside another one), an EXIT statement only causes the LOOP in which it occurs to terminate. If an EXIT is executed in an inner LOOP, control then passes to the statement in the enclosing LOOP following the END statement of the inner LOOP.

Examples

```
(i)    WriteString ('Fatal error - cannot proceed'); WriteLn;
       LOOP
          (* do nothing forever *)
       END;
```

This example really will do nothing for ever, or for as long as the machine keeps running.

```
(ii)   LOOP
          IF CharAtKeyboard THEN
             ReadKeyboard (Character)
          ELSE
             Character := StringTerminator
          END;
          IF AuxPortOK THEN
             Send (Character)
          ELSE
             EXIT
          END;
```

```
      IF CharAtAuxPort THEN
        ReadAuxPort (Character)
      ELSE
        Character := StringTerminator
      END;
      IF Character <> StringTerminator THEN
        Display (Character)
      END
    END;
```

The example above shows a LOOP statement used to control input from the keyboard and output to a port. The loop can terminate via the EXIT statement in the second IF statement.

18.12 WITH STATEMENT

The WITH statement simplifies access to the fields of records; it allows the field identifiers to be used without the record's name.

Syntax

```
with statement =
    "WITH", designator, "DO", statement sequence, "END";
```

The designator must refer to a record variable.

Description of execution

The designator is evaluated before the statement sequence is executed. All fields belonging to the designated record which are used within the statement sequence need not be preceded by the record variable's identifier. WITH statements may be nested.

Care must be taken when fields within the initially designated record are also designators, as the WITH statement can introduce an ambiguity if field identifiers have been chosen in a manner that could clash (without their 'protective' designator). Because the record designator is evaluated *before* the statement sequence (and only once), access to fields of a record which has been pointed to may be faster. The same is true when a record is an element of an array. For example,

```
WITH a[x + y] DO
   f1 := p;
   f2 := q;
   f3 := r
END;
```

is both clearer to read and will probably be faster to execute than:

```
a[x + y].f1 := p;
a[x + y].f2 := q;
a[x + y].f3 := r;
```

Since the designator is always evaluated before the statement sequence, any iteration statement to process different records must contain any WITH statement being used. (The WITH should not include the iteration.) For example, the following is incorrect:

```
i := 1;
WITH RecArray[i] DO     (*WRONG ORDER*)
  WHILE i <= 10 DO
    Field1 := 0;
    Field2 := FALSE;
    Field3 := 'Y'
  END
END;
```

This piece of code will initialize the fields of RecArray[1] 10 times. The correct loop to initialize all 10 elements is:

```
i := 1;
WHILE i <= 10 DO        (*CORRECT ORDER*)
  WITH RecArray[i] DO
    Field1 := 0;
    Field2 := FALSE;
    Field3 := 'Y'
  END;
  INC(i)
END;
```

18.13   EXIT STATEMENT

The EXIT statement is used to terminate execution of the LOOP statement.

Syntax

```
exit statement = "EXIT" ;
```

An EXIT statement is only allowed within a LOOP statement sequence.

Description of execution

The EXIT statement causes execution to transfer to the END of the LOOP statement in which it is encountered. Note that this only applies to the LOOP in which the EXIT statement appears. (See Section 18.11.)

Example

```
LOOP
  CardinalNumber := PortIO.ReadCard();
```

```
    IF NOT PortIO.Done() THEN
      EXIT
    END;
    ProcessNumber(CardinalNumber)
  END;
```

This example shows how a LOOP statement can be terminated with the EXIT statement, subject to some condition (in this case that PortIO.Done() returns FALSE).

18.14 RETURN STATEMENT

The RETURN statement causes execution of a block to terminate. In a procedure body it is equivalent to transferring control to just before the END of the procedure. In a function procedure, its use with a result expression is the only valid way to complete execution of the function procedure.

RETURN may also be used to terminate execution of a module body.

Syntax

```
return statement = "RETURN", [expression];
```

The RETURN statement usually occurs in a function procedure. In a function procedure it must be followed by an expression which is assignment compatible (see Chapter 16) with the result type of the function procedure.

Description of execution

The effect of the RETURN in a function procedure is to terminate execution of the function procedure *and* to return the value of the expression following the RETURN to the expression which invoked the function procedure. Thus, for example, if the expression on the right hand side of the following assignment makes a call to the function procedure LowerCase:

```
    IsOK := (LowerCase(Reply) = 'y');
```

then the RETURN statement would both terminate the function procedure and pass back the value for testing in the Boolean expression.

```
    PROCEDURE LowerCase(Character: CHAR): BOOLEAN;
      BEGIN
        IF Character IN SetOfChar{"A".."Z"} THEN
          RETURN CHR(ORD(Character) + 32)
        END
      END LowerCase;
```

Executing a RETURN statement is the *only* valid way to terminate a *function* procedure (see Chapter 14).

Although a RETURN expression is used in function procedures, it is syntactically incorrect to use an expression with RETURN in either a proper procedure or a module (there is nowhere for the expression to be returned to). The RETURN statement (without a RETURN expression) is only used exceptionally to terminate execution of a procedure or a module.

In the case of procedures, the RETURN statement causes control to be transferred to the statement after the procedure call. The effect of a RETURN statement in a module body is different for program and implementation modules. In a program module it causes the program to be terminated as if the last statement in the main module had been executed. In an implementation module body a RETURN statement will abort the initialization but will not terminate the program.

Examples

(i)
```
        PROCEDURE Max(List: ARRAY OF REAL): REAL;
          VAR
            CurrentMax: REAL;
            CurrentElement: CARDINAL;
          BEGIN
            CurrentMax := List[0];
            FOR CurrentElement := 1 TO HIGH(List) DO
              IF List[CurrentElement] > CurrentMax THEN
                CurrentMax := List[CurrentElement]
              END
            END;
            RETURN CurrentMax
          END Max;
```

This example shows the normal use of a RETURN statement in a function procedure. (The procedure finds the maximum value in an array of REAL values.)

(ii)
```
        BEGIN (* DatabaseManager module *)
          IF DataBaseEmpty THEN RETURN END;
          (* Read Data from database and initialize data structure *)
          ...
        END DatabaseManager.
```

This example illustrates the use of a RETURN statement to abort the initialization code of an implementation module.

18.15 PORTABILITY ISSUES

There are surprisingly few portability issues to be described for statements. Several issues could arise out of procedure calls, but these are dealt with in Chapter 14.

Order of evaluation of assignment statements

The assignment statements have the following syntax:

```
assignment = designator ":=" expression;
```

The order of evaluation of the designator and the expression is implementation dependent, and could therefore occur in either order. You cannot even rely on a compiler always doing it one way round: it could vary for the same compiler with different assignment statements. Problems arise when the same identifier occurs on both sides of the statement, or when the value of an identifier that occurs on one side is modified by a function call that occurs on the other side. For example:

```
Larry[x] := fiddle(x);
```

In this case, `fiddle` is a function procedure which could modify the value of x. If the right hand side is evaluated first, then a different component of the array called `Larry` will have a new value assigned. The best way of preventing such potential problems is to avoid the use of the functions with side-effects—and where possible—avoid using the same identifier on both sides of an assignment statements.

Topspeed Modula-2 evaluates assignment statements in both orders, depending upon circumstances. Do not assume a particular order.

Failure to match CASE labels

As described in Section 18.7, the failure of a CASE statement to match a label to the value of its index expression should result in an exception. However, some Modula-2 compilers will not detect this and the most likely outcome is that the statement following the CASE statement will be executed. It is prudent always to include ELSE parts in CASE statements.

Repetition in CASE label lists

Some Modula-2 compilers prohibit the repetition of case labels in case label lists. This can occur in two ways, as illustrated by the following examples:

```
CASE example1 OF
  a, x, a : maynotbelegal := TRUE;
  ...
END;

CASE example2 OF
  2, 1..3 : maynotbelegal := TRUE;
  ...
END;
```

In the first case, the repetition is explicit. In the second case, the repetition occurs between the explicit value and value range. The practice is best avoided. Topspeed Modula-2 does not allow case label list repetition.

Threatening of FOR loop control variables

In the original definition of Modula-2, Professor Wirth states that the value of a FOR loop control variable:

> *'...should not be changed by the statements sequence...'*

Most Modula-2 compiler implementors have noted the use of the word 'should', rather than the stronger 'must' that Professor Wirth uses when he is more prescriptive, and have taken this to mean that they are not mandated to provide the associated threatening checks in their products.

Since, in general, the threatening checks will not be there to assist you, it is strongly recommended that no assignments ever be made to FOR loop control variables. If assignments are made, quite bizarre and unpredictable performance could arise.

Topspeed Modula-2 does not check for threatening.

Post-execution access to FOR loop control variables

When introducing the FOR statement in the introductory part of his book (*Programming in Modula-2*), Professor Wirth states that :

> *'...The value of the control variable must be considered*
> *as undefined after the FOR statement is terminated...'*

However, this statement is not repeated in the book's more formal *'Report on the Programming Language Modula-2 '*. As a result, many Modula-2 compilers do not enforce this rule, so the FOR loop control variable may be accessible after termination of the loop. Nevertheless, it is extremely poor programming practice to try to access this value, and the results of doing so will be unpredictable.

Topspeed Modula-2 does not enforce this check.

Order of evaluation of FOR loop start and end expressions

FOR loops are controlled by start and end expressions. The order of evaluation of these two expressions is implementation dependent, and could therefore occur in either order. You cannot rely on a compiler always doing it one way round: it could vary for the same compiler with different FOR statements. Problems arise when the same identifier occurs in both expressions, or when the value of an identifier that occurs in one expression is modified by a function procedure call that occurs in the other expression. For example:

```
FOR dodgy := start TO fiddle(end) DO ...
```

In this case, if the function called fiddle modifies the value of start, then unpredictable results could arise if the end expression is evaluated first. The best way of preventing such potential problems is to avoid the use of functions with side-effects, and—where possible—avoid using the same identifier (directly or indirectly) in both the start and end expressions.

Topspeed Modula-2 evaluates the start and end expressions in both orders, depending upon circumstances.

FOR *loop control variable type compatibility rules*

Originally, Modula-2 required the FOR loop control variable to be assignment compatible with the start and end expressions. The rule is now expression compatibility, which is stronger than assignment compatibility. Therefore, older compilers may implement the weaker rule, but any code which takes advantage of this will not be portable.

Topspeed Modula-2 implements the newer, expression compatibility rule.

18.16 REVIEW QUESTIONS AND EXERCISES

Q18.1 What is short-circuit Boolean evaluation?

Q18.2 What is the least number of times that a WHILE loop statement sequence will be executed?

Q18.3 What is the least number of times that a REPEAT loop statement sequence will be executed?

Q18.4 What is the purpose of the EXIT statement?

Q18.5 What is the RETURN statement usually used for?

Q18.6 Consider the following CASE statement sequence:
```
CASE Index OF
   1 :... |
   2 :... |
   3 : ...
END;
```
IF the value of Index were to be 4, the program should terminate with a suitable error message. However, some compilers do not trap this error and allow the program to continue. How could you write a portable CASE sequence which would always trap an invalid CASE index?

Q18.7 Consider the following declarations:
```
TYPE
   StringType = ARRAY StringRange OF CHAR;
   YearRange = [1900..1999];
   MediumType = (Vinyl, Cassette, CD);
   MusicType = (Rock, Jazz, Folk, Classical, Light);
   AlbumRec = RECORD
               Medium: MediumType;
               Title, Artists, CatalogueNumber: StringType;
               Year: YearRange;
               Music: MusicType
            END;
VAR Album: AlbumRec;
```
Rewrite the following assignment (which uses the **non-portable** structured value constructors) using a WITH statement.
```
Album :=
   AlbumRec{Vinyl, "Sgt. Pepper's Lonely Hearts' Club Band",
        "The Beatles", PCS 7027", 1967, Rock};
```

19 ARRAYS

19.1 INTRODUCTION

Arrays are used where there are many variables of the same type that are treated in the same way. Typically, they are used to implement tables or lists of data. An array type consists of a fixed number of components which can be of any single type, but must all be of the same type, called the *component type*. Associated with these components there is an index which is used to select an individual component of the array. This index type must be an ordinal type. The number of components that an array contains is determined by the number of values in the index type. Array types are specified using the array type constructor. (The special case of using character arrays as string types is covered in Chapter 10.)

19.2 ARRAY TYPE DECLARATIONS

An *array type constructor* is provided in order to specify array types from an index type and a component type.

Syntax

> array type = "ARRAY", ordinal type, {",", ordinal type}, "OF", type;

Note that the syntax allows more than one index of ordinal type to be declared; arrays with more than one index are termed multi-dimensional.

Examples

```
TYPE
  Array1 = ARRAY [1..40] OF CARDINAL;
```

```
Array2 = ARRAY [0..79] OF CHAR;
Array3 = ARRAY [1..5], [1..10] OF CARDINAL;
Index1 = [1..20];
Index2 = [1..5];
Array4 = ARRAY Index1, Index2 OF INTEGER;
Rainbow = (Red,Orange,Yellow,Green,Blue,Indigo,Violet);
Array5 = ARRAY Index1 OF Rainbow;
Array6 = ARRAY Rainbow OF REAL;
Alphabet = ['A'..'Z'];
Array7 = ARRAY Alphabet OF BOOLEAN;
```

19.3   ARRAY VARIABLES

In order to denote a component of an array variable, the variable name is written followed by the index expression in square brackets. For example, given these variable declarations:

```
VAR
  MyArray : Array1;
  Value : CARDINAL;
```

then values of type CARDINAL can be assigned to components of the array variable MyArray in the following manner:

```
MyArray[1] := 25;
MyArray[4] := 3*6;
```

Similarly the values of individual components are assigned to variables of the component's type in the following manner :

```
Value := MyArray[1]; (* Value = 25 *)
Value := MyArray[4]; (* Value = 18 *)
```

The most frequent mistake that is made in processing arrays is to try to index an array with a value which is outside the index range. Strictly speaking a Modula-2 implementation should detect this type of mistake and report an exception. However, many compilers permit this checking to be suppressed for the sake of efficiency (see *Portability Issues* below).

An array can be manipulated as a single variable. Given the declarations:

```
VAR
  ArrayA, ArrayB : Array1;
```

then the following assignment statement is possible:

```
ArrayA := ArrayB;
```

this is almost equivalent to writing:

```
FOR Count := 1 TO 40 DO
  ArrayA[Count] := ArrayB[Count]
END;
```

However, the assignment statement is *not* equivalent to the above FOR loop because the loop imposes an order on copying the components; the array assignment implies no order of copying.

Arrays and assignment compatibility

If two arrays were declared anonymously as:

```
VAR
    ArrayA, ArrayB : ARRAY [1..40] OF CARDINAL;
```

then the same assignment statement:

```
ArrayA := ArrayB;
```

would still be legal Modula-2. However, care must be taken. Remember that Modula-2 is a strongly typed language. Given the following variable declarations:

```
VAR
    ArrayC : ARRAY [1..40] OF CARDINAL;
    ArrayD : ARRAY [1..40] OF CARDINAL;
```

then:

```
ArrayC := ArrayD;
```

is an illegal statement. This is because ArrayC and ArrayD are *not* identical (as ArrayA and ArrayB are) and therefore do not meet the assignment compatibility rules. (See Chapter 16 for more details on compatibility.)

However, with the same declarations of ArrayC and ArrayD :

```
FOR Count := 1 TO 40 DO
   ArrayC[Count] := ArrayD[Count]
END;
```

is legal because the array components are identical (both are of type CARDINAL) and therefore assignment compatible.

19.4 SINGLE-DIMENSION ARRAYS

A *single-dimension array* is an array whose components are themselves not arrays. Thus to access a component requires a *single* index—hence the term. They are the simplest array structures to implement and are frequently used to model lists. The following example demonstrates how to create and access a single-dimensional array.

```
MODULE MyClass;
TYPE
   Surname = (Harvey, Austin, Turner, Stock);
   List = ARRAY [1..4] OF Surname;
VAR
   Class : List;
   Student : Surname;
   Counter : CARDINAL;
BEGIN
```

```
      Student := Harvey;
      FOR Counter := 1 TO 4 DO
        Class [Counter] := Student;
        IF Student <> Stock THEN INC(Student) END
      END
   END MyClass.
```

The result of running this program would be to create an array called `Class` of type `List`. The array components have had the following values assigned to them:

Index	1	2	3	4
Class	Harvey	Austin	Turner	Stock

The assignment statement:

```
   Student := Class[3];
```

would result in the variable `Student` being assigned the value `Turner`.

It should be noted that an array data structure can define two distinct relationships. First, there is the relationship between a given index and the component in the array it identifies. This is demonstrated in the example above. Second, there is the relationship that can exist between individual data items due to the order they are held in the array. The example above will be rewritten to reflect this second type of relationship. Instead of entering values of `Surname` into the array in enumeration order, we shall pretend that an examination has just taken place and therefore values of `Surname` will be entered into positions in the array depending on how well each candidate did in the examination. For this example a function procedure called `ReadName` will be assumed which prompts the user for each candidate's name, in order of achievement, and returns values of type `Surname` as its result.

```
   MODULE ExamArray;
   FROM PortIO IMPORT ReadString;
   TYPE
      Surname = (Harvey, Austin, Turner, Stock);
      List = ARRAY [1..4] OF Surname;
   VAR
      Examinees: List;
      Student: Surname;
      Counter: CARDINAL;
   PROCEDURE ReadName() : Surname;
      BEGIN
         (* Reads a string which is mapped onto *)
         (* a value of type Surname.            *)
      END ReadName;
   BEGIN
      FOR Counter := 1 TO 4 DO
        Examinees[Counter] := ReadName()
      END
   END ExamArray.
```

The result of running this program would be to create an array called Examinees of type List. The value Austin has been assigned to the first component of the array as that candidate came top in the examinations. The value Stock has been assigned to the second component as that candidate came second, etc.

Index	1	2	3	4
Examinees	Austin	Stock	Harvey	Turner

The assignment statement:

```
Student := Examinees[1];
```

will assign to the variable Student, the name of the person who came first in the examination.

It is now possible to establish how well each student did in relation to the others, but there is no information on what each candidate's mark was. If the array is declared slightly differently these marks can be captured. This can be done by using the enumeration type Surname as the index to the array Examinees and by using the components of the array to hold the marks each candidate achieved. In the following example a function procedure called ReadFromTerminal will be assumed that takes as its parameter the candidate's name and prompts a terminal user for that candidate's marks which it returns as its result.

```
MODULE StudentsMarks;
FROM PortIO IMPORT WriteString, ReadCard;
TYPE
   Surname = (Turner, Harvey, Stock, Austin);
   Marks = [0..100];
   List = ARRAY Surname OF Marks;
VAR
   Examinees: List;
   Name: Surname;
   Result: Marks;
PROCEDURE ReadFromTerminal(Name : Surname) : Marks;
   BEGIN
   ...
   END ReadFromTerminal;
BEGIN (*StudentsMarks*)
   ...
   FOR Name := MIN(Surname) TO MAX(Surname) DO
     Examinees[Name] := ReadFromTerminal(Name);
   END;
END StudentsMarks.
```

The diagram below represents the array created by the above program:

Index	Turner	Harvey	Stock	Austin
Examinees	55	63	70	59

The assignment statement:

```
Result := Examinees[Turner];
```

would assign the value 55 to the variable `Result`.

Searching arrays

It is often important to search array structures in order to determine whether a particular value exists in one of the array's components. Consider the example module `StudentsMarks`. It would have been useful to be able to search the array `Examinees` to determine if any student achieved a particular mark in that examination.

In the next example the following strategy is adopted. The array type `List` is declared one component larger by adding the enumeration constant `SearchDummy` to the type `Surname`. `SearchDummy` will become the low bound index of the array variable `Examinees`. This extra component is only used when searching the array, and is used to store the mark that is being searched for.

```
MODULE ExamResults;
FROM PortIO IMPORT WriteString, ReadCard;
TYPE
   Surname = (SearchDummy, Turner, Harvey, Stock, Austin);
   Marks = [0..100];
   List = ARRAY Surname OF Marks;
VAR
   Examinees: List;
   Name: Surname;
   Result: Marks;

PROCEDURE ReadFromTerminal(Name: Surname) : Marks;
   BEGIN
     CASE Name OF
       Harvey : WriteString('Harvey = ') |
       Turner : WriteString('Turner = ') |
       Stock  : WriteString('Stock = ') |
       Austin : WriteString('Austin = ')
     END;
     RETURN ReadCard();
   END ReadFromTerminal;

PROCEDURE EasySearch(Result : Marks; Examinees : List): Surname;
   VAR Name : Surname;
   BEGIN
     Examinees[SearchDummy] := Result; Name := Austin;
     WHILE Result <> Examinees[Name] DO
       DEC(Name)
     END;
     RETURN Name
   END EasySearch;

PROCEDURE ArrayQuery(Examinees:List);
   VAR Result : Marks;
   BEGIN
     WriteString('Enter mark to search for : ');
```

```
            Result := ReadCard();
            CASE EasySearch(Result,Examinees) OF
              Harvey : WriteString('Harvey')  |
              Turner : WriteString('Turner')  |
              Stock : WriteString('Stock')  |
              Austin : WriteString('Austin')  |
              SearchDummy : WriteString('Mark not achieved')
            END;
          END ArrayQuery;

      BEGIN (*Body of ExamResults*)
        FOR Name := Turner TO Austin DO
          Examinees[Name] := ReadFromTerminal(Name);
        END;
        ArrayQuery(Examinees)
      END ExamResults.
```

The body of the module `ExamResults` looks similar to the body of the module `StudentsMarks` except for the call of the procedure `ArrayQuery`. This procedure prompts the user to enter an examination mark. With this value it calls the procedure `EasySearch` which works in the following manner. Starting at the high bound index of the array `Examinees`, which is at `Examinees[Austin]`, a test is made to see whether this matches the value being searched for. The other components in the array are tested in descending order until a match is found. It should be noted that a match is always achieved because the component `Examinees[SearchDummy]` holds the target value. If at the end of the search the match is found at `Examinees[SearchDummy]`, then the search has failed.

The reason for adopting this strategy is that it removes the need for a count to detect the lower bound of the array, as the array is searched only until a match is found, and of course this is always the case. `EasySearch` then returns the index to the component where the search value was found to `ArrayQuery`.

19.5 MULTI-DIMENSIONAL ARRAYS

Modula-2 does not *explicitly* provide a ***multi-dimensional array*** data structure; the only form of array structuring provided is that of the single-dimensional array. However, because the components of an array can be of any type, it is possible to have arrays whose components are themselves arrays. This provides the ability to model the properties of multi-dimensional arrays.

The following example demonstrates the declarations that would be needed to declare a two-dimensional array that models a chess board:

```
TYPE
  ChessPiece =
      (NoPiece, King, Queen, Knight, Bishop, Rook, Pawn);
  Column = (A, B, C, D, E, F, G, H); (*standard chess notation*)
  Row = [1..8];
  ChessBoard = ARRAY Column OF ARRAY Row OF ChessPiece;
```

The declaration of ChessBoard is rather cumbersome, so Modula-2 provides a shorthand syntax:

```
ChessBoard = ARRAY Column, Row OF ChessPiece;
```

The variable declarations are:

```
VAR
    x: Column; y: Row;
    Board: ChessBoard;
```

In order to reference a position on the chess board one of two methods can be used, either:

```
Board[x][y];
```

or:

```
Board[x, y];
```

Note that the methods are equivalent and completely interchangeable, regardless of how the array was declared. The second method is simply a shorthand version of the first.

The model of a two-dimensional array differs from a true two-dimensional array in one important respect. A *slice* through the array variable Board can be referenced by a variable of type Column. For example, Board[x] will give a slice of eight board positions. However, there is no way of getting a slice of eight board positions by giving a variable of type Row. This is because the 'two-dimensional' array is really an array of arrays, and therefore the Row coordinates are dependent on first selecting a Column coordinate.

Recall the example module in Section 19.4 called StudentsMarks, which demonstrated how to store students' marks in a single-dimensional array. What if each candidate sat more than one examination each year? How could the marks for each examination be captured? A two-dimensional array needs to be modelled.

In the following example, it will be assumed that the function procedure ReadFromTerminal now takes as its parameters the candidate's name and subject and prompts a user for three marks for each candidate, which it returns as its result. (The SearchDummy value of Surname has been omitted.)

```
MODULE StudentsMarks2;
FROM PortIO IMPORT WriteString, WriteLn, ReadCard;
TYPE
    Surname = (Turner, Harvey, Stock, Austin);
    Subject = (Maths, English, French);
    Marks = [0..100];
    Students = ARRAY Surname, Subject OF Marks;
VAR
    MyStudents : Students;
    Name : Surname;
    Result : Marks;
    Subj : Subject;
```

```
PROCEDURE ReadFromTerminal(Name: Surname; Subj: Subject): Marks;
  BEGIN
     (* Modified version of ReadFromTerminal which prompts for
        Subject as well as Name.*)
  END ReadFromTerminal;

BEGIN (*body of StudentsMarks2*)
  ...
  FOR Name := MIN(Surname) TO MAX(Surname) DO
    FOR Subj := MIN(Subject) TO MAX(Subject) DO
      MyStudents[Name, Subj] := ReadFromTerminal(Name, Subj)
    END
  END
END StudentsMarks2.
```

Notice the use of the nested FOR loop in the body of StudentsMarks. Through the mechanism of this nested loop every component of the two-dimensional array can be accessed. The result of this module would be to create an array that could be represented graphically by the diagram below:

	Turner	Harvey	Stock	Austin
Maths	55	70	33	85
English	63	45	89	59
French	70	65	73	61

An assignment statement of the form:

```
Result := MyStudents[Turner, French];
```

would assign the value 70 (corresponding to the marks the student Turner attained in French) to the variable Result.

The strategy used for two-dimensional arrays can be extended to three dimensions by having an array of arrays of arrays!

19.6   OPEN ARRAY PARAMETERS

Modula-2 provides the means of declaring procedures that are able to process arrays that differ in their index types while sharing the same component type. This is achieved by declaring the array in the formal parameter list of the procedure as an *open array parameter*. An example of a procedure declaration with an open array parameter follows:

```
PROCEDURE MySort(VAR AnArray : ARRAY OF CARDINAL);
```

You will notice that the declaration of the array differs from the normal array declaration, in that the index bounds of the array are omitted. See Chapter 14 for the full syntax for open array parameters.

By declaring an open array parameter, the index range of the actual array that is passed to the procedure is mapped onto the cardinal numbers $0 . . n-1$, where n represents the number of components in the actual array.

In order to process an array that is passed to the procedure it would be necessary to find the high bound index of the array. This is found by using the built-in function procedure HIGH, which returns the value of the upper limit of an open array.

```
UpperLimit := HIGH(AnArray);
```

Procedures that are passed arrays via open array parameters can only process those arrays component by component. For example, given the following procedure heading:

```
PROCEDURE Assign (Oarray1, Oarray2: ARRAY OF CARDINAL);
```

Within this procedure it would be illegal to make the following assignment statement:

```
Oarray1 := Oarray2;
```

Instead the components of Oarray2 would have to be assigned to the components of Oarray1, element by element.

Note that the consequence of mapping the index range of the actual open array parameter onto the CARDINAL subrange [0..n-1] is that the index type of the actual array is unknown to the procedure. Therefore, if a search procedure is defined to return the index of some known value, then the index returned must be adjusted by adding the lower bound of the actual array's index range to the returned index. For example:

```
MODULE ArrayIndex;
FROM SomeModule IMPORT Index; (* subrange *)
TYPE
   ArrayOfCards = ARRAY Index OF CARDINAL;
VAR
   CardArray : ArrayOfCards;
   IndexOfCard : Index;
   Value : CARDINAL;

PROCEDURE Search(A: ARRAY OF CARDINAL; C: CARDINAL): CARDINAL;
   BEGIN
      (* returns an index of A where C is found *)
   END Search;

BEGIN
   ...
   IndexOfCard := Search(CardArray, Value) + MIN(Index);
   ...
END ArrayIndex.
```

Notice that the value returned by Search is adjusted by adding the lower bound of the actual array's index range to the returned value.

Procedures with open array parameters are often used to sort the elements of arrays. The following example demonstrates the well-known bubble sort method.

```
PROCEDURE BubbleSort(VAR IntArray : ARRAY OF INTEGER);
   VAR
```

```
      Bubble, Count : CARDINAL;
      SortFlag : BOOLEAN;
  PROCEDURE Swap(VAR Upper, Lower : INTEGER);
    VAR
      Temp : INTEGER;
    BEGIN
      Temp := Upper;
      Upper := Lower;
      Lower := Temp
    END Swap;

  BEGIN
    Count := 0; SortFlag := TRUE;
    WHILE (Count < HIGH(IntArray)) AND SortFlag DO
      Bubble := HIGH(IntArray); SortFlag := FALSE;
      REPEAT
        IF IntArray[Bubble] < IntArray[Bubble - 1] THEN
          Swap(IntArray[Bubble], IntArray[Bubble - 1]);
          SortFlag := TRUE
        END;
        DEC(Bubble);
      UNTIL Bubble = Count;
      INC(Count);
    END;
  END BubbleSort.
```

19.7   PORTABILITY ISSUES

There are a number of portability issues associated with arrays. These include the provision of structured array values, the restriction that some compilers place on open array parameters, the type of the value that HIGH returns, and, finally, compilers that economize on memory by packing character arrays.

Structured array values

During the standardization of Modula-2, the need to be able to denote structured values was recognized and a new feature—structured value constructors—was introduced into the language. Some implementations of Modula-2 have already incorporated this feature. An array value constructor allows a sequence of expressions which compute a value corresponding to each and every component of an array to be assigned to an array variable or constant.

Syntax

```
value constructor =
   array constructor | record constructor | set constructor;
array constructor = array type identifier, array definition;
array type identifier = qualified identifier;
array definition = "{", component, {",", component},"}";
component = expression;
```

Examples

(i)
```
TYPE
  ArrayType = ARRAY [1..5] OF CARDINAL;
VAR
  AnArray : ArrayType ;
  x : CARDINAL;
CONST
  InitialValue = ArrayType{0,0,0,0,0};
BEGIN
  AnArray := ArrayType{52, x DIV 4, 101, x * 3, 99};
```

In this example, AnArray is assigned six values in one statement.

(ii)
```
PROCEDURE SumArray(AnArray : ArrayType) : CARDINAL;
  BEGIN
    . . .
  END SumArray;
BEGIN
  . . .
  x := SumArray
        (ArrayType{52, x DIV 4, 101, x * 3, 99});
```

A value constructor can also be used to pass values to an actual array parameter.

(iii)
```
CONST
  ArrayConst = ArrayType{52, x DIV 4, 101, x * 3, 99};
```

A value constructor can be used to pass values to an array constant. Note that the array type identifier is required to form an array value constructor, therefore anonymous types cannot be used.

Some implementors, whilst incorporating structured value constructors in their compilers, have evolved non-standard syntaxes. For example, in Topspeed Modula-2 an array constant would be constructed as follows:

```
ArrayConst = ArrayType(542, 324, 1061,3, 199);
```

Notice the difference; the use of round brackets rather than curly brackets (braces).

Use of the function procedure HIGH

Many compilers allow HIGH to be applied to non-open array parameters. The usefulness of this is questionable; if the parameter is a non-open array parameter then the upper bound index is known to the procedure from the procedure heading. Therefore, to maintain the portability of your code, avoid the use of HIGH in these circumstances.

Also, many compilers restrict the value which HIGH returns to those values of $\mathbb{Z}$ which are also CARDINAL values, even though enormous chunks of memory addressed by LONGCARDs may be passed to open arrays. Furthermore, some compilers have HIGH return an INTEGER value, rather than a value of type $\mathbb{Z}$.

Problems with string representation

If an array is declared as ARRAY [0..n-1] OF CHAR, some compilers will *pack* such an array in order to save memory. This means that instead of storing the characters of the array in n contiguous memory locations of size equal to SIZE(CHAR), the compiler will instead store the characters in n contiguous memory locations of size equal to SIZE(WORD) DIV SIZE(CHAR). The result of this is that many implementations will prohibit the passing of an element of a packed array as an actual VAR-parameter. To overcome this, a temporary variable must be used.

Multi-dimensional open arrays

A few implementations allow multi-dimensional open array parameters of the form:

```
PROCEDURE Dimentia(X: ARRAY OF ARRAY OF REAL);
```

These allow actual parameters which are multi-dimensional arrays. HIGH(X) gives the extent of the first dimension, HIGH(X[0]) gives the extent of the second dimension, HIGH(X[0,0]) the third, etc. Although multi-dimensional open array parameters have been proposed for the standard, they are not common enough to be considered portable.

Index type of arrays

Some compilers insist that the index type of an array is a subrange type (it need only be an ordinal type). Such a restriction is properly regarded as a bug, but you may want to restrict your code.

19.8 REVIEW EXERCISES

Q19.1 Declare a subrange type called Age that will encompass the cardinal values 0–105. Then declare an array type with 20 components that will hold values of type Age.

Q19.2 Given a variable of type ArrayOfAge, write a code fragment that will calculate the number of people who are over the age of 25.

Q19.3 Given an array variable of type ArrayOfAges, write a code fragment to move each value in the array up by one position; e.g. the value in ArrayVar[1], is moved to the component ArrayVar[2], the value in ArrayVar[2] is moved to the component ArrayVar[3], etc. Finally the value in ArrayVar[20] is moved to the component ArrayVar[1].

Q19.4 Reverse the values in a variable of type ArrayOfAges, such that the values in ArrayVar[1] and ArrayVar[2] are exchanged, the values in ArrayVar[2] and ArrayVar[19] are exchanged, etc.

Q19.5 Each type of item in a warehouse is identified by a part number. Declare a two-dimensional array that can store, for 20 item types, both the part number and the number of associated items that are currently held in stock. Assume that both part numbers and the number of items are represented by cardinal values.

Q19.6 Given an array variable of the above type, initialize all its components to zero.

Q19.7 Write a procedure that will search the array for a particular part number and output to the screen the number of associated items that are currently in stock .

Q19.8 In the `StudentsMarks2` example the marks each candidate achieved in three examinations were captured. Write a module to capture the attainment record of each candidate over a three-year period. `ReadFromTerminal` will now take as its parameters the candidate's name, and the year and subject and prompts a terminal user for that candidate's marks for that subject during that particular year, which it returns as its result.

20 RECORDS

20.1 INTRODUCTION

A record is a data structure which allows a number of variables of different types to be stored under a single name. Thus, in contrast to arrays whose components are homogeneous, components of a record type have different types.

20.2 RECORD TYPE DECLARATIONS

A record consists of a number of components which are called fields. Each of these fields has a unique identifying name called the field identifier, by which the value in the field can be accessed. The complete record structure is referenced by the record identifier name. The syntax of a record type declaration is as follows.

Syntax

```
record type = "RECORD", field list sequence, "END";
field list sequence = field list, {";", field list};
field list =
    identifier list, ":", type |
    "CASE", [tag identifier], ":", tag type, "OF", variant, {"|", variant},
    ["ELSE", field list sequence], "END";
variant = [case label list, ":", field list sequence];
```

From the above syntax for a *field list,* it can be seen that the field list of a record can take two forms. Either the field identifier list is followed by its type or by a construction which is similar to the CASE statement. This CASE construct is used to define records that may assume different forms. Records so constructed are termed *variant records* and will be described in detail in Section 20.4. Records which have a fixed structure are called *non-variant records* and will form the basis of discussion until Section 20.4.

Examples

(i)   TYPE
       ValidNo = [0..100];
       StockItem = (Spanner, Hammer, Screwdriver, Wrench);
       MyStock = RECORD
             Item : StockItem;
             NoOfItems : ValidNo
          END;

The example above declares a record called MyStock which has two fields denoted by the field identifiers Item and NoOfItems. The field list sequence consists of those declarations between the reserved words RECORD and END. Each of the lines making up the field list sequence are the field lists, both of which in this example consist of a single identifier followed by a colon and then the type name.

(ii)   TYPE
       Name = ARRAY [0..23] OF CHAR;
       JobTitle = (Carpenter, Plumber, Bricklayer, Electrician);
       Dollars = [100..600];
       Employee = RECORD
             Surname : Name;
             Forename : Name;
             Job : JobTitle;
             Wages : Dollars
          END;

The above example declares a record type called Employee which has four fields. Because Surname and Forename are of the same type, the record declaration could be written as:

   Employee = RECORD
          Surname, Forename : Name;
          Job : JobTitle;
          Wages : Dollars
       END;

The record still has four fields, but now the first field list contains two identifiers.

20.3   RECORD VARIABLES

The fields of a record variable are selected by using the record *field selector*. This takes the form of a period (full-stop) between the variable name and the record field. For example, given these declarations:

   TYPE
     ValidNo = [0..100];
     StockItem = (Spanner, Hammer, Screwdriver, Wrench);
     MyStock = RECORD

```
                Item : StockItem;
                NoOfItems : ValidNo
             END;
   VAR
     StockA, StockB, StockC : MyStock;
```

then values can be assigned to the fields of the record variable `StockA`, by denoting the field with the period and the record field name.

```
   StockA.Item := Hammer;
   StockA.NoOfItems := 20;
```

A record can be manipulated as a single entity. This permits assignment statements of the following form:

```
   StockC := StockA;
```

This is equivalent to the following (but without the order implied below):

```
   StockC.Item := StockA.Item;
   StockC.NoOfItems := StockA.NoOfItems;
```

WITH statement

Modula-2 provides the `WITH` statement to simplify reference to record variables. Consider the following example which uses the record type `Employee` declared in Section 20.2:

```
   VAR
     Worker : Employee;
   BEGIN
     Worker.Surname := 'Moriarty';
     Worker.Forename := 'Dean';
     Worker.Job := Plumber;
     Worker.Wages := 500;
```

A more economical and clear way of writing the assignment statements in the above example would have been to use the `WITH` statement. By making use of this construct, the record identifier need only be specified once; thereafter within the `WITH` statement sequence, the field names can be used without their prefix.

```
   WITH Worker DO
     Surname := 'Moriarty';
     Forename := 'Dean';
     Job := Plumber;
     Wages := 500
   END;
```

Example

The syntax of record type declarations given in Section 20.2 shows that the field of a record can be of any type. This allows us to have fields which are themselves structured types, such as arrays and records.

Consider a name and address in the format of :

```
Mr John Smith,
1604, Ocean Boulevard,
Tampa,
Florida,
23234.
```

The name and address could be modelled as a record called `NameAddress`, which has two fields which are themselves records, as follows:

NameRecord	AddressRecord

`NameRecord` has the fields:

Title	Forename	Surname

and `AddressRecord` has the fields:

Number	Street	City	State	Zip

It is unlikely that anyone would write a program to manipulate a single record, therefore in the following example an array will be used to hold a collection of records.

```
MODULE MyAddressBook;
FROM PortIO IMPORT WriteLn, WriteString, ReadString, ReadCard;
TYPE
   AlphaType = ARRAY [0..23] OF CHAR;
   TitleType = (Mr, Mrs, Miss, Ms);
   NameRecord = RECORD
                   Title : TitleType;
                   Forename, Surname: AlphaType;
                END;
   AddressRecord = RECORD
                      Number : CARDINAL;
                      Street, City, State: AlphaType;
                      Zip : CARDINAL
                   END;
   NameAddress = RECORD
                    Name : NameRecord;
                    Address : AddressRecord
                 END;
   Pages = [1..50];
   AddressBookType = ARRAY Pages OF NameAddress;
VAR
   AddressBook : AddressBookType;
   Counter : Pages;
BEGIN
   FOR Counter := MIN(Pages) TO MAX(Pages) DO
     WITH AddressBook[Counter] DO
       WriteString('Enter 1 for Mr'); WriteLn;
       WriteString('Enter 2 for Mrs');WriteLn;
       WriteString('Enter 3 for Miss'); WriteLn;
       WriteString('Enter 4 for Ms'); WriteLn;
```

```
      CASE ReadCard() OF
        1 : Name.Title := Mr |
        2 : Name.Title := Mrs |
        3 : Name.Title := Miss |
        4 : Name.Title := Ms
      END;
      WriteString('Enter Forename : ');
      ReadString(Name.Forename);
      WriteLn;
      WriteString('Enter Surname : ');
      ReadString(Name.Surname);
      WriteLn;
      WriteString('Enter Street No. : ');
      Address.Number := ReadCard();
      WriteLn;
      WriteString('Enter Street Name : ');
      ReadString(Address.Street);
      WriteLn;
      WriteString('Enter City : ');
      ReadString(Address.City);
      WriteLn;
      WriteString('Enter State : ');
      ReadString(Address.State);
      WriteLn;
      WriteString('Enter Zip Code : ');
      Address.Zip := ReadCard()
    END;
  END;

END MyAddressBook.
```

20.4   VARIANT RECORDS

Modula-2 has a mechanism that allows the programmer to declare records that can take alternative, mutually exclusive, field list sequences. These field list sequences can differ both in the number of fields and in their type. Such records are known as *variant records*. For convenience, the syntax of a record field list is repeated below.

Syntax

```
field list =
    identifier list, ":", type |
    "CASE", [tag identifier], ":", tag type, "OF", variant, {"|", variant},
    ["ELSE", field list sequence], "END";
variant = [case label list, ":", field list sequence];
```

Declaration of variant records

The declaration of a variant field list sequence is achieved by the use of a construction similar to a CASE statement (see Chapter 18). The tag field of the record follows the reserved word CASE. The tag field consists of the tag identifier followed by its type. The case labels are constants which are also of the tag type. Note that if the tag field is omitted (see below) the colon symbol and a tag type must be given.

```
TYPE
   ResortType = (Ski, Sun);
   SkiResortName = (Valdisere, Zermatt, StMoritz, Arosa);
   SunResortName = (StTropez, Ibiza, Santorini, Capri);
   Centimetres = CARDINAL;
   RunType = (Green, Blue, Red, Black);
   Degrees = [-50..100];
   Hours = [1..12];

   HolidayDestinations =
     RECORD
       CASE Resort : ResortType OF
         Ski :
           SkiResort : SkiResortName;
           AverageSnowDepth : Centimetres;
           ChairLift, ButtonLift: BOOLEAN;
           EasiestRun, HardestRun : RunType |
         Sun :
           SunResort : SunResortName;
           AverageTemperature : Degrees;
           AverageHoursOfSun : Hours;
           Beach : BOOLEAN
       END
     END;
```

Description of use

The value that is given to the tag field determines which of the variant field list sequences are to become active. For example, if the value assigned to the tag field is equal to a value which is equal to a case label, then the field list sequence prefixed by that label becomes the active variant.

The record type HolidayDestinations (declared in the previous subsection) holds information about various holiday resorts. However, a potential tourist needs to know different types of information about a particular resort depending on whether he or she wishes to go on a skiing holiday or have a holiday in the sun. Consider the following program fragment:

```
VAR
   Holidays : HolidayDestinations;
...
   WITH Holidays DO
     Resort := Sun;
     SunResort := Capri;
```

```
   AverageTemperature := 85;
   AverageHoursOfSun := 9;
   Beach := TRUE
END;
```

This code creates a variable of type `HolidayDestinations`, called `Holidays`. When assigning a value to a variant record it is important that the first assignment should be to the tag field of the record. Therefore the first assignment statement in the above example is to `Resort` (the tag field of the record). This is done to flag the record as being an instance of a variant record in which only the field list sequence selected by the case label `Sun` is of any interest.

Similarly, when accessing values stored in a variant record, such as the one created above, it is important that the tag field of the record be examined first. Once again, this is done in order to establish the active variant. Attempts to access values in the inactive field list sequence will give unpredictable results.

For example, if we declared a variable called `Name` of type `SunResortName` we should only assign the value of the `SunResort` field of `Holidays` after first checking which field list was active.

```
WITH Holidays DO
   IF Resort = Sun THEN
     Name := SunResort
   END
END;
```

If `Resort` did not equal `Sun`, then we would not make the assignment statement `Name := SunResort` (see *Portability Issues*).

Records with both variant and non-variant parts

Records are not restricted to being variant or non-variant in type. In practice records are often declared that are a mixture of the two, having both non-variant and variant sections.

```
TYPE
   ContractType = (Sold, OnHire);
   CarMakeType = (Ford, Chrysler, Pontiac, Nissan);
   LicencePlateType = CARDINAL;
   Dollars = REAL;
   ValidMonth = [1..12];
   ValidDay = [1..31];
   ValidYear = [1987..2050];
   Date = RECORD
           Month : ValidMonth;
           Day : ValidDay;
           Year : ValidYear;
         END;
   NameLength = [0..23];
   Name = ARRAY NameLength OF CHAR;
   CarRecordType = RECORD
                    CarMake : CarMakeType;
                    LicencePlate : LicencePlateType;
```

```
                    Customer : Name;
                    CASE Contract : ContractType OF
                      Sold :
                        Price : Dollars;
                        DateSold : Date |
                      OnHire :
                        ChargePerWeek, TotalHireCost : Dollars;
                        DateOut, DateIn : Date;
                    END;
                  END;
```

The above example models the kind of record that a car dealer might use if the business was involved in both hiring and selling cars. The non-variant part of the record consists of the first three fields. These are `CarMake`, `LicencePlate`, and `Customer`. This information will always be needed no matter whether a car is being hired or sold. The two variant parts of the record denoted by the case labels `Sold` and `OnHire` reflect the different kinds of information that a car dealer would need depending on whether a particular car had been sold or put out on hire.

20.5   PORTABILITY ISSUES

The portability issues that need to be addressed for records are mainly due to the evolution of the language. Structured record values are being introduced and the syntax for tag-less variant records has altered slightly.

Tagless variant records

A tag-less variant record is a variant record where the tag variable identifier is omitted. Early compilers insist that the colon following the tag variable identifier is also omitted. Tag-less variant records are considered extremely bad programming practice as they allow variants to be selected without explicitly making the variant active with the tag field.

Structured record values

During the standardization of Modula-2, the need to be able to denote structured values was recognized and a new feature—structured value constructors—was introduced into the language. Some implementations of Modula-2 have already incorporated this feature. A record value constructor allows a sequence of expressions which compute a value corresponding to each and every field of a record to be assigned to a record variable or to define a constant.

Syntax

```
value constructor =
    array constructor | record constructor | set constructor;
record constructor = record type identifier, record definition;
record type identifier = qualified identifier;
record definition = "{", field value, {",", field value}, "}";
field value = expression;
```

Note that the record type identifier is required to form a record value constructor, therefore anonymous types cannot be used.

Examples

(i)
```
      TYPE
        StockItem = (Spanner, Hammer, Screwdriver, Wrench);
        MyStock = RECORD
                     Item : StockItem;
                     NoOfItems : ValidNo
                  END;
      VAR
        Stock : MyStock; Tool: StockItem;
      BEGIN
        ...
        Stock := MyStock{Tool, 50};
```

Note that the values of the variable Stock are listed after the record type name, in the order that they were declared in the record type declaration.

(ii)
```
      PROCEDURE WriteStockLevel(ARecord : MyStock);
      BEGIN
        ...
      END WriteStockLevel;
      BEGIN
        ...
        x := WriteStockLevel(MyStock{Wrench, 30});
```

A value constructor can also be used to pass values to an actual record parameter.

(iii)
```
      CONST
        RecordConst = MyStock{Hammer, 20};
```

A value constructor can be used to assign values to an array constant.

Some implementors, whilst incorporating structured value constructors in their compilers, have evolved a non-standard syntax. In Topspeed Modula-2, for example, a record constant (called an *aggregate*) would be constructed as follows:

```
      RecordConst = MyStock(Hammer, 20);
```

Note the difference; the use of round brackets rather than curly brackets (braces).

Accessing inactive fields in variant records

It should be noted that in most implementations of Modula-2 there is nothing to prevent a programmer accessing the inactive field list sequence of a variant record. Attempts to assign values to the inactive variant could result in the active field list being over-written. This is because the two variants usually share the same storage locations in memory. Because of this, reading the inactive variant can cause strange results. Indeed instances of tag-less variant records[1] are used to perform type transfer; i.e. to interpret a value of one type as a value of another.

Example

```
TYPE
   NumTransfer = RECORD
                    CASE : BOOLEAN OF
                       TRUE : CardNum : CARDINAL |
                       FALSE : Letter : CHAR
                    END
                 END;
VAR
   Transfer : NumTransfer;
BEGIN
   Transfer.CardNum := 65;
   WriteChar(Transfer.Letter);
```

The statement `WriteChar(Transfer.Letter)` will output the character A to the screen because of the way Topspeed Modula-2 aligns cardinal and character variables in a record. This is generally not a portable practice and should be avoided.

20.6   REVIEW EXERCISES

Q20.1   A library needs a database to hold details of all its books. This database consists of a number of records, one for each book the library has in stock. Each record holds the following information: the title, the author, and a field that indicates whether the book is out on loan. Give the type declarations for such a record, using the type identifier name `LibraryBook`.

Q20.2   Declare an array to hold 2000 book records.

Q20.3   Write a procedure to search an array of type `Library` for a particular book title. The procedure should return a Boolean variable that indicates whether the book has been found and, if found, also return the index to the book record. Assume a variable `BookArray` of type `Library` has been declared globally in the main program.

---

[1] A tag-less variant record is a variant record in which the tag variable identifier is omitted. Early compilers insist that the colon following the tag variable identifier is also omitted. Tag-less variant records are considered to be extremely bad programming practice as they allow variants to be altered without explicitly making the variant active using the tag field.

Q20.4 Rewrite the type declaration for a `LibraryBook` with a variant section. The variant section will have the Boolean variable `OnLoan` as the tag identifier. If `OnLoan` is `TRUE` then the active variant field sequence will consist of a field indicating the date that the book is due to be returned by, and a field which will indicate whether another borrower has requested that this book be reserved on its return into stock. If the value `OnLoan` is `FALSE` then the active variant field sequence will consist of a single field which will store the date that the book was returned.

Q20.5 Using this revised declaration of `LibraryBook`, write a procedure that updates a record when a book is borrowed. Once again assume a variable `BookArray` of type `Library` has been declared globally in the main program. The procedure should have two parameters: the title of the book and the date the book should be returned by. Hint: use the search procedure that was the answer to Q20.3 to retrieve the record.

Q20.6 Using the revised declaration of `LibraryBook`, write a procedure that updates a record when a book that is on loan is requested to be reserved by a borrower.

Q20.7 Using the revised declaration of `LibraryBook`, write a procedure that updates a record when a book is returned by a borrower. Assume a procedure `LateReturn` which takes two parameters: the date that the book is due back and the date that the book is actually returned. If the book is returned after the due-back date, the procedure returns `TRUE`.

Q20.8 Write a (large) `WITH` statement to print a report of a record variable `Holidays` of type `HolidayDestinations`.

21 SETS

21.1 INTRODUCTION

A set consists of an unordered collection of elements (also termed members), which must all be of the same type, called the base type of the set. In Modula-2, this base type must be of some ordinal type. The range of values that a set type can take is the set of all possible sets consisting of elements from the base type. More generally it can be said that if the base type (E) of a set (S) has n distinct values then its set type consists of 2^n sets. The set S is said to be the *powerset* of the base type (E). Set types are specified using the set type constructor. Note that many implementations of Modula-2 restrict the number of elements in a set's base type to no more than 16. This is ignored in the main discussion of sets; it is discussed in *Portability Issues*.

21.2 SET TYPE DECLARATION

A set type is declared using the *set type constructor*.

Syntax

> set type = "SET", "OF", ordinal type;

As the base type of a set in many implementations of Modula-2 is limited, it is often necessary to declare the base type as a subrange or enumeration type before declaring a set type.

```
TYPE
   Transport = (Car, Bus, Train, Plane, MotorBike, Bicycle);
   SmallNos = [0..3];
   Number = [0..9];
```

318

Now that the base types have been declared, it is possible to declare the set types:

```
SetOfTransport = SET OF Transport;
SetOfSmallNos = SET OF SmallNos;
SetOfNumber = SET OF Number;
SetOfBoolean = SET OF BOOLEAN;
```

21.3   THE SET VALUE CONSTRUCTOR

Values of a set type are assigned to variables and constants of that type through the mechanism of the *set value constructor* (not to be confused with the set type constructor).

Syntax

```
value constructor =
    array constructor | record constructor | set constructor;
set constructor = base type identifier, set definition;
base type identifier = qualified identifier;
set definition = "{", [element, {",", element}], "}";
```

Given the type declarations in the previous section, and the syntax of the set value constructor, the following constant declarations can be made:

```
CONST
  TwoWheels = SetOfTransport{MotorBike, Bicycle};
  MyNumbers = SetOfNumber{0,1,2,3,4,5,6,7,8,9};
```

A set value constructor may also be used with a range specification, as in the following examples:

```
CONST
  AllTransport = SetOfTransport{Car..Bicycle};
  MyNumbers = SetOfNumber{0..9};
```

Given the type declarations in the previous section, the following variable declarations can be made:

```
VAR
  NoTransport, MyTransport, TransportSet : SetOfTransport;
  NumberSet : SetOfNumber;
  BooleanSet : SetOfBoolean;
```

Values are assigned to a set with the set value constructor.

```
NoTransport := SetOfTransport{};    (* the empty set *)
MyTransport := SetOfTransport{Car,Bicycle};
NumberSet := SetOfNumber{1,3,4};
BooleanSet := SetOfBoolean{TRUE};
```

A set value constructor can also contain expressions that are expression compatible with the base type of the set:

```
PROCEDURE NumberSet;
TYPE
  Number = [0..100];
  SetOfNumber = SET OF Number;
VAR
  MyNumbers : SetOfNumber;
BEGIN
  MyNumbers := SetOfNumber{ 0, 3*2, 8 DIV 2, 10+5}
END NumberSet;
```

Note that the use of the name of the set type in a set value constructor allows set values to be strictly typed. Therefore, given the following type definitions:

```
S1type = SET OF [1..3];
S2type = SET OF [1..3];
```

the following assignment is illegal:

```
S1type := S2type{1,2}
```

21.4   IN OPERATOR

Testing for set membership is accomplished by use of the asymmetric operator IN. This operator takes on its right hand side a set value and on its left hand side a value of that set's base type. The result of evaluating an expression using the IN operator is a value of type BOOLEAN (i.e. TRUE or FALSE).

Consider the following procedure which demonstrates the use of the operator IN and the denotation of set values:

```
PROCEDURE IsMember;
  TYPE
    Transport = (Car, Bus, Train, Plane, MotorBike, Bicycle);
    SetOfTransport = SET OF transport;
  CONST
    TwoWheels = SetOfTransport{MotorBike, Bicycle};
  VAR
    IsMine, CanFly, HasTwoWheels : BOOLEAN;
    ModeOfTravel : Transport;
    MyTransport : SetOfTransport;
  BEGIN
    ModeOfTravel := Bus;
    HasTwoWheels := ModeOfTravel IN TwoWheels;          (* FALSE *)
    ModeOfTravel := Plane;
    CanFly := ModeOfTravel IN SetOfTransport{Plane};   (* TRUE *)
    MyTransport := SetOfTransport{Car};
    IsMine := ModeOfTravel IN MyTransport              (* FALSE *)
  END IsMember.
```

21.5   SET OPERATORS

There are four set operators which take two sets of the same type and return a third set value of the same type. The four set operators are:

Operation	Type operator
set union	+
set difference	−
set intersection	*
symmetric set difference	/

Set union

The *set union operator* is analogous to the Boolean operator OR. The result of using the set union operator on two sets S1 and S2 is a set value, which consists of elements that exist either in S1 or in S2.

Order is not significant when using the set union operator, so:

```
S3 := S1 + S2;
```

is equivalent to:

```
S3 := S2 + S1;
```

Examples

(i)
```
TYPE
   Numbers = [0..6];
   SetOfNumber = SET OF Numbers;
VAR
   MyNumbers : SetOfNumber;
BEGIN
   MyNumbers := SetOfNumber{2,3,4} + SetOfNumber{1,3,5};
```

In this example MyNumbers takes the value SetOfNumbers{1,2,3,4,5}.

(ii)
```
PROCEDURE Union;
TYPE
   Transport = (Car, Bus, Train, Plane, MotorBike, Bicycle);
   SetOfTransport = SET OF Transport;
VAR
   AllTransport,RoadTransport,OtherTransport: SetOfTransport;
BEGIN
   RoadTransport := SetOfTransport{Car,Bus,MotorBike,Bicycle};
   OtherTransport := SetOfTransport{Train,Plane};
   AllTransport := RoadTransport + OtherTransport;
   AllTransport := SetOfTransport{Train,Plane} +
                   SetOfTransport{Car,Bus,MotorBike,Bicycle};
END Union;
```

In both assignments to AllTransport, the set variable takes the value SetOfTransport{Car, Bus, Train, Plane, MotorBike, Bicycle}.

Set difference

The result of using the *set difference operator* on two sets S1 and S2 is a third set S3, which contains only those members that are present in S1 but absent in S2.

Order *is* significant[1] when using the set difference operator, so:

```
S3 := S1 - S2;
```

is *not* equivalent to:

```
S3 := S2 - S1;
```

Examples:

(i)
```
        MyNumbers := SetOfNumber{2,3,4} - SetOfNumber{3,4,5};
        MyNumbers := SetOfNumber{3,4,5} - SetOfNumber{2,3,4};
```

In the first assignment of this example, `MyNumbers`, takes the value of `SetOfNumber{2}`. In the second assignment it takes the value `SetOfNumber{5}`.

(ii)
```
        PROCEDURE Difference;
        TYPE
           Transport = (Car, Bus, Train, Plane, MotorBike, Bicycle);
           SetOfTransport = SET OF Transport;
        VAR
           AllTransport,
           OnHire,
           NotHired : SetOfTransport;
        BEGIN
           AllTransport := SetOfTransport{Car..Bicycle};
           OnHire       := SetOfTransport{Car..MotorBike};
           NotHired     := AllTransport - OnHire
        END Difference;
```

In this further example of the set difference operator, the set variable `NotHired` takes the value `SetOfTransport{Bicycle}`.

Set intersection

The result of using the *set intersection operator* on two sets `S1` and `S2`, is a third set `S3`, which consists of elements that exist in both `S1` and in `S2`.

Order is not significant when using set intersection, so

```
S3 := S1 * S2;
```

is equivalent to:

```
S3 := S2 * S1;
```

Examples

(i)
```
        MyNumbers := SetOfNumber{2,3,4} * SetOfNumber{3,4,5};
```

`MyNumbers` takes the value `SetOfNumber {2,3,4,5}`.

---

[1]The set difference operator is sometimes called the *asymmetric set difference operator*.

(ii)
```
TYPE
   Transport = ( Car, Bus, Train, Plane, MotorBike, Bicycle);
   SetOfTransport = SET OF Transport;

PROCEDURE Dangerous
   (DueForService, OnHire: SetOfTransport): BOOLEAN;
BEGIN
   RETURN DueForService * OnHire <> SetOfTransport{}
END Dangerous;
```

This function procedure returns TRUE if the set of vehicles on hire intersects the set of those due for service.

Symmetric set difference

The **symmetric set difference operator** is analogous to the Boolean operator known as the 'EXCLUSIVE OR'. The result of using this operator on two sets S1 and S2 is a third set S3, which consists of those elements that exist only in S1 or only in S2.

Order is not significant when using the symmetric set difference operator, so:

```
S3 := S1 / S2;
```

is equivalent to:

```
S3 := S2 / S1;
```

Examples

(i)   `MyNumbers := SetOfNumber{2,3,4} / SetOfNumber{3,4,5};`

The variable MyNumbers takes the value SetOfNumber{2,5}.

(ii)
```
TYPE
   Transport = (Car,Bus,Train,Plane,MotorBike,Bicycle);
   SetOfTransport = SET OF Transport;
PROCEDURE NotThreateningLife
   (DueForService, OnHire: SetOfTransport): SetOfTransport;
BEGIN
   RETURN (DueForService / OnHire)
END NotThreateningLife;
```

Thus:

```
NotThreateningLife(SetOfTransport{Car..Plane},
                   SetOfTransport{Plane..Bicycle});
```

would return:

```
SetOfTransport{Car,Bus,Train,MotorBike,Bicycle}
```

Relational operators and sets

Four of the relational operators can be applied to sets. They take two sets of the same type and return a Boolean value.

The following table lists the relational operators applicable to sets:

Relation	Operator
equality	=
not equal	<>
is a subset of	<=
contains the subset	>=

To understand how relational operators apply to sets, it is important to understand the notion of a subset.

Definition of a subset

In mathematics, a set S1 is defined to be a subset of S2 if all elements of S1 are also elements of S2. (In classical set theory this is denoted $S1 \subseteq S2$.) If S1 is not equal to S2 it is called a proper subset. Modula-2 does not provide an operation for proper set inclusion; rather >= and <= are provided as implementations of the mathematical operators $\supseteq$ and $\subseteq$. The following table illustrates the meaning of these operators.

Maths/Modula-2	Result
$\{0, 1, 4\} \subseteq \{0, 1, 2, 3, 4\}$ `SetOfNumber{0,1,2,4} <= SetOfNumber{0,1,2,3,4}`	TRUE
$\{0, 4, 6\} \subseteq \{0, 2, 3,\ 4, 5\}$ `SetOfNumber{0,4,6} <= SetOfNumber{0,2,3,4,5}`	FALSE
$\{1, 2, 3\} \supseteq \{1, 2, 3\}$ `SetOfNumber{1,2,3} >= SetOfNumber{1,2,3}`	TRUE

Given the following declarations:

```
VAR
    AllTransport, DueForService, OnHire : SetOfTransport;
```

and the assignment statements:

```
OnHire := SetOfTransport{Car..Bicycle};
AllTransport := SetOfTransport{Car..Bicycle};
DueForService := SetOfTransport{Plane};
```

The following table demonstrates the use of relational operators with the above variables:

Boolean expression	Result of expression
AllTransport = OnHire;	TRUE
AllTransport = DueForService;	FALSE
AllTransport <> OnHire;	FALSE
OnHire <> DueForService;	TRUE
DueForService <= OnHire;	TRUE
DueForService >= OnHire;	FALSE
OnHire <= DueForService;	FALSE
OnHire >= DueForService;	TRUE

21.6   THE PROCEDURES EXCL AND INCL

Modula-2 provides two built-in procedures for use with sets. EXCL is used to exclude a member from a set variable and INCL is used to include a member in a set variable. They both take two parameters: a variable of a set type and any simple expression compatible with the base type of the set.

Example

```
MyNumbers := SetOfNumber{1,2,3,4,5};
EXCL(MyNumbers, 5);       (* Exclude 5 from the set *)
EXCL(MyNumbers, 2*2);     (* Exclude 4 from the set *)
INCL(MyNumbers, 9);       (* Include 9 in the set *)
INCL(MyNumbers, 4*2);     (* Include 8 in the set *)
```

Further details of EXCL and INCL can be found in Chapter 23.

21.7   BITSET

All Modula-2 implementations provide the standard type BITSET, which is a predefined SET OF [0..WordLength-1] where WordLength is the number of bits in a word of storage. The word on your particular computer will typically be 8, 16, 24, 32, or 64 bits in length.

Although the smallest addressable unit on IBM-PC/ATs and compatibles is 8 bits, Topspeed Modula-2 implements BITSET as if it were defined as the type SET OF [0..15].

The usefulness of the type BITSET is easier to appreciate in the context of how data is represented at the machine level. At this level all data is represented in storage as a series of zeros and ones, i.e. as binary digits. Inclusion of a cardinal n (where $0 \leq n \leq$ WordLength) in a BITSET will set the nth bit of the word to one. Similarly, exclusion of a valid cardinal will clear the nth bit to zero.

The definition of BITSET is inherently machine dependent. However, it is quite portable (as discussed in Chapter 25) despite the variety of ways it is provided by implementations. Some implementations require it to be imported from SYSTEM (this is what the Modula-2 standard will ratify) but many implementations include it as a pervasive type name. Others allow the omission of the set type from a value constructor to signify the value is of the type BITSET. Therefore, except for the example below, we postpone full discussion of BITSET until Section 25.5.

Given the following variable declaration:

```
VAR
  MyBitset : BITSET;
```

The following assignment statements may be used in Topspeed Modula-2

```
MyBitset := BITSET{};
(* The word addressed by MyBitset is set to 0000000000000000 *)

MyBitset := BITSET{2,6,9};
(* The word addressed by MyBitset is set to 0000001001000100 *)

MyBitset := BITSET{0..15};
(* The word addressed by MyBitset is set to 1111111111111111 *)
```

21.8 PORTABILITY ISSUES

There are only two portability issues that concern sets. However, these issues are most significant and fundamentally effect the usefulness of the set data type. The issues are the limitations that some compilers apply to the number of set elements and a restriction that some place on the set's base type.

Limitations on the number of set elements

Many early implementations of Modula-2 limit sets to 16 or 32 elements. Therefore, the base type must be restricted to an enumeration type (with a cardinality of 16 or less) or a subrange type. Later compilers have a much higher limit, which makes set types more useful. For example, Topspeed Modula-2 allows a set to contain up to 65536 elements. Therefore, in Topspeed Modula-2 a set can be constructed from the types CHAR, BOOLEAN, CARDINAL, enumeration types, and subranges of all these.

If your compiler does limit sets to 16 or 32 elements, the use of sets can be avoided. For example, set inclusion tests of simple values in a contiguous range can be mimicked by testing using relational operators. For example:

```
ch IN SetOfChar{'0'..'9'}
```

can be replaced by:

```
(ch >= '0') AND (ch <= '9')
```

A more general approach is to use Boolean arrays to model sets. The index to such a Boolean array would be the values you would wish to include in a pseudo set type. Given the following type declarations:

```
TYPE
   PseudoSet = ARRAY['a'..'z'] OF BOOLEAN;
VAR
   CharSet = PseudoSet;
```

if the components of the array variable `CharSet` were all initialized to TRUE, then this test of set membership:

```
IF ch IN SetOfChar{'a'..'z'} THEN ...
```

could be replaced by:

```
IF CharSet[ch] THEN ...
```

See Section 21.9 for exercises in modelling sets.

Restriction on the set base type

Many Modula-2 compilers use an implementation technique for sets which assumes that the smallest value in the base type is zero. This has implications for the storage needed for sets, with consequent restrictions placed on programmers. In general, if the base type contains ordinal values n..m (where $0 < n \le m$), these compilers allocate storage as if the base type was from 0..m. Such compilers limit the storage for sets and so programmers using such systems are told to limit the size of their set *base types*. Such strictures are not completely accurate: if the limitation is 16, the constraint is *actually* that $m+1 \le 16$, and not that $m+1-n \le 16$.

For example, on many systems which only allow 16 elements per set, the first set type (`LegalSet`), is acceptable, and the second (`IllegalSet`) is not (even though there are the same number of values in each base type):

```
TYPE
   Base1 = [0..15];
   LegalSet = SET OF Base1;

   Base2 = [10..25];
   IllegalSet = SET OF Base2;
```

The second consequence of this kind of representation is that negative values in a base type are prohibited. Thus, the following is illegal on very many compilers:

```
TYPE
   NegBase = [-5..5];
   IntSet = SET OF NegBase;
```

This restriction is more common. Implementations with large upper limits on base types often forbid negative values. This is the case with Topspeed Modula-2; CARDINAL is in the list of permissible set base types and INTEGER is not.

21.9   REVIEW EXERCISES

Q21.1   Give a suitable alternative data structure for a set of values in range -5 to +5. Declare a variable of the type and write the assignment statements necessary to represent {-4, 2}.

Q21.2   Write a predicate (i.e. a function procedure that returns a Boolean value) to mimic the IN operator.

Q21.3   Write a procedure to mimic the built-in function INCL.

Q21.4   Write a procedure to mimic the built-in procedure EXCL.

Q21.5   Write a function procedure to mimic the set difference operator.

Q21.6   Write a function to mimic the set union operator.

22 POINTERS

22.1 INTRODUCTION

A pointer is used to store the address of a variable of any type. Normally they are used in a more abstract fashion to point to dynamic variables. Dynamic variables can be used to construct dynamic data structures such as trees and linked lists, which are not provided for in the language. Pointers can also be used to point to static variables (see Section 22.6). Once a pointer has been set to point to a variable, the latter can then be accessed *indirectly* through that pointer.

22.2 POINTER DECLARATIONS

When you declare a pointer, the type of the variable which you wish the pointer to reference has to be specified. The pointer can then only refer to variables of that type.

Syntax

> pointer type = "POINTER", "TO", type;

Pointer variables can be declared to point to any named type of arbitrary complexity.

Example

```
TYPE
  PointerToCardinal = POINTER TO CARDINAL;
VAR
  Ptr : PointerToCardinal;
```

In the above example `PointerToCardinal` is declared as a pointer type, variables of which can only hold the address of a `CARDINAL` variable. `Ptr` is a pointer variable. Note that the `VAR` declaration causes storage for a static variable `Ptr` to be allocated which can only be assigned the *address* of a `CARDINAL` variable. It does not create any storage for a `CARDINAL` variable that `Ptr` could reference.

22.3   POINTER OPERATIONS

Before a pointer variable can be used to access a dynamic variable, storage for a dynamic variable must be explicitly requested with a call of NEW[1] (see Section 22.4), or the address of a static variable must be assigned to it (see Section 22.6). Alternatively, a pointer variable can be assigned the value of another pointer variable which already points to another dynamic or static variable.

Dereferencing pointers

If a pointer variable is used on the left hand side of an assignment statement or as an actual VAR-parameter in a procedure call, it would refer to the address of a variable of the type specified in its declaration, otherwise it would refer to the address of a value of the type specified in its declaration.

The unary operator ^ is used to access the value stored in a variable that is referenced by a pointer. This is known as dereferencing a pointer. The ^ operator is placed after the pointer variable's name. For example, the identifier `Ptr^` is a `CARDINAL` variable (using the declaration given in Section 22.2).

Pointers and assignment statements

Given the following declarations:

```
VAR
   P1, P2 : PointerToCardinal;
   B : CARDINAL;
```

and the statements:

```
NEW(P1);
P1^ := 18;
```

then the following assignment statement can be made:

```
B := P1^;
```

This statement assigns to B the cardinal value pointed to by P1 (i.e. 18). Pointers of the *same* type can be assigned to one another. For example:

```
P1^ := 15;
P2 := P1;
```

---

[1]NEW may not be provided by a Modula-2 implementation. In this case the procedure ALLOCATE must be imported from the standard procedure `Storage` and used instead. See *Portability Issues* in Section 22.7.

The first statement assigns the cardinal value 15 to the variable pointed to by P1. The second statement assigns to P2 the value of P1 which is the *address* of the variable with the cardinal value of 15.

```
NEW(P2);
P2^ := 45;
P1^ := P2^;
```

The effect of the final assignment statement above is to copy the value of the variable pointed to by P2 to the variable pointed to by P1.

Pointers and relational operators

The only relational operations that can be applied to pointers are tests for equality or inequality. Two pointers are considered equal only if they both point to the same variable or if they both have the value NIL (see Section 22.5).

Examples

```
(i)     NEW(P1);
        P1^ := 34;
        P2 := P1;
        IF P1 = P2 THEN ...
```

The Boolean expression in the IF statement would evaluate to TRUE.

```
(ii)    NEW(P1);   P1^ := 34;
        NEW(P2);   P2^ := 34;
        IF P1 = P2 THEN ...
```

The Boolean expression in the IF statement would evaluate to FALSE as P1 and P2 point to different dynamic variables, i.e. they do not have the same address value. The fact that the dynamic variables they point to happen to have the same value is not being tested here.

```
(iii)   NEW(P1);   P1^ := 34;
        NEW(P2);   P2^ := 34;
        IF P1^ = P2^ THEN ...
```

This time the Boolean expression in the IF statement would evaluate to TRUE as it is the values of the dynamic variables that are being tested.

22.4 NEW AND DISPOSE

Pointers are normally used to point at dynamic variables; therefore it is useful at this juncture to restate the differences between static and dynamic variables.

Static variables are declared in the declaration part of a procedure or module, in a VAR declaration. Storage is allocated for static variables that are declared in a procedure as soon as the procedure is called, and storage is deallocated when that procedure is left. Static variables that are declared in a separate module have storage allocated for them as soon as the program that uses that module is executed and this is not deallocated until that program ends.

Dynamic variables, however, are not declared in this manner (although a pointer which refers to them must be). Storage for dynamic variables is under program control and must be explicitly requested. Similarly, storage for a dynamic variable may exist beyond the lifetime of the pointer variable that refers to it and must be explicitly deallocated by the program. If this deallocation of storage is not carried out before the end of a procedure which declares a dynamic variable is reached, the 'chunk' of memory associated with it cannot be reused (as the only reference to it, the pointer variable, is lost when the procedure is left).

The creation and disposal of dynamic variables is handled by the supplied module `Storage`, which makes use of two procedures `ALLOCATE` and `DEALLOCATE`. The programmer does not normally use these procedures directly, but if provided, uses the built-in procedures `NEW` and `DISPOSE`.

Allocation of storage

Allocation of storage for dynamic variables is achieved via the procedure `ALLOCATE`. The procedure takes two parameters: a pointer variable, and a `CARDINAL` value which is equivalent to the number of addressable storage units required to store a dynamic variable of the type indicated by the pointer's type declaration.

Example

```
TYPE
   PointerToInteger = POINTER TO INTEGER;
VAR
   Ptr1 : PointerToInteger;
BEGIN
   ALLOCATE(Ptr1, SIZE(INTEGER));
```

The call of the procedure `ALLOCATE` above allocates the number of storage units (which is implementation defined) needed to store an `INTEGER` value. Note the use of the built-in procedure `SIZE` which is used to return the number of addressable storage units required to store a variable of the type indicated by its parameter (See Chapter 23).

Relationship between ALLOCATE and NEW

If it is provided by the compiler, it is preferable to use the built-in procedure `NEW` instead of `ALLOCATE`. The procedure `NEW` does not have to be imported as it is one of Modula-2's built-in procedures. However, you must import the procedure `ALLOCATE` into your program. The reason for this is that the procedure `NEW` is like a macro: the compiler translates a call of `NEW` into a call of `ALLOCATE`. Thus, for example:

```
NEW(Ptr1);
```

is translated by the compiler to:

```
ALLOCATE(Ptr1, SIZE(INTEGER));
```

As the procedure NEW is a macro, you can substitute your own procedure to handle storage for dynamic variables. However you must name this procedure ALLOCATE and provide it with a parameter list which is identical with the parameter list of ALLOCATE in Storage. Also you must ensure that the ALLOCATE procedure in the module Storage is not visible as it would cause a clash of identifier names.

Deallocation of storage

Disposal of storage for dynamic variables is achieved via the procedure DEALLOCATE. This procedure, like ALLOCATE, takes two parameters: a pointer variable, and a CARDINAL value which is equivalent to the number of addressable storage units being used to store a dynamic variable.

Example

```
TYPE
   PointerToChar = POINTER TO CHAR;
VAR
   Ptr2 : PointerToChar ;
BEGIN
   ALLOCATE(Ptr2, SIZE(CHAR));
   ...
   DEALLOCATE(Ptr2, SIZE(CHAR));
```

Depending on the implementation, the procedure DEALLOCATE may mark the storage associated with the dynamic variable as being reusable and make that memory location inaccessible to that pointer variable. Otherwise the procedure may just set the pointer variable to NIL.

Relationship between DEALLOCATE and DISPOSE

As for ALLOCATE, your compiler may provide a simpler alternative to DEALLOCATE—the procedure DISPOSE. The procedure DISPOSE does not have to be imported as it is one of Modula-2's built-in procedures. However, you must import the procedure DEALLOCATE into your program. The reason for this is that the procedure DISPOSE is like a macro: the compiler translates a call of DISPOSE into a call of DEALLOCATE. Thus, for example:

```
DISPOSE(Ptr2);
```

is translated by the compiler to:

```
DEALLOCATE(Ptr2, SIZE(CHAR));
```

As with the allocation of storage, you can declare your own procedure to deallocate storage.

Dangling pointers

When you dispose of a dynamic variable that is pointed to by more than one pointer variable, care should be taken that a pointer variable is not left *dangling*.

Example

```
VAR
  Tom, Dick : PointerToCardinal;
BEGIN
  NEW(Tom);
  Tom^ := 32;
  Dick := Tom;
```

Dick and Tom now point to the same dynamic variable, which is a cardinal variable with the value of 32.

```
DISPOSE(Tom);
```

The call of DISPOSE has made the storage for the dynamic variable pointed to by Tom inaccessible to Tom. Dick is now what is termed a *dangling pointer*. It still points to the same area of memory, but this area of memory may have been reallocated and could store some other value, of some other type! It would therefore be an error to try and dereference Dick as its value is undefined. The correct way of disposing of the dynamic variable pointed to by Tom and Dick would be:

```
DISPOSE(Tom);
Dick := NIL;
```

22.5 NIL

Pointer variables should be initialized to some sensible value before they are used. They are initialized by assigning them the value NIL. NIL is a predefined constant (and therefore does not have to be imported) which can be assigned to a pointer of any type. Its use indicates that a pointer points to 'nothing'. Pointer variables should be assigned the NIL value in two instances: before storage is allocated for a dynamic variable and after the disposal of a dynamic variable.

Before storage is allocated for an associated dynamic variable, the value of a pointer variable is undefined. It is quite likely that the pointer variable will have some random address value. Therefore attempts to dereference it will, at best, cause an address exception at run-time which will halt your program; or worse still, garbage will be introduced into your program which will be hard to detect, giving curious and unpredictable results.

After storage for a dynamic variable has been released with a call of DISPOSE or DEALLOCATE, the value of a pointer variable is likely to be undefined. Once again, attempts to dereference the pointer variable will either halt the program or give unpredictable results.

Assigning the value `NIL` to a pointer variable in these circumstances will allow you to program in a defensive manner. You will be able to check that a pointer variable is not equal to `NIL` before you dereference it.

Examples

(i)
```
IF Ptr <> NIL THEN
   Ptr^ := SomeVar
ELSE
   HALT
END;
```

(ii)
```
IF Ptr <> NIL THEN
   Ptr^ := SomeVar
ELSE
   NEW(Ptr);
   Ptr^ := SomeVar
END;
```

These examples show two different strategies for finding a pointer equal to `NIL`: the first just halts, and in the second a new dynamic variable is created and assigned a value.

22.6   THE ADR FUNCTION PROCEDURE

Modula-2 provides a procedure called `ADR`[1] which is used to return the address of a static variable in order that it might be assigned to a pointer variable. The function `ADR` takes a single parameter, a variable of any type, and returns the address at which that variable is stored. The statement:

```
P1 := ADR(A);
```

assigns the address of `A` to the variable `P1`, which is then said to point to `A`. Note in the assignments:

```
P1 := ADR(A);
P2 := ADR(B);
P2 := P1;
```

The value of the variable `B` is not changed. This is because assigning to `P2` only affects the address that `P2` stores.

The table that follows lists a series of operations involving pointers and the `ADR` function, together with equivalent actions. They require the following declarations:

```
TYPE
   Ptr = POINTER TO CHAR;
VAR
```

---

[1]ADR must be imported from `SYSTEM` in many implementations of Modula-2; it is a built-in procedure in Topspeed Modula-2.

```
P1, P2 : Ptr;
A, B : CHAR;
```

Pointer operation	Equivalent action
`P1 := ADR(A);` `B := P1^;`	`B := A;`
`P1 := ADR(A);` `P2 := ADR(A);`	`P2 := P1;`
`P1 := ADR(A);` `P1^ := 'D';`	`A := 'D';`

ADR and low-level programming

The type ADDRESS is provided in Modula-2 (see Chapter 25) to facilitate low-level programming. This type is defined to be assignment compatible with all pointer types. The function procedure ADR returns a value of the type ADDRESS and so can be used to circumvent Modula-2's strict type compatibility rules. ADR and ADDRESS are usually available from the SYSTEM module.

Example

```
TYPE
   FourteenChars = ARRAY [0..13] OF CHAR;
   SixChars = ARRAY [0..5] OF CHAR;
   Ptr = POINTER TO SixChars;
VAR
   A   : FourteenChars;
   Str1Ptr, Str2Ptr : Ptr;
BEGIN
   Str1Ptr := NIL;                (* Initialise pointer *)
   Str2Ptr := NIL;
   A := 'Topspeed Modula-2';  (* Initialise string A *)
   Str1Ptr := ADR(A[0]);      (* Str1Ptr points to 'Topspe' *)
   Str2Ptr := ADR(A[9]);      (* Str2Ptr points to 'Modula' *)
```

In the above example the variable A (which is of type FourteenChars) is assigned the literal string value 'Topspeed Modula-2'. By assigning the address of A's zero component to Str1Ptr (which is of type SixChars), it is set to point to the string 'Topspe'. This last assignment is equivalent to Str1Ptr := ADR(A). Similarly, by assigning the address of A's ninth component to Str2Ptr, it is set to point at the string 'Modula'.

Note that pointer variables cannot be set to point to an area of memory that is larger than the storage needed for a variable of the type that the pointer has been declared to reference. For this reason the effect of assigning ADR(A[0]) to Str1Ptr is to set it to point to an area of memory that is large enough to hold six characters rather than 14 characters.

See Chapter 25 for more details of ADR.

22.7 PORTABILITY ISSUES

Most of the portability issues associated with pointers arise over the allocation and deallocation of storage for dynamic variables. Most of these are due to the evolution of the language, whilst others are due to the architecture and the operating system of the machine for which the compiler was written.

Function procedures and structured types

Many compilers do not allow function procedures to return structured types such as sets, arrays, and records. However, there is no restriction on functions returning pointers to variables of these types. Therefore we recommend, in the interests of portability, that even if your particular compiler does allow structured types to be returned, that you return a pointer to a structured type instead.

Example

```
CONST
  AddressError = "Address error";
  DivByZeroError = "Divide by zero error";
TYPE
  ErrorMessage = ARRAY[0..23] OF CHAR;
  ErrorPtr = POINTER TO ErrorMessage;
  ErrorRange = [1..2];
VAR
  Error : ErrorPtr;
PROCEDURE LookUpError(ErrorNo : ErrorRange) : ErrorPtr;
  VAR
    Err : ErrorPtr;
  BEGIN
    NEW(Err);
    CASE ErrorNo OF
      1: Err^ := AddressError |
      2: Err^ := DivByZeroError
    END;
    RETURN Err
  END LookUpError;
BEGIN
  . . .
  Error := LookUpError(1);
  WriteString(Error^);
  . . .
```

DEALLOCATE

It must not be assumed that DISPOSE or DEALLOCATE reclaim storage associated with redundant dynamic variables. Many implementations merely make that storage inaccessible to the pointer variable. Others may also mark the storage as reusable, but do not reclaim the storage until some later stage in your program. If the amount of free memory is critical to your program you would be advised to maintain your own free list of dynamic variables. (See the section on *Memory limitations* below.)

SIZE

In the second edition of *Programming in Modula-2*, SIZE was not included as one of Modula-2's built-in procedures. Instead it was specified along with TSIZE as being exported from the standard module SYSTEM. Furthermore, SIZE could only be applied to variables, the procedure TSIZE being applied to type identifiers. Therefore, if your compiler complies with this specification of Modula-2, your calls of the procedures ALLOCATE and DEALLOCATE must use the procedure TSIZE which you must import from SYSTEM. For example:

```
ALLOCATE(Ptr, SYSTEM.TSIZE(CARDINAL))
```

By the third edition of *Programming in Modula-2*, SIZE became one of Modula-2's built-in procedures, being applicable to both variables and types. This removed the need for TSIZE, which was retained to maintain the portability of code written for compilers that conformed in this area, to the second edition of the book.

NEW and DISPOSE

In the third edition of *Programming in Modula-2*, Professor Wirth dropped the built-in procedures NEW and DISPOSE from the language, only providing allocation and disposal of dynamic storage directly through calls of ALLOCATE and DEALLOCATE. However, although there are some compilers that conform to this, many have maintained NEW and DISPOSE and it seems likely that the forthcoming standard will also allow allocation and disposal of dynamic storage through calls of NEW and DISPOSE.

Memory limitations

Given that computers have finite memories, you cannot continue requesting storage for dynamic variables *ad infinitum*. Of course, you can help matters by disposing of dynamic variables when they are no longer needed, but it is not inconceivable that a program that has a high incidence of pointer usage could, under certain circumstances, exhaust available memory.

If a call of NEW or ALLOCATE fails because there is not enough free memory to allocate storage for a dynamic variable, the procedure will halt your program. In most cases this is fine, especially if your program could not continue without the requested storage. However, you may wish your program to avoid such circumstances. In order to facilitate this, some implementations include the procedure Available in the standard module Storage. This procedure takes a single parameter, a CARDINAL value representing the number of bytes you need and returns a Boolean value, which will be true if that number of bytes can be allocated, false if not. For example:

```
VAR
  Ptr : PointerToChar;
  ...
IF Available(SIZE(CHAR)) THEN
  NEW(Ptr)
ELSE
  (* Some program defined recovery procedure *)
END;
```

If the amount of free memory is critical to a program, you would be advised to maintain your own free list of redundant dynamic variables that you can reuse at some later stage in your program. In other words, you should keep a queue of redundant dynamic variables which would be added to instead of calling the DISPOSE procedure. Then, whenever a new dynamic variable is needed, you would first check to see if there was any in the queue that could be reused, before calling the procedure NEW.

NIL

Note that it is an error to dereference a pointer variable that has been initialized to NIL. What will actually happen if you do varies between compilers. Either the program will continue, giving no indication you have dereferenced a pointer with the value NIL, or the program will abort with a run-time error. (This is what Topspeed Modula-2 does.)

22.8   REVIEW EXERCISES

Q22.1   It was stated in Section 22.7 that if the amount of free memory is critical to a program, you should maintain your own free list as a queue of redundant dynamic variables. Details of implementing a queue can be found in Chapter 11. Write a module to implement the following procedures:

- AddToFreeList — to add redundant dynamic variables to the queue.

- TakeFromFreeList — to remove a dynamic variable from the queue in order that it may be reused.

- EmptyFreeList — to check if the queue is empty or not.

Q22.2   Write a code fragment to indicate how you would use the TakeFromFreeList procedure.

23 BUILT-IN PROCEDURES

23.1 INTRODUCTION

Modula-2 provides a set of predefined procedures which operate on the standard types and which can be considered to be an extension to the standard operators. Some of these procedures are *generic* in nature, that is to say they can 'serve many masters'. To be precise, they can operate on a number of different types and may also provide a choice in the number of arguments that their parameter lists may take. It would be impossible to declare explicitly many of these procedures in Modula-2 because of this generic nature.

Note that Modula-2 does not provide mathematical functions such as trigonometric, hyperbolic, and logarithmic functions. These are usually provided in a library module (see Section 13.9).

23.2 ABS

ABS is a function procedure that takes as its parameter an INTEGER, REAL, or LONGREAL number and returns the absolute value of the same type.

Examples

ABS(-78)	returns 78	ABS(3.56)	returns 3.56
ABS(99)	returns 99	ABS(-5.1)	returns 5.1

23.3 CAP

CAP is a function procedure that takes a parameter of type CHAR. If the character set used by the implementation is ASCII or EBCDIC, then it will map a lower-case character to the corresponding upper-case character. If the parameter is an upper-case character or any non-alphabetic character, the result is implementation defined. Topspeed Modula-2 will return the same character.

Examples

```
CAP(a)  returns 'A'
CAP(B)  returns 'B'   (in Topspeed Modula-2)
CAP(?)  returns '?'   (in Topspeed Modula-2)
```

23.4 CHR

CHR is a function procedure that takes a parameter of type CARDINAL and returns the character whose ordinal value is equal to it. For example, in the ASCII character set the letter A is represented by the number 65 and the letter c by the number 99.

Note that CHR is, strictly speaking, a type conversion function which should report any problems in delivering a CHAR value. However, in practice it may be implemented as a type transfer function and so is not as 'safe' as it might be.

Examples

```
CHR(65)  returns A  (for ASCII implementations of CHAR)
CHR(99)  returns c  (for ASCII implementations of CHAR)
```

23.5 DEC

DEC is a proper procedure that takes a parameter of any ordinal type (i.e. CARDINAL, INTEGER, CHAR, enumeration, or subrange types). DEC will return the predecessor of the parameter. For numeric types DEC(x) is equivalent to writing the expression $x := x - 1$. DEC can also take a second parameter, n say, in which case the value of the first parameter will be replaced by its nth predecessor. When DEC is used with two parameters, the second parameter must be of $\mathbb{Z}$. Note that DEC is the inverse of INC.

Examples

(i)
```
i := 25;
DEC(i);        results in  i = 24.
```

(ii)
```
c := 'B';
DEC(c);        results in  c = 'A'.
```

(iii)
```
TYPE
   DaysOfTheWeek = (Sun, Mon, Tue, Wed, Thu, Fri, Sat);
VAR
  x : DaysOfTheWeek;
BEGIN
```

```
        x := Sat;
        DEC(x, 2);   results in  x = Thu
```

23.6   DISPOSE

DISPOSE is a proper procedure that takes as its parameter a pointer variable.
DISPOSE makes the dynamic variable pointed to by its parameter inaccessible,
and sets its parameter to NIL. Usually, DISPOSE deallocates storage for a
dynamic variable whose memory address is assigned to the parameter. DISPOSE
makes use of a procedure called DEALLOCATE which can be found in the
standard library module Storage. Therefore any program which makes use of
DISPOSE must first import the procedure DEALLOCATE from the module
Storage.

Example

```
MODULE DynamicStore;
FROM Storage IMPORT ALLOCATE, DEALLOCATE;
TYPE
  Name = RECORD
           Forename, Surname : ARRAY[0..20] OF CHAR
         END;
  NamePointer = POINTER TO Name;
VAR
  NamePtr : NamePointer;
BEGIN
  NEW(NamePtr);
  NamePtr^.Forename := John;
  NamePtr^.Surname  := Smith;
  ...
  DISPOSE(NamePointer)
END DynamicStore.
```

For further details of DISPOSE see Chapter 22.

23.7   EXCL

EXCL is a proper procedure that excludes an element from a set. The first
parameter is a variable of set type (including BITSET); the second parameter is
the element to be excluded, which can be any simple expression that is
compatible with the element type of the set.

Example

```
TYPE
  Colour = (Red, Gold, Green);
  SetOfColour = SET OF Colour;
VAR
  x : SetOfColour;
  y : Colour;
```

```
BEGIN
  y := Green;
  x := SetOfColour{Red,Gold,Green};
  EXCL(x,y);
```

The result of the call to EXCL is that the set x has the value {Red, Gold}.

Further examples of EXCL can be found in Chapter 21.

23.8 FLOAT

FLOAT is a function procedure that takes a whole number expression as its parameter and returns the equivalent REAL value.

Some implementations allow FLOAT to be used with a LONGREAL parameter, to perform a type conversion from LONGREAL to REAL.

Examples

(i)   FLOAT(65)   returns 6.5000E+1
         FLOAT(3*5) returns 1.5000E+1

(ii)   VAR
           x: LONGREAL;
         ...
           x := 3.62379426195263;
           FLOAT(x) returns 3.62379 (but this is not portable)

23.9 HALT

HALT is a proper procedure that terminates the execution of a program. Normally a Modula-2 program terminates execution when it reaches the final END in the program code, or when it executes a RETURN statement in the program module. However, occasionally it may be desirable to terminate a program's execution at some other point in the code. This would usually be after your program had discovered an unrecoverable condition.

Some implementations report a runtime error when HALT occurs. (This is most often used to invoke a debugging system.)

Example

```
IF (StockNo < 0) OR (StockNo > 999) THEN
  WriteString('Stock No. out of range'); WriteLn;
  WriteString('***Program Aborts***');
  HALT
END
```

23.10 HIGH

HIGH is a function procedure that takes a parameter corresponding to an open array parameter and returns a value of $\mathbb{Z}$ type, which is the index of the last element of the array.

However, many implementations return either a CARDINAL or INTEGER value. Other implementations return a value of an extended whole number type (e.g. LONGCARD). Because of this lack of portability, a type conversion to CARDINAL is often needed. Furthermore, in some implementations HIGH can also be given ordinary arrays and array constants. This is not portable.

Example

```
PROCEDURE  ZeroAnyArray (VAR AnyArray : ARRAY OF INTEGER);
  VAR Count : CARDINAL;
  BEGIN
    FOR Count := 0 TO HIGH (AnyArray) DO
      AnyArray[Count] := 0
    END
  END ZeroAnyArray;
```

It can be seen that the procedure ZeroAnyArray will initialize to all zeros any single-dimensional array whose components are of type INTEGER. Further details of HIGH can be found in Chapter 19.

23.11 INC

INC is a proper procedure that takes a parameter of any ordinal type (i.e. CARDINAL, INTEGER, CHAR, enumeration, or subrange types) and returns the successor of the parameter. For numeric types, INC (x) is equivalent to writing the expression x := x + 1. INC can also take a second parameter, n say, in which case x will be replaced by its nth successor. When INC is used with two parameters, the second parameter must be of $\mathbb{Z}$ type. Note INC is the inverse of DEC.

Examples

(i)   x := 25;
         INC (x);   results in x = 26

(ii)   ch := 'B';
         INC (ch);   results in ch = 'C'.

(iii)   TYPE
           DaysOfTheWeek = (Sun, Mon, Tue, Wed, Thu, Fri, Sat);
        VAR
         x : DaysOfTheWeek;
        BEGIN

```
x := Wed;
INC(x, 2);   results in x = Fri
```

23.12 INCL

INCL is a proper procedure that includes an element in a set. The first parameter is a variable of set type (including BITSET); the second parameter is the element to be included, which can be any simple expression which is assignment compatible with the element type of the set.

Example

```
TYPE
   Colour = (Red, Gold, Green);
   SetOfColour = SET OF Colour;
VAR
   x : SetOfColour;
   y : Colour;
BEGIN
   y := Green;
   x := SetOfColour{Red,Gold};
   INCL(x,y);
```

The result of the call to INCL is that the set x has the value {Red,Gold,Green}.
Further examples of INCL can be found in Chapter 21.

23.13 LFLOAT

LFLOAT is a function procedure that takes a whole number expression as its parameter and returns the equivalent LONGREAL value. LFLOAT may take a parameter of type REAL, to perform a type transfer to type LONGREAL.

LFLOAT is not available on all compilers. Some use other names (such as FLOATD).

Examples

```
LFLOAT(65)   returns 6.5000E+1
LFLOAT(3*5)  returns 1.5000E+1
```

23.14 MAX

MAX is a function procedure that takes as its parameter any ordinal type and returns the maximum value of that type.

Examples

```
(i)     MAX(INTEGER)   returns 32767 in Topspeed Modula-2
        MAX(CARDINAL)  returns 65535 in Topspeed Modula-2
```

(ii)   `TYPE Colour = (Red, Gold, Green);`
           `MAX(Colour)` **returns** `Green`

23.15 MIN

`MIN` is a function procedure that takes as its parameter any ordinal type and returns the minimum value of that type.

Examples

(i)   `MIN(INTEGER)` returns `-32768` in Topspeed Modula-2
       `MIN(CARDINAL)` returns `0` in all implementations of Modula-2

(ii)   `TYPE Colour = (Red, Gold, Green);`
        `MIN(Colour)` **returns** `Red`

23.16 NEW

`NEW` is a proper procedure that takes as its parameter a variable of a pointer type. `NEW` allocates storage for a dynamic variable and assigns its memory address to the pointer variable parameter. `NEW` makes use of a procedure called `ALLOCATE` which can be found in the standard library module `Storage`. Therefore any program which makes use of `NEW` must first import the procedure `ALLOCATE` from `Storage`.

Example

```
MODULE DynamicStore;
FROM Storage IMPORT Allocate;
TYPE
   Index = [0..20];
   Name = RECORD
             Forename, Surname  : ARRAY Index OF CHAR
          END;
   NamePointer = POINTER TO Name;
VAR NamePtr : NamePointer;
BEGIN
   NEW(NamePtr);
   NamePtr^.Forename := John;
   NamePtr^.Surname  := Smith;
   ...
END DynamicStore.
```

Further details of `NEW` can be found in Chapter 22.

23.17 ODD

`ODD` is a function procedure that takes as its parameter a whole number expression (x) and returns the result of the Boolean expression x `MOD 2 <> 0`.

Examples

```
ODD(64) returns FALSE
ODD(53) returns TRUE
```

23.18 ORD

ORD is a function procedure that takes as its parameter a value of any ordinal type (i.e. INTEGER, CARDINAL, CHAR, enumeration, or subrange types) and returns the ℤ value corresponding to the ordinal value of its parameter. Note that many implementations do not allow negative integer parameters; such implementations return a value of type CARDINAL. Strictly speaking ORD is a type conversion function which should report problems of converting an ordinal value to ℤ. In practice, because of the common way in which ordinal types are implemented, ORD may actually be a type transfer function and therefore less 'safe' than it might be.

Examples

(i) ORD('A') returns 65 in implementations that use ASCII
     ORD(31) returns 31

(ii)
```
TYPE
   COLOUR = (Red, Gold, Green);
VAR
   Col : COLOUR;
   y: CARDINAL;
BEGIN
   Col := Red;
   y:= ORD(Col)     results in      y = 0
```

23.19 SIZE

SIZE is a function procedure that takes as its parameter any type x or a variable identifier x and returns a CARDINAL value which is equivalent to the number of addressable storage units required to represent x. For further information about SIZE see Chapter 22.

Examples

```
SIZE(INTEGER)    returns 2 in Topspeed Modula-2 (see Chapter 25)
SIZE(LONGREAL)   returns 8 in Topspeed Modula-2 (see Chapter 25)
```

(See also TSIZE in Chapter 25.)

23.20 TRUNC

TRUNC is a function procedure that takes as its parameter a positive REAL number, truncates its fractional part, and returns the corresponding CARDINAL value.

If you pass a negative REAL to TRUNC the value returned is implementation defined. (Topspeed Modula-2 returns a number in the range 32767..65535.)

Examples

```
TRUNC(2.1)      returns 2
TRUNC(32766.9)  returns 32766  in Topspeed Modula-2
```

23.21 VAL

VAL is a function procedure used for converting values between types. It takes two parameters: the first is the name of a result (or destination) type which should be expression compatible with operands in the expression containing VAL. The second parameter is an expression which is the source value to be converted to a value in the destination type.

Originally, VAL was defined on ordinal types only. However, its semantics have been extended and modified by many implementations. Some profess it to be a type transfer function while implementing type conversion, others implement type transfer semantics. According to the forthcoming Modula-2 Standard, VAL should implement type *conversion* semantics only (see *Portability Issues*).

The forthcoming standard for Modula-2 allows parameters which obey the following rules. At least one rule must apply for the use of VAL to be valid:

- the type of the source value and the type of the result type are both numeric (i.e. whole numbers or reals);

- the result type is a whole number type and the source value is any ordinal type;

- the type of the source value is a whole number type and the result type is any ordinal type.

Examples

```
(i)    VAL(BOOLEAN,1)      returns TRUE
       VAL(INTEGER,TRUE)   returns 1
       VAL(REAL,5)         returns 5.0000E+0   (in Topspeed Modula-2 )
       VAL(CHAR,65)        returns 'A'         (in Topspeed Modula-2 )
       VAL(INTEGER,5.6)    returns 5           (in Topspeed Modula-2 )
       VAL(INTEGER,-6)     returns -6
```

(ii)   Given the following type declaration :

```
TYPE Colour = (Red,Gold,Green);
```

then:

```
VAL(Colour,2)        returns Green
VAL(CARDINAL,Green) returns 2
```

(See Chapter 25 for further information on type transfer.)

23.22 PORTABILITY ISSUES

There are a number of portability problems with built-in procedures. They are discussed in alphabetical order.

CAP
: In many implementations a call of CAP with a non-lower-case argument returns a value which is not equal to the argument. (For example, on some implementations, CAP('R') = 'z' !) To guarantee correctness, you should write your own procedure.

HIGH
: In some implementations, HIGH returns a type which is not expression compatible with CARDINAL (i.e. it does not return a value of type $\mathbb{Z}$). Some implementations return INTEGER and others return a type which is an extension of cardinals. (Indeed, the provision of a new type, such as a LONGCARD, can often compromise the meaning of built-in procedures.) Because of this a type conversion with HIGH is sometimes needed.

LFLOAT
: LFLOAT is not yet common, but many implementations provide an alternative (e.g. FLOATD), but the semantics will not necessarily be those described.

MAX
: Some implementations allow MAX to be applied to real types. This is not portable. (In some implementations MAX is called LAST.)

MIN
: Some implementations allow MIN to be applied to real types. This is not portable. (In some implementations MIN is called FIRST.)

ORD
: The most common problem with ORD is that most implementations will not permit its argument to be an negative integer. A less common problem is that ORD might return an INTEGER or a LONGCARD.

VAL
: The confusion between type conversion and type transfer semantics is the main problem when using VAL. These are described above and in Section 25.4.

23.23 REVIEW QUESTIONS AND EXERCISES

Q23.1   What type does ABS return?

Q23.2 Write a code fragment, which guards against the implementation defined nature of CAP, for ASCII or EBCDIC character sets.

Q23.3 What is the result of DEC(0) on your implementation, if it is assigned (a) to a CARDINAL or (b) to an INTEGER.

Q23.4 Given the following piece of code

```
TYPE
   Cars = (XR3, GTI, XJS, TVR, RX7);
   MyCars = SET OF CARS;
VAR  x : MyCars;
BEGIN
   x := MyCars{XR3, XJS};
```

using only INCL and EXCL change x to contain only TVR, XJS, and RX7.

Q23.5 What is the maximum value FLOAT will return on your system?

Q23.6 Write out three instances when calling HALT is justified.

Q23.7 See if your implementation will accept ordinary array variables or even constants as parameters to HIGH. Why is it unnecessary for an implementation to do this?

Q23.8 Using ORD and ODD find out if '?' is odd or even?

Q23.9 Find out on your system if the largest CARDINAL has the same ordinal value as the smallest INTEGER.

Q23.10 Write a program to print out the number of addressable units used to store the data types provided by your implementation.

Q23.11 Given the following declaration

```
TYPE
   BigArray = ARRAY [0..MAX(CARDINAL)] OF REAL;
```

What does SIZE(BigArray) return? How should this effect your use of SIZE?

Q23.12 What happens when you pass 10.0 as a parameter to TRUNC? Why should TRUNC be used sparingly in portable programs?

Q23.13 Give equivalents of VAL conversions using ORD, FLOAT, and TRUNC.

Q23.14 The following module is illegal: why?

```
MODULE x;
VAR  Intptr: POINTER TO INTEGER;
BEGIN
   NEW(Intptr);
   Intptr^ := 1;
   DISPOSE(Intptr);
END;
```

PART III—PROGRAMMING FOR PORTABILITY

24 DEVELOPING PORTABLE SOFTWARE

24.1 INTRODUCTION

Throughout this book, we have attempted to identify and explain those aspects of the Modula-2 language which are not portable. The purpose of this chapter is to draw upon these aspects in order to establish some principles for portable program design. Even if your programs are never intended to be moved to another implementation, it is sensible to make the code as independent of the implementation as possible. Avoiding the poorly defined areas of the language will make programs more understandable and reliable.[1]

The portability of a program is dependent upon two factors:

- The percentage of code which does not have to be changed when a program is moved from one system to another.

- The ease with which those portions of the program that will have to be changed when the program is moved to a new implementation can be identified and modified.

These factors roughly correspond to programming issues and design issues, respectively.

An example of a programming issue is the range of CARDINAL. If you write code that requires CARDINAL values be in the range $0...2^{32}-1$ (i.e. requiring 32 bits) then the program will not be portable, since there are many Modula-2 implementations that only provide 16-bit CARDINALs. To transfer such code to another implementation could require the addition of many type conversions (to LONGCARD, if it is available), which could be quite tedious and error prone—as

---

[1]In parallel with the development of the program, self-checking test programs should also be developed. These are not discussed in the book. Self-checking test programs are supplied with the portable modules on a disk available through McGraw-Hill.

virtually all expressions could be affected. A better approach would be to declare a 32-bit subrange type, such that if the implementation does not support the design assumption then a compile-time error will result.

The design issues are more difficult to isolate. However design principles can be summarized. We enumerate nine in this chapter. The first two follow:

Principle 1: Isolate those portions of the code which are implementation specific.

Principle 2: Try not to make assumptions in the design which will force unnecessary coding restrictions on the programmer (e.g. the design should not assume a 32-bit CARDINAL range unless these values are output).

Principle 3: Document any decisions which will affect portability.

Although this book is not about program design *per se*, in order to illustrate practical portable programming this chapter will discuss the process of designing a portable file I/O library (similar in functionality to PortIO). Not all of the portability issues raised in the book are addressed in this case study, but it does provide guidance on designing other portable programs. The module to be studied is called PortFileIO. It provides a portable interface to input and output to and from disc text files.

24.2   THE SPECIFICATION OF PortFileIO

PortFileIO has to be able to read and write INTEGER, CARDINAL, string, and character values from and to files. It should provide constant semantics across both record- and character-based file systems.[1] The module is designed to be compatible with PortIO (see Chapter 9 for further information), and therefore the same procedures are provided with one extra parameter, the file descriptor. In addition to this file and the procedures which correspond to those in PortIO, the following procedures are provided:

- Open(FileName) — Searches the file system for a file that matches Filename. If a file exists then this file is opened for reading and a file descriptor linked to that file is returned.

- Create(FileName) — Opens an external file, called FileName, for writing to. It will overwrite pre-existing files of the same name. Create returns a file descriptor linked to this file.

- Append(FileName) — Searches the file system for a file that matches Filename. If a file exists then this file is opened for writing so that new data

---

[1]In a character-based file system a file consists of characters separated by special end-of-line characters. In a record-based file system a file consists of records for each line of a file which contains those characters that make up that line. A record-based system therefore does not necessarily have an end-of-line character.

is appended to the end of the file, and a file descriptor linked to that file is returned.

- `Close(FileDescriptor)` — Takes a `FileDescriptor` and closes the associated file. (This flushes the buffers if the file was in write mode.)

- `OpenFiles()` — Returns the number of files currently open.

- `MaxFiles` — Is a constant which is the maximum number of files that a client program is allowed to open.

`INPUT` and `OUTPUT` are two file descriptors which are pre-assigned by `PortFileIO` to the keyboard and the screen, respectively.

The success or failure of any of the above operations can be checked by a call to the function procedure `Done`.

The model of a text file assumed by `PortFileIO` is a series of lines terminated with a special end-of-file character. Each line consists of a sequence of characters terminated by an end-of-line character.

24.3   THE DESIGN OF PortFileIO

In order to keep the interface between `PortFileIO` and the operating system both small and simple, and therefore to minimize the amount of code which has to be changed when reimplementing `PortFileIO`, all I/O is based upon operations to open and close a file and read a character. These operations are usually provided as primitives within each file system that supports a Modula-2 implementation. If they are not present, then this design is not portable. The next guiding principle of portable programming can be expressed thus:

Principle 4:   Always design around the lowest common denominator. If a design is to be portable the basic assumptions must be made clear, and they must be true for all the implementations to which the program may be moved.

The implementation dependent features which `PortFileIO` needs are isolated in a separate module called `ImplDep` (an acronym for implementation dependent). This module encapsulates and isolates implementation dependent code which will have to be changed. The fifth portability design principle is thus:

Principle 5:   Separate modules should be used to isolate non-portable code from portable code. This may conflict with the normal design goal of each module implementing one task; however, it enables easy identification of the features which have to be changed.

`ImplDep` provides five constants, which will change from implementation to implementation; these are as follows:

- The string terminator (imported from `PortStrings`).

- The end-of-line character (defined within `ImplDep` and exported to `PortIO`).

- The end-of-file character.

- The maximum number of files which can be open at any one time.

The first constant is imported from another module; this ensures consistency and reduces the amount of work that has to be done in moving module PortFileIO to a new system. We called this module ImplDep.

The modules which this book assumes (PortIO and PortStrings) have to be altered for each new implementation. Therefore it makes sense to use constants declared in PortIO and PortStrings rather than redeclare them within ImplDep, and run the risk of one being changed without the other.

There is a difference between the above constants. The string terminator is determined by the Modula-2 implementation; it must be whatever the assignment statement uses at the end of a string literal when it has been copied to a larger character array (see Chapter 10). However, the end-of-file and end-of-line characters are not tied to a Modula-2 implementation; they are internal representations of the conventions used by the file system and do not need to change when the module is recompiled on another Modula-2 implementation. They are used to define the *internal* environment and are not related to the external environment. (The way they are implemented in the external environment can be very different. For example, on a record-based file system, the implementation of PortFileIO may not be able to use suitable characters for end-of-line and end-of-file characters.)

ImplDep provides a number of procedures that interface with the operating system; these are four file management procedures: Open, Append, Create, Close and two I/O procedures: ReadLine and WriteLine. PortFileIO uses these procedures to implement its fuller range of I/O functions. A further principle is:

Principle 6: Isolate the primitive operations that need to interface to the external environment and reduce them to a small number of primitive operations. These primitives can be isolated in a separate module and all the major functions implemented in terms of these primitives. This avoids inconsistency as well as easing implementation.

The procedures provided within by ImplDep are described below.

- Open(FileName, FileBuffer) — Opens a file bound to the name specified by filename and prepares it for reading. The file buffer is assigned to the file.

- Append(FileName, FileBuffer) — Opens a file bound to the name specified by filename and prepares it to be appended to. The file buffer is assigned to the file.

- `Create(FileName, FileBuffer)` — Creates a new file overwriting any old file with the same name. It prepares the file for writing. A correspondence is set up between the file buffer and the file.

- `Close(FileBuffer)` — Closes the external file and deallocates the file buffer; any further attempt to access the file will cause a run-time error.

- `ReadLine(F: FILE)` — `ReadLine` is the only procedure which reads from a file directly. It reads a line of characters into the input buffer associated with the individual file descriptor whilst translating the end-of-line and end-of-file markers to the logical representation defined within `PortFileIO`. As `PortFileIO` only performs text I/O, this can be done safely without corrupting data.

- `WriteLine(F: FILE)` — `WriteLine` writes the output buffer to a file. It translates the `Impldep` defined end-of-line character to the implementation dependent equivalent character (or system call). It does not translate the end-of-file character.

24.4 THE STRUCTURE OF PortFileIO

We have listed the definitions and procedures upon which `PortFileIO` is based. Now we will examine parts of the code itself to see why it is portable. A complete listing of the implementation is given in Appendix 3.

Different operating systems have different file structures and store different information about the files that have been opened. None of this information needs to be accessible to the user. The hiding of information about the file structure is accomplished in `PortFileIO` by the use of an opaque type. This not only ensures that the programmer cannot use information specific to the system on which the program was compiled, but also ensures that file descriptors cannot be tampered with by user programs. This leads to a further principle:

Principle 7: A portable program should limit the visibility of implementation dependent features. User programs should not be able to access implementation dependent code directly, only through well-defined procedures whose semantics can remain constant across Modula-2 implementations.

The number of files that can be opened on the system is defined by the constant `MaxFiles`. The predicate `OpenFiles` returns the number of files that are open. This use of predicates illustrates another design principle:

Principle 8: A portable program should contain validation code to check operations before it uses them. This is because the effect of an illegal operation differs between implementations. The program should not rely on the operating system to terminate the program if a logical error has occurred, like opening too many files, because the consequences are unknown to the program.

The validation code contained within `PortFileIO` is limited; for example it checks that `CARDINAL` and `INTEGER` values are within range. The method used relies on overflow wrapping around and not being detected as an exception by the implementation. Very little has been said so far in this book about exceptions. In this context, exceptions are errors in your program which are detected by the hardware, operating system, or by checks inserted in the code by the compiler. An example of an exception would be an attempt to read from a file which had not been opened.

Implementations may provide a mechanism for trapping these exceptions and continuing the program. This is usually termed *exception handling*. The semantics of exception handlers differ and therefore they should be used sparingly in portable programs. If an operation is likely to cause an exception the program itself should check that the operation is legal before attempting it. Exception handlers should only be used where program logic cannot determine in advance the success or failure of an operation (e.g. file I/O operations). If exception handlers are used, they should be isolated to a particular module, to ease identification and change when reimplementing the code.

The names used by `PortFileIO` should not clash with those used by common extensions to the language, nor should they clash with the names defined in the library modules provided with the implementation. An example of a quirky choice of name to ensure that a name clash does not occur is `Fiel`. `Fiel` is the component of the file descriptor which represents the implementation dependent file type. The principle which arises from this is:

Principle 9:   Name clashes that can cause confusion are best avoided. This is good coding practice and an aid to portability.

The rest of the code is reasonably portable, there is one circular dependency (see Chapter 13) but there is as little dependence on the external environment as possible. The residual portability problems which could arise with this module are:

- The implementation may not support Modula-2 types properly. For example, a compiler might pack character arrays and prevent indexed character arrays from being used as the actual parameter to a procedure which expects a `VAR` parameter (see comment in `PortIO.ReadLine`).

- The linker/compiler may not support names of longer than six characters. This is a problem on older operating systems and linkers. All our programs rely on the number of significant characters in an identifier being at least 12.

- File names have different formats on different operating systems. For example, some operating systems are case sensitive (e.g. UNIX) and others (e.g. MS-DOS) are not. `ImplDep` could translate file names into the correct format for the operating system. The problem with this approach is that this translation is invisible to the programmer. When moving a program to a different system the program would read and write files with different file names.

`PortFileIo` is considerably less efficient than the Topspeed I/O module `FIO`, because `FIO` closely models the IBM PC file system. Portability has been gained in `PortFileIo` at the cost of efficiency.

24.5 CONCLUSIONS

Writing portable code is not difficult. Occasionally code has to be written in an inelegant manner in order to cope with awkward implementations, but in general you just have to stick to a simple design and good coding practices. Some compromises have to be made: a portable module will often run slower than a well written non-portable module, as it will not use the system facilities to their full potential.

However, some functions cannot be written in a portable fashion. For example, REAL number I/O is a problem, because the internal representation of floating point numbers and the rounding rules used by the processor has to be known in order to avoid rounding errors. Problems can arise from decimal numbers which have not got an exact binary representation being inaccurately read. Whilst it is possible (using binary coded decimal (BCD) calculations and BCD to REAL conversions) to produce an accurate portable REAL I/O package, the performance overhead of reading in REALs this way is often too great to be acceptable.[1]

In this book we have tried to describe those areas of the language which are likely to differ from implementation to implementation. As long as you are aware of the assumptions made about the underlying hardware when you start to design and code your programs, and you follow the nine simple principles we have proposed, your programs will be as portable as you want them to be.

---

[1] The BCD representation of a decimal number is a string of decimal digits. Each decimal digit of that number is stored in four bytes and calculations are performed digit by digit ensuring the accuracy of the result.

25 SYSTEMS PROGRAMMING WITH MODULA-2

25.1 INTRODUCTION

Modula-2, though a high-level language, provides sufficient low-level access to make it an excellent tool for systems programming. For the purpose of this book, we classify systems programs as follows:

- software which directly interacts with the operating system or file system (e.g. an input/output module such as `PortFileIO`);

- software which needs to access the computer it runs on at a low level (e.g. at the level of bits, bytes, or words);

- software which can only be implemented with knowledge of how data is represented by an implementation (e.g. procedure for converting a `REAL` value to a string).

The first category has already been discussed in Chapter 24. This chapter is primarily concerned with the second and third categories. (However, the address of variables has already been discussed in Chapter 22, and concurrency facilities are described in Chapter 26.)

Because of the inherently non-portable nature of systems programming, you might be tempted to dismiss portability considerations. This would be a mistake: the high cost of software development increases the likelihood that the investment which software represents will be protected by implementing the software on many systems. Also, there is a high degree of similarity between compilers for machines on which software might be reimplemented, and so properly designed systems programs can be fairly portable in practice.

25.2 SYSTEM MODULES

To a large extent, the use of systems programming facilities is risky: you abandon the 'safety' of normal Modula-2 for the more 'dangerous' low-level world. You are therefore obliged to make explicit your use of dangerous facilities by importing them from a module in which they are isolated.

Inevitably, the systems programmer needs to break out of the straitjacket which Modula-2 quite properly imposes on applications programmers. This means that the systems programmer needs to use facilities in a way which the rules of the language do not usually permit and needs those facilities to possess properties not normally available in the language. Therefore, systems programming facilities cannot be expressed in Modula-2 but have to be provided by an implementation—through the module mechanism. The term *system module* is coined to describe the special status of this type of module.

At the time of writing, most implementations implement only one system module—called SYSTEM. However, there are a number of implementations which divide up the systems programming facilities between system modules. (For example, the forthcoming standard specifies a system module for coroutines, which are at present mostly provided for in SYSTEM; hence we deal with coroutines in Chapter 26.)

The facilities provided by instances of SYSTEM vary considerably. In a given implementation, it is likely to contain all the low-level facilities the implementors found useful when producing their system. (See *Portability Issues* for examples of these facilities.) In this chapter we will only describe the following:

(i)   data representation (as in Topspeed Modula-2) and the general approach to discovering how an implementation represents data values;

(ii) bit, byte, and word manipulation;

(iii) access to computer addresses;

(iv) development of generic procedures.

We begin our discussion by looking at how data is represented in Topspeed Modula-2.

25.3 DATA REPRESENTATION

All variables require some number of units of storage in a computer to represent them. The size of these storage units depends firstly on the variety of addressing methods of the target computer,[1] and secondly how the programming language implementation exploits these addressing methods. The number of such units depends on the data type and how the Modula-2 compiler implements them.

---

[1] If an implementation is generating code for another computer, then the architecture of the target computer must be considered, not that of the host implementation.

On the PC/AT family of computers there are two addressable units of storage—the *byte* (which is 8 bits in size) and the *word* (16 bits). In Topspeed Modula-2 the byte is taken to be more common, and it is the number of bytes of a data type or variable which the SIZE procedure returns (see Chapter 23). The elementary types are implemented using 1, 2, 4 or 8 bytes, while the size of structured types is the sum of the sizes of their components.

Elementary types

The following table shows the typical size of variables of elementary types. (The sizes below are correct for Topspeed Modula-2 as well as many other compilers.)

Data type	Size in bytes
CARDINAL (or subrange)	2
INTEGER (or subrange)	2
REAL	4
LONGREAL	8
BOOLEAN	1
CHAR (or subrange)	1
enumeration types with <= 256 values	1
enumeration types with > 256 values	2
pointer types	4

(All of these sizes can be confirmed using the predefined SIZE procedure.)

For the ordinal types the size of the storage allocated to a type determines the range of values which they can take. This is because n bits can represent 2^n values: 0 to ($2^n - 1$). Thus, for example, in Topspeed Modula-2 CHAR can have 256 values. (Chapter 17 provides a table of these minima and maxima for Topspeed Modula-2.)

The way in which bit patterns are interpreted depends on the type. The bit pattern 00000001 is interpreted as the ASCII control code SOH (Ctrl-A) in the type CHAR, and TRUE in BOOLEAN. Examples of how to print the bit patterns of values are given below.

Representation of structured types

The structured types, i.e. arrays and records, are represented as a number of storage units which are contiguous in memory. The size of the units will depend on the size of the components of the structure if it is an array, and will typically be mixed if the structured type is a record. The total size of the data structure is usually the sum of the sizes of all components or fields.

For example, if an array A is declared as:

```
A: ARRAY [0..9] OF CHAR;
```

then the size of A is 10 bytes, since each component is a byte in size and there are 10 in A.

If R is a record, then the size of the fields must be calculated and added:

```
R: RECORD
      name: ARRAY [0..29] OF CHAR;
      code: CARDINAL;
      height, weight: REAL
   END;
```

Thus the size of R is $30 + 2 + (2 \times 4) = 40$ bytes.

The following program illustrates the use of the function procedure SIZE[1] and shows how the above discussion can be confirmed.

```
MODULE sizes;
FROM PortIO IMPORT WriteCard, WriteLn, WriteString;
TYPE
  ptr = POINTER TO boolarray;
  boolarray = ARRAY [0..9] OF BOOLEAN;
  rec = RECORD
              i: INTEGER;
              b: BOOLEAN
           END;
BEGIN
  WriteString('size of Boolean=');
  WriteCard(SIZE(BOOLEAN)); WriteLn;
  WriteString('size of Char=');
  WriteCard(SIZE(CHAR)); WriteLn;
  WriteString('size of Real=');
  WriteCard(SIZE(REAL)); WriteLn;
  WriteString('size of ptr=');
  WriteCard(SIZE(ptr)); WriteLn;
  WriteString('size of boolarray=');
  WriteCard(SIZE(boolarray)); WriteLn;
  WriteString('size of rec=');
  WriteCard(SIZE(rec)); WriteLn;
END sizes.
```

Note that some implementations use less storage for a structured type than the sum of the sizes of its components. Character arrays are often packed. For example, a CHAR may occupy 2 bytes, but an ARRAY [0..3] OF CHAR may only occupy 4.

Conversely, for some implementations the size of storage for some structured types is greater than the sum of the sizes of the components. For example, a CHAR may occupy one byte, but an ARRAY [0..3] OF CHAR may require 8 bytes because the implementation uses 16 bit words for arrays.

---

[1] In some implementations, SIZE may not be applied to types, and SYSTEM.TSIZE might have to be used. (See *Portability Issues*.)

Representation of real types

Real numbers are stored in what is known as *floating point* format. A number such as 1.23E–2 is stored as a sign (+, in this example), a *mantissa* (1.23) and an *exponent* (–2). The format of REAL and LONGREAL numbers in Topspeed Modula-2 follows the IEEE standard for 4 and 8 byte types.

Representation of sets

In Topspeed Modula-2 sets are represented in the same way as BITSETs (see Section 21.7). That is, each value in the base type of the set whose ordinal value is n is allocated one bit—the nth— which is set to 1 if the value is included in the set and cleared to 0 if it is excluded from the set.

In Topspeed Modula-2 , sequences of bits are used to represent sets. A set may only be formed from a base type of positive ordinal values in the range 0..65535 (and so SET OF [0..65535] is allowed). If the maximum ordinal value of a set's base type is n, then 1 + (n DIV 8) consecutive bytes will be required to represent it. The element of a set of value i (where $0 \le \text{ORD}(i) \le n$) is represented by bit number i MOD 8, in byte number i DIV 8, counting from bit 0 in byte 0.

25.4   TYPE TRANSFER

In systems programming applications, it is often necessary to circumvent the type rules of Modula-2 in order to interpret the bit representation of a value of one type as a value in another type. (This is different from type *conversion* which generates a new value, and new bit pattern, from a value of another type; type conversion is used primarily between numeric types. See VAL in Chapter 23.)

Unfortunately, the means by which type transfers may be carried out is not portable. The verb 'to cast' has been coined to describe performing a type transfer, and so the forthcoming standard for Modula-2 specifies a function procedure called CAST which should be provided in SYSTEM. This function procedure is not yet ubiquitous, and, what is worse, the built-in function VAL is sometimes provided in SYSTEM with type transfer (rather than conversion) semantics. We will describe CAST, explain how its functionality is provided in Topspeed Modula-2, and then show how this can be simulated in a portable fashion (albeit at some cost).

CAST is similar to VAL in that its parameters are a result type and a value. CAST takes the value and returns the bit pattern for that value as if it was a value of the specified result type. (CAST makes no attempt to check whether the bit pattern represents a valid value in the destination type.) Any type may be used with CAST. (VAL usually only accepts elementary types.)

For example, consider an implementation (such as Topspeed) which represents CARDINAL values as ones-complement, 16-bit values, and INTEGER values as twos-complement, 16-bit values.

```
VAR i: INTEGER;
...
i := VAL(INTEGER, 655);  results in i = 655
i := CAST(INTEGER, 65535);  results in i = -1
```

Topspeed Modula-2 does not provide CAST, but does provide *type transfer functions*. These functions are invoked by using a type name as if it is a function procedure name. Thus, in Topspeed Modula-2 the last line in the previous example would need to be rewritten as:

```
i := INTEGER(65535);
```

It is assumed that CAST will be implemented without the compiler generating any type transfer code (the bits of the input value are simply reinterpreted as the destination type, regardless of whether this yields anything sensible). This is in contrast to a proper implementation of VAL for type conversion, which must generate code to check that the conversion is sensible. We can supply a portable version of CAST, which only assumes that BYTE is the smallest addressable unit of storage. (Note: WORD can be substituted for BYTE, if this is appropriate for a particular implementation.) Our version, which will generate executable code, and therefore be less efficient, is as follows:

```
PROCEDURE Cast(in: ARRAY OF BYTE; VAR out: ARRAY OF BYTE);
  VAR c, max: CARDINAL;
  BEGIN
    IF HIGH(in) <= HIGH(out) THEN
      max := VAL(CARDINAL, HIGH(in))
    ELSE
      max := VAL(CARDINAL, HIGH(out))
    END;
    FOR c := 0 TO max DO
      out[c] := in[c]
    END
  END Cast;
```

Note that the use of VAL is unnecessary with Topspeed Modula-2, but it has been included to avoid problems with the result type of HIGH from other compilers.

As a more elaborate example of how type transfer works, consider what happens when values of structured types are cast. The following declarations will be used (assuming that the previously declared CAST is available from a module called PORTSYS):

```
FROM PORTSYS IMPORT CAST;
TYPE
  intpair = ARRAY [1..2] OF INTEGER;
  rec = RECORD
          b: BOOLEAN;
          ch: ['A'..'C'];
          i: intpair;
        END;
VAR
  r: rec;
```

```
big: LONGREAL;
str: ARRAY [0..5] OF CHAR;
```

Notice that both the variables r and str are represented in 6 bytes (in Topspeed Modula-2), while big requires 8 bytes. In Topspeed Modula-2 the components of a structured variable are stored, byte by byte, in the order in which they are declared. Thus, in r the first byte is used for the field b; the next byte is used for ch; the last four bytes are used for i.

These variables are to be initialized as shown below. The bit patterns of each byte of the variable are shown to the right:

```
WITH r DO                            r  byte  0  00000001
  b := TRUE;                            byte  1  01000001
  ch := 'A';                            byte  2  11111111
  i[1] := -1;                           byte  3  11111111
  i[2] := 2;                            byte  4  00000010
END;                                    byte  5  00000000

big := 1234.56789;                  big  byte  0  11100110
                                         byte  1  11000110
                                         byte  2  11110100
                                         byte  3  10000100
                                         byte  4  01000101
                                         byte  5  01001010
                                         byte  6  10010011
                                         byte  7  01000000

str := 'ABCDEF';                    str  byte  0  01000001
                                         byte  1  01000010
                                         byte  2  01000011
                                         byte  3  01000100
                                         byte  4  01000101
                                         byte  5  01000110
```

The following type transfers show how our CAST procedure may be used to transfer values between types; again the resultant bit patterns stored in the record are shown to the left.

```
Cast(r.ch, big);                     r  byte  0  00000001
                                         byte  1  11100110
                                         byte  2  11111111
                                         byte  3  11111111
                                         byte  4  00000010
                                         byte  5  00000000
```

Potentially, there is a problem here; the size of r.ch is 1 byte, and the size of big is 8 bytes. If the cast were to be made using a type transfer function, some implementations would transfer the bits of the source value, regardless of whether there was a risk to variables which are neighbours of the destination of the cast; other implementations would refuse to execute the cast. Topspeed Modula-2 only transfers at most the number of bits in the destination. In this case only the least significant byte of big (byte 0) is transferred to r.ch.

Also, note that the assignments to the `ch` field may cause a runtime error if a subrange checking compiler option is enabled. This is because the bit pattern gives a `CHAR` value which is outside the subrange values. This possibility is ignored above. Note that our `CAST` procedure deals explicitly with a mismatch in the sizes of parameters, as in the following type transfer.

```
Cast(r.i, big);          r  byte  0  00000001
                            byte  1  11100110
                            byte  2  11100110
                            byte  3  11000110
                            byte  4  11110100
                            byte  5  10000100
```

25.5   BITSET

A bitset is the Modula-2 mechanism by which individual bits of a storage unit can be manipulated. The size of the storage unit chosen for a bitset is implementation defined. Ideally it should be the size of the smallest addressable unit (see Section 25.6), but it is often the size of the storage unit which the implementor considers most useful. In Topspeed Modula-2 a word (2 bytes) is used.

The type `BITSET` is predefined to be `SET OF [0..unitlength-1]` which is implemented in a unit of storage. If a value n within the range `0..unitlength-1` (i.e. $0 \leq n <$ `unitlength`) is included in a bitset, the nth bit of the `BITSET` storage unit is assigned the value 1; excluding it from the bitset clears the nth bit to zero. Thus, in Topspeed Modula-2 a bitset can include values in the range `[0..15]`.

The usual set operators of union +, intersection *, set difference –, and symmetric set difference / apply. However, because of the way in which `BITSET` variables are implemented, these become the low-level logical operators OR, AND, AND-NOT, and XOR, respectively, and so can be used to perform low-level operations on bit patterns.

Note that in many implementations, `BITSET` is a predefined identifier, and not a type exported by `SYSTEM`. Also, many implementations do not require that the identifier `BITSET` precede a value of the type. Topspeed Modula-2 has `BITSET` as a predefined identifier, and does not require it in a bitset value constructor.

Example

```
VAR b: BITSET;
BEGIN
  b := BITSET{};
  (* will set the word used for b to 0000000000000000 *)
  b := BITSET{15, 3, 0, 1};
  (* will result in 1000000000001011 in the variable b *)
```

This shows the usefulness of BITSET in systems programming because of the ease with which individual bits can be set or cleared. Note that the result of the last assignment shows the least significant byte as the rightmost 8 bits.

25.6   WORD AND BYTE

We have already mentioned the need for Modula-2 compilers to provide at least one predefined type which represents a storage unit and which can be used to circumvent the type checking rules of Modula-2. Previous chapters have discussed how strong typing can help you as a programmer—allowing the compiler to check your logic. This can be a little too restrictive for systems programmers, who necessarily have to write programs which deal with the low-level representation of data types.

Ideally, the *smallest addressable unit* should be defined in SYSTEM and other common units of storage defined in terms of them. This would provide a portable framework for systems programmers, and implementors would not feel obliged to provide a byte-sized type if it was not appropriate for an implementation.

Topspeed Modula-2 defines the types WORD and BYTE. Both are pervasive (i.e. predefined and not in SYSTEM). Many other compilers also make these special types pervasive.

The type WORD is common to all Modula-2 implementations. It is generally implemented as a type which has the same size as the type CARDINAL; typically this can be between 2 and 4 bytes. However, many computers can address bytes as well as words, and it is fairly common for certain built-in types (e.g. CHAR) to be implemented as bytes. Therefore the 8 bit type BYTE is also provided. Thus it may suit your application to use BYTE rather than WORD according to the following rules.

- Any actual parameter of *any* type and whose size is the same as the size of WORD will match a formal parameter of type WORD.

- Any 8-bit actual parameter of *any* type will match a formal parameter of type BYTE.

- A parameter of *any* type of at least the size of a WORD will match a formal parameter of ARRAY OF WORD.

- Any parameter of *any* type of at least 8 bits in size will match a formal parameter of ARRAY OF BYTE.

These last two rules allow procedures to be written which can take virtually any actual parameter. The following example shows WORD, BYTE, and BITSET being used in a module which flips the bytes of word-sized data structures.

Example

```
MODULE flip;
FROM PortIO IMPORT
  WriteCard, WriteInt, WriteChar, WriteLn, WriteString;
TYPE twobytes = ARRAY [0..1] OF BYTE;
VAR
  c: CARDINAL;
  i: INTEGER;

PROCEDURE WriteWordBits(w: WORD);
  VAR card: CARDINAL;
  BEGIN
    FOR card := 15 TO 0 BY -1 DO
      IF card IN WordBits(w)
      THEN WriteChar('1')
      ELSE WriteChar('0')
      END
    END;
    WriteLn
  END WriteWordBits;

PROCEDURE flipbytes(VAR b: ARRAY OF BYTE);
  VAR temp: BYTE;
  BEGIN
    temp := b[1];
    b[1] := b[0];
    b[0] := temp
  END flipbytes;

BEGIN
  c := 519;
  WriteString('bits representing 519 are: ');
  WriteBitset(WordBits(c));
  flipbytes(c);
  WriteString('value of flipped 519 =');
  WriteCard(c); WriteLn;
  WriteString('bits representing flipped value :');
  WriteWordBits(WordBits(c));   (* CAST(WordBits, c) *)
  flipbytes(c);
  WriteString('value of flipped back ='); WriteCard(c);
  WriteLn;
END flip.
```

The output from this program is shown below.

```
bits representing 519 are: 0000001000000111
value of flipped 519 =  1794
bits representing flipped value: 0000011100000010
value of flipped back =  519
```

Note that the type transfer of the CARDINAL and INTEGER values has been performed using BYTE as the formal parameter of flipbytes, even though both CARDINAL and INTEGER are the same size as WORD. The purpose of flipbytes is to flip *bytes* and so clearly using BYTE is the most natural choice. (See Exercise Q25.1 on the consequences of choosing WORD.)

25.7   GENERIC PROCEDURES AND DATA STRUCTURES

In Chapter 14 open array parameters were described. These are a means by which general-purpose procedures can be written to process arrays of the same component type but different index types.

This is adequate for constructing modules which provide operations on a particular data type, or on a number of data types which can be considered to be instances of the same type but of different sizes. This is the case, for example, with the PortStrings module: open array parameters allow strings of different sizes to be catered for.

However, the restriction that the component types be the same impedes the use of ordinary open array parameters for implementing more abstract types such as queues, lists, stacks, etc. Modula-2 does not have such types built in the same way as, say, arrays are. These abstract data types have to be built from other components of the language using knowledge of the way built-in types are represented. But, if the implementor must know about these types, the programmer who might use them generally does not, maybe should not, know about them.

For example, consider a queue, which is a data structure which can have data items added to the end of it. If you want to implement a module which will allow queues of a variety of types of item to be manipulated, you must allow *queue types* to be declared (and identified) and you must provide operations which can apply to any queue variable.

Before considering the implementation, you of course need to write the definition module. To begin with, you should make the queue type opaque (see Chapter 14). Making the implementation of queue hidden in this way will prevent the users of the module from making assumptions about the implementation. However, the items to be stored in the queue must be represented somehow and open arrays of BYTE are chosen here.

Having made these decisions, then we must define what operations the module will offer. Obviously, a queue must be created—hence Createq. We must also allow items to be added to the queue—hence AddToq. Finally, the procedure Processq is defined in order to allow the user to define how he or she wants each item in the queue to be processed; this also needs the procedure type Action to be defined (see Chapter 14). The full definition module is given below:

```
DEFINITION MODULE QMod;
TYPE
  Queue;
  Action = PROCEDURE(VAR ARRAY OF BYTE);
PROCEDURE Processq(VAR q: Queue; Process: Action);
```

```
PROCEDURE AddToq(VAR q: Queue; ItemValue: ARRAY OF BYTE);
PROCEDURE Createq(VAR q: Queue);
END QMod.
```

The implementation of the queue data structure is a straightforward linked list with each item being a record containing a value (an array of bytes) and a pointer to the next item. The `Queue` opaque type is itself defined as a pointer to a pair of pointers, which point to the head and tail of the list.

Thus creating a queue involves creating a new head and tail record (using `NEW(q)`) and a first, dummy item (using `NEW(q^.head)`). The `NextItem` pointer of the first item is then set to `NIL`, because there are no other items, and the `Tail` field of the queue record is set to be the same as the head—i.e. pointing to the first item.

Adding a new value involves creating a new item, with the old tail's `NextItem` pointer pointing to it (`NEW(q^.Tail^.NextItem)` in `AddToq`) and resetting the `Tail` to point to it. Then the value must be copied into the new item. (Note that calls to the `ALLOCATE` procedure from `STORAGE` are given as alternatives to `NEW`, in case `NEW` is not provided by an implementation.)

`Processq` is relatively simple: a loop steps through the list from the head to the tail applying the `Process` procedure (supplied by the client module) to the value of each item.

The full implementation module is given below.

```
IMPLEMENTATION MODULE QMod;
FROM STORAGE IMPORT ALLOCATE, DEALLOCATE;
CONST MaxSize = 64;
TYPE
  Itemptr = POINTER TO Item;
  Item = RECORD
           Value: ARRAY [0..MaxSize -1] OF BYTE;
           NextItem: Itemptr
         END;
  Queue = POINTER TO RECORD
                       Head, Tail: Itemptr
                     END;

PROCEDURE AddToq(VAR q: Queue; ItemValue: ARRAY OF BYTE);
  VAR x: CARDINAL;
  BEGIN
    NEW(q^.Tail^.NextItem);
    (*ALLOCATE(q^.Tail^.NextItem, SIZE(ItemValue));*)
    q^.Tail := q^.Tail^.NextItem;
    WITH q^.Tail^ DO
      FOR x := 0 TO HIGH(ItemValue) DO
        Value[x] := ItemValue[x]
      END
    END;
    q^.Tail^.NextItem := NIL
  END AddToq;
```

```
PROCEDURE Processq(VAR q: Queue; Process: Action);
  VAR ThisItem: Itemptr;
  BEGIN
    ThisItem := q^.Head^.NextItem;
    WHILE ThisItem <> NIL DO
      Process(ThisItem^.Value);
      ThisItem := ThisItem^.NextItem
    END
  END Processq;

PROCEDURE Createq(VAR q: Queue);
  BEGIN
    NEW(q);
    (* ALLOCATE(q, SIZE(Queue)); *)
    NEW(q^.Head);
    (* ALLOCATE(q^.Head, SIZE(Itemptr));*)
    q^.Head^.NextItem := NIL;
    q^.Tail := q^.Head
  END Createq;
END QMod.
```

The following example shows how the QMod module may be used. Two integer queues are manipulated—one to hold negative numbers, the other to hold non-negative integers (somewhat erroneously called 'positive' below). The procedure which processes the queue prints the values of each item.

```
MODULE IntQ;
FROM QMod  IMPORT Queue, Processq, Createq, AddToq;
FROM PortIO IMPORT
  ReadInt, WriteLn, WriteString, WriteInt, Done;
VAR
  Number: INTEGER;
  PositiveQ, NegativeQ: Queue;
PROCEDURE WriteLnInt(VAR IntegerBytes: ARRAY OF BYTE);
  BEGIN
    WriteInt(VAL(INTEGER, IntegerBytes[0])); WriteLn
  END WriteLnInt;
BEGIN
  Createq(PositiveQ);  Createq(NegativeQ);
  WriteString('Input integer in range ');
  WriteInt(MIN (INTEGER)); WriteString('..');
  WriteInt(MAX (INTEGER)); WriteString(':');
  Number := ReadInt();
  WHILE Done() DO
    CASE Number < 0 OF
      TRUE: AddToq(NegativeQ, Number) |
      FALSE: AddToq(PositiveQ, Number)
    END;
    WriteString('Input integer: ');
    Number := ReadInt()
  END;
  WriteString('Positive Queue -'); WriteLn;
  Processq(PositiveQ, WriteLnInt);
  WriteString('Negative Queue -'); WriteLn;
```

```
    Processq(NegativeQ, WriteLnInt);
END IntQ.
```

25.8   ADDRESSES AND POINTERS

Systems programming frequently involves address manipulation. This might be in order to access some device like a clock, or graphics display. Alternatively it might be needed so that the use of memory can be controlled, as might happen in an operating system. At a high level, pointers can be used in many applications of this nature, but inevitably addresses must be computed and operated on. Support for this requirement is discussed below.

The ADDRESS type

A pointer is implemented as an address. An address on the 8086/80286/80386 family of computers consists of a segment number and an offset. In Topspeed Modula-2 these two values are both CARDINALs. Thus a pointer in Topspeed Modula-2 is essentially a record containing a segment number and offset field.

Pointer variables are subject to the type checking rules of Modula-2, which are often too restrictive for systems programmers. In particular, generic pointer manipulation routines are difficult to implement because of the type checking between actual and formal parameters. The type ADDRESS is therefore provided—either as a predefined type, or, more properly, in SYSTEM. It is considered to be defined thus:

```
TYPE ADDRESS = POINTER TO WORD;
```

This definition shows that ADDRESS is expression compatible (see Chapter 16) with any pointer type. Thus the type ADDRESS may be used (much like WORD or BYTE) to construct generic procedures for pointer types.

For example, an application may have two types of linked lists—one with forward linking only, another with two-way linking. In the example below the types Element1 and Element2 and associated pointer types define these types of lists, respectively. The type and variable declarations are as follows:

```
TYPE
  Element1Ptr = POINTER TO Element1;
  Element1 = RECORD
                Value: INTEGER;
                Next: Element1Ptr
             END;
  Element2Ptr = POINTER TO Element2;
  Element2 = RECORD
                Size: INTEGER;
                Next, Last: Element2Ptr
             END;
VAR
  r1: Element1; r2: Element2;
  p1: Element1Ptr; p2: Element2Ptr;
```

A function procedure to return the value held in an element of either of these lists could be implemented as:

```
PROCEDURE ElementValue(Ptr: ADDRESS): INTEGER;
  BEGIN
    RETURN INTEGER(Ptr^)   (* CAST(INTEGER, Ptr^) *)
  END ElementValue;
```

Since in both records the INTEGER value is the first word, then simply dereferencing the pointer and casting it to INTEGER suffices. The assignments and calls might be:

```
NEW(p1); p1^.Value := 99;
NEW(p2); p2^.Size := 123;
WriteInt(ElementValue(p1)); WriteLn;
WriteInt(ElementValue(p2)); WriteLn;
```

This code will output the values 99 and 123.

The predefined function procedure ADR takes any variable as a parameter and returns its address, which may be assigned to a pointer. This is particularly useful when you want to access static variables (i.e. those created when the program is compiled) using procedures whose parameters are pointers to dynamically created variables. For example, the procedure ElementValue above takes a pointer value and so normally could not be applied to the variables r1 or r2 declared above. ADR may be used effectively to point at these variables:

```
WriteInt(ElementValue(ADR(r1))); WriteLn;
```

Address constructor

Frequently, the address of a variable, not necessarily a pointer, must be specified. This is done by giving the address when the variable is declared.

Syntax

```
variable declaration = variable identifier list, ":", type ;
variable identifier list =  identifier, [address], {",", identifier, [ address]};
address =
   '[', cardinal constant, ":", cardinal constant,']'; (* in Topspeed *)
cardinal constant = constant expression;
```

Note that the constant expressions used to specify the location of the variables are often given in hexadecimal or octal.

Example

```
MODULE IBMConfig;
(* Program to print out hardware configuration of an IBM PC. *)

FROM SYSTEM IMPORT BITSET;   (* not needed if BITSET predefined *)
```

```
FROM PortIO IMPORT
  WriteCard, WriteLn, WriteString;

VAR
  EquipmentAttached [ 0000H : 0410H ] : BITSET;

(* Equipment installed information bits are stored at
   location 0000H : 0410H on IBM PCs.
   Hence, declaration of variable EquipmentAttached at this
   location gains access to bit values stored there.
   Bit numbers and functions are:
       15  14      13      12          11  10   9       8
        \   /              game         \      /
        # of print        port         # of RS-232
        ports 0-3         used          ports 0-4


        7   6       5     4         3   2    1       0
         \   /       \    /          \   /   8087     |
        # of        video mode      RAM     or       no
        disk-       at boot up      00=16K  80287     disk
        ettes       00=EGA          01=32K            drive
         1-4        01=CGA-40       10=48K            if 0
        if bit      10=CGA-80       11=64K
        0 = 1       11=MDA-80       (old PCs)                  *)

TYPE
  DriveRange = [1..4];
VAR
  NumberOfDrives: DriveRange ;
BEGIN
  IF  1 IN EquipmentAttached THEN
    WriteString('8087 or 80287 attached'); WriteLn;
  END;
  IF  NOT(0 IN EquipmentAttached) THEN
    WriteString('No floppy disc drives attached');
  ELSE
    IF 7 IN EquipmentAttached THEN
      NumberOfDrives:= 2;
      WriteString(' bit 7 set'); WriteLn;
    ELSE
      NumberOfDrives := 0;
    END;
    IF 6 IN EquipmentAttached THEN
      NumberOfDrives := NumberOfDrives + 2;
    ELSE
      NumberOfDrives := NumberOfDrives + 1;
    END;
    WriteCard(NumberOfDrives);
    WriteString(' floppy disk drives are attached'); WriteLn;
  END;
  IF BITSET{5,4} <= EquipmentAttached THEN
    WriteString('Monochrome monitor'); WriteLn;
  ELSIF  5 IN EquipmentAttached THEN
    WriteString('CGA 80 column monitor'); WriteLn;
  ELSIF  4 IN EquipmentAttached THEN
    WriteString('CGA 40 column monitor'); WriteLn;
```

```
    ELSE
      WriteString('EGA monitor');
    END;
    IF  12 IN EquipmentAttached THEN
      WriteString('Games port attached'); WriteLn;
    END;
  END IBMConfig.
```

This program examines the value of a specific address to check the configuration of the machine; it is highly IBM-PC specific.

25.9 PORTABILITY ISSUES

Systems programming is inherently unportable. However, a great deal of source code can be preserved if only the most common facilities are used. We therefore discuss what kinds of facilities are provided by system modules and how type transfer and type conversion operations may be confused.

SYSTEM facilities

A large number of facilities may be provided by an implementation of SYSTEM. These can include several types for storage units (e.g. SHORTWORD = 2 bytes, when WORD = 4 bytes), address arithmetic (i.e. procedures to increment or decrement addresses), register manipulation procedures, interrupt handling routines, bit shifting routines, and operating system function call facilities. None of these are portable.

The portable set of facilities should include:

- the types BYTE, WORD, BITSET, ADDRESS;

- the procedures ADR, TSIZE, and (when a Modula-2 standard is established) CAST.

Note, however, that the types may be predefined (as all are in Topspeed Modula-2). It is less common to find the procedures being built-in, but, as has been mentioned before, they may be provided by other means. Topspeed has ADR as a built-in procedure; it provides, but does not document TSIZE (the built-in SIZE is equivalent); casting is provided to some extent through type transfer functions (see below).

The relevance of TSIZE is historical. Originally, SIZE was provided for obtaining the storage requirements of variables, and TSIZE for types; both were originally in SYSTEM. Later compilers have SIZE as a predefined procedure and either discard TSIZE or keep it as a redundant feature of SYSTEM.

Type transfer functions

The use of type transfers and type conversions has become confused in the development of Modula-2. Originally VAL, FLOAT, TRUNC, ORD, and CHR were defined as type conversion procedures. They are mostly to be used with numeric types, or between ordinal types. They are 'safe' in that they are expected to report invalid conversions (e.g. such as between a REAL value and a BOOLEAN). Only two type transfer functions were originally described by Professor Wirth. These were INTEGER and CARDINAL; they were not assumed to be safe, but were assumed to allow a bit pattern of one whole number type to be interpreted as a value of the other. For all known implementations, this works for the range of non-negative whole number values.

However, these facilities were seen to be inadequate by many implementors, and a number of divergent extensions were introduced. Some implementations allow VAL to have two roles: type conversion for numeric types, and type transfer for all others. (Topspeed implements this extension.) Some implementations have VAL as a type transfer function only; at least one places it in SYSTEM (effectively making it CAST).

A great number of implementations have generalized the numeric type transfer functions and permit any type name to be used to cast a value of one type as a value of another. Topspeed Modula-2 implements this, and it is a reasonably portable extension.

25.10 REVIEW EXERCISES

Q25.1 Reimplement flipbytes using a WORD formal parameter.

Q25.2 Using the generic module QMod, create two string queues—one for holding strings beginning with upper-case letters, and one for holding strings with lower-case letters. Provide a procedure which processes the queues and prints the values of each item.

26 COROUTINES

26.1 INTRODUCTION

All the programs we have looked at so far have been sequential, based on a single thread of control; if a procedure P calls a procedure Q then it must wait for the termination of Q before it resumes. This is not always a convenient way to model real-life problems, so Modula-2 provides a non-sequential control mechanism called coroutines. Actually, as this facility is only defined for uniprocessors, it is not parallelism; however, coroutines allow many threads of control to exist at the same time.

26.2 WHAT ARE COROUTINES?

The relationship between two procedures specified as coroutines is one of mutual control. When a procedure P invokes a coroutine Q (a coroutine can be considered as a form of procedure), the execution of P is suspended and the current state - the point of execution and the values of local variables - is stored. At some later point, Q can restart P from precisely the point from which P invoked Q by calling it as a coroutine. Now Q is suspended, but it remembers its state. P and Q may call each other alternately, and each time the procedure restarts at the place immediately after the point it was last suspended (and control transferred).

Coroutines are the natural facility of Modula-2 to use when modelling the following:

- problems involving several tasks or operations which have equal priority;

- real-time events, such as programs which are time dependent or which depend upon hardware interrupts;

- simulation.

Confusingly the Modula-2 literature uses the term *process* both in relation to coroutines and to another concurrency abstraction (a 'process') which is usually provided by a separate library module. We will not discuss this latter feature and will use the terms process and coroutine interchangeably in the following text.[1]

Modula-2 allows you to create any number of coroutines with the special procedure NEWPROCESS. These coroutines transfer control from one to another synchronously at predetermined points in a program using the special procedure TRANSFER, or asynchronously in response to an interrupt following a call to the special procedure IOTRANSFER. ('Synchronous' and 'asynchronous' are explained in Sections 26.4 and 26.5.) If any coroutine reaches the end of its procedure body, the entire program, including all other coroutines, is automatically terminated.

Coroutines are considered to be system-dependent facilities and therefore their associated type (PROCESS) and the procedures to operate on them (NEWPROCESS, TRANSFER, and IOTRANSFER) have to be imported from the module SYSTEM, as follows:

```
FROM SYSTEM IMPORT
    PROCESS, NEWPROCESS, TRANSFER, IOTRANSFER;
```

26.3 CREATING A COROUTINE

To create a coroutine a variable must be declared of type PROCESS (imported from SYSTEM).

An example declaration is:

```
VAR Coroutine1, Coroutine2 : PROCESS;
```

The variables Coroutine1 and Coroutine2 can then be bound to a particular coroutine by the SYSTEM procedures NEWPROCESS, TRANSFER, and IOTRANSFER.

A Modula-2 program may have two or more coroutines. They can all interact with each other. Indeed, the main program module (or an implementation module) becomes a coroutine when it creates a new coroutine. In the case of the main program being a coroutine, the body of the coroutine is the body of the program module. Similarly, a procedure called from the main program can become a coroutine, in which case the body of the coroutine is the remaining program code.

Since NEWPROCESS requires a parameter of type ADDRESS, we remind you of ADDRESS and ALLOCATE.

---

[1]The forthcoming Modula-2 standard will remove this ambiguity. The system type PROCESS will be renamed COROUTINE and the procedure NEWPROCESS will re-named NEWCOROUTINE, but it will be some time before this is widely implemented.

ADDRESS is a predefined type in Topspeed Modula-2 and is considered to be defined as:

```
TYPE ADDRESS = POINTER TO WORD;
```

The ADDRESS type is compatible with all pointers (and also in Topspeed Modula-2 with CARDINAL). It can therefore be used for address computations and the results of such computations can be passed as pointers to procedures. The ALLOCATE procedure, imported from Storage, is used for dynamic data creation and can be considered to be defined as:

```
PROCEDURE ALLOCATE(VAR Where : ADDRESS; HowMuch : CARDINAL);
```

ALLOCATE returns a pointer to an area of free memory which is big enough to accommodate the demand specified in the HowMuch parameter. ALLOCATE is system dependent, and handles the task by direct interaction with the operating system (see Chapter 22 for more details).

NEWPROCESS

The procedure NEWPROCESS is used to create a new coroutine in the following manner:

```
NEWPROCESS(ProcedureName, Space, Size, ProcessName);
```

NEWPROCESS takes four parameters:

- ProcedureName is the name of a procedure which will form the coroutine. The procedure must be declared at the outermost block in the surrounding program or implementation module (i.e. it cannot be nested within other procedures). This procedure must be parameterless, and the body of the procedure forms the executable code of the coroutine.

- Space is a variable of type ADDRESS and is the start address of the workspace needed both to allocate the local variables of the coroutine and to store its state (i.e. the stack and other information) when it is suspended. Care must be taken with this parameter; the usual method is to create the space using the procedure ALLOCATE.

- Size is of type CARDINAL and is the size of the workspace allotted to the coroutine in bytes (in Topspeed Modula-2). Again, care must be taken over the selection of this parameter, to ensure that sufficient memory is allocated to meet requirements (see next subsection for details).

- ProcessName is a variable of type PROCESS, which must have been declared in the program. NEWPROCESS associates (or binds) the procedure ProcedureName to the coroutine variable identified by ProcessName.

NEWPROCESS only prepares a coroutine for execution, it does not cause it to begin execution.

Coroutine workspace requirements

The workspace requirements vary among systems. MS-DOS imposes a basic requirement for 512 bytes per coroutine. In addition, each coroutine will need further space allocated for its stack, any local variables, and for any nested procedures. The coroutine procedure overhead is about 20–30 bytes, and local variables require storage space according to their type (in the normal way). Nested procedures require space for parameters (as if they are local variables) as well as a stack space of around 30 bytes (increasing by 10 bytes or so, for each extra level of nesting). These overheads look quite small, 1000 bytes will do in most cases, but the space requirement increases dramatically if any local procedures within the coroutine are recursive.

26.4 SYNCHRONOUS TRANSFER BETWEEN COROUTINES

Synchronous transfers simply proceed from one coroutine to another, suspending the old one and preserving its state. The way in which execution takes place is entirely determined by the logic of the program, as distinct from asynchronous transfers—which are governed by external events (in the form of interrupts). Asynchronous transfers are explained in Section 26.5.

TRANSFER

The procedure TRANSFER allows you to make synchronous transfers, by stopping one coroutine and starting another. The syntax is as follows:

```
TRANSFER(Process1, Process2);
```

TRANSFER takes two parameters: both are of type PROCESS. The first parameter is a variable, which is associated with the current thread of control (which could be in a procedure or module body). TRANSFER causes this thread of control to be suspended and assigned to Process1. The second parameter, Process2, is the coroutine to be activated. TRANSFER can be used in two ways to start execution of the first coroutine.

- The first method is to declare one more PROCESS than is needed for the intended coroutines and to make an initial transfer from this to the first coroutine. This method makes the main program (or implementation module) into a suspended coroutine and allows transfer back. In these circumstances, it can be helpful to call this extra PROCESS something like main so that the name will be meaningful on subsequent reading of the source text.

- The second method is simply to call a procedure from the main program (or implementation module) which contains the first TRANSFER statement. This is more efficient (in the number of coroutines at least) but there is no main to transfer back to if problems arise.

Example of first method

The following program has two coroutines, the first (`Tick`) prints the word TICK to the screen, and then transfers control to other coroutine `Tock` which prints the word TOCK to the screen and then transfers control back to `Tick`. This is repeated 15 times and then the process stops.

```
MODULE TickTock;
FROM PortIO IMPORT WriteLn, WriteCard, WriteString;
FROM SYSTEM IMPORT
   (* many of following may be built-in by an implementation *)
   TRANSFER, NEWPROCESS, ADDRESS, PROCESS;
FROM Storage IMPORT ALLOCATE;
CONST
   size = 1000; (* Space required for process in bytes *)
(* TYPE PROCESS = ADDRESS; needed if no PROCESS in implementation*)
VAR
   WorkSpace1, WorkSpace2 : ADDRESS;
   Main, Process1, Process2 : PROCESS;
   Count : [0..100];

PROCEDURE Tick;
   BEGIN
     WHILE Count <= 30 DO
       Count := Count + 1;
       WriteString(' TICK  ');
       WriteCard(Count);
       WriteLn;
       TRANSFER(Process2, Process1) (* Transfer to Tock *)
     END;
       TRANSFER(Process2, Main); (* Transfer back at the end.*)
   END Tick;

PROCEDURE Tock;
   BEGIN
     LOOP
       Count := Count + 1;
       WriteString(' TOCK  ');
       WriteCard(Count);
       WriteLn;
       TRANSFER(Process1, Process2) (* Transfer to Tick *)
     END;
   END Tock;

BEGIN
   Count := 0;
   (* Create new process called Tock *)
   ALLOCATE (WorkSpace1, size);
   NEWPROCESS (Tock, WorkSpace1, size , Process1);
   (* Create new process called Tick *)
   ALLOCATE (WorkSpace2, size);
   NEWPROCESS (Tick, WorkSpace2, size , Process2);
   (* Suspend the main process and transfer control to Tick *)
   TRANSFER(Main, Process2);
```

```
    WriteString('Tick-Tock terminated'); WriteLn;
END TickTock.
```

In the main program body, `Count` is initialized and then space is allocated for the coroutine to run in. The call to `NEWPROCESS` associates `Process1` with the procedure `Tock` so that when it is activated it will act like a call to the procedure `Tock`. This is repeated for `Tick` with `Process2`. We now have three coroutines, two associated with `Tick` and `Tock` (which are suspended) and the `Main` coroutine. The call to `TRANSFER` suspends the main process, saving its state, and activates `Tick`. On activating `Tick` it increments the counter by one, writes `TICK` to the screen, and then calls `TRANSFER`. This call suspends execution of `Tick`, assigns the current state of the coroutine to `Process2` (`Tick`), and activates the coroutine `Process1` (`Tock`). The code for `Tock` is almost identical. After outputting `TICK` 16 times the loop condition becomes false and `Tick` transfers back to the main process.

Example of second method

This example copies characters from input to output. The first takes keyboard input and converts all instances of the input string AA to B; meanwhile there is a second coroutine which converts all instances of the string BB to C.

```
MODULE AAtoBandBBtoC;
FROM PortIO IMPORT WriteLn, WriteChar, WriteString, ReadChar;
FROM SYSTEM IMPORT
    (* many of following may be built-in by an implementation *)
    TRANSFER, NEWPROCESS, ADDRESS, PROCESS;
FROM Storage IMPORT ALLOCATE;
CONST
    size = 1000; (* Space (in bytes) required for coroutine *)
(* TYPE PROCESS = ADDRESS; needed if PROCESS not available *)
VAR
    WorkSpace : ADDRESS;
    Process1, Process2 : PROCESS;
    Ch, Ch1 : CHAR;

PROCEDURE AAtoB;
    BEGIN
        WriteString('Input some characters --> ');
        LOOP
            Ch := ReadChar();
            (* exit (and terminate program) if input character is Z *)
            IF Ch = 'Z' THEN EXIT END;
            IF Ch = 'A' THEN
                Ch := ReadChar();
                IF Ch = 'A' THEN
                    Ch := 'B'
                ELSE
                    Ch1 := Ch;
                    Ch := 'A';
                    TRANSFER(Process2, Process1);
                    Ch := Ch1;
```

```
            END;
          END;
          TRANSFER(Process2, Process1)
        END;
        WriteString('Terminating...'); WriteLn;
      END AAtoB;

  PROCEDURE BBtoC;
    BEGIN
      LOOP
        IF Ch = 'B' THEN
          TRANSFER(Process1, Process2);
          IF Ch = 'B' THEN
            WriteChar('C')
          ELSE
            WriteChar('B');
            WriteChar(Ch);
          END;
        ELSE
          WriteChar(Ch);
        END;
        TRANSFER(Process1, Process2)
      END;
    END BBtoC;

  BEGIN
    (* Create new process called BBtoC *)
    ALLOCATE(WorkSpace, size);
    NEWPROCESS(BBtoC, WorkSpace, size, Process1);
    (* Call AAtoB as a procedure, rather than a coroutine *)
    AAtoB;
  END AAtoBandBBtoC.
```

Space is allocated in the module body for the coroutine Process1 (BBtoC) and a new coroutine (BBtoC) is created and assigned to Process1. This process is not yet activated. The call of the procedure AAtoB gets the computation started. In AAtoB there is a loop controlling the main computation, which terminates if the character Z is input. A character is read into ch. If it is an A then a second character is read. If the second character is also an A then B is assigned to ch and Process1 is activated, and the current process is suspended and assigned to Process2. Process1 is also activated if the first character is not an A. If the first A is not followed by a second A, then A is assigned to ch and Process1 activated, ch is set to the following input character and Process1 activated again. The procedure BBtoC is similar in its construction and we can see that coroutines provide a simple solution to this problem, without requiring buffering.

26.5 ASYNCHRONOUS TRANSFER BETWEEN COROUTINES

The IBM-PC/AT family of computers contain one central processor and several smaller processors which control peripheral devices like the keyboard and serial ports. When a key is pressed on the keyboard, for example, the keyboard processor sends a message to the central processor to tell it a key has been pressed. This message is called an interrupt. Asynchronous transfers depend upon interrupts to control their execution.

IOTRANSFER

The procedure IOTRANSFER allows you associate a particular interrupt with a coroutine transfer. The syntax is as follows:

```
IOTRANSFER(ProcessName1, ProcessName2, InterruptNumber);
```

IOTRANSFER takes three parameters:

- The first, ProcessName1, is the name of the coroutine from which control is to be transferred. The parameter must be of type PROCESS.

- The second, ProcessName1, is the name of the coroutine to which control is to be transferred. The parameter must be of type PROCESS.

- The third, InterruptNumber, is the interrupt number[1] which will cause transfer to take place. This must be of type CARDINAL on the IBM-PC/AT family.

IOTRANSFER associates the current process with the interrupt number given as the third parameter. It then suspends the current process, saves its state, and activates the new process. However, when the central processor receives an interrupt, it checks if it has been associated with a particular process by IOTRANSFER. If it has, it suspends the current process and activates the process associated with the interrupt; otherwise the interrupt is ignored. Once an interrupt and a resultant transfer has occurred, the interrupt is no longer associated with that process. If you want an interrupt to continue to be associated with the process, IOTRANSFER must be called again.

Three steps are generally involved in setting up an interrupt-driven transfer:

- First, the coroutines must be created using NEWPROCESS (just as with synchronous coroutines).

- Second, TRANSFER must be used to start the execution of a process.

- Finally, IOTRANSFER can be used within executing processes to transfer on interrupt.

The second step can be omitted, but then the interrupt handler becomes the main process. IOTRANSFER must be imported from SYSTEM.

---

[1]The CARDINAL values representing the various kinds of interrupts can be found in the reference manual provided with your machine.

Priority

Modules can be assigned a priority when they are declared. The syntax is as follows:

```
program module =
   "MODULE", module identifier, [priority], ";",
   {import}, block, module identifier, ".";
priority = "[", constant expression, "]";
```

Priority expressions are generally either set or ordinal (usually CARDINAL) constants. In Topspeed Modula-2, priority expressions are CARDINALs and, if no priority is explicitly provided, modules are assigned a default priority of 0 by the compiler, unless it is a local module. Local modules inherit their priority from their surrounding module. The priority facility provides a method for controlling the action of a program which is subject to external interrupts.[1]

In Topspeed Modula-2 the effect of priority depends on the machine on which the program is being run and the type of interrupt that the coroutine is associated with. When the coroutine is activated (via IOTRANSFER) the bit representation of the interrupt number and the priority are logically OR-ed together and are placed in the interrupt controller. This means the same priority may have different meanings for different interrupts. As the IBM-PC has an 8-bit interrupt controller and the IBM-PC/AT has a 16-bit interrupt controller, priorities should be chosen to work with the PC/AT (they will then automatically work with the PC).

Priority in Topspeed Modula-2 can be any cardinal value. The simplest way to use priority is to use two values: 0 which is the default value and means the process is interruptable, and MAX (CARDINAL) which ensures that the process cannot be interrupted. If these are coded as constants, they will be easier to change if you reimplement the code; however, due to scope problems, this can only be done for local or implementation modules. You should only use other values for the priority of a module if you have access to reference information for the machine.

Note that, when using the interruptable/non-interruptable schema, you will have to explicitly enable keyboard and other I/O interrupts.

Monitors in Modula-2

When two coroutines are to share data, or write to the screen, they must often be synchronized so that one is not allowed to tamper with the data while the other is using it. The method used to achieve this in Modula-2 is to use a *monitor*. In Modula-2, a monitor is a module in which all the procedures for modifying global or imported data are encapsulated. This module must be assigned a higher

---

[1]The Modula-2 notation of priority must not be confused with the concept of importance in a concurrent system in which a scheduler decides which process to execute next. In Modula-2, priority relates to the ability to be interrupted.

priority than the modules in which any coroutines which call these encapsulated procedures are found.

The monitor priority guarantees that only one process may be executing a procedure in the monitor at a particular time and this procedure must complete before another process is allowed to enter the monitor.

An example of a monitor using IOTRANSFER

The example is of a simple alarm coroutine. The program prompts you for a delay in seconds. It then calculates the prime numbers between 1000 and 2000, periodically writing to the screen the time remaining and the number of primes found. It is IBM-PC specific, and the module `Screen` is the monitor.

```
MODULE Time;

FROM SYSTEM IMPORT IOTRANSFER, NEWPROCESS, TRANSFER, PROCESS;
FROM Storage IMPORT ALLOCATE;
FROM PortIO IMPORT
  ReadCard, WriteChar, WriteString, WriteLn, WriteCard;
CONST
  Bell = 07C;
  NONINTERRUPTABLE = MAX( CARDINAL );
VAR
  Delay, I, K, NoPrimes : CARDINAL;

MODULE Screen[ NONINTERRUPTABLE ];
(* This is a Monitor which stops an interrupt
   occurring while the program is writing to the screen. *)
IMPORT WriteString, WriteLn, WriteCard;
EXPORT Output, OutCard;
PROCEDURE Output(STR : ARRAY OF CHAR);
  BEGIN
    WriteString( STR ); WriteLn;
  END Output;
PROCEDURE OutCard(Card : CARDINAL; STR : ARRAY OF CHAR);
  BEGIN
    WriteCard(Card); WriteString(STR); WriteLn;
  END OutCard;
END Screen;


MODULE EnableKeyboard [ 0 ];
(* This module is interruptable and therefore allows keyboard
   I/O to take place (keyboard I/O relies on interrupts on
   the IBM PC). This schema can only be used because this
   module is executed before IOTRANSFER has been used.*)
IMPORT Output, ReadCard, Delay;
PROCEDURE ReadDelay;
  BEGIN
    Output( 'Input Delay in seconds' );
    Delay := ReadCard()*20; (* convert it to 1/20's of a sec *)
  END ReadDelay;
BEGIN
```

```
      ReadDelay;
   END EnableKeyboard;


   MODULE Timer[ NONINTERRUPTABLE ];
   IMPORT ALLOCATE, IOTRANSFER, NEWPROCESS, TRANSFER, PROCESS,
     Output, OutCard, ReadCard, Delay;
   EXPORT Finish;
   VAR
     AD : ADDRESS;
     Main, P2 : PROCESS;
   PROCEDURE Finish(): BOOLEAN;
     (* This function procedure stops the wait loop in the Main
        process.It can't be interrupted by CountDown as it has the
        same priority. *)
     BEGIN
       RETURN Delay = 0;
     END Finish;
   PROCEDURE CountDown;
     BEGIN
       REPEAT
         IOTRANSFER( P2, Main, 08H);
         (* Transfer to main process but return here when an
            interrupt 8 occurs *)
         DEC( Delay );
         IF Delay MOD 20 = 0 THEN           (* Output the time left *)
           OutCard( Delay DIV 20,' SECONDS ');     (* every second *)
         END;
       UNTIL Delay = 0;                              (* UNTIL time up *)
       Output( 'Times up' );
       TRANSFER( P2, Main );            (* return to the main process*)
     END CountDown;
   BEGIN (* body of Timer *)
     ALLOCATE( AD, 8000 );            (* Workspace for the NEWPROCESS *)
     NEWPROCESS( CountDown, AD, 8000, P2 ); (* Create the process *)
     TRANSFER( Main, P2 );             (* Transfer to the new process *)
   END Timer;
   BEGIN (* body of main program *)
     LOOP
       (* find primes between 1000 and 8000 *)
       NoPrimes := 0;
       FOR I := 1000 TO 2000 DO
         K := 2;
         WHILE ( K - 1 ) < ( I DIV 2 ) DO
           IF ( I MOD K ) = 0 THEN
             K := 10000;
           ELSE
             K := K + 1;
             IF ( K - 1 ) = ( I DIV 2 ) THEN
               NoPrimes := NoPrimes + 1;
             END;
           END;
         END;
       END;
       OutCard( NoPrimes, ' primes between 1000 and 2000' );
```

```
    IF Finish() THEN EXIT END;
END;
    WriteChar( Bell );                    (* ring the bell *)
END Time.
```

The main module has three local modules. The first is Screen. This acts as a monitor protecting screen I/O from interruption. The second module, EnableKeyboard, reads from the keyboard. This must have interrupts enabled as the keyboard is interrupt driven on the IBM-PC. The third local module is Timer. On execution of the module Time, the body of the local module Timer is executed first. This creates a new process called CountDown and performs a TRANSFER to it. CountDown enters a loop and executes an IOTRANSFER which passes control back to the main process. This associates CountDown with interrupt 8 (which occurs about 20 times per second on an IBM-PC/AT). The main process exits the body of the local module and enters the body of the main module Time. It calls the procedure ReadDelay, which inputs the time the program is to run for and stores it in the variable Delay. Then main process enters a loop which counts the prime numbers between 1000 and 2000 until the function procedure Finish returns TRUE. This loop is interrupted approximately every 1/20th of a second and CountDown is activated. CountDown decrements Delay and outputs the time left every 20 activations (about once a second). While Delay is not 0, CountDown executes an IOTRANSFER back to the main process and continues to calculate primes. If Delay is 0, CountDown executes a TRANSFER back to the main process which stops calculating primes on its next call to the procedure Finish. The bell is then rung.

The different modules are given two different priorities. The monitor used to protect screen I/O from interruption (Screen) was made non interruptable as is the interrupt handler (Timer). The main module had implicitly been given priority 0, and was therefore interruptable by Timer.

26.6   PORTABILITY ISSUES

There are two types of coroutines described in this chapter. Those that use IOTRANSFER and those that do not. If a coroutine does not use IOTRANSFER then the portability issues are restricted to:

- The size of workspace allocated for the procedure to run in. If the workspace is declared as a constant and marked at the beginning of the module it can be changed when the program is ported.

- The capacity of the machine. If a program is too big or has too many coroutines then it will not be portable.

If the coroutines use IOTRANSFER then they are not easily portable, since they associate highly machine-specific interrupt numbers with coroutines. Interrupt numbers, and their functionality, differ from machine to machine. The interrupt used in the above example happens about 20 times per second on an IBM-PC/AT. It may not have an equivalent on other machines, or it could be that the establishment of an equivalent interrupt will affect other interrupts or degrade program performance to an unacceptable level.

The scope of priority expressions

Implementation modules may have an associated priority expression, as in the following example:

```
IMPLEMENTATION MODULE Fred [priority];
```

The priority expression must follow the rules of constant expressions, and can therefore contain identifiers and operators. However, there is some confusion over which block contains the priority expression, and so confusion of the scope of any identifier occurring in the priority expression. The best approach, for portability, is to qualify the identifiers with the appropriate module name. Whether or not this works, the compiler should reveal what it is trying to do in its diagnostic messages.

Topspeed Modula-2 allows both literal constants constant identifiers to be priority expressions.

Priority in program modules

Although the syntax of Modula-2 allows a priority expression in a program module, this has no portable meaning (and is not implemented by all compilers).

Priority is used to protect programs from interrupts. Priority constants are associated by the compiler with some machine dependent characteristic. In general, you should only rely on a machine providing two states: interruptable or non-interruptable. If you use more than two levels of priority in your programs they may not be portable.

The interrupts and timer problems make it very difficult to write portable concurrent programs. The interrupt problems can be overcome by:

- only using two levels of priority, corresponding to interruptable and non-interruptable;

- the use of monitors for critical code segments;

- not allowing interruptable coroutines to be associated with interrupts.

This type of programming can lead to potential starvation of processes. If a program is monitoring three events associated with interrupts all of equal importance, but one of the interrupts is assigned a higher priority by the hardware than the other two, then the lower priority of two of the processes can lead to loss of data. This could arise because more data has been input, but the lower priority processes are unable to consume it. Therefore you need to know that the processor can monitor all three events with an arbitrary ordering of priority. These timing problems are difficult to predict. You need to know the maximum number of interrupts of each type that can occur in a set time period, whether the interrupts are periodic, aperiodic, or a mixture of both, whether they have to synchronize with other tasks, and the time it takes to process each interrupt (this may not be a constant value).

26.7 REVIEW QUESTIONS

Q26.1 What is a coroutine?

Q26.2 One of the parameters to the procedure NEWPROCESS specifies the size of the workspace used by the coroutine. What is this workspace used for?

Q26.3 What do you have to do in order to create and run a coroutine?

Q26.4 What is the difference between TRANSFER and IOTRANSFER?

Q26.5 Why should you not associate an interrupt with a coroutine which is interruptable?

APPENDICES

APPENDIX 1
MODULA-2 SYNTAX

A1.1 COLLECTED CONCRETE SYNTAX

The following syntax definition uses the variant of BNF defined by the British Standard: *BSI Syntactic Metalanguage*, BS 6154 (1981). (See Chapter 12 for explanation of metalanguages.)

The rules which follow describe Modula-2 as the authors believe it will be defined in the forthcoming standard. A certain degree of redundancy has been employed in order to make the syntax more readable and to impart some of the semantics of the language.

Note that an index of non-terminals, which gives the rule numbers in which these are defined, is included after the set of rules.

```
1    compilation unit =
         definition module | implementation module | program module;

     (*———————Definition Module———————*)
2    definition module =
         "DEFINITION", "MODULE", module identifier, ";", {import},
         {definition}, "END", module identifier, "." ;
3    module identifier = identifier;

4    definition =
         "CONST", {constant declaration, ";"} |
         "TYPE", {(type declaration |  opaque type), ";"} |
         "VAR", {variable declaration, ";"} |
         procedure heading, ";";

5    opaque type = identifier;

     (*———————Program and implementation modules———————*)
6    implementation module = "IMPLEMENTATION", program module;
7    program module =
         "MODULE", module identifier, [priority], ";", {import},
         block, module identifier, ".";

8    import = ["FROM", module identifier], "IMPORT", identifier list, ";";

9    priority = "[", constant expression, "]";
```

10   block = {declaration}, ["BEGIN", statement sequence], "END";

11   statement sequence = statement, {";", statement};

      (*————Declarations————*)

12   declaration =
       data declaration | procedure declaration | module declaration;

      (*————Data Declaration————*)

13   data declaration =
       "CONST", {constant declaration, ";"} |
       "TYPE", {type declaration, ";"} |
       "VAR", {variable declaration, ";"};

14   constant declaration =
       identifier, "=", (constant expression | constant identifier);

15   constant expression = expression (* which is evaluated by compiler *);

16   constant identifier = identifier;

17   variable declaration = variable identifier list, ":", type ;

18   variable identifier list =
       identifier, ["[", address,"]"], {",", identifier, "[", [address], "]" };

19   address =
       ? Implementation defined. For Topspeed Modula-2 address is
        cardinal constant expression, ":", cardinal constant expression?;

20   type declaration = identifier, "=", type;

      (*————Procedure declaration————*)

21   procedure declaration = procedure heading, ";", block, procedure identifier;

22   procedure heading =
       "PROCEDURE", procedure identifier, [formal parameter list];

23   procedure identifier = identifier;

24   formal parameter list =
       "(", [formal parameter section, {";", formal parameter section}], ")",
       [function result];

25   formal parameter section = ["VAR"], identifier list, ":", formal type;

26   formal type = {"ARRAY", "OF"}, qualified identifier;

27   function result = ":", qualified identifier;

      (*————Module Declaration————*)

28   module declaration =
       "MODULE", module identifier, [priority], ";", {import}, [export],
       block, module identifier;

29   export = "EXPORT", ["QUALIFIED"], identifier list, ";";

(*—————————Statements—————————*)
30   statement =
          null statement |
          assignment |
          procedure call |
          if statement |
          case statement |
          loop statement |
          while statement |
          repeat statement |
          for statement |
          with statement |
          return statement |
          exit statement (* only allowed in LOOP statement sequence *);

31   null statement = ;

32   assignment = designator, ":=", expression;

33   procedure call = designator, [actual parameters];

34   actual parameters = "(", [expression list], ")";

(*—————————Selection statements - IF and CASE—————————*)
35   if statement =
          "IF", boolean expression, "THEN", statement sequence,
          {"ELSIF", boolean expression, "THEN", statement sequence},
          ["ELSE", statement sequence], "END";

36   boolean expression = expression;

37   case statement =
          "CASE", expression, "OF", case, {"|", case},
          ["ELSE", statement sequence], "END";
38   case = [case label list, ":", statement sequence];

(*———————Iteration statements - LOOP, FOR, REPEAT and WHILE ———————*)
39   loop statement = "LOOP", statement sequence, "END" ;

40   while statement =
          "WHILE", boolean expression, "DO", statement sequence, "END";

41   repeat statement =
          "REPEAT", statement sequence, "UNTIL", boolean expression;

42   for statement =
          "FOR", identifier, ":= ", expression, "TO", expression,
          ["BY", constant expression], "DO", statement sequence, "END";

43   with statement = "WITH", designator, "DO", statement sequence, "END";

44   return statement = "RETURN", [expression] ;

45   exit statement = "EXIT" ;

(*————————Types————————*)
46   type =
        qualified identifier | enumeration | subrange type | array type |
        record type | set type | pointer type | procedure type;

47   enumeration = "(", identifier list, ")";

48   identifier list = identifier, {",", identifier};

49   subrange type =
        [range type], "[", constant expression, "..", constant expression, "]";
50   range type = qualified identifier ;

(*————————ARRAY, SET and POINTER types————————*)
51   array type = "ARRAY", ordinal type, {",", ordinal type}, "OF", type;

52   set type = "SET", "OF", ordinal type;

53   ordinal type =
        qualified identifier (* but not real, pointer, set or structured types *) |
        enumeration | subrange type;

54   pointer type = "POINTER", "TO", type;

(*————————RECORD type————————*)
55   record type = "RECORD", field list sequence, "END";

56   field list sequence = field list, {";", field list};

57   field list =
        identifier list, ":", type |
        "CASE", [tag identifier], ":", tag type, "OF", variant, {"|", variant},
        ["ELSE", field list sequence], "END";

58   variant = [case label list, ":", field list sequence];

59   case label list = case labels, {",", case labels};
60   case labels = constant expression, ["..", constant expression];

61   tag identifier = identifier;
62   tag type = qualified identifier (*of ordinal type*);

(*————————Procedure types————————*)
63   procedure type = "PROCEDURE", [formal parameter type list];
64   formal parameter type list =
        "(", [formal parameter type, {",", formal parameter type}], ")",
        [function result] ;
65   formal parameter type = ["VAR"], formal type;

(*————————Expressions ————————*)
66   expression = simple expression, [relation, simple expression];
67   simple expression = ["+" | "-"], term, {add operator, term};

68   term = factor, {multiply operator, factor};
69   factor =
       numeric literal | string literal | "(", expression, ")" | not operator, factor |
       designator, [actual parameters] | value constructor;

70   numeric literal = whole number literal | real number literal;

71   whole number literal =
       digit, {digit} | octal digit, {octal digit}, "B" | digit, {hex digit}, "H";

72   real number literal = digit, {digit}, ".", {digit}, [scale factor];
73   scale factor = "E", ["+" | "-"], digit, {digit};

74   string literal =
       ' " ', {character -' " '}, ' " ' | " ' ", {character - " ' "}," ' " |
   character number literal;
75   character number literal = octal digit, {octal digit}, "C";

76   designator = qualified identifier, {".", identifier | "[", expression list, "]" | "^" };

77   expression list = expression, {",", expression};

78   qualified identifier = identifier, {".", identifier};

79   identifier = letter, {letter | digit};

(*————————Value constructors————————*)
80   value constructor = array constructor | record constructor | set constructor;

81   array constructor = array type identifier, array definition;
82   array type identifier = qualified identifier;
83   array definition = "{", component, {",", component},"}";
84   component = expression;

85   record constructor = record type identifier, record definition;
86   record type identifier = qualified identifier;
87   record definition = "{", field value, {",", field value}, "}";
88   field value = expression;

89   set constructor = base type identifier, set definition;
90   base type identifier = qualified identifier;
91   set definition = "{", [element, {",", element}], "}";
92   element = expression, ["..", expression];

```
          (*————————Operators————————*)
93    add operator = "+" | "-" | "OR";
94    multiply operator = "*"  | "/" | "DIV" | "MOD" | "REM"| and operator;
95    not operator = "NOT" | "~" ;
96    and operator =  "AND" | "&" ;
97    not equal = "<>" | "#" ;
98    relation = "=" | not equal  | "<" | "<= " | ">" | ">=" | "IN";

          (*————————Lexical definitions————————*)
99    octal digit = "0" | "1" | "2", | "3" | "4" | "5" | "6" | "7";
100   digit = octal digit | "8" | "9";
101   hex digit = digit | "A" | "B" | "C" | "D" | "E" | "F";

102   character =
          ? any printable character, or graphic character  from implemented
              character set?;

103   letter = ? "a".."z" | "A".."Z" | "_" ? .
```

Index for syntax rules

The following index of non-terminal symbols may be used either with the above
BNF rules, or with the syntax diagrams which follow.

Non-terminal	Rule no.	Non-terminal	Rule no.
function result	27	record constructor	85
hex digit	101	record type identifier	86
identifier list	48	record definition	87
identifier	79	record type	55
if statement	35	relation	87
implementation	6	repeat statement	41
import	8	return statement	44
letter	103	scale factor	73
loop statement	39	set constructor	89
module declaration	28	set definition	91
module identifier	3	set type	52
multiply operator	94	simple expression	67
not equal	97	statement sequence	11
not operator	95	statement	30
null statement	31	string literal	74
numeric literal	70	subrange type	49
octal digit	99	tag identifier	61
opaque type	5	tag type	62
ordinal type	53	term	68
pointer type	54	type declaration	20
priority	9	array type identifier	82
procedure call	33	type	46
procedure declaration	21	value constructor	80
procedure heading	22	variable declaration	17
procedure identifier	23	variable identifier list	18
procedure type	63	variant	58
program module	7	while statement	40
qualified identifier	78	whole number literal	71
range type	50	with statement	43
real number literal	72		

A1.2 MODULA-2 SYNTAX DIAGRAMS

As an alternative to the BNF rules above, the following syntax diagrams describe Modula-2 as it is believed it will appear in the forthcoming standard.

Terminal symbols are enclosed by rounded rectangles, for example:

(END)

Non-terminals are enclosed in rectangles, for example:

definition module

Non-terminals are defined by a rule which is numbered according to the production rules in A1.1. Hence, the index at the end of A1.1 may be used to look up the syntax diagrams below.

For consistency, the redundancy used in A1.1. is maintained here. Simple syntactic equivalences are denoted using = (cf. rule 3).

Note that iteration is often shown as a clockwise loop (terminating in a leftward arrow).

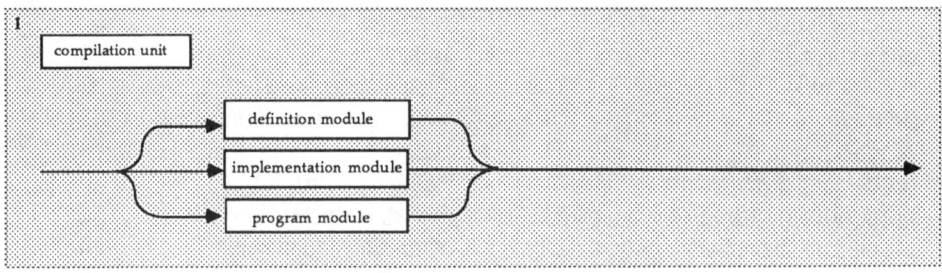

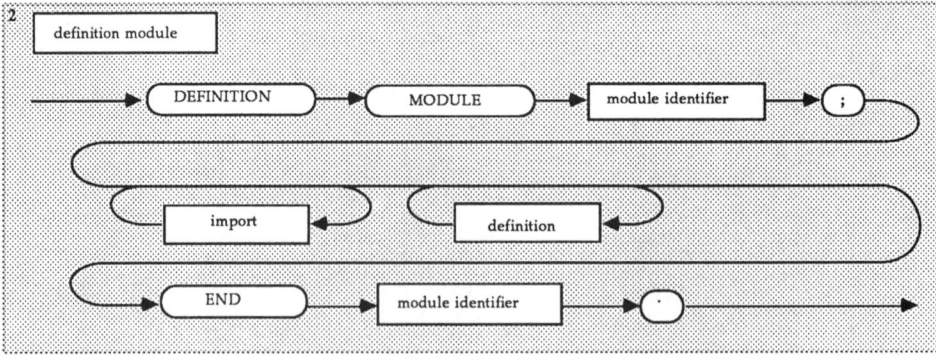

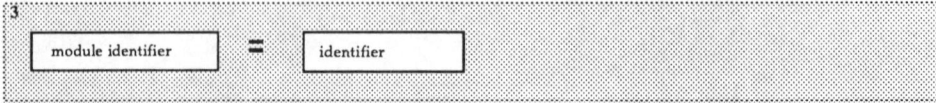

4

definition

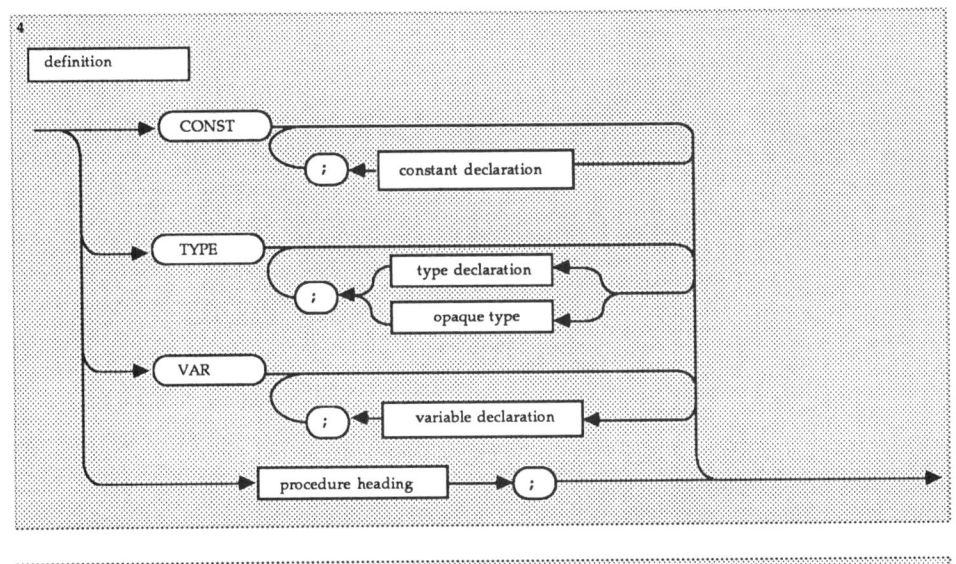

5

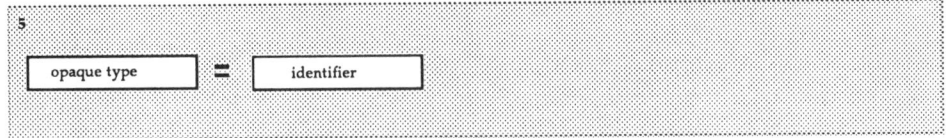

6

implementation module

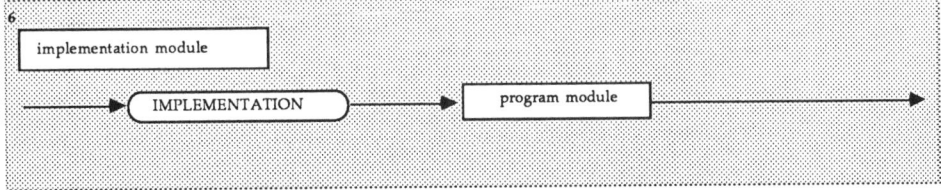

7

program module

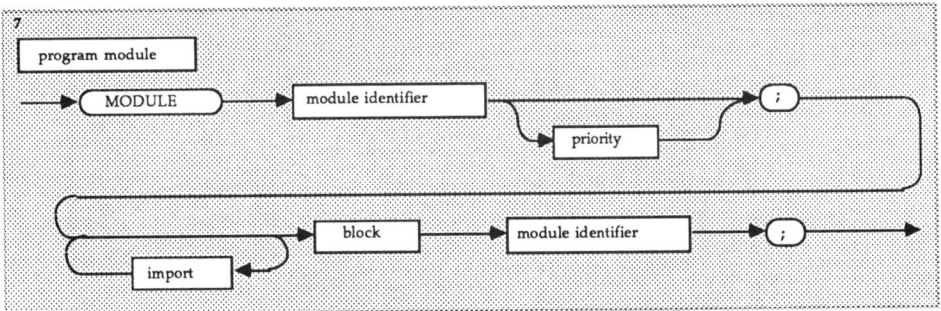

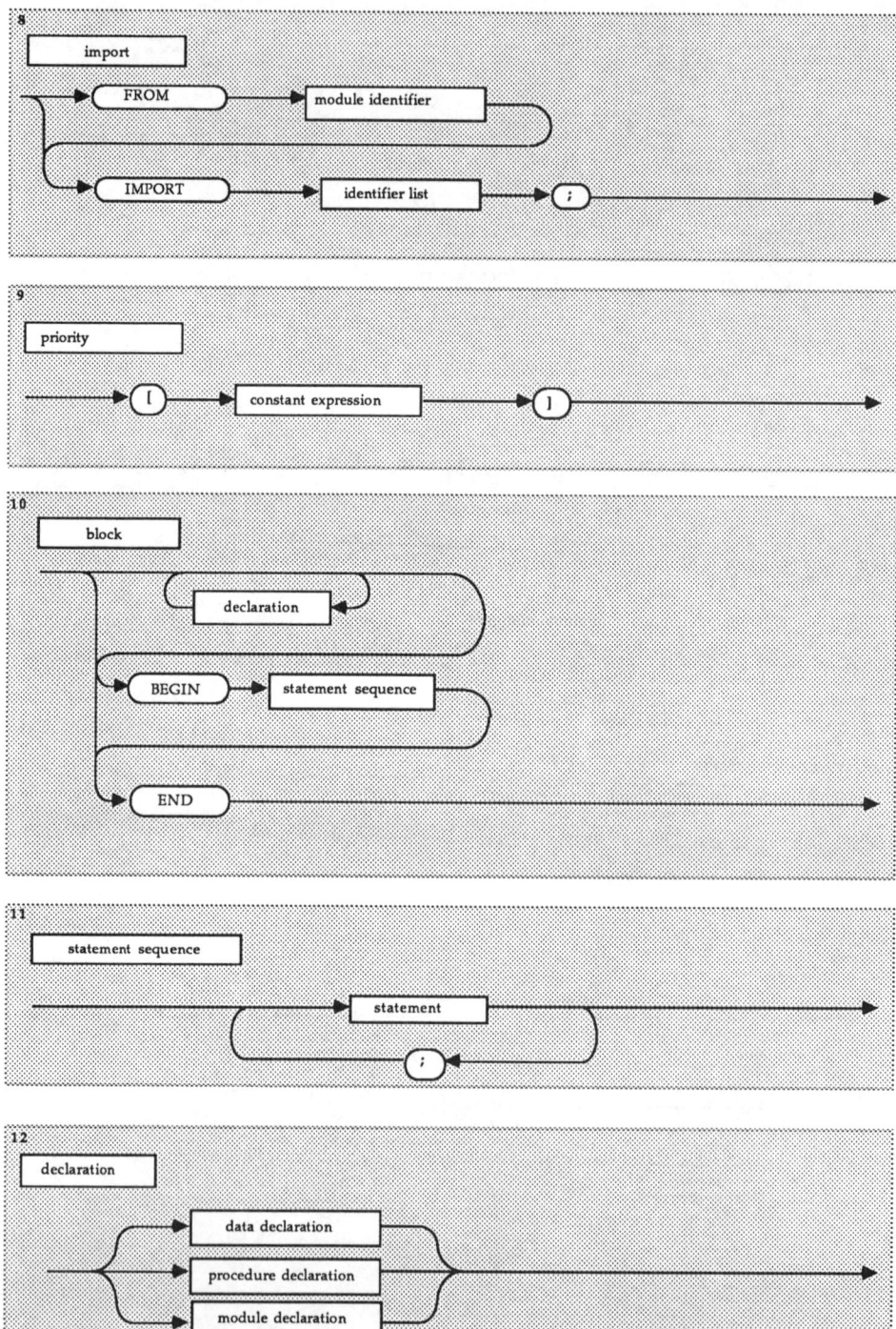

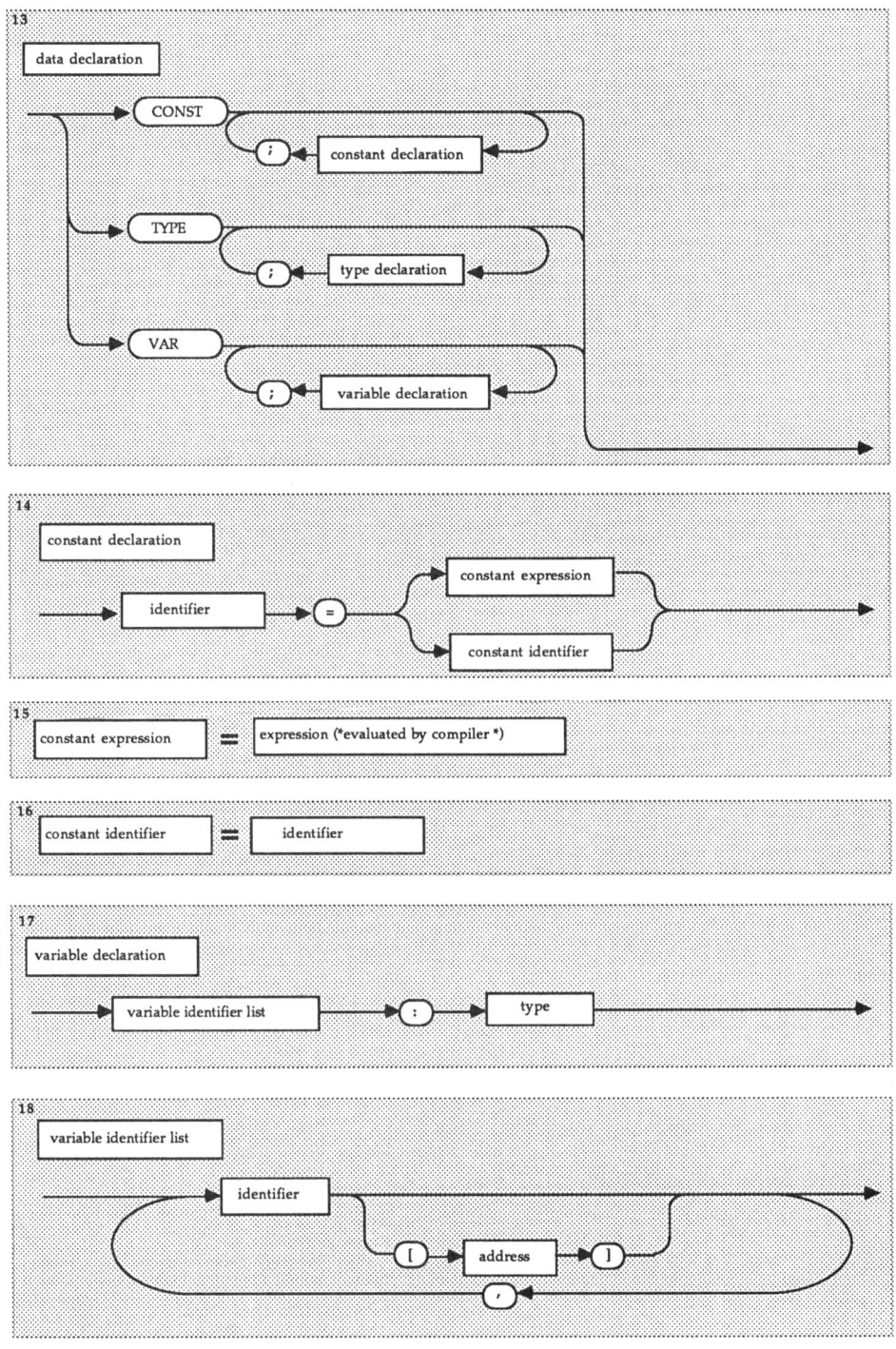

13 data declaration

CONST
; constant declaration

TYPE
; type declaration

VAR
; variable declaration

14 constant declaration

identifier = constant expression
constant identifier

15 constant expression = expression (*evaluated by compiler *)

16 constant identifier = identifier

17 variable declaration

variable identifier list : type

18 variable identifier list

identifier
[address]
,

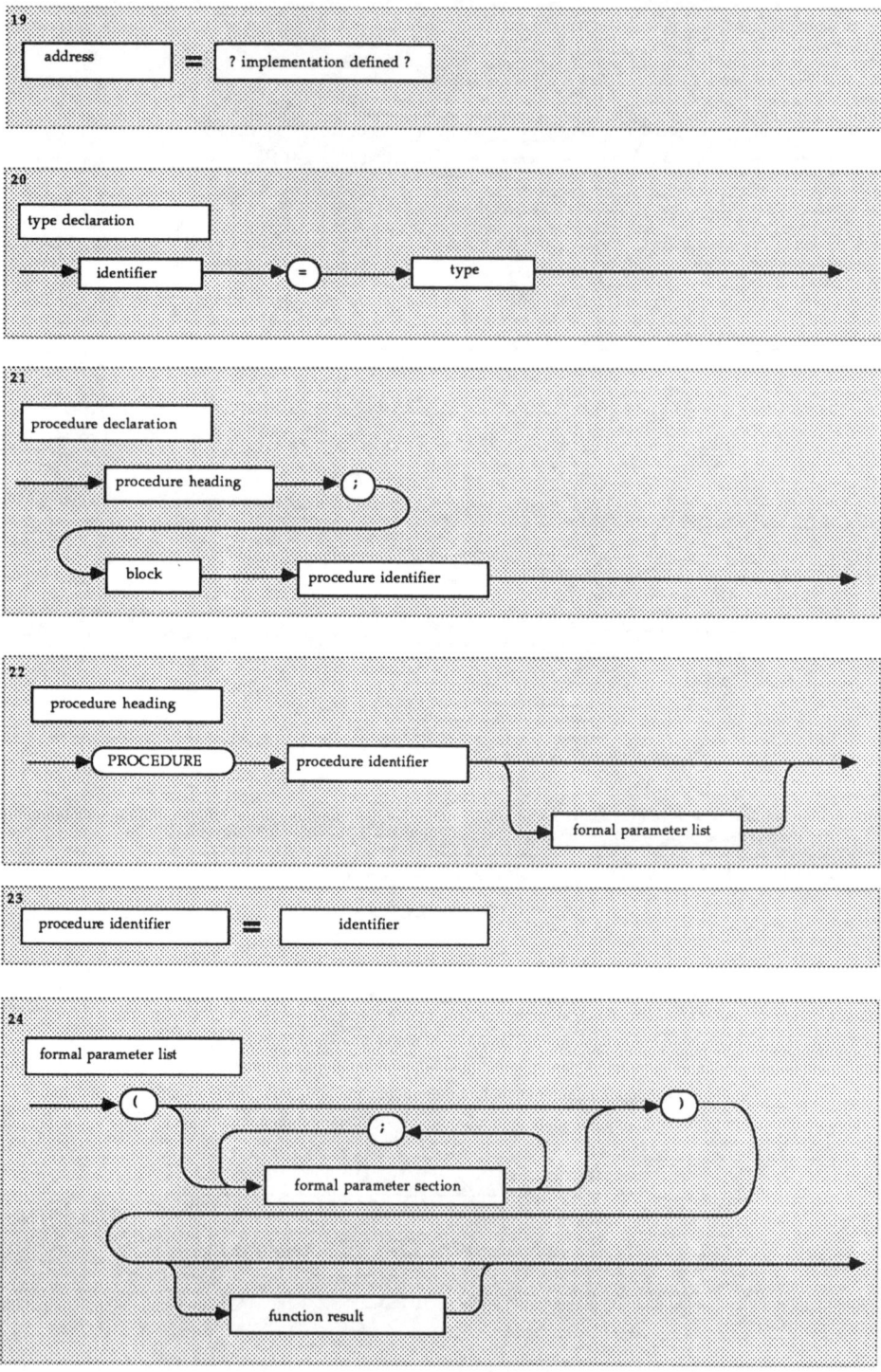

19

address ═ ? implementation defined ?

20

type declaration

→ identifier → = → type →

21

procedure declaration

→ procedure heading → ; →

→ block → procedure identifier →

22

procedure heading

→ PROCEDURE → procedure identifier →

formal parameter list

23

procedure identifier ═ identifier

24

formal parameter list

→ (→

;

formal parameter section

function result

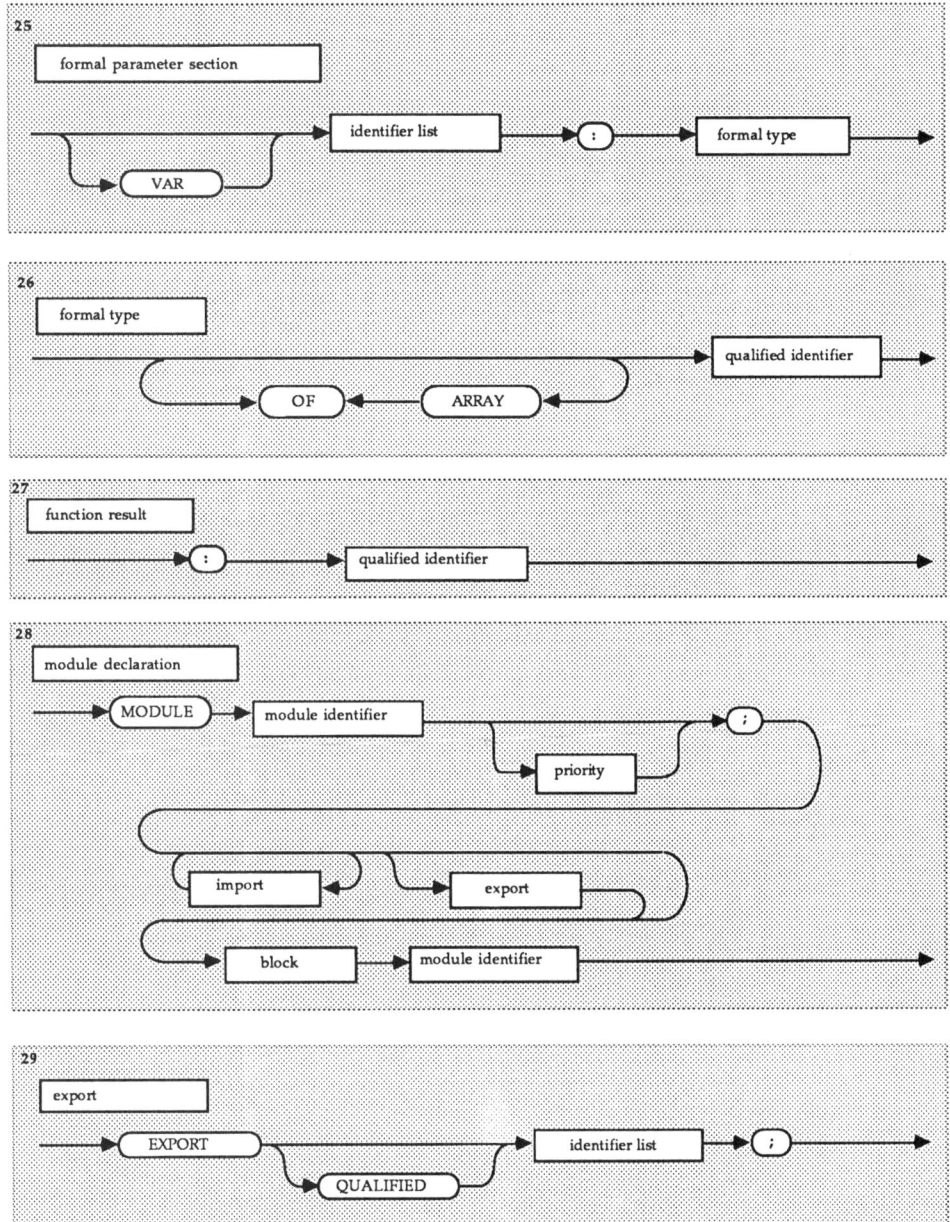

25 formal parameter section

26 formal type

27 function result

28 module declaration

29 export

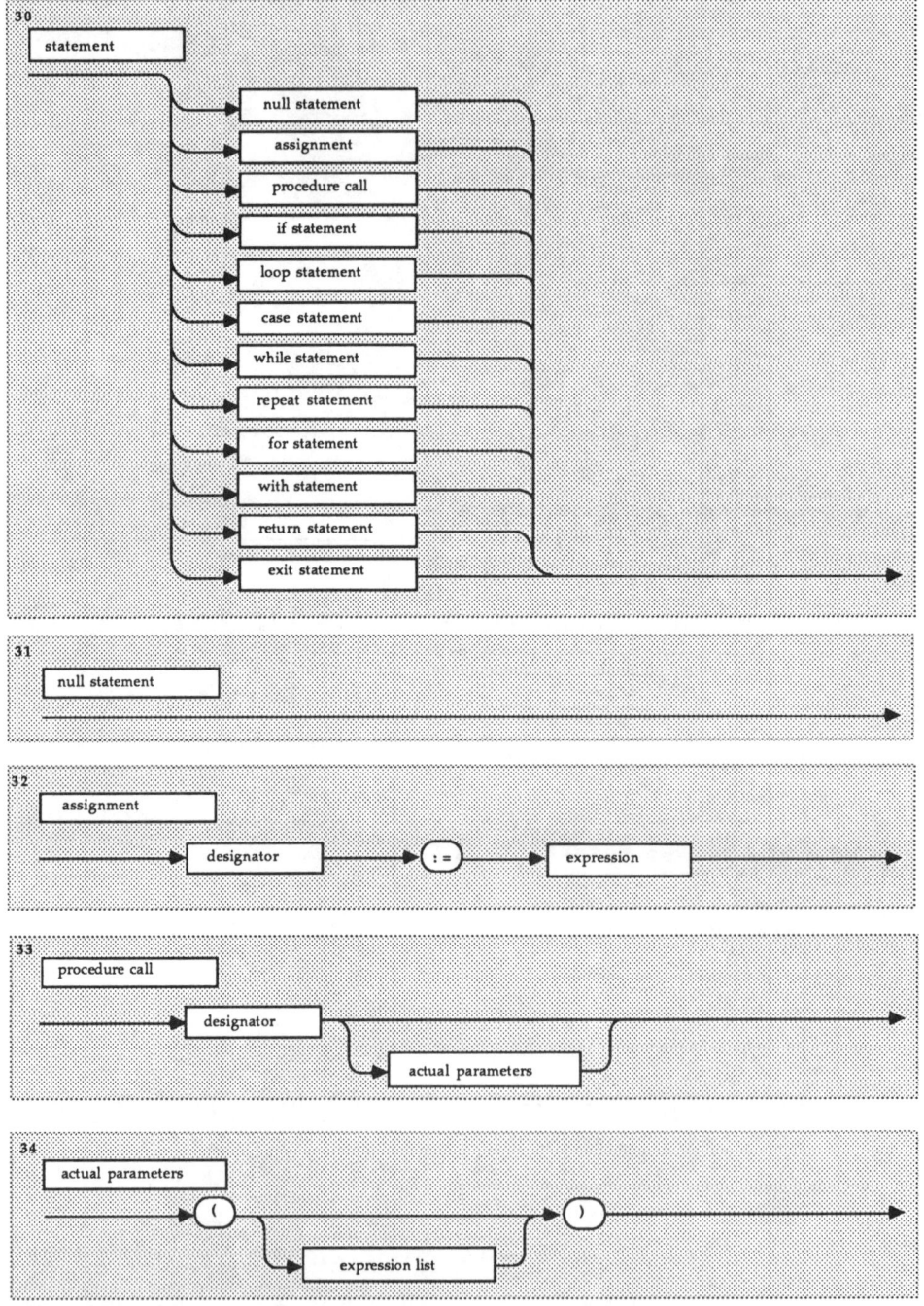

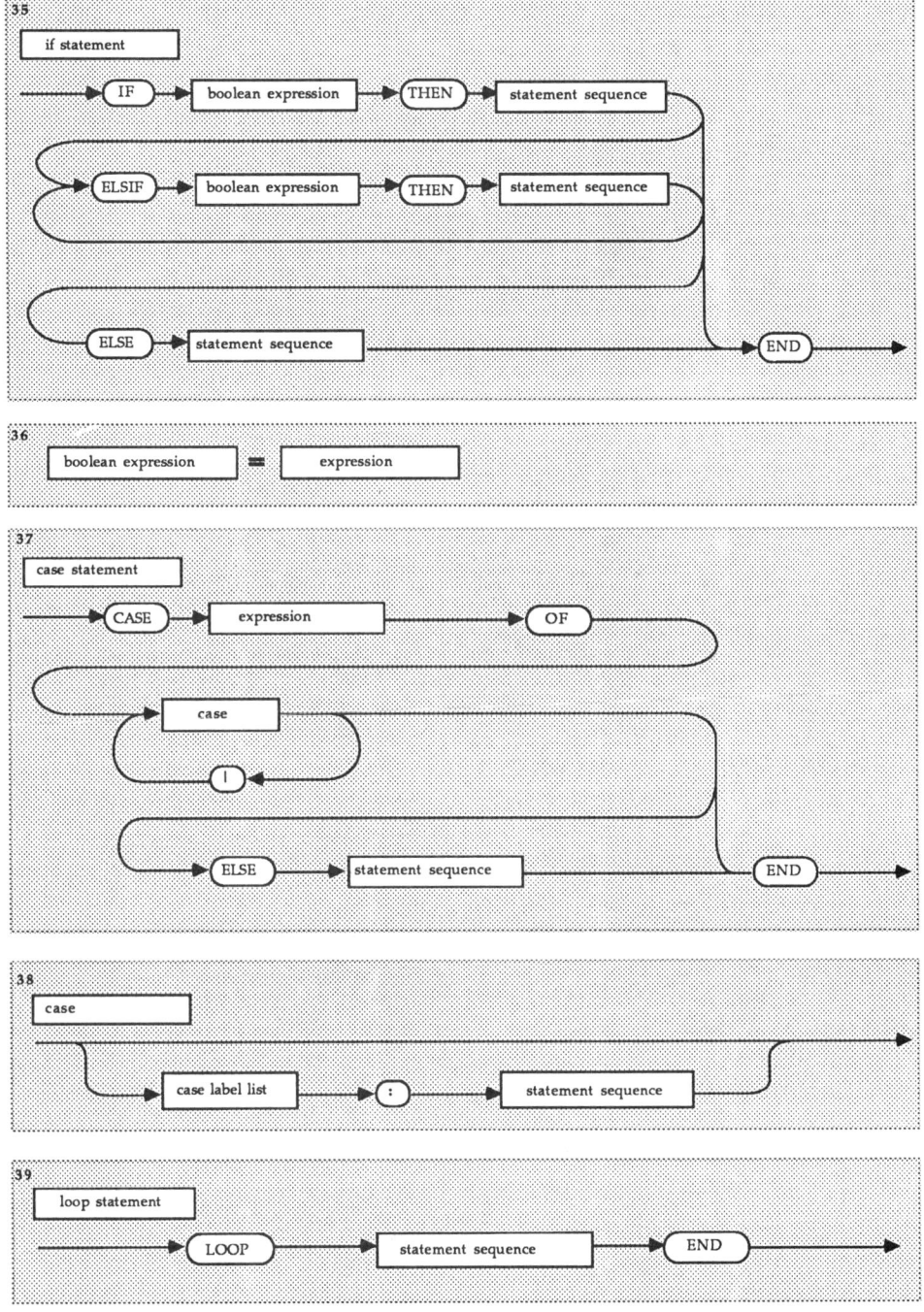

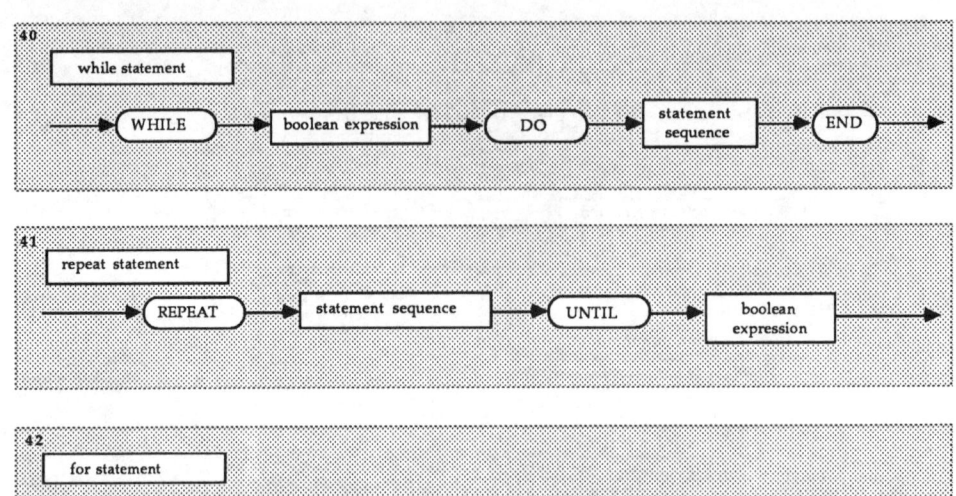

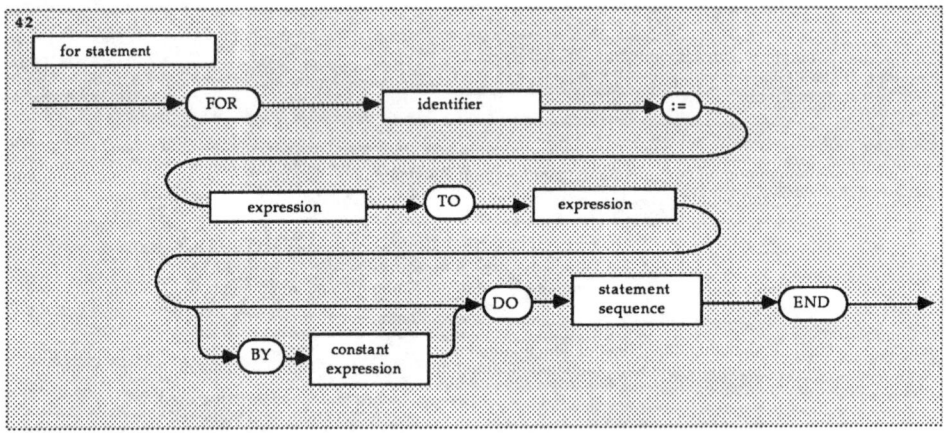

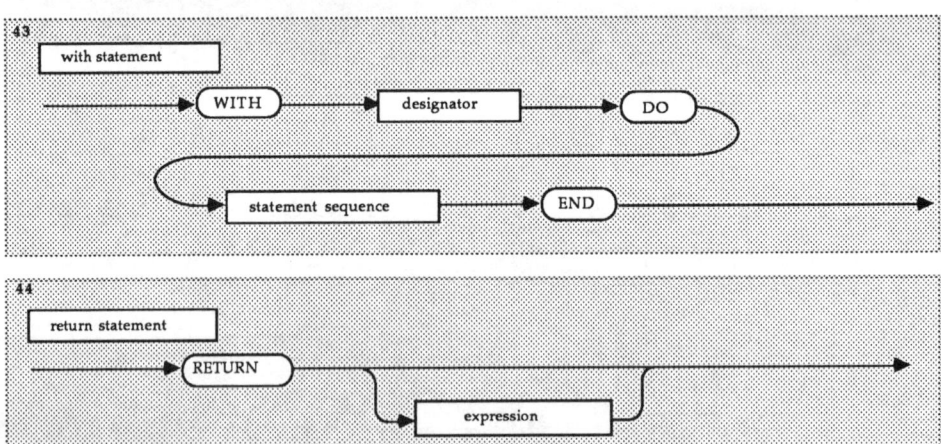

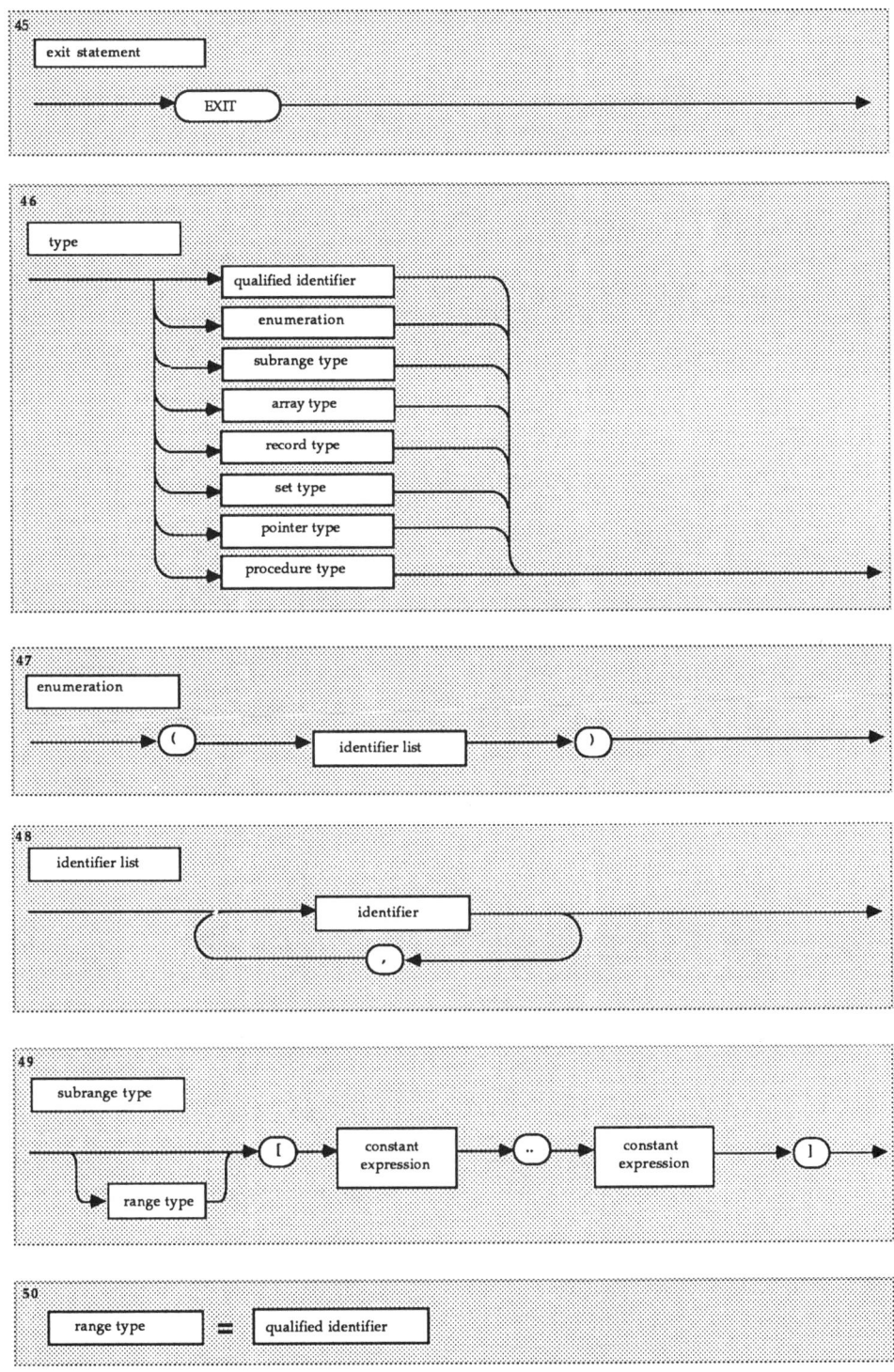

45
exit statement

EXIT

46
type

qualified identifier

enumeration

subrange type

array type

record type

set type

pointer type

procedure type

47
enumeration

(identifier list)

48
identifier list

identifier

,

49
subrange type

range type

[constant expression .. constant expression]

50
range type = qualified identifier

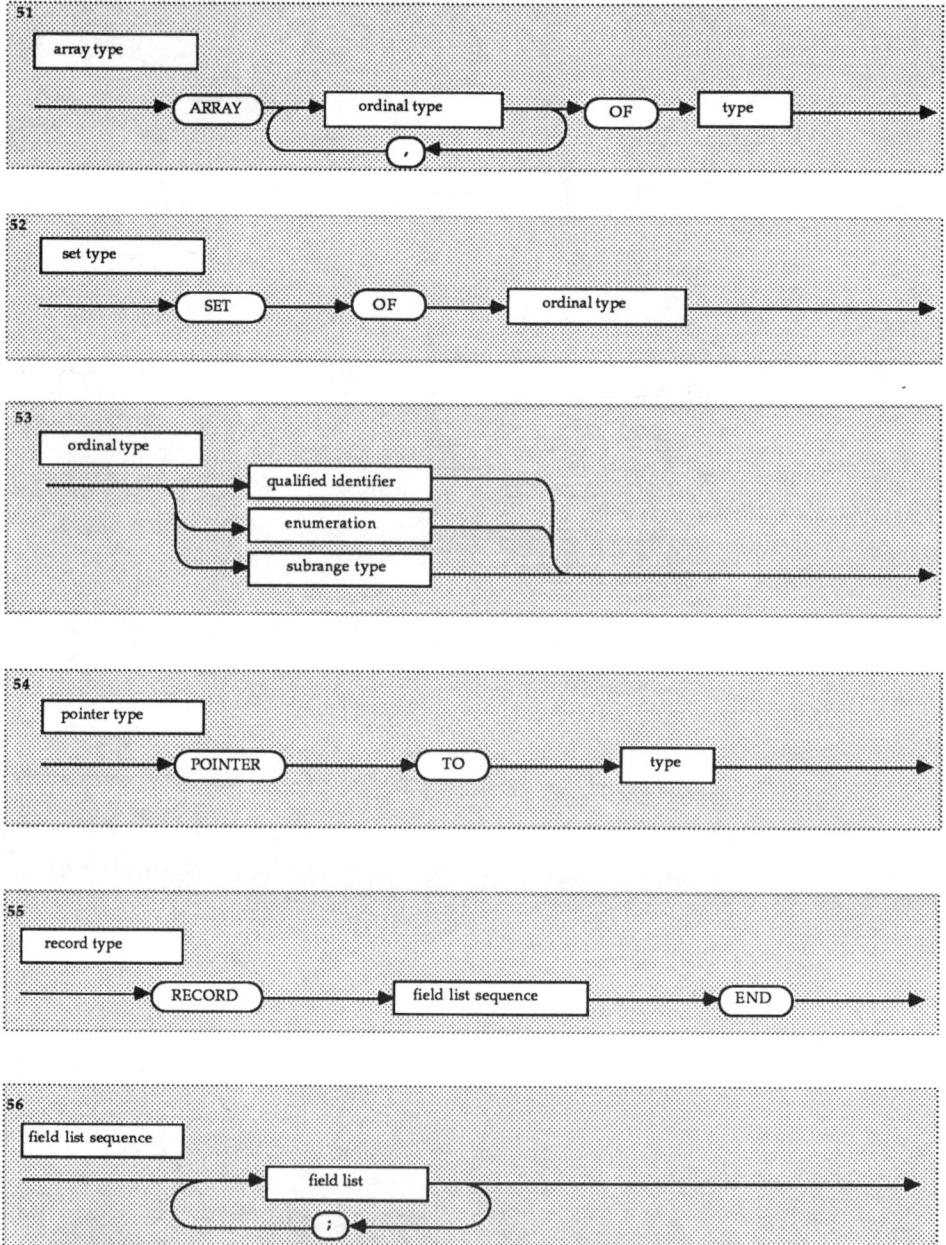

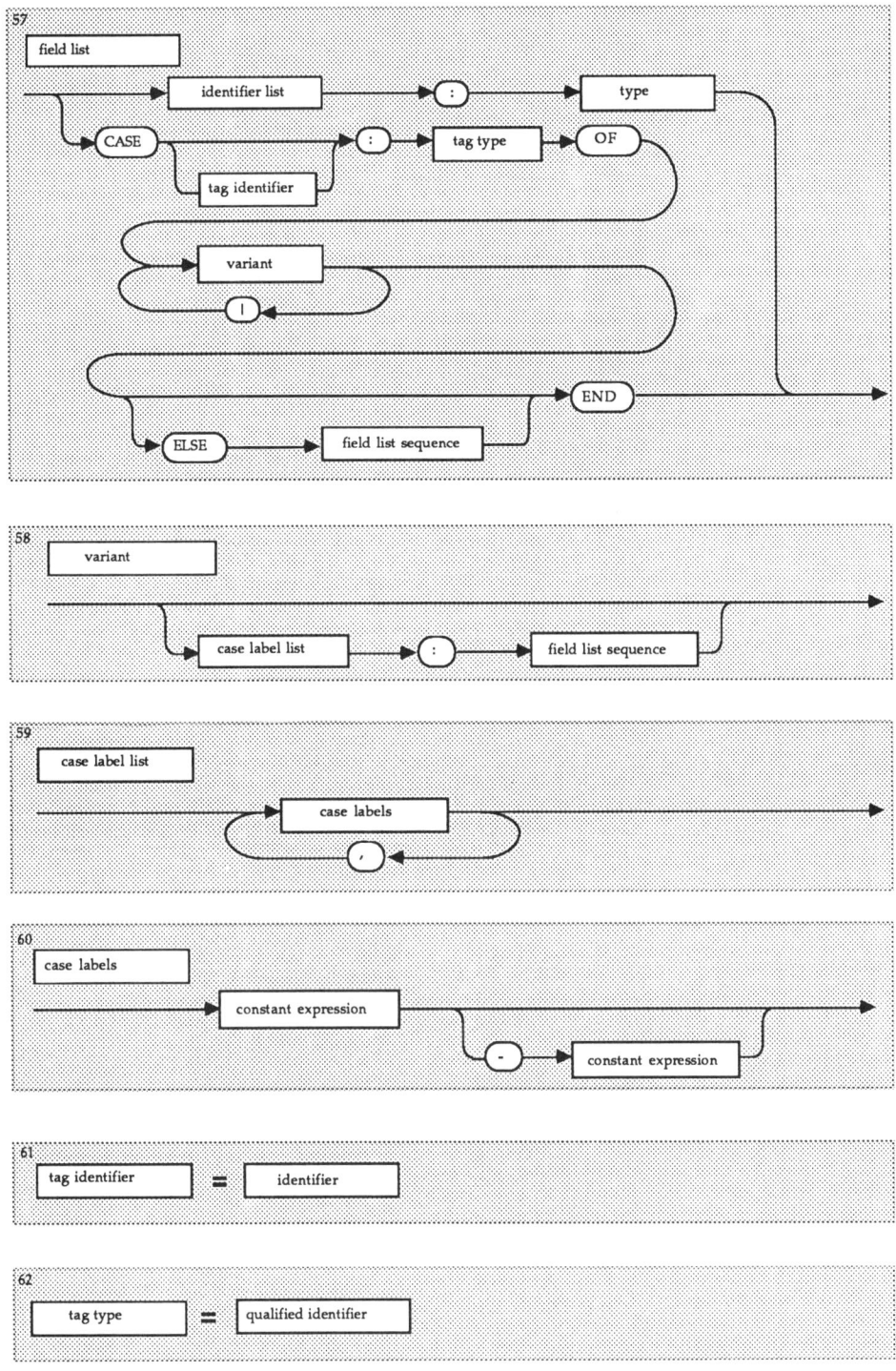

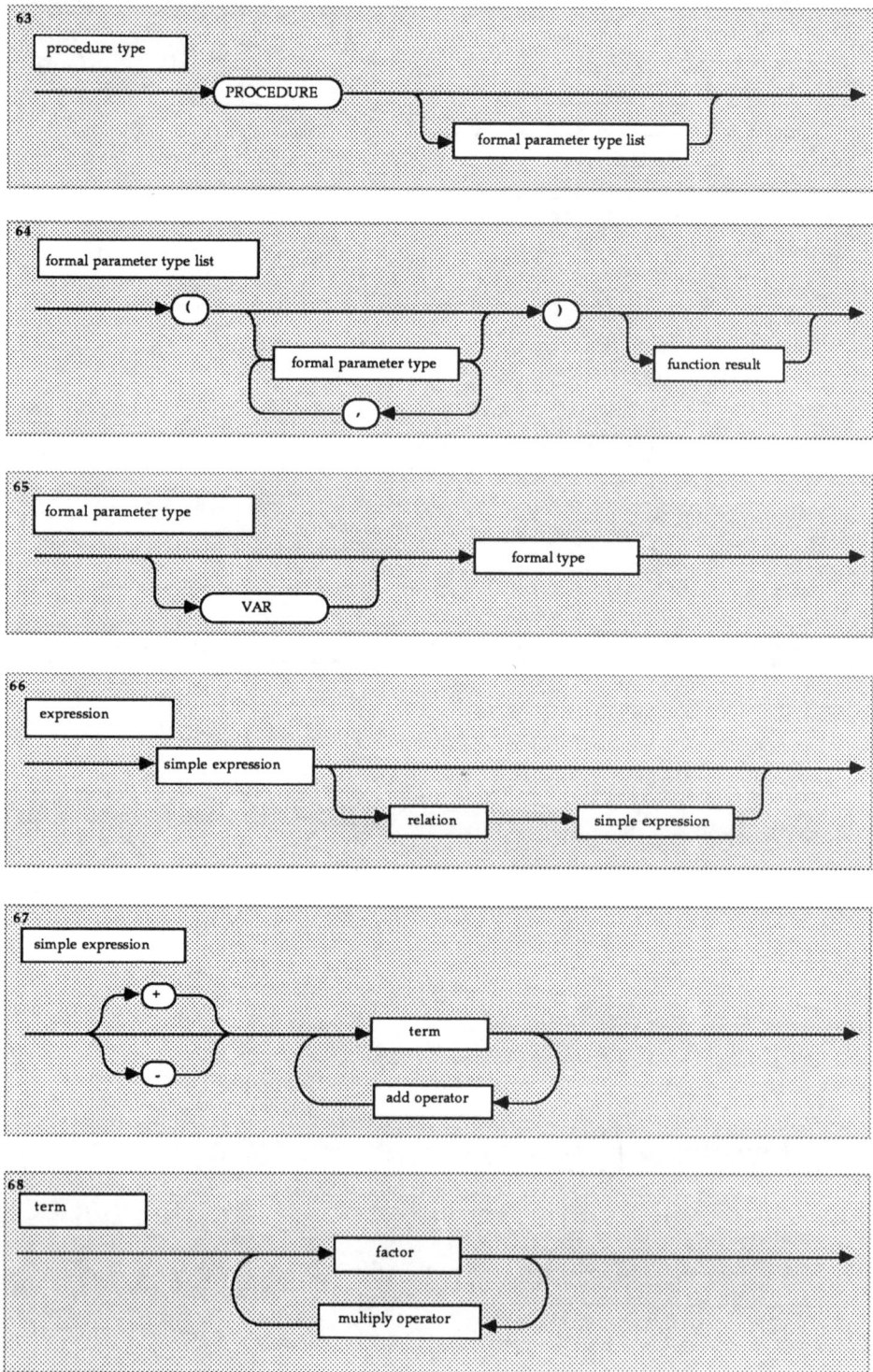

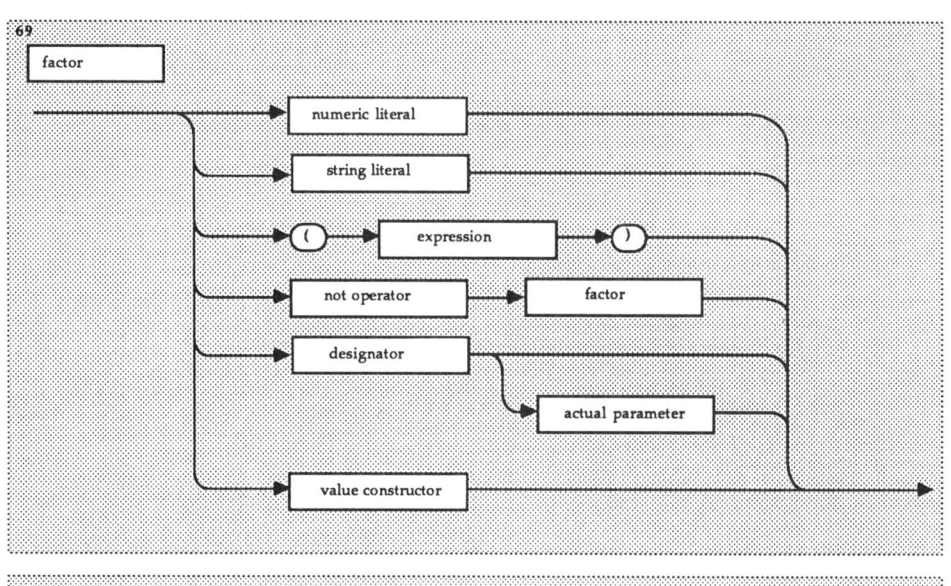

69 factor

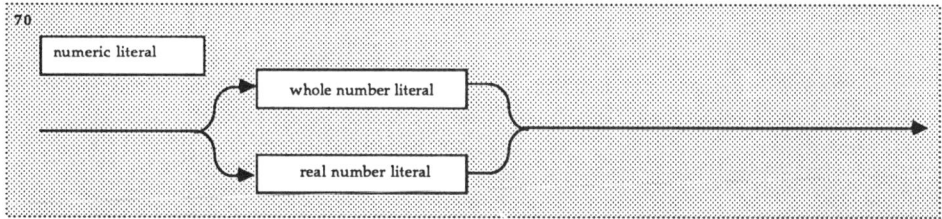

70 numeric literal

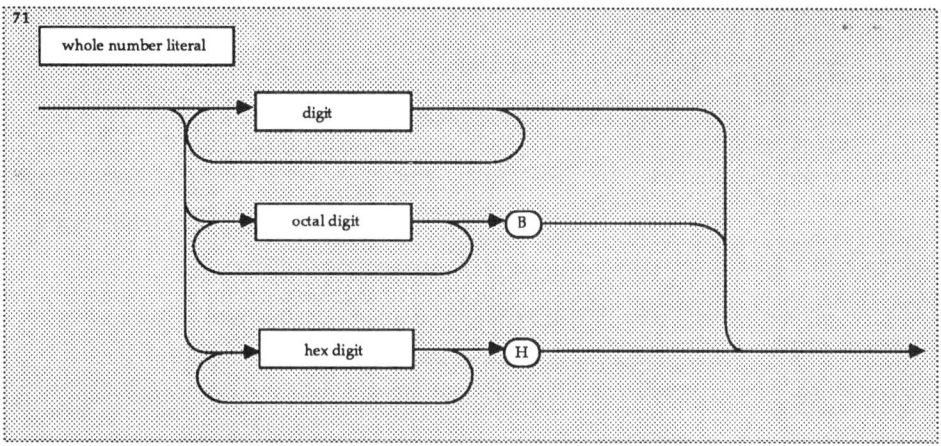

71 whole number literal

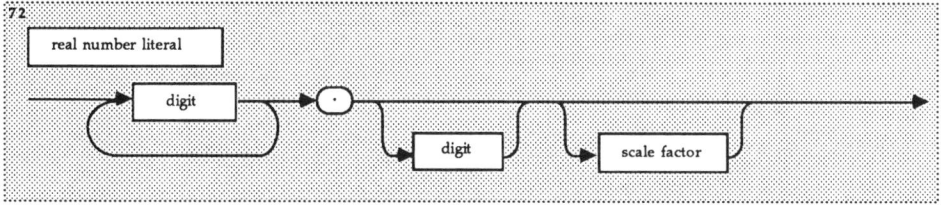

72 real number literal

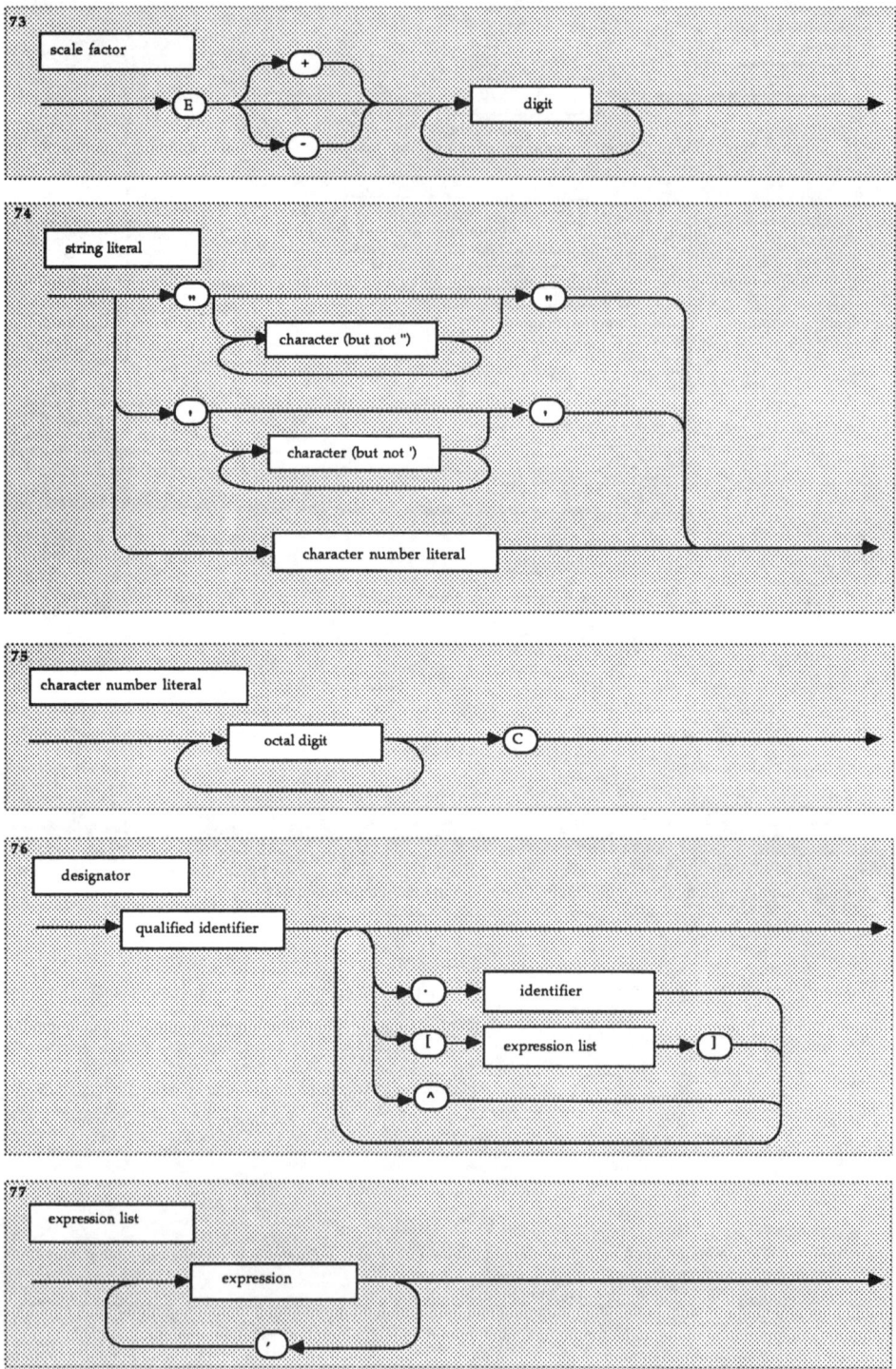

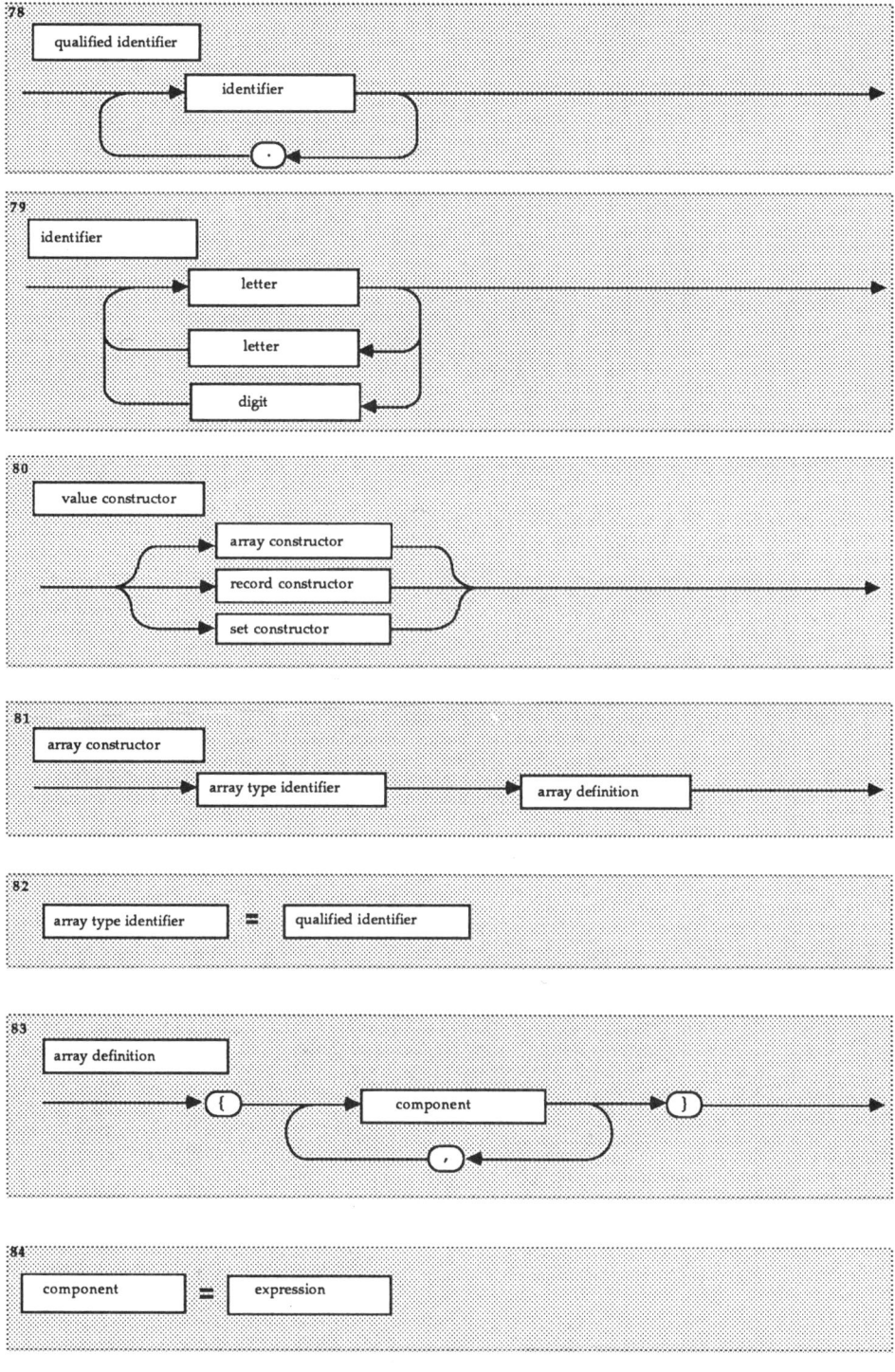

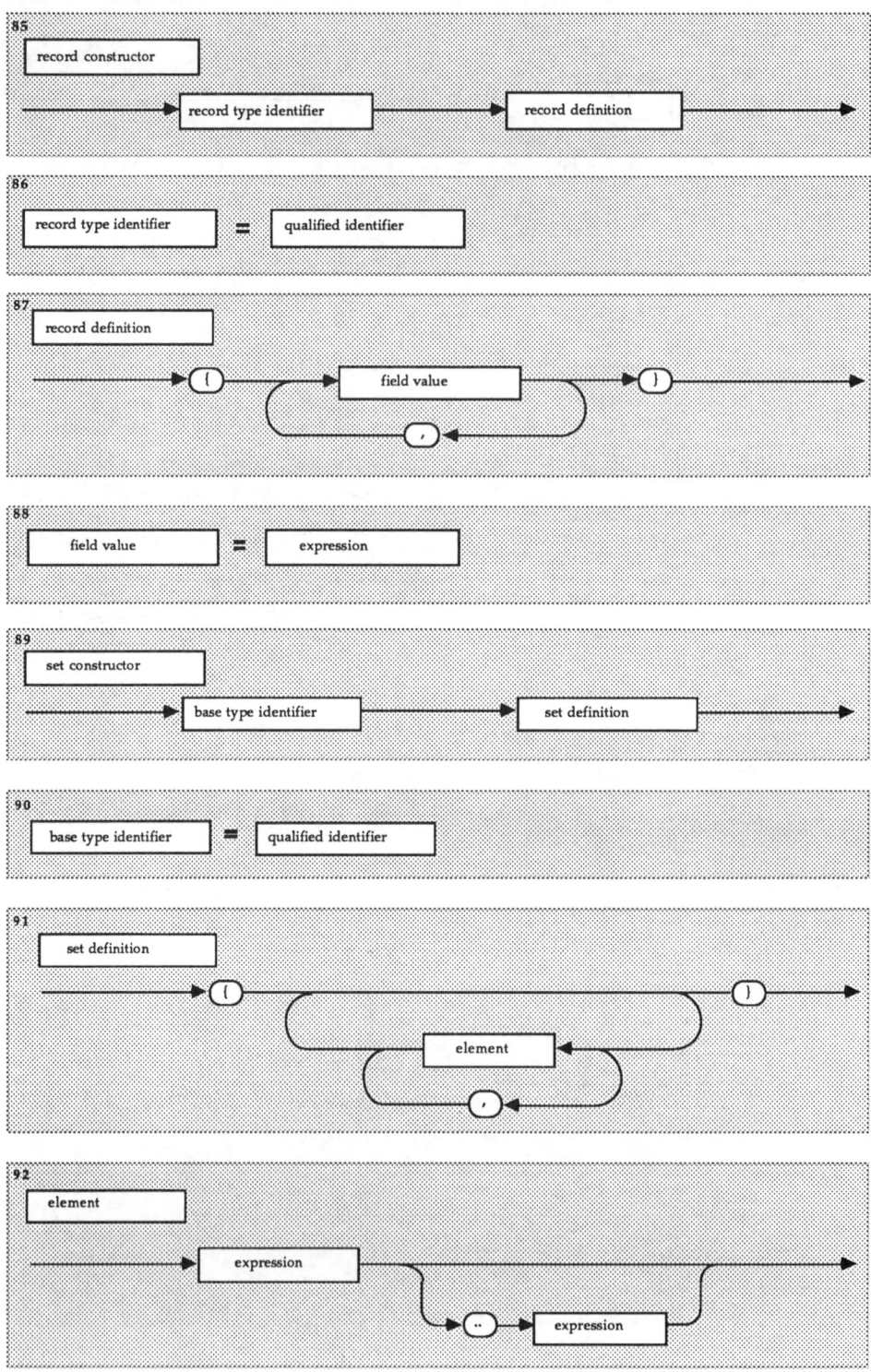

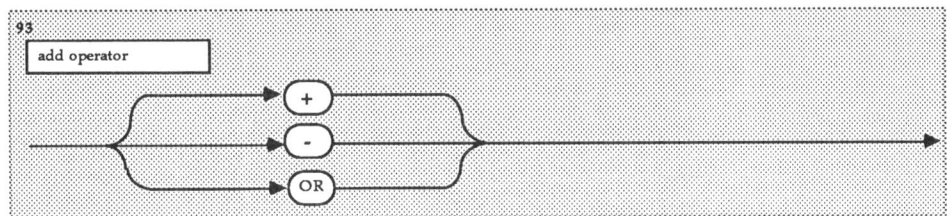

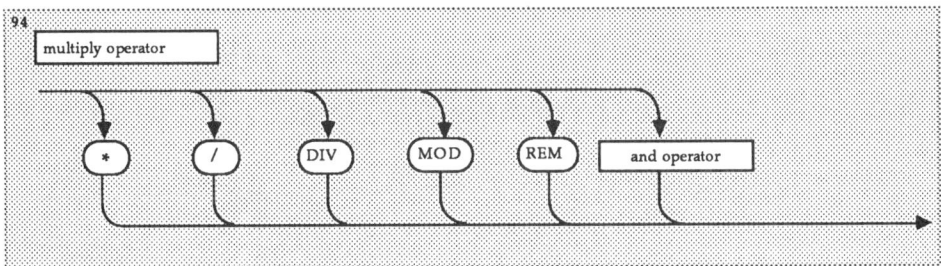

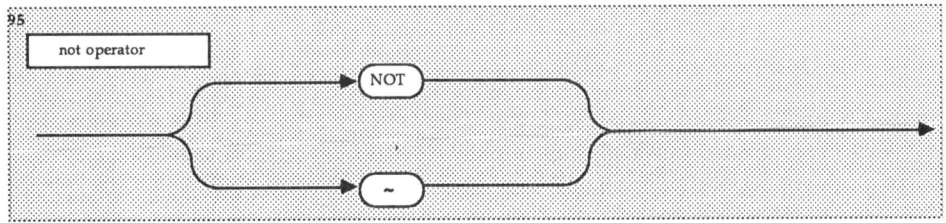

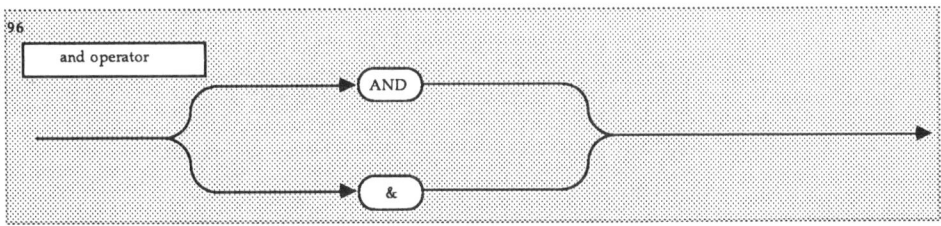

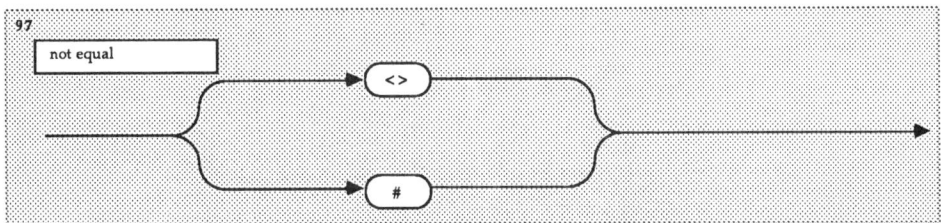

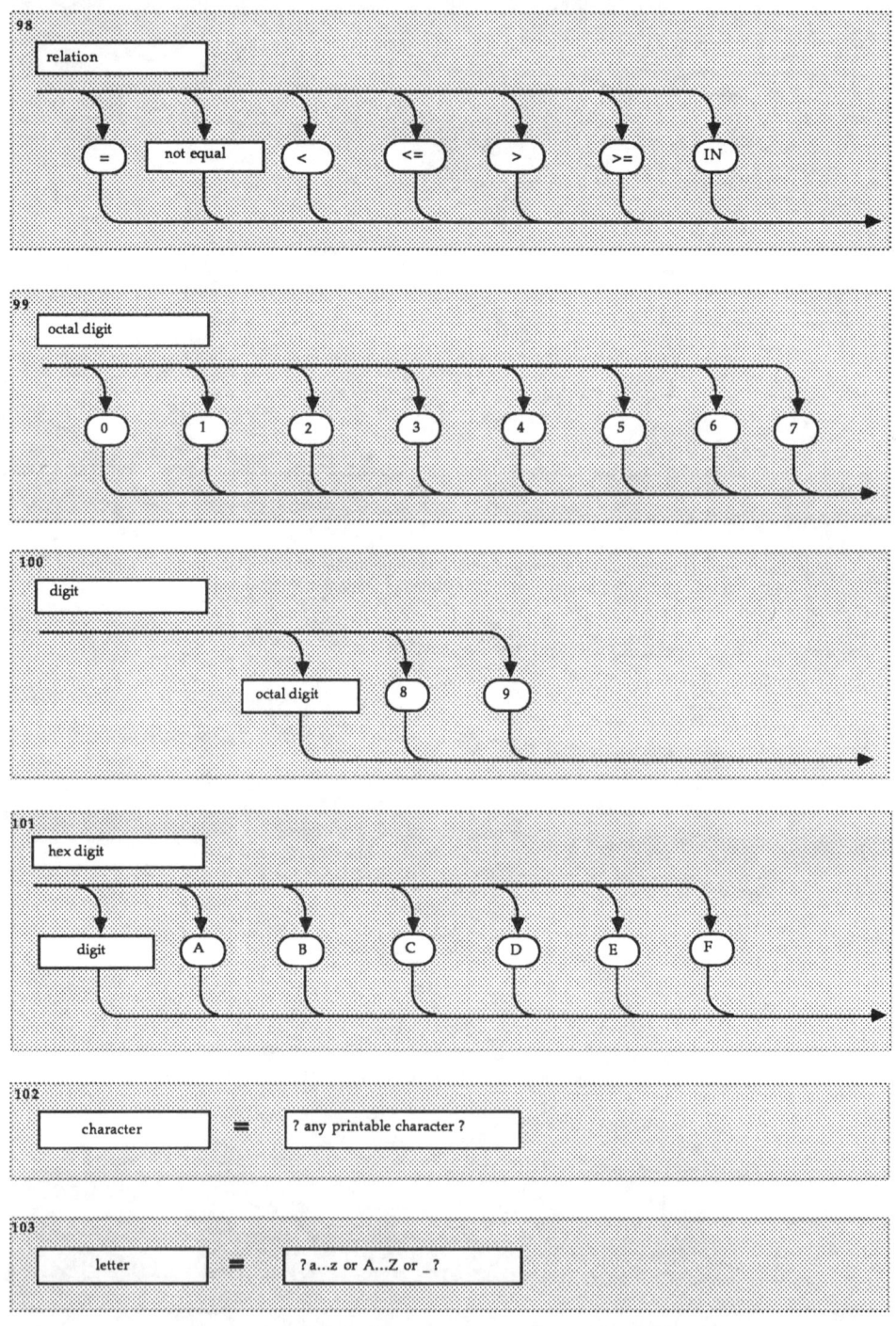

APPENDIX 2
TOPSPEED MODULA-2 EXTENSIONS

A2.1 INTRODUCTION

Extensions are the additions made to the Modula-2 language by compiler implementors. Some of these extensions have been added by implementors in anticipation of the forthcoming standard, whilst others have been added in an ad hoc manner, as a means of making their compilers more attractive to the consumer. This appendix lists those extensions which are available in Topspeed Modula-2, some of which may be found in other implementations. By their very nature, extensions are not portable, therefore they should be avoided if at all possible.

A2.2 POINTER CONSTRUCTOR

The pointer constructor simplifies address arithmetic and allows the programmer to access particular locations in memory in an elegant manner.

Syntax

```
designator =
    qualified identifier, {".", identifier |
    "[", expression list, "]" | "^" | pointer constructor };

pointer constructor =
    "[", cardinal expression, ":", cardinal expression,
    [type identifier], "]";
```

The optional type identifier in the second syntax rule may be used to inform the compiler that the variable at the specified address has a type which it, the compiler, already knows about. The compiler can therefore generate appropriate code for accessing the value or component value, at that address. In other words, if you want to deal with the whole variable, then its address is sufficient, but if you want to access some component, you need to tell the compiler what the structure of the variable at that address is. This information is available to the compiler through the type identifier (because only the declaration of that identifier will indicate whether the variable is an array or a record, for example).

Example

If the type `Packet` is needed for a communications program and is defined thus:

```
Packet = RECORD
            header: ARRAY [0..3] OF BITSET;
            data: ARRAY [0..39] OF BYTE;
            control: ARRAY [0..7] OF BITSET
         END;
```

Given this declaration, if a sequence of 30 such packets had been stored at segment `SegNo`, offset `Offset` in memory, and the 5th bit of the first control word had to be set (for some reason to do with the communications protocol), then the following code could be used:

```
FOR p := 1 TO 30 DO
  INCL([SegNo : Offset Packet].control[0], 5);
  INC(Offset, SIZE(Packet))
END;
```

Extreme care must be exercised when manipulating memory directly, because the operating system is unprotected.

A2.3 BUILT-IN PROCEDURES AND TYPES

In Topspeed Modula-2, unlike some other Modula-2 implementations, you do not have to import: `BYTE`, `WORD`, `ADDRESS`, `ADR`, `SIZE`, `NEW`, `DISPOSE`, or `BITSET`.

Topspeed also provides a function procedure called `VSIZE` which takes a field identifier of a record as a parameter, and returns the size of the record up to that field.

A2.4 AGGREGATES

Topspeed Modula-2 provides aggregates (structured *constant* constructors) for defining constants. The syntax is different from that proposed in the Modula-2 standard for structured value constructors, see the sections on *Portability Issues* in Chapters 19 and 20.

A2.5 FORWARD

As Topspeed Modula-2 is a single-pass compiler, a procedure declaration must precede a call to that procedure. The keyword `FORWARD` allows you to separate declaration of the procedure header from the procedure body. This allows two procedures which both call each other to share the same module. You do not need to use `FORWARD` if the procedure in question has been declared in the definition module. If you declare a forward procedure you must put the procedure body in later! (See the section on *Portability Issues* in Chapter 14 for further information.)

A2.6 INFIX PROCEDURE CALLS

Topspeed Modula-2 gives you the choice of how you call a procedure or function procedure with two parameters; this can be done in the normal way or by using a special infix notation. A procedure or function procedure is declared in the same way, whether it is going to be used as an infix operator or not. The only difference is in the way in which it is called. To call a procedure as an infix operator, simply append a '\' to each end of the procedure name and place it between its parameters.

Syntax

```
infix procedure call =
  parameter1, "\", procedure name, "\", parameter2;
```

Example

Consider a procedure called `Concat` which appends one string onto another. Its procedure heading might be:

```
PROCEDURE Concat(VAR Str1 : String; Str2 : String);
```

the result of calling it is to copy the contents of `Str2` to the end of `Str1`. You can either call `Concat` in the traditional way as a prefix operator like this:

```
Concat(String1,String2);
```

or as an infix operator like this:

```
String1 \Concat\ String2;
```

A2.7 PROCEDURE CONSTANTS AND ALIASING

Topspeed Modula-2 has the facility of allowing you to rename an imported procedure by aliasing it via a constant declaration.

Example

```
FROM PortIO IMPORT WriteString;
CONST WrString := WriteString; (* note the different syntax*)
BEGIN
  WrString('Hello');
```

A2.8 SHORT AND LONG NUMERICS

Topspeed Modula-2, in common with many other implementations, provides short and long INTEGERs and CARDINALs as well as LONGREALs. For details of these types and examples see Chapter 17.

A2.9 SHIFT OPERATORS

It is a common need in systems programming to move groups of bits around in a storage location. To make the shifting of bits easier, Topspeed Modula-2 provides left and right shift operators (<< and >>) which work on SHORTCARD, CARDINAL, and LONGCARD values.

Syntax

> shift operation =
> cardinal expression, ("<<" | ">>"), cardinal expression;

The shift operators << and >> perform left and right shifts of their left operands by the number of bit positions given by the right operand. Thus:

    X << 2

means shift X left by two positions, filling the space vacated with zeros.

    X >> 2

means shift X right by two positions, filling the space vacated with zeros. Note that both the operands of the shift operators must be of type CARDINAL.

A2.10 VAL

VAL is provided as a built-in function by most Modula-2 compilers while some other compilers implement VAL as being exportable from the module SYSTEM (See Chapter 23). However, the reason for including VAL in this appendix is that VAL works slightly differently in Topspeed Modula-2 than in most other implementations.

VAL takes two parameters and in many Modula-2 implementations these must be any ordinal type name and an ordinal value. Topspeed Modula-2, however, has extended VAL so that its type name parameter can be any type, and its value parameter can be of any type. If the value can be interpreted sensibly as a value of the named type, a type conversion is performed. For example VAL (CHAR, 65.253) will result in the character 'A': the 65.253 is truncated to the whole number 65 and a type conversion performed. If the value has no logical relationship with the destination type, a type transfer (i.e. a bit copy) is performed. Examples of this use can be found in Chapter 25.

A2.11 VSIZE

VSIZE is provided by a number of compilers and acts like the built-in procedure SIZE (see Chapter 23). However, it is more powerful than the procedure SIZE, in that if the parameter of VSIZE is the field of a record then it returns the size of the record up to that field.

Example

```
MODULE Treasure;
FROM PortIO IMPORT WriteCard, WriteLn;
TYPE
   TreasureType = ( Gold, Silver);
   Name = ARRAY [0..100] OF CHAR;
   Wreck = RECORD
               Longitude : CARDINAL;
               Lattitude : CARDINAL;
               CASE Legend : TreasureType OF
                 Gold:
                    Nuggets : CARDINAL;
                    Bars : CARDINAL;
                    Coins : CARDINAL;
                    Jewels : CARDINAL; |
                 Silver:
                    Ingots : CARDINAL;
               END; (* CASE *)
               NameOfWreck: Name;
             END; (* RECORD *)
VAR Legend: TreasureType;
BEGIN
   WriteCard(VSIZE(Wreck.Lattitude));    (* outputs 4*)
   WriteLn;
   WriteCard(VSIZE(Wreck.Ingots));       (* outputs 7*)
   WriteLn;
   WriteCard(VSIZE(Wreck.Jewels));       (* outputs 13*)
   WriteLn;
   WriteCard(SIZE(Wreck.NameOfWreck));   (* outputs 114*)
   WriteLn;
END Treasure.
```

The ability to find out the exact location of a particular field of a record is useful in systems programming. For details of systems programming, see Chapter 25.

A2.12 TYPE TRANSFER FUNCTIONS

Many compilers allow type identifiers to be used as type transfer functions. In such cases, the type identifier name acts as a function identifier, with the variable to be converted being passed as a parameter to the function. It should be noted that such type transfer functions do not involve any computation but act merely as a flag to the compiler to relax Modula-2's normally strict type checking. Because of this, these type transfer functions can only be used to transfer between types whose variables occupy the same number of words in memory. Some compilers will not report an error if you attempt to transfer between variables that occupy differing amounts of memory, which will give 'unpredictable' results.

Example

```
VAR
  i : INTEGER;
  c : CARDINAL;
  ch : CHAR;
BEGIN
  ...
  ch := 'A';
  c := 66;
  i := INTEGER(c);    (* i = 66 *)
  c := CARDINAL(ch);  (* c = 65 *)
  ch := CHAR(i);      (* ch = 'B' *)
```

See Chapter 25 for further details of type transfer functions.

Topspeed Modula-2 for DOS or OS/2 is available directly from Jensen & Partners. Substantial discounts are offered to educational establishments and students.

U.S.A. and Canada:

Jensen & Partners International Inc.
1101 San Antonio Road
Mountain View
CA 94043
U.S.A.

Technical: + 1 415-967-3200
Fax: + 1 415-967-3288
Orders: 1-800-543-5202 in the U.S.A.
                1-800-543-5202 in Canada

United Kingdom and the rest of the world:

Jensen & Partners (UK) Ltd.
63 Clerkenwell Road
London EC1M 5NP
U.K.

Phone: + 44 (01) 253-4333
Fax: + 44 (01) 251-1442

You can call or write for a pricelist or see leading computer magazines for advertisments on Topspeed compilers from Jensen & Partners.

APPENDIX 3

PORTABLE LIBRARY MODULES

A3.1 PortStrings DEFINITION MODULE

```
DEFINITION MODULE PortStrings;
(* PortStrings provides a series of functions to manipulate   *)
(* strings. The functions provided in this Module are described *)
(* in detail inChapter 10, the exception is Reverse with which  *)
(* the module has been extended.                               *)

(* The following may be required by older Modula-2 implementations:
EXPORT QUALIFIED
   CompareResult, Length, CanAssign, Assign, AssignChar,
   CanExtract, Extract, CanDelete, Delete, CanInsert, Insert,
   InsertChar, CanReplace, Replace, CanAppend, Append, AppendChar,
   Compare, Find, FindChar, Reverse (* new procedure *),
   StringTerminator;                 *)

CONST
   StringMax = 255;                        (* maximum string size *)
   StringTerminator = 0C; (* same as implemented by compiler *)
TYPE
   String1Type = ARRAY [0..0] OF CHAR;
   String2Type = ARRAY [0..StringMax] OF CHAR;
   CompareResult = (less,equal,greater); (* result of a comparison*)

PROCEDURE Length(String: ARRAY OF CHAR): CARDINAL;

PROCEDURE CanAssign
   (Source: ARRAY OF CHAR;
    VAR Destination: ARRAY OF CHAR):BOOLEAN;

PROCEDURE Assign
   (Source: ARRAY OF CHAR; VAR Destination: ARRAY OF CHAR);

PROCEDURE AssignChar
   (SourceChar: CHAR; VAR Destination : ARRAY OF CHAR);

PROCEDURE CanExtract
   (Source: ARRAY OF CHAR;
    StartIndex :CARDINAL; NumberToExtract: CARDINAL;
    VAR Destination: ARRAY OF CHAR): BOOLEAN;

PROCEDURE Extract
   (Source: ARRAY OF CHAR;
    StartIndex :CARDINAL; NumberToExtract: CARDINAL;
    VAR Destination: ARRAY OF CHAR);
```

```
PROCEDURE CanDelete
   (VAR String : ARRAY OF CHAR; StartIndex: CARDINAL;
    NumberToDelete: CARDINAL): BOOLEAN;

PROCEDURE Delete
   (VAR String : ARRAY OF CHAR; StartIndex: CARDINAL;
    NumberToDelete: CARDINAL);

PROCEDURE CanInsert
   (SourceLength: CARDINAL; StartIndex: CARDINAL;
    VAR Destination : ARRAY OF CHAR): BOOLEAN;

PROCEDURE Insert
   (Source: ARRAY OF CHAR; StartIndex: CARDINAL;
    VAR Destination : ARRAY OF CHAR);

PROCEDURE InsertChar
   (SourceChar: CHAR; VAR s1 : ARRAY OF CHAR;
    StartIndex : CARDINAL);

PROCEDURE CanReplace
   (Length : CARDINAL; StartIndex: CARDINAL;
    VAR Destination: ARRAY OF CHAR): BOOLEAN;

PROCEDURE Replace
   (Source: ARRAY OF CHAR; StartIndex: CARDINAL;
    VAR Destination: ARRAY OF CHAR);

PROCEDURE CanAppend
   (Length : CARDINAL;
    VAR Destination : ARRAY OF CHAR):BOOLEAN;

PROCEDURE Append
   (Source: ARRAY OF CHAR; VAR Destination: ARRAY OF CHAR);

PROCEDURE AppendChar
   (SourceChar: CHAR; VAR Destination: ARRAY OF CHAR);

PROCEDURE Compare
   (String1: ARRAY OF CHAR;
    String2: ARRAY OF CHAR):CompareResult;

PROCEDURE Find
   (Pattern: ARRAY OF CHAR; String: ARRAY OF CHAR;
    VAR Position: CARDINAL; VAR Found: BOOLEAN);

PROCEDURE FindChar
   (Char: CHAR; String: ARRAY OF CHAR;
    VAR Position: CARDINAL; VAR Found: BOOLEAN);

PROCEDURE Reverse
   (VAR Str: ARRAY OF CHAR);

END PortStrings.
```

A3.2 PortStrings IMPLEMENTATION MODULE

```
IMPLEMENTATION MODULE PortStrings;
(* PortStrings provides a series of functions to manipulate    *)
(* strings. The functions provided in this Module are described *)
(* in detail inChapter 10, the exception is Reverse with which  *)
(* the module has been extended.                                *)

(* The following IMPORT statement is only necessary for those   *)
(* implementations which do not include VAL as a built-in       *)
(* procedure but instead have it exportable from the module     *)
(* SYSTEM. Furthermore VAL is only needed for implementations in *)
(* which HIGH does not return a type compatible with CARDINAL.  *)
(* (See StringHIGH.)                                            *)
(* FROM SYSTEM IMPORT VAL; *)

PROCEDURE StringHIGH(VAR String: ARRAY OF CHAR): CARDINAL;
VAR temp: INTEGER; temp2: CARDINAL;
(* This procedure is only needed because some Modula-2         *)
(* implementations return INTEGER or LONGCARDINAL from HIGH.   *)
BEGIN
   temp := HIGH(String);
   RETURN VAL(CARDINAL,temp)
END StringHIGH;

PROCEDURE Length(String: ARRAY OF CHAR): CARDINAL;
VAR High, Len : CARDINAL;
(* Length returns the length of a string *)
BEGIN
   High := StringHIGH(String); Len := 0;
   (* The next line relies on left to right
      short circuit evaluation *)
   WHILE (Len <= High) AND (String[Len] # StringTerminator) DO
     INC(Len);
   END;
   RETURN Len;
END Length;

PROCEDURE CanAssign
   (Source: ARRAY OF CHAR;
    VAR Destination: ARRAY OF CHAR):BOOLEAN;
(* tests if you can assign a string to an array without        *)
(* truncation of the string taking place.                      *)
BEGIN
   RETURN (Length(Source) <= (StringHIGH(Destination)+1));
END CanAssign;

PROCEDURE Assign
   (Source: ARRAY OF CHAR; VAR Destination: ARRAY OF CHAR);
(* Assign assigns one string to another, it truncates the      *)
(* String if it is too long .                                  *)
VAR
   HSource, HDestination, Index, Max: CARDINAL;
BEGIN
   HDestination := StringHIGH(Destination)+1;
   HSource := Length(Source);
```

```
    IF HSource > HDestination THEN              (* string too long *)
      Max := HDestination                       (* truncate it      *)
    ELSE
      Max := HSource
    END;
    FOR Index := 1 TO Max DO    (* assign characters *)
      Destination[Index-1] := Source[Index-1];
    END;
    IF Max < HDestination THEN
      Destination[Max] := StringTerminator;
    END;
END Assign;

PROCEDURE AssignChar
            (SourceChar: CHAR; VAR Destination : ARRAY OF CHAR);
(* Assigns a character to a string *)
BEGIN
  Destination[0] := SourceChar;
  IF StringHIGH(Destination) > 0 THEN
      Destination[1] := StringTerminator;
  END;
END AssignChar;

PROCEDURE CanExtract
   (Source: ARRAY OF CHAR;
    StartIndex: CARDINAL; NumberToExtract: CARDINAL;
    VAR Destination: ARRAY OF CHAR): BOOLEAN;
(* returns true if you can extract a string from Source, of *)
(* length NumberToExtract starting from index.             *)
BEGIN
  RETURN
     (StartIndex+NumberToExtract <= Length(Source)) AND
     (StringHIGH(Destination)+1 >= NumberToExtract);
END CanExtract;

PROCEDURE Extract
   (Source: ARRAY OF CHAR;
    StartIndex: CARDINAL; NumberToExtract: CARDINAL;
    VAR Destination: ARRAY OF CHAR);
(* Extract, extracts one string from another, it truncates *)
(* the String if it is too long.                           *)
VAR
  Ind, Ind1, High, LSource: CARDINAL;
BEGIN
  High := StringHIGH(Destination); LSource := Length(Source);
  (* Work out number of characters to extract *)
  IF High < NumberToExtract THEN
      NumberToExtract := High+1;
  END;
  Ind := StartIndex+1; Ind1 :=1;
  WHILE (Ind <= LSource) AND
         (Ind <= StartIndex+NumberToExtract) DO
    Destination[Ind1-1] := Source[Ind-1];   (* copy characters *)
    INC(Ind1); INC(Ind);
  END;
  IF High >= Ind1 THEN
```

```
      Destination[Ind1-1] := StringTerminator;
    END;
END Extract;

PROCEDURE CanDelete
   (VAR String : ARRAY OF CHAR; StartIndex: CARDINAL;
    NumberToDelete: CARDINAL): BOOLEAN;
(* CanDelete returns TRUE if you can delete NumberToDelete *)
(* characters  from String starting at StartIndex.        *)
VAR
   LString : CARDINAL;
BEGIN
   LString := Length(String);
   RETURN
      (StartIndex < LString) AND
      (StartIndex + NumberToDelete <= LString);
END CanDelete;

PROCEDURE Delete
   (VAR String : ARRAY OF CHAR; StartIndex: CARDINAL;
    NumberToDelete: CARDINAL);
   (* Delete, deletes NumberToDelete characters from String *)
   (* starting at StartIndex, or the maximum number of      *)
   (* characters left.                                      *)
VAR Ind, LSource, High : CARDINAL;
BEGIN
   High := StringHIGH(String); LSource := Length(String);
   IF StartIndex+1 > LSource THEN ; (* Do nothing *)
   ELSE
      (* Work out number of characters to delete *)
      IF LSource < NumberToDelete+StartIndex THEN
         NumberToDelete := LSource-StartIndex;
      END;
      Ind := StartIndex+1;
      (* Shuffle characters back *)
      WHILE (Ind <= LSource-NumberToDelete) DO
         String[Ind-1] := String[Ind+NumberToDelete-1];
         INC(Ind);
      END;
      IF High+1 >= Ind THEN
         String[Ind-1] := StringTerminator;
      END;
   END;
END Delete;

PROCEDURE CanInsert
   (SourceLength: CARDINAL; StartIndex: CARDINAL;
    VAR Destination: ARRAY OF CHAR):BOOLEAN;
   (* CanInsert returns TRUE if it is possible to insert   *)
   (* SourceLength characters in Destination starting from *)
   (* StartIndex.                                          *)
BEGIN
   RETURN
      ((StartIndex < Length(Destination)) AND
      (SourceLength + Length(Destination) <=
```

```
      StringHIGH(Destination) + 1))
END CanInsert;

PROCEDURE Insert
   (Source: ARRAY OF CHAR; StartIndex: CARDINAL;
    VAR Destination: ARRAY OF CHAR);
(* Insert, inserts Source into Destination at position *)
(* StartIndex truncating both strings if necessary.    *)
VAR
  LDestination, LSource, HDestination,NumberOfChars, Ind: CARDINAL;
BEGIN
  LDestination := Length(Destination);
  HDestination := StringHIGH(Destination)+1;
  LSource := Length(Source);
  IF StartIndex > LDestination THEN ; (* Do nothing *)
  ELSE
    IF LSource + LDestination > HDestination THEN
       IF LSource + StartIndex + 1 > HDestination THEN
          LSource := HDestination -StartIndex ;
          LDestination := StartIndex;
       ELSE
         LDestination := HDestination-LSource;
                             (* Distance to move them*)
       END;
    END;
    (* Shuffle Destination characters along *)
    FOR Ind := LDestination TO StartIndex + 1 BY -1 DO
       Destination[Ind + LSource-1] := Destination[Ind-1];
    END;
    (* Copy Source into Destination *)
    FOR Ind := 1 TO LSource DO
       Destination[Ind + StartIndex-1] := Source[Ind-1];
    END;
    IF LSource+LDestination < HDestination THEN
      Destination[LDestination + LSource] := StringTerminator;
    END;
  END;
END Insert;

PROCEDURE InsertChar
   (SourceChar: CHAR; VAR Destination : ARRAY OF CHAR;
    StartIndex : CARDINAL);
(* InsertChar inserts a character into Destination at StartIndex *)
VAR
  LDestination, HDestination, Ind : CARDINAL;
BEGIN
  LDestination := Length(Destination);
  HDestination := StringHIGH(Destination) + 1;
  IF LDestination = HDestination THEN
     RETURN;           (* No room for the character *)
  END;
  (* Shuffle Destination character along *)
  FOR Ind := LDestination TO StartIndex+1 BY -1 DO
    Destination[Ind] := Destination[Ind-1];
  END;
  (* Copy SourceChar into Destination *)
```

```
      Destination[StartIndex] := SourceChar;
      IF LDestination+1 < HDestination THEN
        Destination[LDestination + 1] := StringTerminator;
      END;
END InsertChar;

PROCEDURE CanReplace
    (SourceLength : CARDINAL; StartIndex: CARDINAL;
     VAR Destination: ARRAY OF CHAR): BOOLEAN;
(* CanReplace returns TRUE if it is possible to replace  *)
(* SourceLength characters in  Destination starting from *)
(* StartIndex.                                           *)
BEGIN
  RETURN ((SourceLength + StartIndex) <= Length(Destination))
END CanReplace;

PROCEDURE Replace
    (Source: ARRAY OF CHAR; StartIndex: CARDINAL;
     VAR Destination: ARRAY OF CHAR);
(* Replace replaces a slice of Destination by Source at *)
(* StartIndex truncating the Source if it is too long.  *)
VAR
  LDestination,LSource,HDestination,Ind : CARDINAL;
BEGIN
  LDestination := Length(Destination); LSource := Length(Source);
  (* Work out how many characters to replace *)
  IF LSource + StartIndex+1 > LDestination THEN
     LSource := LDestination-StartIndex;
  END;
  (* Copy Source into Destination *)
  FOR Ind := 1 TO LSource DO
    Destination[Ind + StartIndex-1] := Source[Ind-1];
  END;
END Replace;

PROCEDURE CanAppend
    (Len: CARDINAL; VAR Destination: ARRAY OF CHAR):BOOLEAN;
(* CanAppend returns TRUE if it is possible to Append Len *)
(* characters to Destination.                             *)
BEGIN
  RETURN (Length(Destination) + Len)<= (StringHIGH(Destination)+1)
END CanAppend;

PROCEDURE Append
    (Source: ARRAY OF CHAR; VAR Destination: ARRAY OF CHAR);
(* Append appends Source to Destination truncating if necessary *)
VAR
  LDestination, LSource, HDestination,Ind : CARDINAL;
BEGIN
  LDestination := Length(Destination);
  HDestination := StringHIGH(Destination) + 1;
  LSource := Length(Source);
  (* Work out how many characters to append *)
  IF LSource + LDestination > HDestination THEN
     LSource := HDestination - LDestination;
  END;
```

```
  (* Copy Source into Destination *)
  FOR Ind := 1 TO LSource DO
    Destination[Ind-1+LDestination] := Source[Ind-1];
  END;
  IF LSource+LDestination < HDestination THEN
    Destination[LDestination + LSource] := StringTerminator;
  END;
END Append;

PROCEDURE AppendChar
  (SourceChar: CHAR; VAR Destination: ARRAY OF CHAR);
(* AppendChar appends a character to Destination if possible *)
VAR
  LDestination, HDestination, Ind : CARDINAL;
BEGIN
  LDestination := Length(Destination);
  HDestination := StringHIGH(Destination) + 1;
  IF LDestination = HDestination THEN
    RETURN;                    (* No room for the character *)
  END;
  Destination[LDestination] := SourceChar;
  IF (LDestination + 1) <> HDestination THEN
    Destination[LDestination + 1] := StringTerminator;
  END;
END AppendChar;

PROCEDURE Compare
  (String1: ARRAY OF CHAR;
   String2: ARRAY OF CHAR):CompareResult;
(* Compare compares two strings and returns equal, less or   *)
(* greater, depending on the ordinal value of the characters *)
(* they contain and their length.                            *)
VAR
  Ind : CARDINAL;
  Len1, Len2: CARDINAL;
  rval : CompareResult;
BEGIN
  Len1 := Length(String1); Len2 := Length(String2);
  (* Compare the lengths first *)
  IF Len1 < Len2 THEN
    rval := less;
  ELSE
    IF Len1 > Len2 THEN
      rval := greater; Len1 := Len2;
    ELSE
      rval := equal;
    END;
  END;
  (* compare the characters *)
  FOR Ind := 1 TO Len1  BY 1 DO
    IF String1[Ind-1] # String2[Ind-1] THEN
      IF String1[Ind-1] < String2[Ind-1] THEN
        RETURN less;
      ELSE
        RETURN greater;
      END;
```

```
    END;
  END (* FOR *);
  RETURN rval;  (* equal *)
END Compare;

PROCEDURE Find
   (Pattern: ARRAY OF CHAR; String: ARRAY OF CHAR;
    VAR Position: CARDINAL; VAR Found: BOOLEAN);
(* Find locates the first occurrence of Pattern in String *)
VAR
  HPattern, HString, Sind, Pind: CARDINAL;
BEGIN
  HPattern := StringHIGH(Pattern); HString := StringHIGH(String);
  Position  := 0; Found := FALSE;
  LOOP
    IF (Position > HString) OR
       (String[Position] = StringTerminator)
    THEN
      RETURN
    END;
    Pind := 0; Sind := Position;
    LOOP
      IF (Pind > HPattern) OR
         (Pattern[Pind] = StringTerminator) THEN
        Found := TRUE;
        RETURN
      END;
      IF Sind > HString THEN RETURN END;
      IF String[Sind] # Pattern[Pind] THEN EXIT END;
      INC(Sind); INC(Pind);
    END;
    INC(Position);
  END;
END Find;

PROCEDURE FindChar
   (Char: CHAR; String: ARRAY OF CHAR;
    VAR Position: CARDINAL; VAR Found: BOOLEAN);
(* FindChar locates the first occurrence of Char in String *)
VAR
  HString : CARDINAL;
BEGIN
  HString := StringHIGH(String);
  Position := 0; Found := FALSE;
  LOOP
    IF (Position > HString) THEN RETURN; END;
    IF (String[Position] = StringTerminator) THEN RETURN; END;
    IF String[Position] # Char THEN
      INC(Position);
    ELSE
      Found := TRUE;
      RETURN
    END
  END
END FindChar;
```

```
PROCEDURE Reverse(VAR s: ARRAY OF CHAR);
VAR
  ch : CHAR;
  l, h : CARDINAL;
BEGIN
  l := 0; h := Length(s)-1;
  WHILE l < h DO
    ch := s[l];
    s[l] := s[h]; s[h] := ch;
    INC(l); DEC(h);
  END;
END Reverse;

END PortStrings.
```

A3.3   PortIO DEFINITION MODULE

```
DEFINITION MODULE PortIO;
(* PortIO reads and writes Strings, integers, cardinals and  *)
(* characters to the default input and output devices. I/O is *)
(* buffered by line.                                          *)

(* Indicates whether the last input was successful. *)
PROCEDURE Done():BOOLEAN;

(* Input procedures *)
PROCEDURE ReadChar(): CHAR;
PROCEDURE ReadCard(): CARDINAL;
PROCEDURE ReadInt(): INTEGER;
PROCEDURE ReadString(VAR str : ARRAY OF CHAR);
PROCEDURE ReadLn();
PROCEDURE SetPrompt(prompt: ARRAY OF CHAR);

(* Output procedures *)
PROCEDURE WriteChar(ch : CHAR);
PROCEDURE WriteCard(c : CARDINAL);
PROCEDURE WriteInt(i : INTEGER);
PROCEDURE WriteString(str : ARRAY OF CHAR);
PROCEDURE WriteLn;

(* set the default field width for whole number output *)
PROCEDURE SetFieldWidth(W: CARDINAL);
PROCEDURE FieldWidth():CARDINAL;

(* Returns the next of any pending characters *)
PROCEDURE NextChar(): CHAR;

(* Returns logical end of file character *)
PROCEDURE EolChar(): CHAR;

END PortIO.
```

A3.4   PortIO IMPLEMENTATION MODULE

```
IMPLEMENTATION MODULE PortIO;
(* PortIO reads and writes Strings, integers, cardinals and  *)
```

```
(* characters to the default input and output devices. I/O is     *)
(* buffered  by line. *)

IMPORT IO;            (* Dependant on Topspeed implementation      *)
(* To implement on other systems, you may have to import           *)
(* InOut and replace the IO procedures with InOut procedures.      *)
(* See Section 9.3.                                                 *)
FROM ImplDep IMPORT EOLN;                    (* End-of-line character *)
FROM PortStrings IMPORT StringTerminator;
IMPORT PortStrings;
CONST
  MaxLine = 80;                      (* maximum input line length *)
  Space = ' ';
TYPE
  Buffer = RECORD
             Count: CARDINAL;
             Line : ARRAY [0..MaxLine-1] OF CHAR;
           END;
VAR
   Input          : Buffer;                        (* Input buffer *)
   CharsRead      : CARDINAL;
   FieldWidthVal  : CARDINAL;      (* Default field width for I/O *)
   DONE           : BOOLEAN;       (* Result of the last operation *)
   PromptStr      : ARRAY [0..20] OF CHAR;       (* prompt string *)

PROCEDURE EolChar(): CHAR;
(* EolChar returns the logical end of line character. *)
BEGIN
  RETURN EOLN;
END EolChar;

PROCEDURE SetPrompt(Prompt: ARRAY OF CHAR);
(* Sets the input prompt to the string passed as its parameter.    *)
BEGIN
  PortStrings.Assign(Prompt,PromptStr);
  (* prompt is truncated if too long *)
END SetPrompt;

PROCEDURE ReadLine(); (*** IMPLEMENTATION DEPENDENT ***)
(* ReadLine reads a line from the terminal, and stores it in the *)
(* input buffer. It is local to this module and will require      *)
(* changing for different implementations. The TopSpeed           *)
(* procedure IO.Read is used. It assumes it will always read to   *)
(* the end of the line. It will not allow a carriage control      *)
(* character or line feed character to be read. Some              *)
(* implementations 'pack' arrays whose components are smaller     *)
(* than the size of a word (e.g. ARRAYs OF CHAR). You then need   *)
(* a temporary variable for reading characters into, prior to     *)
(* updating the buffer.                                           *)

(* VAR UnpackedChar : CHAR;                                       *)

BEGIN
  Input.Count := 0;
  IO.WrStr(PromptStr);                  (* Write prompt to string *)
  LOOP
```

```
      Input.Line[Input.Count]:=IO.RdChar();        (* TopSpeed read *)

   (* Example of read using a temporary variable.              *)
   (* InOut.Read(UnpackedChar);                                *)
   (* Input.Line[Input.Count]:= UnpackedChar;                  *)

   (* In some implementations you will need to echo to screen  *)
   (* InOut.Write(Input.Line[Input.Count]);                    *)

   (* This section filters out carriage control line feed pairs *)
   IF Input.Line[Input.Count] = CHR(10) THEN
      Input.Line[Input.Count] := IO.RdChar();        (* Ignore CR *)
      (* InOut.Read(UnpackedChar);         use temporary variable? *)
      (* Input.Line[Input.Count]:= UnpackedChar                    *)
   END;

   IF Input.Line[Input.Count]= CHR(13) THEN (* when end of line *)
      Input.Line[Input.Count] := EOLN;
      (* InOut.WriteLn;             echo to screen if necessary *)
      EXIT
   END;
   IF Input.Count < MaxLine-1 THEN INC(Input.Count); END;
  END (* LOOP *);
  DONE := (Input.Count <> 0);
END ReadLine;

PROCEDURE Done(): BOOLEAN;
(* Done is a function, which returns whether the last operation *)
(* was successful by returning the value of the global variable *)
(* DONE which is maintained by all procedures.                 *)
BEGIN
  RETURN DONE;
END Done;

PROCEDURE Numeric(ch: CHAR): BOOLEAN;
(* The function procedure Numeric would best be implemented     *)
(* using:SET OF CHAR. For example:                              *)
(*    TYPE setofchar = SET OF CHAR;                             *)
(*    CONST Numbers = setofchar{'0'..'9'};                      *)
(*    RETURN ch IN Numbers;   Unfortunately SET OF CHAR is not  *)
(*                       available on all implementations.      *)
BEGIN
  RETURN (ch >= '0') AND (ch <= '9')
END Numeric;

PROCEDURE NumericValue(ch: CHAR): CARDINAL;
(* NumericValue is an internal function which returns the       *)
(* cardinal value of a numeric character. This is needed because *)
(* you cannot rely on the character representations of digits   *)
(* being sequential.It might have to be changed for non ASCII   *)
(* implementations.                                             *)
BEGIN
  RETURN (ORD(ch) - ORD('0'))
   (* Note: depends on the ASCII collating sequence *)
END NumericValue;

PROCEDURE NextChar():CHAR;
(* Returns next of any pending characters. If there are no      *)
```

```
(* pending characters it returns the end of line character.      *)
BEGIN
  IF (CharsRead = 0) OR (CharsRead > Input.Count) THEN
    RETURN EOLN
  ELSE
    RETURN Input.Line[CharsRead]
  END;
END NextChar;

PROCEDURE ReadChar (): CHAR;
(* This reads the next character from the input buffer. ReadChar *)
(* calls ReadLine to fill the buffer when the contents of the    *)
(* current buffer have been used. It returns the next character  *)
(* in the buffer which has not been read. ReadChar does not      *)
(* assume buffered I/O. This makes it less efficient but ensures *)
(* that it will work with unbuffered devices.                    *)
VAR t : CARDINAL;
BEGIN
  IF CharsRead > Input.Count THEN
    CharsRead := 0; ReadLine;
  END;
  IF (CharsRead <= Input.Count) THEN
    INC(CharsRead);
    RETURN (Input.Line[CharsRead-1]);
  ELSE
    RETURN EOLN;
  END;
END ReadChar ;

PROCEDURE ReadLn();
(* ReadLn reads all the characters on the current line. ReadLn   *)
(* calls ReadLine, which discards the current contents of the    *)
(* buffer and loads the next line into the buffer.               *)
VAR ch : CHAR;
BEGIN
  REPEAT
    ch := ReadChar();
  UNTIL ch = EOLN;
END ReadLn;

PROCEDURE ReadString  (VAR v : ARRAY OF CHAR ) ;
(* ReadString reads a string into the array given. It reads      *)
(* characters into the array until either the array is full or   *)
(* the end of line character is reached. It will not read past   *)
(* the end of a line. It sets the end of file to true if no      *)
(* characters could be read into the string and sets end of line *)
(* to true if the end of line is reached.                        *)
VAR
  index,high : CARDINAL;
  ch : CHAR;
BEGIN
  DONE := TRUE; index := 0; high := HIGH(v);
  LOOP
      IF index > high THEN EXIT END;   (* If string is full return *)
      ch := ReadChar();
      IF ch = EOLN THEN                       (* when end of line *)
```

```
          v[index] := StringTerminator;
          (* terminate string at end of line*)
          EXIT;
        ELSE
          v[index] := ch; INC(index);
        END
    END
END ReadString;

PROCEDURE ReadCard(): CARDINAL;
(* ReadCard reads a cardinal value from the terminal. It ignores *)
(* whitespace at the beginning of the number. Whitespace         *)
(* includes the EOLN character. If it fails to find a cardinal   *)
(* it sets Done to fail. ReadCard reads characters until it      *)
(* finds a separator. It then translates the characters into a   *)
(* cardinal number. It does not checkthat the number is in range.*)
(* How would you add checks to ensure the cardinal value read in *)
(* is not out of bounds? The method used here uses a LONGCARD    *)
(* and converts this to a CARDINAL only if it is less than       *)
(* MAXCARD, contrast this with the method used for PortFileIO.    *)
(* If it is out of bounds what sort of error should it give?      *)
(* If it continues what should it return?                        *)

CONST
  Ten = LONGCARD(10);              (* constants for overflow checking *)
  MaxCard = LONGCARD(MAX(CARDINAL));
VAR
  ch : CHAR;
  LongCard : LONGCARD;
BEGIN
  DONE := TRUE; LongCard := 0;
  REPEAT
    ch :=ReadChar();
  UNTIL (ch <> Space) AND (ch <> EOLN);
  LOOP
    IF NOT Numeric(ch) THEN (* illegal character *)
      DONE := FALSE;
      RETURN VAL(CARDINAL,LongCard)
    END;
    LongCard := (LongCard*10)+VAL(LONGCARD,NumericValue(ch));
    IF LongCard > MaxCard THEN (* Overflow check *)
      DONE := FALSE;
      RETURN 0
    END;
    ch := ReadChar();
    IF (ch = Space) OR (ch = EOLN) THEN
      RETURN VAL(CARDINAL,LongCard)
    END
  END
END ReadCard;

PROCEDURE ReadInt(): INTEGER;
(* Read integer reads an integer value from a terminal. It       *)
(* ignores whitespace (and EOLN) at the beginning of the number, *)
(* but not between the optional sign and the number. If it fails *)
(* to find an integer it sets Done to fail. ReadCard reads       *)
```

```
(* characters until it finds a separator. It translates the    *)
(* characters into an integer. It does not check that the      *)
(* integer is in range.                                        *)
CONST                              (* Constants for overflow checking *)
  Zero = LONGCARD(0);
  One = LONGCARD(1);
  Ten = LONGCARD(10);
  MaxInt = LONGCARD(MAX(INTEGER));
  MinInt = ABS(LONGCARD(MIN(INTEGER)));
VAR
  LongCard : LONGCARD;
  Int : INTEGER;
  ch : CHAR;
BEGIN
  DONE:= TRUE; LongCard := Zero;
  REPEAT                (* Remove whitespace *)
    ch := ReadChar();
  UNTIL (ch <> Space) AND (ch <> EOLN);
  Int := 1;
  IF ch = '+' THEN      (* read sign information *)
    ch := ReadChar();
  ELSIF ch = '-' THEN
    ch := ReadChar(); Int := -1
  END;
  LOOP
    IF NOT Numeric(ch) THEN (* illegal character*)
      DONE := FALSE;
      RETURN (VAL(INTEGER, LongCard) * Int)
    END;
    LongCard := (LongCard*Ten) + VAL(LONGCARD,NumericValue(ch));
    ch := ReadChar();
    IF ((Int < 0)  AND (LongCard>MinInt))      (* Overflow check *)
       OR ((Int > 0) AND (LongCard > MaxInt)) THEN
      DONE := FALSE;                      (* Overflow has happened *)
      RETURN 0
    END;
    IF (ch = Space) OR (ch = EOLN) THEN
      IF LongCard = Zero THEN
          (* Needed to cope with MinInt > MaxInt *)
          RETURN 0;
      ELSIF Int < 0 THEN
        RETURN ((VAL(INTEGER,LongCard-One)*Int)-1);
      ELSE
        RETURN (VAL(INTEGER,LongCard) * Int)
      END
    END
  END
END ReadInt;

PROCEDURE WriteChar(ch : CHAR);
(* Write Char writes characters to a the terminal. It translates *)
(* ImplDep.EOLN to the implementation defined end of line.       *)
(* character. If the line length is exceeded it will output a    *)
(* new line and starts again.                                    *)
BEGIN
```

```
    (* Input.Count := 0;          flush input buffer *)
  IF (ch = EOLN) THEN
    IO.WrLn;
  ELSE
    IO.WrChar(ch);
  END
END WriteChar;

PROCEDURE WriteLn();
(*WriteLn writes a new line to the output.*)
BEGIN
  WriteChar(EOLN);
END WriteLn ;

PROCEDURE WriteString(v : ARRAY OF CHAR);
(*WriteString writes a string to the terminal.*)
VAR
  index,high : CARDINAL;
  ch : CHAR;
BEGIN
  index := 0; high := HIGH(v);
  LOOP
    IF (index > high) OR (v[index] = StringTerminator) THEN
      EXIT                       (* When end of line *)
    END;
    WriteChar(v[index]); INC(index);
  END
END WriteString;

PROCEDURE WriteCard(v : CARDINAL);
(* WriteCard writes a cardinal value to the screen. It uses the  *)
(* variable FieldWidthVal to justify it.                         *)
VAR
  Str : ARRAY [0..21] OF CHAR;
  Ind : CARDINAL;
BEGIN
  Ind := 0;
  (* write out the digits of the number into a string *)
  REPEAT
    Str[Ind] := CHR((v MOD 10) + ORD('0'));
    INC(Ind); v := v DIV 10;
  UNTIL v = 0;
  Str[Ind] := StringTerminator; PortStrings.Reverse(Str);
  WHILE (Ind < FieldWidthVal) DO    (* Justify the output *)
    PortStrings.InsertChar(Space,Str,0);
    INC(Ind)
  END;
  WriteString(Str)
END WriteCard;

PROCEDURE WriteInt(v : INTEGER);
(* WriteInt writes an integer to the terminal. It uses the     *)
(* global variable FieldWidthVal to determine the field width in *)
(* which to place the Integer.                                 *)
VAR
  Str : ARRAY [0..20] OF CHAR;
```

```
    Ind,TMP : CARDINAL;
BEGIN
   IF v < 0 THEN                    (* Convert v to a positive cardinal *)
      v := v+1;                            (* cope with MaxInt < MinInt *)
      TMP := ABS(v); INC(TMP);
   ELSE
      TMP := v
   END;
   Ind := 0;
   (* write the digits of the number into a string *)
   REPEAT
      Str[Ind] := CHR( (TMP MOD 10) + ORD('0'));
      INC(Ind); TMP := TMP DIV 10;
   UNTIL TMP = 0;
   Str[Ind] := StringTerminator;
   PortStrings.Reverse(Str);
   IF v < 0 THEN                              (* add '-' if necessary *)
      PortStrings.InsertChar('-',Str,0);
      INC(Ind);
   END;
   WHILE (Ind <FieldWidthVal) DO      (* Justify the output *)
      PortStrings.InsertChar(Space,Str,0); INC(Ind);
   END;
   WriteString(Str);
END WriteInt;

PROCEDURE SetFieldWidth(W: CARDINAL);
(* SetFieldWidth changes the default output width for integer    *)
(* and cardinal values.                                          *)
BEGIN
   IF W > 20 THEN
      FieldWidthVal := 20;
   ELSE
      FieldWidthVal := W;
   END;
END SetFieldWidth;

PROCEDURE FieldWidth():CARDINAL;
(* FieldWidth returns the current field width for INTEGER and    *)
(* CARDINAL I/O.                                                 *)
BEGIN
   RETURN  FieldWidthVal;
END FieldWidth;

(* The main body of PortIO is used to initialise the the default *)
(* field FieldWidthVal for INTEGER and CARDINAL I/O to 6 and to  *)
(* initialise the variables associated with input buffering.     *)

BEGIN(*main body of PortIO*)
   PromptStr := '';                (* Initialise prompt to null string *)
   FieldWidthVal := 6;                      (* Default field width *)
   Input.Count := 0;
   CharsRead := 999;                 (* ensure ReadLine is called *)
END PortIO.
```

A3.5 PortFileIO DEFINITION MODULE

```
DEFINITION MODULE PortFileIO;
IMPORT ImplDep;
CONST MaxFiles = ImplDep.MaxFiles;
(* Define file type *)
TYPE FILE = POINTER TO ImplDep.Buffer;
(* Declare terminal I/O *)
VAR INPUT,OUTPUT: FILE;

(* indicates whether the last input was successful *)
PROCEDURE Done(F: FILE):BOOLEAN;

(* file management procedures *)
PROCEDURE Open(FileName: ARRAY OF CHAR): FILE;
PROCEDURE Append(FileName: ARRAY OF CHAR): FILE;
PROCEDURE Create(FileName: ARRAY OF CHAR): FILE;
PROCEDURE Close(VAR F: FILE);

(* input procedures *)
PROCEDURE ReadChar(VAR F: FILE): CHAR;
PROCEDURE ReadCard(VAR F: FILE): CARDINAL;
PROCEDURE ReadInt(VAR F: FILE): INTEGER;
PROCEDURE ReadString(VAR F: FILE; VAR str : ARRAY OF CHAR);
PROCEDURE ReadLn(VAR F: FILE);

(* output procedures *)
PROCEDURE WriteChar(VAR F: FILE; ch : CHAR);
PROCEDURE WriteCard(VAR F: FILE; c : CARDINAL);
PROCEDURE WriteInt(VAR F: FILE; i : INTEGER);
PROCEDURE WriteString(VAR F: FILE; str : ARRAY OF CHAR);
PROCEDURE WriteLn(VAR F: FILE);

(* set the default field width for whole number output *)
PROCEDURE SetFieldWidth(VAR F: FILE; W: CARDINAL);
PROCEDURE FieldWidth(F: FILE):CARDINAL;

(* Returns the next of any pending characters *)
PROCEDURE NextChar(F: FILE): CHAR;

(* Returns logical end of line and file characters *)
PROCEDURE EolChar(): CHAR;
PROCEDURE EofChar(): CHAR;

(* Returns the number of files currently open *)
PROCEDURE OpenFiles(): CARDINAL;

END PortFileIO.
```

A3.6 PortFileIO IMPLEMENTATION MODULE

```
IMPLEMENTATION MODULE PortFileIO;
(* PortIO reads and writes Strings, integers, cardinals and    *)
(* characters to text files. I/O is buffered by line.          *)

FROM PortStrings IMPORT StringTerminator;
IMPORT ImplDep, PortStrings, IO;
```

```
FROM Storage IMPORT ALLOCATE, DEALLOCATE;
CONST Space = ' ';

PROCEDURE EolChar(): CHAR;
(* EolChar returns the logical end of line character.          *)
BEGIN
  RETURN ImplDep.EOLN;
END EolChar;

PROCEDURE EofChar(): CHAR;
(*EofChar returns the logical end of file character.*)
BEGIN
  RETURN ImplDep.EOF;
END EofChar;

PROCEDURE OpenFiles(): CARDINAL;
(* OpenFiles returns the number of currently open.files.       *)
BEGIN
  RETURN ImplDep.FilesOpen;
END OpenFiles;

PROCEDURE Done(F: FILE): BOOLEAN;
(* Done is a function, which returns whether the last operation *)
(* was successful.A  Boolean associated with the last operation *)
(* is accessed and the result returned.                         *)
BEGIN
  RETURN F^.DONE;
END Done;

PROCEDURE Open(FileName: ARRAY OF CHAR):FILE;
(*Opens a file.*)
VAR F : FILE;
BEGIN
  NEW(F);
  ImplDep.Open(FileName,F^);
  (* Initialise the field of the file *)
  F^.Count := 0;
  F^.FieldWidth := 0;
  F^.CharsRead := 999;           (* ensure readline gets called *)
  RETURN F;
END Open;

PROCEDURE Append(FileName: ARRAY OF CHAR):FILE;
(* Opens a file for for appending to.                          *)
VAR F : FILE;
BEGIN
  NEW(F);
  ImplDep.Append(FileName,F^);
  (* Initialise the field of the file *)
  F^.Count := 0;
  F^.FieldWidth := 0;
  F^.CharsRead := 999;           (* ensure readline gets called *)
  RETURN F;
END Append;

PROCEDURE Create(FileName : ARRAY OF CHAR):FILE;
```

```
(* Create creates a new file and prepares it for writing to.    *)
VAR F : FILE;
BEGIN
  NEW(F);
  ImplDep.Create(FileName,F^);
  F^.Count := 0; F^.CharsRead := 999; F^.FieldWidth := 0;
  RETURN F;
END Create;

PROCEDURE Close(VAR F: FILE);
BEGIN
  ImplDep.Close(F^); DISPOSE(F);
END Close;

PROCEDURE Numeric(ch: CHAR): BOOLEAN;
(* An internal function which returns whether a character is a   *)
(* numeric. The function procedure Numeric would best be         *)
(* implemented using: setofchar = SET OF CHAR;                   *)
(* CONST                                                         *)
(*    Numbers = setofchar{'0'..'9'};                             *)
(* However this is not available on all implementations          *)
BEGIN
  RETURN (ch >= '0') AND (ch <= '9')
END Numeric;

PROCEDURE NumericValue(ch: CHAR): CARDINAL;
(* NumericValue is an internal function which returns the        *)
(* cardinal value of a numeric character.                        *)
BEGIN
  RETURN(ORD(ch) - ORD('0'))
END NumericValue;

PROCEDURE NextChar(F: FILE):CHAR;
(* Returns next of any pending characters. If there are no       *)
(* pending characters it returns the end of line character.      *)
BEGIN
  IF (F^.CharsRead = 0) OR (F^.CharsRead > F^.Count) THEN
    RETURN ImplDep.EOLN
  ELSE
    RETURN F^.Line[F^.CharsRead]
  END;
END NextChar;

PROCEDURE ReadChar (VAR F: FILE): CHAR;
(* Reads the next character from the input buffer.               *)
(* ReadChar calls IMPDEP.ReadLine to fill the buffer when the    *)
(* contents of the current buffer have been used. It returns the *)
(* character in the buffer which has not been read.              *)
(* ReadChar does not assume buffered I/O. This makes it less     *)
(* efficient but ensures it will work with unbuffered devices.   *)
VAR t : CARDINAL;
BEGIN
  IF F^.CharsRead > F^.Count THEN
    F^.CharsRead := 0; ImplDep.ReadLine(F^);
  END;
  IF (F^.CharsRead < F^.Count) THEN
```

```
      INC(F^.CharsRead);
      RETURN (F^.Line[F^.CharsRead-1]);
    ELSE
      INC(F^.CharsRead);
      RETURN (F^.Line[F^.Count]);
    END;
END ReadChar ;

PROCEDURE ReadLn(VAR F: FILE);
(* ReadLn reads all the characters on the current line. It calls *)
(* ImplDep.ReadLine, which discards the current contents of the  *)
(* buffer and loads the next line into the buffer.               *)
VAR ch : CHAR;
BEGIN
  REPEAT
    ch := ReadChar(F);
  UNTIL (ch = ImplDep.EOLN) OR (ch = ImplDep.EOF);
END ReadLn;

PROCEDURE ReadString  (VAR F: FILE; VAR v : ARRAY OF CHAR );
(* Readstring reads a string into the array given. It reads      *)
(* characters into the array until either the array is full      *)
(* or the end of line character is reached. It will not read     *)
(* past the end of a line. It sets  the end of file to  true if  *)
(* no characters could be read into the string and sets end of   *)
(* line to true if the end of line is reached.                   *)
VAR
  index,high : CARDINAL;
  ch : CHAR;
BEGIN
  F^.DONE := TRUE; index := 0; high := HIGH( v );
  LOOP
    IF index > high THEN EXIT END;    (* If string is full return *)
    ch := ReadChar(F);
    IF (ch = ImplDep.EOLN) OR (ch = ImplDep.EOF) THEN
      (* when end of line *)
      v[index] := StringTerminator;
      (* terminate string at end of line*)
      EXIT;
    ELSE
      v[index] := ch; INC(index);
    END;
  END;
END ReadString;

PROCEDURE ReadCard(VAR F: FILE): CARDINAL;
(* Read cardinal reads a cardinal value from the terminal. It     *)
(* ignores  whitespace at the beginning of the number.Whitespace *)
(* includes the ImplDep.EOLN character. If it fails to find a      *)
(* cardinal it sets Done to fail. ReadCard reads characters       *)
(* until it finds a separator. It then translates the characters *)
(* into a cardinal number. It does not check that the number is   *)
(* in range. The check to ensure the cardinal read in is not out *)
(* of bounds requires range checking to be disabled. If it is     *)
(* out of bounds what sort of error should it give?               *)
VAR
```

```
    ch : CHAR;
    OldCard, Card : CARDINAL;
BEGIN
  F^.DONE := TRUE; Card := 0;
  (* skip leading spaces and end-of-lines *)
  REPEAT
    ch := ReadChar(F);
  UNTIL (ch <> Space) AND (ch <> ImplDep.EOLN);
  LOOP
    IF (NOT Numeric(ch)) THEN (* illegal character *)
      F^.DONE := FALSE;
      RETURN Card;
    END;
    OldCard := Card;
    Card := (Card * 10) + NumericValue(ch);
    (* Following test relies on overflow not causing a runtime   *)
    (* error, but wrapping round to zero. If wrapround happens,   *)
    (* then old value will be greater than current.              *)
    IF OldCard <> Card DIV 10 THEN              (* Numeric overflow *)
      F^.DONE := FALSE;
      RETURN Card;
    END;
    ch := ReadChar(F);
    IF (ch = Space) OR (ch = ImplDep.EOLN) THEN RETURN Card END;
  END;
END ReadCard;

PROCEDURE ReadInt(VAR F: FILE): INTEGER;
(* Read integer reads an integer value from a terminal. It       *)
(* ignores whitespace (and ImplDep.EOLN) at the beginning of the *)
(* number, but not between the optional sign andthe number. If   *)
(* it fails to find an integer it sets Done to fail. ReadCard    *)
(* reads characters until it finds a separator. It translates    *)
(* the characters into an integer.It does not check that the     *)
(* integer is in range.                                          *)
CONST
  MinInt = VAL(CARDINAL,ABS(MIN(INTEGER)));
  MaxInt = VAL(CARDINAL,MAX(INTEGER));
VAR
  OldCard, Card: CARDINAL;
  Int : INTEGER;
  ch : CHAR;
BEGIN
  F^.DONE := TRUE; Card := 0;
  REPEAT                      (* Remove whitespace *)
    ch :=ReadChar(F);
  UNTIL (ch <> Space) AND (ch <> ImplDep.EOLN);
  Int := 1;
  IF ch = '+' THEN        (* read sign information *)
    ch := ReadChar(F);
  ELSIF ch = '-' THEN
    ch := ReadChar(F); Int := -1
  END;
  LOOP
    IF NOT Numeric(ch) THEN (*illegal character*)
      F^.DONE := FALSE;
```

```
          RETURN(VAL(INTEGER, Card) * Int);
        END;
        OldCard := Card;
        Card := (Card * 10) + NumericValue(ch);
        (* Following test relies on overflow not causing a runtime   *)
        (* error, but wrapping round to zero. If wrap around          *)
        (* happens, then old value will be greater than current.      *)
        IF (OldCard <> Card DIV 10) OR              (* Numeric overflow *)
               ((Card > MaxInt) AND (Int =1))
               OR ((Card > MinInt) AND (Int = -1)) THEN
          (* Only true on 2's complement machines*)
          F^.DONE := FALSE;
          RETURN Card;
        END;
        ch :=ReadChar(F);
        IF (ch = Space) OR (ch = ImplDep.EOLN) THEN
          IF Card = 0 THEN      (* Needed to cope with MinInt > MaxInt *)
            RETURN 0;
          ELSIF Int < 0 THEN
            RETURN (VAL(INTEGER,Card-1)*Int)-1;
          ELSE
            RETURN VAL(INTEGER,Card);
          END
        END
      END
    END
END ReadInt;

PROCEDURE WriteChar(VAR F: FILE; ch : CHAR );
(* Write Char writes characters to a the terminal. It translates *)
(* PortIO.ImplDep.EOLN to the implementation defined end of line *)
(* character.If the line length is exceeded it will output a new *)
(* line and starts again.                                        *)
VAR t : CARDINAL;
BEGIN
  IF ImplDep.MaxLine = F^.Count THEN
    ImplDep.WriteLine(F^);
  END;
  INC(F^.Count); F^.Line[F^.Count]:= ch;
END WriteChar ;

PROCEDURE WriteLn(VAR F: FILE);
(* WriteLn writes a new line to the output.*)
BEGIN
  WriteChar(F,ImplDep.EOLN); ImplDep.WriteLine(F^);
END WriteLn;

PROCEDURE WriteString (VAR F: FILE; v : ARRAY OF CHAR );
(*WriteString writes a string to the terminal.*)
VAR
  index,high : CARDINAL;
  ch : CHAR;
BEGIN
  index  := 0; high  := HIGH( v );
  LOOP
    IF (index > high) OR (v[index] = StringTerminator) THEN
      EXIT       (* When end of line *)
```

```
        END;
        WriteChar(F, v[index]); INC( index );
      END
END WriteString ;

PROCEDURE WriteCard    (VAR F: FILE; v : CARDINAL);
(* WriteCard writes a cardinal value to the screen. It uses the   *)
(* variable FieldWidth to justify it.                             *)
VAR
    Str : ARRAY [0..21] OF CHAR;
    Ind : CARDINAL;
BEGIN
    Ind := 0;
    (* write out the digits of the number into a string *)
    REPEAT
        Str[Ind] := CHR((v MOD 10) + ORD('0'));
        INC(Ind); v := v DIV 10;
    UNTIL v = 0;
    Str[Ind] := StringTerminator;
    PortStrings.Reverse(Str);
    WHILE (Ind <F^.FieldWidth) DO            (* Justify the output *)
        PortStrings.InsertChar(Space, Str, 0); INC(Ind)
    END;
    WriteString(F, Str)
END WriteCard;

PROCEDURE WriteInt(VAR F: FILE; v : INTEGER);
(* WriteInt writes an integer to the terminal. It uses the        *)
(* global variable FieldWidth to determine the field width in     *)
(* which to place the Integer value                               *)
VAR
    Str : ARRAY [0..20] OF CHAR;
    Ind,TMP : CARDINAL;
BEGIN
    IF v < 0 THEN              (* Convert v to a positive cardinal *)
        v := v+1;                        (* cope with MaxInt < MinInt *)
        TMP := ABS(v); INC(TMP);
    ELSE
        TMP := v;
    END;
    Ind := 0;
    (* write the digits of the number into a string *)
    REPEAT
        Str[Ind] := CHR((TMP MOD 10) + ORD('0'));
        INC(Ind); TMP := TMP DIV 10;
    UNTIL TMP = 0;
    Str[Ind] := StringTerminator;
    PortStrings.Reverse(Str);
    IF v < 0 THEN                            (* add '-' if necessary *)
        PortStrings.InsertChar('-', Str, 0);
        INC(Ind);
    END;
    WHILE (Ind <F^.FieldWidth) DO    (* Justify the output *)
        PortStrings.InsertChar(Space, Str, 0);
        INC(Ind);
    END;
```

```
    WriteString(F,Str);
END WriteInt;

PROCEDURE SetFieldWidth(VAR F: FILE; W: CARDINAL);
(* SetFieldWidth changes the default output width for integer   *)
(* and cardinal values.                                         *)
BEGIN
  IF W > 20 THEN
    F^.FieldWidth := 20;
  ELSE
    F^.FieldWidth := W;
  END;
END SetFieldWidth;

PROCEDURE FieldWidth(F: FILE): CARDINAL;
(*FieldWidth returns the current field width for
  INTEGER and CARDINAL I/O*)
BEGIN
  RETURN  F^.FieldWidth;
END FieldWidth;

(* The main body of PortFileIO associates standard input and    *)
(* standard output with the variables INPUT and OUTPUT.         *)

BEGIN(*main body of PortFileIO*)
  INPUT := Open(ImplDep.INPUT);
  OUTPUT := Create(ImplDep.OUTPUT);
END PortFileIO.
```

A3.7 ImplDep DEFINITION MODULE

```
DEFINITION MODULE ImplDep;
(* ImplDep contains all the procedures and constants which will  *)
(* need to be changed if PortFileIO is to be moved to a          *)
(* different implementation.                                     *)

IMPORT FIO;
CONST
  MaxLine = 80;                        (* maximum line length *)
  EOLN = 15C;                   (* logical end of line char *)
  EOF = 30C;                    (* logical end of file char *)
  MaxFiles = 10;            (* Number of files which can be open *)
  INPUT = 'CON';           (* File handles for input and output *)
  OUTPUT = 'CON';                         (* to the terminal *)
TYPE
  Access = (read,write, direct);
  Buffer = RECORD
              Fiel : FIO.File;                    (* File descr *)
              Count : CARDINAL;        (* No. of chars in buffer *)
              Line : ARRAY [0..MaxLine-1] OF CHAR;     (* Buffer *)
              Mode : Access;            (* Mode of use for file *)
              DONE : BOOLEAN;          (* result of last operation *)
              CharsRead : CARDINAL;
                      (* Number of characters taken from line *)
              FieldWidth : CARDINAL;     (*Fieldwidth for output *)
            END;
```

```
VAR FilesOpen: CARDINAL;                          (* number of files open *)

(* File creation procedures *)
PROCEDURE Open(Name : ARRAY OF CHAR; VAR F: Buffer);
PROCEDURE Append(Name : ARRAY OF CHAR; VAR F: Buffer);
PROCEDURE Close(VAR F: Buffer);
PROCEDURE Create(Name : ARRAY OF CHAR; VAR F: Buffer);

(* File input procedures *)
PROCEDURE ReadLine(VAR F: Buffer);

(* File output procedures *)
PROCEDURE WriteLine(VAR F: Buffer);

END ImplDep.
```

A3.8   ImplDep IMPLEMENTATION MODULE

```
IMPLEMENTATION MODULE ImplDep;
(* Contains all the implementation dependent, constants types   *)
(* variables and procedures which will have to bechanged        *)
(* when porting an implementation of PortFileIO.                *)

IMPORT FIO, IO;        (* IMPORT the implementation's file system *)
CONST
  NOFILE = MAX(CARDINAL);        (* implementation dependent value *)
  Space = ' ';

PROCEDURE IOError(s : ARRAY OF CHAR);
(* Procedure IOError is internal to Module IMPDEP. Whenever an   *)
(* I/O error occurs it is called to output an error message to   *)
(* the screen and to terminate the program.                     *)
(* What should IOError do when it is called? Presently it        *)
(* outputs a message to the screen and terminates the program.   *)
(* It would be reasonable for it to also close any open files.   *)
(* It could attempt to continue with the program after setting   *)
(* the variable DONE to fail.                                   *)
BEGIN
  IO.WrStr(s); IO.WrLn;
  HALT;
END IOError;

PROCEDURE Open(name : ARRAY OF CHAR ; VAR F : Buffer);
(* Opens a file if one already exists and assigns it to a file   *)
(* descriptor. Open also checks that too many files have not     *)
(* been opened.It calls the operating system primitive to open   *)
(* the file andassigns the the file descriptor to the file       *)
(* buffer. Should Open create a file if it doesn't exist? Should *)
(* it take parameters on what type of file to open, and in what  *)
(* mode it should be opened? Portable programs cannot rely on    *)
(* more than the minimum file system capabilities, neither can   *)
(* they rely on the file system to trap errors. Should Open try  *)
(* to trap more errors at the expense of inefficiency?           *)
BEGIN
  IF FilesOpen = MaxFiles THEN
    IOError('Error too many files open')
```

```
      END;
    INC(FilesOpen);
    F.Fiel := FIO.Open(name);           (* assign it to the file *)
    F.Mode := read;                                 (* Read only *)
    F.DONE := FIO.OK;
    IF NOT FIO.OK THEN          (* was the operation successful? *)
      IOError('File cannot be opened');
    END
  END Open;

  PROCEDURE Append(name : ARRAY OF CHAR ; VAR F : Buffer);
  (* Opens a file if one already exists in append mode and assigns *)
  (* it to a file descriptor. Append also checks that too many     *)
  (* files have not been opened. It calls the operating system     *)
  (* primitive to open the file and assigns the file descriptor to *)
  (* the file buffer.                                              *)
  BEGIN
    IF FilesOpen=MaxFiles
      THEN IOError('Error too many files open')
    END;
    INC(FilesOpen);
    F.Fiel := FIO.Append(name);         (* assign it to the file *)
    F.Mode := write;                               (* Write only *)
    F.DONE := FIO.OK;
    IF NOT FIO.OK THEN           (* was the operation successful *)
      IOError('File cannot be opened')
    END
  END Append;

  PROCEDURE Close (VAR F: Buffer);
  (* Close flushes the buffer and closes the file associated with  *)
  (* the file descriptor.                                          *)
  BEGIN
    IF F.Fiel <> NOFILE THEN             (* if the file is assigned *)
      WriteLine(F);                      (* flush PortFileIO buffer *)
      FIO.Close(F.Fiel);          (* call O/S primitive to close it *)
      F.DONE := FIO.OK;                              (* set done *)
      IF FIO.OK THEN              (* If the call was successful *)
        DEC(FilesOpen);
      ELSE
        (*IOError('File could not be closed');
        (* otherwise print message *)*)
      END;
    ELSE
      IOError('Error file not open')
    END
  END Close;

  PROCEDURE Create(name : ARRAY OF CHAR ;VAR F : Buffer);
  (* Creates a new file, over writing any previous files.*)
  BEGIN
    IF FilesOpen = MaxFiles THEN
      IOError('Error too many files open')
    END;
    INC(FilesOpen);
    F.Fiel := FIO.Create(name);              (* assign it to the file *)
```

```
    F.Mode := write; F.DONE := FIO.OK;
END Create;

PROCEDURE ReadLine(VAR Input: Buffer);
(* ReadLine reads a line from a File, and stores it in the      *)
(* input buffer.It is local to this module and will require     *)
(* changing for different implementations. The TopSpeed         *)
(* procedure RdChar is used. It assumes it will always read to  *)
(* the end of the line. It will not allow a carriage control    *)
(* character or line feed character to be read.                 *)
BEGIN
  CASE Input.Mode OF
  write:
    Input.DONE := FALSE;
    RETURN; |
  direct:
    WriteLine(Input);
  ELSE (* do nothing *);
  END;
  Input.Count := 0;
  LOOP
    Input.Line[Input.Count] := FIO.RdChar(Input.Fiel);
    IF FIO.EOF THEN  (* when end of file *)
      Input.Line[Input.Count] := EOF;
      EXIT
    END;
    (* This section filters out CR/LF pairs *)
    IF Input.Line[Input.Count] = CHR( 10 ) THEN
      Input.Line[Input.Count] := FIO.RdChar(Input.Fiel);
      (* Ignore CR *)
    END;
    IF Input.Line[Input.Count]= CHR( 13 ) THEN
      (* when end of line *)
      Input.Line[Input.Count] := EOLN;
      EXIT
    END;
    IF Input.Count < MaxLine-1 THEN
      INC(Input.Count)
    END
  END (* LOOP *);
  Input.DONE := (Input.Count <> 0)
END ReadLine;

PROCEDURE WriteLine(VAR Output: Buffer);
(* WriteLine writes the contents of the output buffer to a file. *)
(* It is local to this module and will require changing for      *)
(* different implementations. The TopSpeed procedure WrChar is   *)
(* used. If it encounters an end-of-line character it writes a   *)
(* line to the file.                                             *)
VAR Index: CARDINAL;
BEGIN
  CASE Output.Mode OF
  read:
    Output.DONE := FALSE;
    RETURN; |
  ELSE ;
```

```
    END;
    Output.DONE := TRUE;
    FOR Index := 1 TO Output.Count DO
      IF Output.Line[Index] = EOLN THEN
        FIO.WrLn(Output.Fiel)
      ELSE
        FIO.WrChar(Output.Fiel,Output.Line[Index])
      END; (* IF *)
      Output.DONE := Output.DONE AND FIO.OK
    END; (* FOR *)
    Output.Count := 0
END WriteLine;

BEGIN (* main body of IMPDEP *)
  FilesOpen := 0
END ImplDep.
```

APPENDIX 4

ANSWERS TO REVIEW QUESTIONS AND EXERCISES

A4.1 CHAPTER 1 ANSWERS

A1.1 Professor Niklaus Wirth of ETH Zürich.

A1.2 It means abandoning the evaluation of an expression. It is used with Boolean expressions because with them it is possible to determine what the outcome of evaluating the expression will be early.

A1.3 The LOOP statement.

A1.4 Modules are provided which allow data and procedures to be hidden away together.

A1.5 They are not as such. Character arrays are used to represent strings and a library module is supplied for manipulating them.

A1.6 The type rules might need to be broken in order to mix numeric values such as CARDINAL and INTEGER in an expression or in systems.

A4.2 CHAPTER 2 ANSWERS

A2.1 A program module begins with the keyword MODULE, followed by an identifier which is the module's name, followed by a semicolon. It finishes with an END symbol, the program identifier, and a fullstop.

A2.2 The IMPORT instruction.

A2.3 False (assuming that 'non-trivial' means that the program produces some observable result).

A2.4 False: it matters very much.

A2.5 They are used in implementations which require the explicit exportation of identifiers from a definition module.

A2.6 The source code for all these is given earlier in the chapter.

A2.7 The new implementation module is given below. It must be compiled and then linked with TestMessages before executing the latter. Note that neither the definition module of Messages nor the TestMessages program module need be changed in any way.

```
IMPLEMENTATION MODULE Messages;
FROM PortIO IMPORT WriteString, WriteLn;
PROCEDURE InfoMessage(Message: ARRAY OF CHAR);
BEGIN
   WriteString(Message); WriteLn
END InfoMessage;
PROCEDURE ErrorMessage(Message: ARRAY OF CHAR);
```

```
BEGIN
  WriteString("*** ERROR ***"); WriteLn;
  WriteString(Message); WriteLn
END ErrorMessage;
END Messages.
```

Note that `WriteChar` need no longer be imported because the character to produce a bleep is no longer output.

A4.3 CHAPTER 3 ANSWERS

A3.1 Tokens are sequences of characters which are delimited by punctuation characters, spaces, or end-of-lines.

A3.2 They are all literal constants.

A3.3 `"Don't"`

A3.4 `1.2E-5`

A3.5 It would make `FORWARD` unavailable as an identifier. It might also point to the implementation being unable to handle some Modula-2 programs.

A4.4 CHAPTER 4 ANSWERS

A4.1 With the keyword `VAR`.

A4.2 Anywhere except in the statement parts of modules and procedures.

A4.3 `VAR Length, Height: CARDINAL;`

A4.4 First the values stored in a an b are added. Then the value in c is multiplied with that sum, and the result is stored in x.

A4.5 `366`

A4.5 CHAPTER 5 ANSWERS

A5.1 `CONST ErrorTolerance = 0.00001;`

A5.2
```
IF Measurement < Standard + ErrorTolerance THEN
  WriteString("Measurement is close to standard")
ELSE
  WriteString("Measurement not yet close to standard")
END;
```

A5.3
```
CASE ReadChar() OF
'Y', 'y' : WriteString("Closing down.") |
'N', 'n' : WriteString ("Continuing...")
ELSE
  WriteString("Cannot understand answer!")
END;
```

A5.4
```
VAR ch: CHAR;
...
FOR ch := 'L' TO 'Y' BY 2 DO
  WriteChar(ch)
END;
```

A5.5
```
Ch := 'L';
LOOP
  IF ch <= 'y' THEN
    WriteChar(ch)
  ELSE
    EXIT
  END:
  INC(ch); INC(ch)
END;
```

A5.6 A repeat statement:

```
REPEAT
  Command := ReadChar();
UNTIL command ; 'Q';
```

A5.7 A WHILE statement is the most appropriate because there is a possibility that the body of the loop (in this case the accumulation of the total, and incrementing the count) might never be executed. This would be the case if an invalid first Input was read. Note that an extra BOOLEAN flag, Finished, is required.

```
Total := 0; Number := 0;
Finished := Number < MaxAllowed;
Input := ReadInt();
WHILE (Input >= 5) AND (Input <= 1045)
  AND (NOT Finished) DO
  Total ;= Total + Input;
  Number := Number + 1;
  IF Number = MaxAllowed THEN
    Finished := TRUE
  ELSE
    Input := ReadInt()
  END
END;
```

A4.6 CHAPTER 6 ANSWERS

A6.1
```
TYPE
  MonthNames =  (Jan, Feb, Mar, Apr, May, Jun,
                 Jul, Aug, Sep, Oct, Nov, Dec);
```

A6.2 Jan has an ordinal value of 0.

A6.3 Months takes the value May.

A6.4 It returns Mar.

A6.5 It returns 10.

A6.6 Either MIN(INTEGER) to MAX(INTEGER)
or MIN(CARDINAL) to MAX(CARDINAL)

A6.7 The host type is CARDINAL.

A6.8 You would specify the range type to be INTEGER thus:

```
TYPE Digits = INTEGER[0..9];
```

A4.7   CHAPTER 7 ANSWERS

A7.1   It can be of any type.

A7.2   It must be of some ordinal type.

A7.3
```
TYPE
   letters = ['A'..'Z']
   Alphabet = ARRAY [0..49] OF letters;
```

A7.4
```
MODULE RevCards;
FROM PortIO IMPORT ReadCard, WriteCard, WriteLn;
CONST
   Min = 1; Max = 6;
TYPE
   ArrayOfCards = ARRAY [Min..Max] OF CARDINAL;
VAR
   CardArray : ArrayOfCards; i : CARDINAL;
BEGIN
   FOR i := Min TO Max DO
      CardArray[i] := ReadCard()
   END;
   FOR i := Max TO Min BY -1 DO
      WriteCard(CardArray[i]); WriteLn
   END
END RevCards.
```

A7.5
```
TYPE
   DayRange = [1..31];
   MonthRange = [1..12];
   YearRange = [0..99];
   DateRec = RECORD
               Day: DayRange;
               Month: MonthRange;
               Year: YearRange
             END;
```

A7.6   It must be an enumeration type with a cardinality of 16 or less, or a subrange of an ordinal type.

A7.7
```
TYPE
   Colour = (Red,Orange,Yellow,Green,Blue,Indigo,Violet);
   SetOfColour = SET OF Colour;
```

A4.8   CHAPTER 8 ANSWERS

A8.1   A VAR-parameter returns values from a procedure. An expression may not be used as an actual parameter.

A8.2
```
PROCEDURE Swap(VAR First, Second: CARDINAL);
VAR  Temporary: CARDINAL;
BEGIN
   Temporary := First;  First := Second;
   Second := Temporary
END Swap;
```

A8.3 False: it must terminate via a RETURN statement.

A8.4
```
PROCEDURE Sum(a, b : CARDINAL) : CARDINAL;
BEGIN
  RETURN a + b
END Sum;
```

A8.5
```
IMPLEMENTATION MODULE Birthdays;
FROM Dates IMPORT DateRecord, WriteDate;
FROM PortIO IMPORT WriteString, WriteLn;
CONST
  Lower = 1;
  Upper = 20; (* maximum of 20 birthdays can be stored *)
TYPE
  DateArray = ARRAY [Lower..Upper] OF DateRecord;
VAR
  DateStore : DateArray;
  FreeSlot : CARDINAL;
PROCEDURE SaveBirthday(d : DateRecord);
  BEGIN
    IF FreeSlot > Upper THEN
      WriteString("No space to save date");
    ELSE
      DateStore[FreeSlot] := d;
      INC(FreeSlot)
    END;
  END SaveBirthday;
PROCEDURE PrintBirthdays;
  VAR
    Index : CARDINAL;
  BEGIN
    FOR Index := 1 TO FreeSlot - 1 DO
      WriteDate(DateStore[Index])
    END
  END PrintBirthdays;
BEGIN
  FreeSlot := Lower
END Birthdays.
```

A8.6
```
MODULE CheckDate;
FROM Dates IMPORT
  ReadDay, ReadMonth, ReadYear,
  GetDayName, ValidDate, DateRecord;
FROM PortIO IMPORT ReadChar, WriteLn, WriteString;
FROM Birthdays IMPORT SaveBirthday, PrintBirthdays;
VAR
  Date : DateRecord;
  Quit, Pause : CHAR;
BEGIN
  REPEAT
    ReadDay(Date, IsOk);
    IF IsOk THEN
      ReadMonth(Date, IsOk);
      IF IsOk THEN
        ReadYear(Date, IsOk)
```

```
                IF IsOk THEN
                  ValidDate(Date, IsOk)
                  IF IsOk THEN
                    GetDayName(Date);
                  END
                END
              END
            END;
            SaveBirthday(Date);
            WriteString("Type '!' to quit any key to continue :");
            Quit := ReadChar(); WriteLn;
          UNTIL Quit = '!';
          PrintBirthdays;
          Pause := ReadChar();
        END CheckDate.
```

A4.9   CHAPTER 9 ANSWERS

A9.1
```
MODULE Convert1;
(* program to convert a line from lower to upper case *)
VAR ch : CHAR;
FROM PortIO IMPORT Done, ReadString, WriteString, WriteLn;
FROM PortStrings IMPORT Length;
VAR
  Index : CARDINAL;
  Line  : ARRAY [0..255] OF CHAR;
BEGIN
  ReadString(Line);
  FOR Index := 1 TO Length(Line) DO
    IF (Line[Index] >= 'a') AND (Line[Index] <= 'z') THEN
      (* converts lower to upper case*)
      Line[Index] := CAP(Line[Index]);
    END;
    WriteChar(Line[Index]);
  END;
END Convert1.

MODULE Convert2;
(* program to convert a line from lower to upper case *)
VAR ch : CHAR;
FROM PortIO IMPORT EolChar, ReadChar, WriteChar;
BEGIN
  REPEAT
    ch := ReadChar();
    IF (ch >= 'a') AND (ch <= 'z') THEN
    ch := CAP(ch);         (* converts lower to upper case*)
  END;
    WriteChar(ch);
  UNTIL ch = EolChar();
END Convert2.
```

A9.2   input characters

```
?ab
??
```

```
?a
?
?x
```

Seven characters are read in total due to the end-of-line character being read as a character. This has to be filtered out when it is not significant thus:

```
REPEAT
    h := ReadChar();
  UNTIL (ch <> PortIO.EolChar());
With this change the output of the program becomes:
?ab
??b
?x
```

The '??' is due to two characters being present on one line. The prompt is unnecessarily being printed. This can be overcome either by consuming the line once you have taken one character thus:

```
WriteChar('?');          (* output prompt *)
ch := ReadChar();
ReadLn;                  (* discard the rest of the line*)
```

or by outputting a prompt only when an end-of-line character has been read.

A9.3
```
MODULE OctalConvert;
IMPORT PortIO;
VAR
  Card :CARDINAL;
  OK : BOOLEAN;
PROCEDURE ReadOct(): CARDINAL;
VAR
  ch    : CHAR;
  Card : CARDINAL;
BEGIN
  OK := TRUE; Card := 0;
  REPEAT
    ch := PortIO.ReadChar();
  UNTIL (ch <> ' ') AND (ch <> EolChar());
  LOOP
    IF (ch < '0') OR (ch >'7') THEN (* illegal character *)
      OK := FALSE;
      RETURN Card;
    END;
    Card := (Card*8)+(ORD(ch)-ORD('0'));(* ASCII dependent*)
    ch := PortIO.ReadChar();
    IF (ch = ' ') OR (ch = PortIO.EolChar()) THEN
        RETURN Card
    END;
  END;
END ReadOct;
PROCEDURE WriteOct(c: CARDINAL);
VAR SaveWidth: CARDINAL;
BEGIN
```

```
        SaveWidth:= PortIO.FieldWidth();
        PortIO.SetFieldWidth(20);
        PortIO.WriteCard(c);
        PortIO.SetFieldWidth(SaveWidth)
      END WriteOct;
    BEGIN
      PortIO.WriteString("Input an octal number: ");
      Card := ReadOct()
      IF OK THEN
        PortIO.WriteString("The decimal equivalent of which is:");
        WriteOct(Card);
      ELSE
        PortIO.WriteString("Malformed octal number");
      END;
      PortIO.WriteLn;
    END OctalConvert.
```

A4.10 CHAPTER 10 ANSWERS

A10.1 They are of type CHAR.

A10.2 It must be a CARDINAL subrange which starts at 0.

A10.3 The string terminating character —usually 0C.

A10.4
```
CONST
  Low =1;  High = 14;
TYPE
  ChListRange = [Low..High];
  CharList = ARRAY ChListRange OF CHAR;
```

A10.5
```
MODULE CList;
FROM PortIO IMPORT RdChar;
CONST
  Low = 1;  High = 14;
  Prompt = 'Input a Character:';
TYPE
  ChListRange = [Low..High];
  CharList = ARRAY ChListRange OF CHAR;
VAR
  Index: ChListRange;
  Characters: CharList;
BEGIN
  FOR Index := Low TO High DO
    WriteString(Prompt);
    Characters[Index] := ReadChar(); ReadLn;
  END
END Clist.
```

A10.6 (NumberToExtract <= Length(Source)) AND
(HIGH(Destination) >= NumberToExtract)

A10.7 (Length(Destination) + Length(Source))
         <= (HIGH(Destination) + 1)

A10.8
```
PROCEDURE Reverse(VAR s: ARRAY OF CHAR);
VAR ch : CHAR;
    Low, High : CARDINAL;
BEGIN
  Low := 0; High := Length(s)-1;
  WHILE Low < High DO
    ch := s[Low];
    s[Low] := s[High];
    s[High] := ch;
    INC(Low);
    DEC(High);
  END;
END Reverse;
```

A4.11 CHAPTER 11 ANSWERS

A11.1 Any named legal type.

A11.2 No, a dynamic variable is created with a call of NEW with a pointer variable as its parameter.

A11.3 By assigning to it the value NIL.

A11.4 With a call of DISPOSE with the dynamic variable's associated pointer variable as its parameter.

A11.5 It is undefined.

A11.6 A node is a record which consists of a data field and one or more pointer fields. They are used to construct dynamic data structures, the pointer field (sometimes called the link field) is used to point to the next record in the sequence.

A11.7 Storage for static data structures is set aside when the procedure declaring the data structure is invoked, the storage remaining constant throughout the procedure and being released when that procedure is left. Dynamic data structures can have storage allocated for them at any time during the execution of the procedure they are declared in. The size of the data structure can change during the execution of the procedure, storage being allocated and deallocated on demand. When the procedure is left, storage for the dynamic data structure is not released unless this is explicitly demanded by the program, although storage for the pointer variable that references the data structure is released.

A11.8
```
MODULE StackHandler;
FROM Storage IMPORT ALLOCATE, DEALLOCATE;
TYPE
  NodePtr = POINTER TO Node;
  Node = RECORD
            Data : CARDINAL;
            Link : NodePtr;
         END;
VAR
  PtrToLast : NodePtr;
PROCEDURE InitializeStack;
```

```
  BEGIN
    PtrToLast := NIL;
  END InitializeStack;
PROCEDURE AddToStack(CardVal : CARDINAL);
  VAR
    NewNode : NodePtr;
  BEGIN
    NEW(NewNode);
    NewNode^.Data := CardVal;
    NewNode^.Link := NIL;
    NewNode^.Link := PtrToLast;
    PtrToLast := NewNode;
  END AddToStack;
PROCEDURE RemoveFromStack;
  VAR
    ToBeRemoved : NodePtr;
  BEGIN
    IF PtrToLast <> NIL THEN
      ToBeRemoved := PtrToLast;
      PtrToLast := ToBeRemoved^.Link;
      DISPOSE(ToBeRemoved)
    END
  END RemoveFromStack;
```

A4.12 CHAPTER 12 ANSWERS

A12.1 The BSI Standard Syntactic Metalanguage.

A12.2 A terminal symbol is a token in a language and appears in syntax rules between quotation marks (e.g. "BEGIN", "."). A non-terminal symbol is a place holder in a production rule; it may be replaced by another sequence of symbols in order to determine legal forms of Modula-2 or to check if a piece of text is well-formed Modula-2.

A12.3 It means that a valid household has at least one person in it, and maybe a number of other persons or pets, or both.

A12.4 A pair of '?' symbols may be used to delimit a rule which is informally expressed, for example in English.

A12.5 (i) OK (ii) invalid (iii) OK (iv) OK (v) invalid.

A4.13 CHAPTER 13 ANSWERS

A13.1 Before the execution of the main program block.

A13.2 On reaching the END in the main program block, or on encountering a RETURN statement in the main program block.

A13.3 Qualified and unqualified IMPORT.

A13.4 An example of qualified import is:

```
IMPORT PortIO;
...
PortIO.WriteString("Fred");
An example of unqualified import is:
FROM PortIO IMPORT WriteString;
```

```
...
WriteString("Fred");
```

A13.5 Local modules can use the qualified form of import without having to qualify the identifier name when it is used inside the local module.

A13.6 An opaque type is a type whose name only is declared in the definition module. Its full declaration is then given in the implementation module. An opaque type would be declared if you wished to hide its structure from an importing module.

A13.7 They can only be declared as pointer types.

A13.8 The export statement is only ever used by local modules.

A13.9 To allow the use of identifiers declared within a local module to be accessed by the surrounding scope.

A13.10 It is the lifetime of the program module.

A13.11 It is determined by the lifetime of the surrounding block.

A13.12 The answer is to make module B a local module declared in module A.

A13.13 The procedures `AssignChar`, `InsertChar`, `AppendChar`, and `FindChar` could be deleted from the module `PortStrings`. Instead of these you could use the procedures, `Assign`, `Insert`, `Append`, and `Find` by using the array value constructor as a type transfer function.

```
TYPE
    StringType = ARRAY [0..23] OF CHAR;
    CharStr = ARRAY [0..0] OF CHAR;
VAR
    ch : CHAR;
    String : StringType;
BEGIN
    ...
    Append(CharStr{ch}, String);
    Find(CharStr{ch}, String);
```

A13.14
```
Starting to initialize ST, and calling Q twice
    Local module STM1 initialized
  Procedure Q executed
  The value of I is 43
    Local module STM1 initialized
  Procedure Q executed
  The value of I is 43
Implementation module ST is now initialized
Starting to execute program Life2
Calling procedure ST.Q
    Local module STM1 initialized
  Procedure Q executed
  The value of I is 43
Program Life2 now finished.
```

A4.14 CHAPTER 14 ANSWERS

A14.1 When the END of the procedure is reached or a RETURN statement is executed.

A14.2 A procedures' formal parameters have a scope which is local to the procedure body.

A14.3 The compatibility rules for formal and actual parameters are:
1. The number of actual parameters must match the number of formal parameters.
2. Taken in sequence, each parameter in the actual parameter list must be of a type compatible with the parameter in the formal parameter list.
3. If the formal parameter is a VAR-parameter then the associated actual parameter must be a variable of an identical type.
4. If a formal parameter is declared as a value parameter, then the associated actual parameter must be an expression that is assignment compatible with the formal parameter.

A14.4 `ProcType = PROCEDURE(ARRAY OF CARDINAL; CARDINAL): BOOLEAN;`

A14.5 The variable p has the value 2 after the call of the procedure Add. This is because the formal parameter a which matches with the actual parameter p has been declared as a value parameter. It should have been declared as a VAR-parameter:

```
PROCEDURE Add(VAR a : CARDINAL; b : CARDINAL);
```

A14.6 A single-pass compiler would not accept the procedure declarations, because LovesMeNot is used before it is declared. After the IMPORT statement insert the following: PROCEDURE LovesMeNot(I : CARDINAL);
FORWARD;

A4.15 CHAPTER 15 ANSWERS

A15.1
```
CONST
   Length = 5; Width = 2;
   Area = Length * Width;
```

A15.2 Time is of an anonymous type, as it has no associated type name. This is considered poor programming practice. The declaration of Time would be improved by first declaring a type called TimeType. Also, the anonymous CARDINAL types could be named, thus:

```
TYPE
   HourRange = [0,,24];
   MinRange = [0..60];
   SecRange [0..60]
   TimeType = RECORD
                  Hours : HourRange;
```

```
                    Minutes : MinRange;
                    Seconds : SecRange
                END;
        VAR
          Time : TimeType;
```

A15.3 The type identifier `Index` has been used before it has been declared; this breaks the rule that identifiers must be declared before use in another declaration. The declarations should have been written in the following manner:

```
TYPE
  Index = [0..99];
  ArrayType = ARRAY Index OF CARDINAL;
```

A15.4 No, they are not incorrect. The declare-before-use rule is relaxed in the case of pointers.

A4.16 CHAPTER 16 ANSWERS

A16.1 For structured types assignment compatibility demands the types be identical.

A16.2 Either of the following three solutions should work.
- (i) redefine a2 to be equal to a1;
- (ii) declare both x and y to be of the same type (either a1 or a2);
- (iii) write a FOR loop to assign individual values from x to y.

A16.3 You will need to determine the size of the procedure types using `TSIZE`, and then choose a type of the same size for which equality is defined. For example, if the size of a procedure type is the size of a `CARDINAL`, then the following will work:

```
MODULE Proc;
FROM PortIO IMPORT WriteString;
TYPE p = PROCEDURE(INTEGER, INTEGER, VAR CARDINAL);
VAR x, y : p;
PROCEDURE z1
  (a: INTEGER; b: INTEGER; VAR c : CARDINAL);
  BEGIN
  END z1;
PROCEDURE z2 (r, s : INTEGER; VAR t: CARDINAL);
  BEGIN
  END z2;
BEGIN
  x := z1;
  y := z2;
  IF x = y THEN WriteString('equal');
  ELSE
    WriteString("Not equal");
  END;
END Proc.
```

A16.4
```
PROCEDURE SCompare(S:SmallSet; L:LittleSet):Comparison;
VAR
```

```
        CardS,CardL: CARDINAL; (* for holding number in set *)
        c: CARDINAL;
BEGIN
   CardS := 0;
   CardL := 0;
   FOR c := 0 TO 7 DO
     IF c IN S THEN
       INC(CardS);
       IF c IN L THEN
         INC(CardL);
       ELSE
         RETURN NotEqual
       END;
     ELSIF c IN L THEN
       INC(CardL);
     END;
   END;
   IF CardS < CardL THEN
     RETURN StrictSubSet
   ELSE (* CardS must equal CardL *)
     RETURN Equal
   END
END SCompare;
```

A4.17 CHAPTER 17 ANSWERS

A17.1 They are INTEGER, CARDINAL, REAL, LONGREAL, CHAR, and BOOLEAN.

A17.2 MOD and DIV, they often permit negative right hand operands.

A17.3
```
PROCEDURE MathMod(i, r : INTEGER): INTEGER;
VAR temp : INTEGER;
BEGIN
   IF r < 0 THEN
     WriteString('Error'); WriteLn;
     RETURN 0;
   ELSIF i < 0 THEN
     i := ABS(i);
     temp := i MOD r;
     IF temp <> 0 THEN
       RETURN r - temp
     END;
   ELSE
     RETURN i MOD r
   END
END MathMod;
```

A17.4 Because computers can only represent a limited number of decimal places.

A17.5 Variables of type SHORTCARD only occupy half the space that CARDINAL variables do.

A17.6 B := C * TRUNC(R) * VAL(CARDINAL, I);

A4.18 CHAPTER 18 ANSWERS

A18.1 Short-circuit Boolean evaluation means that the evaluation of a Boolean expression is halted if the value of the expression can be determined without evaluating all the terms of the expression.

A18.2 A WHILE loop statement sequence may never be executed.

A18.3 A REPEAT loop statement sequence is guaranteed to be executed at least once.

A18.4 The EXIT statement is used to terminate execution of a LOOP statement sequence.

A18.5 The RETURN statement is used to terminate the execution of a function procedure and to return a value to the expression that invoked the procedure.

A18.6 You would include an ELSE part in the CASE sequence. For example:

```
CASE Index of
    1 :... |
    2 :... |
    3 ...
    ELSE
       WriteString("Invalid CASE index. Program halting.");
       HALT
END;
```

A18.7 Rewrite the following assignment (which uses unportable structured value constructors) using a WITH statement:

```
WITH Album DO
    Medium := Vinyl;
    Title := "Sgt. Pepper's Lonely Hearts' Club Band";
    Artists := "The Beatles";
    CatalogueNumber := "PCS 7027";
    Year := 1967;
    Music := Rock
END;
```

A4.19 CHAPTER 19 ANSWERS

A19.1
```
TYPE
    Age = [0..105];
    ArrayOfAge = ARRAY [1..20] OF Age;
```

A19.2
```
VAR
    PeoplesAges : ArrayOfAge;
    Count, i : CARDINAL;
BEGIN
    ...
    Count := 0;
    FOR i := 1 TO 20 DO
      IF PeoplesAges[i] > 25 THEN
        Count := Count + 1
      END
```

```
        END;
        ...
```

A19.3
```
        VAR
          PeoplesAges : ArrayOfAge;
          temp1,temp2: CHAR;
          i : CARDINAL;
        BEGIN
          temp1 := PeoplesAges[1];
          FOR i := 2 TO 20 DO
            temp2 := PeoplesAges[i];
            PeoplesAges[i] := temp1;
            temp1 := temp2;
          END;
          PeoplesAges[1] := temp1;
          ...
```

A19.4
```
        VAR
          PeoplesAges : ArrayOfAge;
          High, Low : CARDINAL;
          Temp : Age;
        BEGIN
          ...
          Low := 1;
          High := 20;
          WHILE Low < High DO
            Temp := PeoplesAges[Low];
            PeoplesAges[Low] := PeoplesAges[High];
            PeoplesAges[High] := Temp;
            INC(Low);
            DEC(High)
          END;
          ...
```

A19.5
```
        TYPE
          Column = [1..20];
          Row = [1..2];
          StockArray = ARRAY Column, Row OF CARDINAL;
```

A19.6
```
        VAR
          Stock : StockArray;
          i : Column;
          j : Row;
        BEGIN
          ...
          FOR i := 1 TO 20 DO
            FOR j := 1 TO 2 DO
              Stock[i,j] := 0
            END
          END;
          ...
```

A19.7
```
        PROCEDURE Search
          (CurrentStock : StockArray; PartNo :CARDINAL);
```

```
VAR
  Count  CARDINAL;
BEGIN
  Count := 1
  WHILE PartNo <> CurrentStock[Count,1] AND Count <= 20 DO
    INC(Count);
  END;
  IF PartNo = CurrentStock[Count,1] THEN
    WriteString("No of items = ");
    WriteCard(CurrentStock[Count,2];
  ELSE
    WriteString("Part Number does not exist!")
  END
END Search;
```

A19.8
```
MODULE StudentsMarks3;
FROM PortIO IMPORT WriteString, WriteLn, ReadCard;
TYPE
  Surname = (Turner, Harvey, Stock, Austin);
  Years = [1..3];
  Subject = (Maths, English, French);
  Marks = [0..100];
  Students =
    ARRAY [Turner..Austin], Years, [Maths..French] OF Marks;
VAR
  MyStudents : Students;
  Name : Surname;
  AYear : Years;
  Result : Marks;
  Subj : Subject;

PROCEDURE ReadFromTerminal
  (Name : Surname; AYear : Years; Subj : Subject): Marks;
  BEGIN
    WriteString('For year '); WriteCard(AYear);
    WriteLn;
    WriteString('Please Enter the marks obtained by ');
    CASE Name OF
      Harvey : WriteString('Harvey ') |
      Turner : WriteString('Turner ') |
      Stock  : WriteString('Stock ') |
      Austin : WriteString('Austin ')
    END;
    WriteLn;
    WriteString('In the subject of ')
    CASE Subj OF
      Maths : WriteString('Maths: ') |
      English : WriteString('English: ') |
      French  : WriteString('French: ')
    END;
    RETURN ReadCard();
  END ReadFromTerminal;

BEGIN (*body of StudentsMarks3*)
  FOR Name := Turner TO Austin DO
    FOR AYear := 1 TO 3 DO
      FOR Subj := Maths TO French DO
```

```
        MyStudents[Name,AYear,Subj] :=
            ReadFromTerminal(Name,AYear,Subj)
      END
    END
  END
END StudentsMarks3.
```

The assignment statement:

```
Result := MyStudents[Turner,3,French];
```

will assign to the variable Result, the marks that Turner achieved in year 3 in the French exam.

A4.20 CHAPTER 20 ANSWERS

A20.1
```
TYPE
    String = ARRAY [0..79] OF CHAR;
    LibraryBook = RECORD
                      Title : String;
                      Author : String;
                      OnLoan : BOOLEAN;
                  END;
```

A20.2
```
CONST
    Min = 1;
    Max = 2000;
TYPE
    Index = [Min..Max];
    Library = ARRAY Index OF LibraryBook;
```

A20.3
```
PROCEDURE FindBook
    (BookTitle : String; VAR Found : BOOLEAN;
     VAR i : Index);
BEGIN
  i := Max;
  LOOP
    IF PortString.Compare(BookArray[i].Title, BookTitle) =
      equal THEN
        Found := TRUE;
        EXIT;
    END;
    IF i = Min THEN
      Found := FALSE;
      EXIT;
    END;
    DEC(i)
  END
END FindBook;
```

A20.4
```
TYPE
    DayNums = [1..31];
    MonthNums = [1..12];
    YearNums = [1960..2000];
    Date = RECORD
```

```
                       Day : DayNums;
                       Month : MonthNums;
                       Year : YearNums;
                  END;
          String = ARRAY [0..79] OF CHAR;
          LibraryBook = RECORD
                          Title : String;
                          Author : String;
                          CASE OnLoan : BOOLEAN OF
                            TRUE :
                              ReturnDate : Date;
                              Reserved : BOOLEAN |
                            FALSE :
                              DateReturned : Date;
                          END
                        END;
```

A20.5
```
          PROCEDURE LoanUpdate
            (BookTitle : String; DueBackDate :Date);
          VAR
            Found : BOOLEAN;
            i : Index;
          BEGIN
            Found := FALSE;
            FindBook(BookTitle, Found, i);
            IF Found THEN
              IF NOT BookArray[i].OnLoan THEN
                BookArray[i].OnLoan := TRUE;
                BookArray[i].ReturnDate := DueBackDate;
              ELSE
                 WriteString("Book already out on loan")
              END;
            ELSE
              WriteString("Book not in database");
            END
          END LoanUpdate;
```

A20.6
```
          PROCEDURE Reserve(BookTitle : String);
          VAR
            Found : BOOLEAN;
            i : Index;
          BEGIN
            Found := FALSE;
            FindBook(BookTitle, Found, i);
            IF Found THEN
              IF BookArray[i].OnLoan THEN
                IF NOT BookArray[i].Reserved THEN
                   BookArray[i].Reserved := TRUE;
                ELSE
                   WriteString("Book already reserved")
                END;
              ELSE
                WriteString("Book is not on loan");
              END;
            ELSE
```

```
                     WriteString("Book not in database")
                  END
               END Reserve;


A20.7    PROCEDURE ReturnUpdate
            (BookTitle : String; DateBack : Date);
         VAR
            Found : BOOLEAN;
            i : Index;
         BEGIN
            Found := FALSE;
            FindBook(BookTitle, Found,i);
            IF Found THEN
               IF BookArray[i].OnLoan THEN
                  IF
                     LateReturn(DateBack, BookArray[i].ReturnDate)
                  THEN
                     WriteString("A fine is due on this book");
                  END;
                  BookArray[i].OnLoan := FALSE;
                  BookArray[i].DateReturned := DateBack;
               ELSE
                  WriteString("Book already out on loan")
               END;
            ELSE
               WriteString("Book not in database");
            END;
         END ReturnUpdate;


A20.8    WITH Holidays DO
            CASE Holidays.Resort OF
               Sun :
                  CASE SunResort OF
                     StTropez : WriteString('StTropez') |
                     Ibiza : WriteString('Ibiza') |
                     Santorini : WriteString('Santorini') |
                     Capri : WriteString('Capri')
                  END;
                  WriteLn;
                  WriteString('Average Temperature = ');
                  WriteCard(AverageTemperature);  WriteLn;
                  WriteString('Average Hours of Sun = ');
                  WriteCard(AverageHoursOfSun); WriteLn;
                  IF Beach THEN
                     WriteString('Beautiful sandy beaches');
                  ELSE
                     WriteString('The resort has no beaches')
                  END |
               Ski:
                  CASE SkiResort OF
                     Valdisere : WriteString("Val d'isere") |
                     StMoritz : WriteString('St Moritz') |
                     Zermatt : WriteString('Zermatt') |
                     Arosa : WriteString('Arosa')
                  END;
```

```
                    WriteLn;
                    WriteString('Average depth of snow in centimetres =');
                    WriteCard(AverageSnowDepth); WriteLn;
                    IF ChairLift THEN
                      WriteString('Has ChairLifts'); WriteLn
                    END;
                    IF ButtonLift THEN
                      WriteString('Has ButtonLifts'); WriteLn
                    END;
                    CASE EasiestRun OF
                      Green : WriteString('The easiest run is green') |
                      Blue : WriteString('The easiest run is blue') |
                      Red : WriteString('The easiest run is red') |
                      Black : WriteString('The easiest run is black')
                    END;
                    WriteLn;
                    CASE HardestRun OF
                      Green : WriteString('The hardest run is green') |
                      Blue : WriteString('The hardest run is blue') |
                      Red : WriteString('The hardest run is red') |
                      Black : WriteString('The hardest run is black')
                    END;
                  END
                END;
```

A4.21 CHAPTER 21 ANSWERS

A21.1
```
TYPE
   range = [-5..5];
   NegSet = ARRAY range OF BOOLEAN;
VAR
   NegNums: NegSet;
BEGIN
   ...
   FOR i := MIN(range) TO MAX(range) DO
     NegNums[i] := FALSE
   END;
   NegNums[-4] := TRUE;
   NegNums[2] := TRUE;
```

A21.2
```
PROCEDURE InSet(value: range; set: NegSet) : BOOLEAN;
BEGIN
   RETURN set[value]
END InSet
```

A21.3
```
PROCEDURE InclInSet(value : range; VAR set : NegSet);
BEGIN
   set[value] := TRUE
END InclInSet;
```

A21.4
```
PROCEDURE ExclFromSet
   (value : range; VAR set : NegSet);
BEGIN
```

```
         set[value] := FALSE
       END ExclFromSet;
```

A21.5
```
       PROCEDURE Difference(s1,s2 : NegSet):NegSet;
       VAR
         NewSet : NegSet;
         i : range;
       BEGIN
         FOR i := -5 TO 5 DO
           IF (s1[i] = TRUE) AND (s2[i] = FALSE) THEN
             NewSet[i] := TRUE
           END
         END;
         RETURN NewSet
       END Difference;
```

A21.6
```
       PROCEDURE Union(s1,s2:NegSet):NegSet;
       VAR
         NewSet : NegSet;
         i : range;
       BEGIN
         FOR i := -5 TO 5 DO
           IF (s1[i] = TRUE) OR (s2[i] = TRUE) THEN
             NewSet[i] := TRUE
           END
         END;
         RETURN NewSet
       END Union;
```

A4.22 CHAPTER 22 ANSWERS

A22.1
```
       MODULE FreeListHandler;
       FROM Storage IMPORT ALLOCATE, DEALLOCATE;
       TYPE
         NodePointer = POINTER TO Node;
         DynamicVar = POINTER TO CARDINAL;
         Node = RECORD
                   Data : DynamicVar;
                   Link : NodePointer;
                END;
       VAR
         PtrToFirst, PtrToLast: NodePointer;

       PROCEDURE AddToFreeList(CardVal : DynamicVar);
       VAR
         NewNode : NodePointer;
       BEGIN
         NEW(NewNode);
         NewNode^.Data := CardVal;
         NewNode^.Link := NIL;
         IF PtrToFirst = NIL THEN
           PtrToFirst := NewNode;
         ELSE
           PtrToLast^.Link := NewNode;
         END;
```

```
      PtrToLast := NewNode
    END AddToFreeList;

    PROCEDURE TakeFromFreeList(CardVal : DynamicVar);
    VAR
      ToBeRemoved : NodePointer;
    BEGIN
      IF PtrToFirst <> NIL THEN
        ToBeRemoved := PtrToFirst;
        PtrToFirst := PtrToFirst^.Link;
        CardVal := ToBeRemoved
      END
    END TakeFromFreeList;

    PROCEDURE EmptyFreeList(): BOOLEAN;
    BEGIN
      RETURN (PtrToFirst <> NIL)
    END EmptyFreeList;

    BEGIN (* body of FreeListHandler*)
      PtrToFirst := NIL;
      PtrToLast := NIL;
    END FreeListHandler.
```

A22.2
```
IF EmptyFreeList() THEN
   TakeFromFreeList(Ptr)
ELSE
   NEW(Ptr)
END;
```

A4.23 CHAPTER 23 ANSWERS

A23.1 ABS(x) returns a value of the same type.

A23.2 CAP returns the upper-case equivalent of a lower-case letter. If the character is not a lower-case letter the result is implementation defined.

```
TYPE
   setofchar = SET OF CHAR;
   lowercase = setofchar {'a'..'z'};
BEGIN
   ...
   IF ch IN lowercase THEN
      ch := CAP(ch);
   END;
```

A23.3 This is a portability problem, 0 may be taken as CARDINAL on most systems and either an error raised, or a large positive value returned as a result. If your implementation allows you to compile this then it supports the looser type compatibility rules put forward in the proposed standard.

A23.4
```
INCL(x, TVR);
INCL(x, RX7);
EXCL(x, XR3);
```

A23.5 Print out value of FLOAT(MAX(CARDINAL));

A23.6 If you are not writing real-time embedded applications you should *never* use HALT.

A23.7 If it has been declared statically, then you already know the array bounds or the length of a constant.

A23.8
```
IF ODD(ORD('?')) THEN WriteString('? is odd')
ELSE WriteString('? is even')
END;
```

A23.9
```
IF MAX(CARDINAL) = ORD(MIN(INTEGER))THEN
   WriteString('Yes')
ELSE
   WriteString('No')
END;
```

A23.10 For example, to find the number of storage units needed to store a value of type INTEGER:

```
WriteCard(SIZE(INTEGER));
```

etc.

A23.11 This will either raise an exception or it will return a false value. You should restrict the use of SIZE to types which do not contain tens of thousands of elements.

A23.12 In Topspeed Modula-2, 0 is returned. TRUNC should be used sparingly because REAL arithmetic is not accurate, and values returned may be outside the range of CARDINAL.

A23.13
```
VAL(REAL, x)     = FLOAT(x);
VAL(CARDINAL, x) = ORD(x);
VAL(CARDINAL, x) = TRUNC(x);
```

A23.14 ALLOCATE and DEALLOCATE have not been imported.

A4.24 CHAPTER 25 ANSWERS

A25.1 To have used WORD might have required the following implementation of flipbytes:

```
PROCEDURE flipbytes(VAR b: WORD);
  VAR byte1, byte2: BITSET;
  BEGIN
    byte1 := BITSET(CARDINAL({0..7} * BITSET(b)) * 256);
    byte2 := BITSET(CARDINAL({8..15} * BITSET(b)) DIV 256);
    b := WORD(byte1 + byte2);
  END flipbytes;
```

To produce the same effect as before requires a little more processing and a lot more understanding: the first 8 bits of the word are extracted by masking them (AND-ing them with eight zeros and eight ones) and are then shifted left by 8 bits by multiplying by 256 (2^8). The second 8 bits are shifted right by dividing by 256. The two bytes are then combined using the union/logical-OR operator, +, and transferred back to the type WORD.

Note that in order to perform these arithmetic operations the WORD parameter had first to be transferred to type BITSET, and BITSET expressions turned into CARDINALs (for the multiplication and division) and then reconverted to BITSET.

A25.2
```
MODULE StrQ;
FROM QMod IMPORT Queue, Processq, Createq, AddToq;
FROM PortStrings IMPORT StringTerminator;
FROM PortIO IMPORT
  ReadString, WriteChar, WriteLn, WriteString, Done;
VAR
  String: ARRAY [0..79] OF CHAR;
  UpperCaseQ, LowerCaseQ: Queue;
PROCEDURE WriteLnStr(VAR String: ARRAY OF BYTE);
  VAR x: [0..79];
  BEGIN
    x := 0;
    WHILE
      (x <= HIGH(String)) &
      (CHAR(String[x]) <> StringTerminator) DO
      WriteChar(CHAR(String[x]));
      INC(x)
    END;
    WriteLn
  END WriteLnStr;
BEGIN
  Createq(UpperCaseQ);  Createq(LowerCaseQ);
  WriteString('Input String: '); ReadString(String);
  WHILE String[0] <> '!' DO
    CASE String[0] OF
      'a'..'z': AddToq(LowerCaseQ, String) |
      'A'..'Z': AddToq(UpperCaseQ, String)
      ELSE WriteString('Ignored.'); WriteLn;
    END;
    WriteString('Input String: '); ReadString(String);
  END;
  WriteString('Upper case Queue -'); WriteLn;
  Processq(UpperCaseQ, WriteLnStr);
  WriteString('Lower case Queue -'); WriteLn;
  Processq(LowerCaseQ, WriteLnStr);
END StrQ.
```

A4.25 CHAPTER 26 ANSWERS

A26.1 A coroutine is a parameterless procedure, which is activated by a call to TRANSFER or IOTRANSFER (followed by an interrupt).

A26.2 It is used to store the local variables and the state of the coroutine when it is suspended.

A26.3 (i)   declare a variable of type PROCESS;

(ii)   allocate a workspace for the coroutine;

(iii)   create the coroutine with a call to NEWPROCESS;

(iv)   transfer control to the coroutine via a call to either TRANSFER or IOTRANSFER.

A26.4 IOTRANSFER not only transfers control from one coroutine to another, but sets the processor to transfer control back to the original coroutine when a particular interrupt occurs. TRANSFER is a simpler and more direct process, not dependent upon interrupts.

A26.5 If that coroutine is interrupted by some other coroutine, you run the risk of the original interrupt not being attended to in time and data being lost.

INDEX

In the index a bold page number denotes the defining instance of a term, i.e. the location of the most detailed technical discussion. Bold page numbers are, therefore, usually in Part II, *Modula-2 Reference*. A page number in italics denotes the location of a discussion of a portability issue. The lowest page number is where a term is introduced (which is usually in Part I of the book).

SYMBOLS

* **246**
  CARDINAL multiplication 41, 259
  INTEGER multiplication 43, 260
  REAL multiplication 45, 262
  set intersection 322

\+ **246**
  CARDINAL addition 41, 259
  INTEGER addition 43, 260
  REAL addition 45, 262
  set union 321

\- **246**
  CARDINAL minus 41, 259
  INTEGER minus 43, 260
  INTEGER negation 43, 260
  REAL minus 45, 262
  REAL negation 45, 262
  set difference 322

/ **247**,
  CARDINAL division 41, 259, *268*
  INTEGER division 43, 259, *268*
  REAL division 45, 262
  symmetric set difference 323

< **245**
  CARDINAL less than 41
  INTEGER less than 44
  REAL less than 45

<= **245**
  CARDINAL less or equal to 41
  INTEGER less or equal to 44
  REAL less or equal to 45
  superset of 324

<> **244**
  CARDINAL not equal to 41
  INTEGER not equal to 44

  REAL not equal to 45

\# *30*, **244**

= **244**
  CARDINAL equal to 41
  INTEGER equal to 44
  REAL equal to 45

> **245**
  CARDINAL greater than 41
  INTEGER greater than 44
  REAL greater than 45

>= **245**
  CARDINAL greater or equal to 42
  INTEGER greater or equal to 44
  REAL greater or equal to 45
  subset of 324

& [AND] 245, **264**

~ [NOT] 246, **264**

$\mathbb{R}$ [reals] 49, 233, **238**

$\mathbb{S}$ [strings] 49, 126, 233, **238**

$\mathbb{Z}$ [whole numbers] 49, 233, **238**

A

ABS 45, **340**
actual open array parameters 221
actual parameters 92, 93, *100*, *210*, 273
  bad actual VAR-parameters *225*
  order of evaluation *226*
address constructor 235, 374
address on the 8086/80286/80386 373
address type 373
addresses and pointers 373
ADR 335, 374
  its use in low-level programming 336
aggregates *304*, *314*, *422*
ALLOCATE 145, *160*, **332**
  relationship with NEW 332